New Concepts in Investment and Technology

Volume I

New Concepts in Investment and Technology
Volume I

Edited by **Perry Stinson**

CLANRYE INTERNATIONAL

New Jersey

Published by Clanrye International,
55 Van Reypen Street,
Jersey City, NJ 07306, USA
www.clanryeinternational.com

New Concepts in Investment and Technology: Volume I
Edited by Perry Stinson

International Standard Book Number: 978-1-63240-373-5 (Hardback)

Printed in the United States of America.

Contents

Preface

The origins of the term Technology can be traced to its Greek roots, 'techne' which means skill or cunning of hand. It essentially refers to any skill, knowledge of tools, machines and techniques which are used to modify and create existing systems for various purposes. These purposes could include achieving a goal or solving a problem for performing a specific function, which would significantly affect humans.

Scientists suggest that the use of the term Technology has changed drastically over the last 200 years. It was only in the 20th century, that the term rose to prominence with the Second Industrial Revolution. Today, as we understand the term Technology is very different. However, technological interventions and creations have been into existence from ancient times. In fact, the use of technology began with the conversion of natural resources into simple tools. The creation of fire and invention of the wheel were also technological advancements as they helped humans in travelling in and controlling their environment.

The advantages and benefits of technology have been manifold. It has made a significant impact in almost every sphere of life. However, it has also led to the production of some unwanted by-products, which deplete natural resources and degrade the Earth's environment. Thus, it has its share of pros and cons but when invested in consciously, technology will reap good benefits.

I would like to thank all the contributors of this book who not only shared their knowledge but also gave us their valuable time to make this book possible.

Editor

Stylistic Differences across Hedge Funds as Revealed by Historical Monthly Returns

Hany A. Shawky[1*], Achla Marathe[2]
[1]*Center for Institutional Investment Management School of Business, University at Albany, Albany, USA*
[2]*Virginia Bioinformatics Institute, Virginia Tech, Blacksburg, USA*

Abstract

This paper utilizes two clustering techniques to provide an objective method for classification of hedge funds. A data driven classification framework that utilizes monthly hedge fund returns as inputs, is shown to provide better comparisons among fund categories and can help investors in identifying common factors that can lead to better diversification strategies. Our clustering results indicate that other than the managed futures category, there are only three unique hedge fund styles. These three categories are the Equity Hedge, Fund of Hedge Funds and the Emerging Markets categories. None of the other hedge fund classifications such as Global macro, Distressed Securities, Merger Arbitrage, Convertible Arbitrage appear as a unique and independent category.

Keywords: Hedge Funds, Clustering, Management Style, Dynamic Trading Strategies

1. Introduction

In a seminal paper, Sharpe [1] proposed an elegant asset class factor model for performance attribution and style analysis of mutual fund managers. The model shows that with only a limited number of asset classes, it is possible to replicate the performance of a large universe of mutual funds. The success of Sharpe's model in capturing stylistic differences between mutual fund managers is largely attributed to the fact that most mutual fund managers are typically constrained to hold assets from a well-defined number of standard asset classes and are expected to perform according to relative return targets within their asset classes.

In theory, it should be possible to extend Sharpe's style factor analysis by adding regressors to proxy for the returns of the various hedge fund strategies. However, in practice, implementing such a strategy may not be feasible due to the infinite number of dynamic trading strategies that are used by hedge fund managers. As an alternative to the Sharpe's approach, which requires identifying factors a priori, we use cluster analysis to identify the dominant styles in hedge funds. We use monthly returns to cluster the data and our goal is to see if there are unique style categories that are consistent with the return data.

Fung and Hsieh [2] were the first to extend the basic intuition of the Sharpe asset class factor model to the hedge fund industry through the use of Factor analysis. They factor analyze 409 hedge funds and CTA pools over the period January 1991 to December 1995, and find that there are five dominant investment styles in hedge funds. They were able to associate the five dominant styles generated quantitatively to the qualitative styles based on the trading strategies described in the disclosure document of hedge funds.

Brown and Goetzmann [3,4] study the monthly returns of 1296 hedge funds over the period 1989 through January 2000 and find that there are indeed a number of distinct styles of management[1] They use two different algorithms in their classification process. The first is a Generalized Style Classification methodology in which funds are assigned to categories through finding a local optimum via the minimization of a "within-group" sum of squares criterion over a specified time period[2], the second approach is a Style Classification algorithm in which the number of styles is pre-specified. They report the presence of at least eight distinct styles currently employed by hedge fund managers.

---

[1]Brown and Goetzmann [4] use the TASS data where funds are classified into 17 different types.
[2]The details of the Generalized Style Classification algorithm are described in Brown and Goetzmann [3]. This procedure resembles switching regression and is also analogues to cluster analysis.

Although there are many statistical techniques that can be used to classify data, the technique that appears to be most directly suitable for the present application is cluster analysis[3]. We use both K-means Clustering and Hierarchical Clustering techniques to cluster the monthly returns for 2397 hedge funds for the period January 1994 through December 2003. Such a data driven classification framework can help in identifying common factors that can lead to better performance evaluation of hedge fund strategies. As pointed out by Liang [5], to understand the differences and similarities across investment classes, it is necessary to classify hedge funds into major investment classes in terms of performance, risk and fee structures.

Our results obtained through both clustering techniques indicate that other than the managed futures category, there are only three unique hedge fund categories. These three categories are the Equity Hedge, Fund of funds (FOF) and the Emerging Markets categories. None of the other hedge fund strategies such as Global Macro, Distressed Securities, Merger Arbitrage or Convertible Arbitrage appears as a unique and independent cluster. Moreover, we find that there are three unique clusters within the Equity Hedge category, two clusters for Fund of funds (FOF) and four independent clusters for the managed futures category.

Hedge funds use a wide variety of dynamic trading strategies. On one hand, macro funds are most directional, employing a top-down macro view to take advantage of the expected returns of various asset classes. On the other hand, there are market-neutral relative value arbitrage funds that aim to exploit temporary price anomalies between related assets, in equities or fixed income markets. In between these two extreme strategies, there are funds that aim to uncover undervalued asset opportunities in debt or equity markets without necessarily being market neutral.

Unlike mutual funds, hedge funds' focus primarily on absolute returns rather than benchmarks or relative performance. Hedge fund managers have the freedom to pursue a wide range of alternative investment strategies such as the use of derivatives, short selling and leverage, without having to adhere to the stringent SEC regulations and disclosure requirements[4]. As a result, hedge funds often have low or sometimes negative correlations with traditional market indices. Because of these unique characteristics, hedge funds as an asset class is considered to be an attractive complement to traditional investment strategies that can further help in portfolio diversification.

2. Data and Descriptive Statistics Data Sources

The hedge fund data used in this study is obtained from the CISDM at the University of Massachusetts at Amherst. It covers 4,693 hedge funds from March 1972 through December 2003[5]. Of the total hedge funds in the database, 2397 are live funds and 2296 are defunct funds. The sample includes both U.S. domiciled funds and offshore funds. The variables reported in the database are fund name, strategy, management fee, incentive fee, minimum account size, management company, returns, assets, and net asset value per share[6].

The database is survivor-bias free in the sense that it includes both live and dead funds. However, it may still be subject to reporting bias as some funds may at times deliberately choose not to disclose their information publicly[7]. We choose the period 1990-2003 as the sample period for this study for three reasons. First, this period was characterized by rapid growth of the hedge fund industry. Second, the pre-1990 fund data may be back-filled, as no funds covered in the database are reported as defunct before 1990. Thus, there may be a survival bias in the pre-1990 period. Third, this time period is long enough to cover more than one business cycle.

Four primary hedge fund database providers are common among researchers and industry professionals. Each of these data providers offers a different product. Hedge Fund Research (HFR) database has twenty-six categories of hedge funds. The TASS database is produced through the research subsidiary of Credit Suisse First Boston Tremont Advisors, has nine categories classified based on the investment styles of hedge fund mangers. The Van Hedge maintains an extensive database and also provides detailed generic performance information on hedge fund styles. Finally, the CISDM hedge fund database, which presently incorporates both the ZCM/Hedge and the former MAR/Hedge provides a comprehensive coverage of all hedge funds and is the database used in this paper.

It is clear that database providers classify hedge funds in very different ways. All databases have their own indices based on their classifications. Hedge fund categories are all based on self-reported style classifications that are listed in a particular database. None of the databases seem to provide information on the complete hedge fund universe, and they seem to differ in the definition and identification of a hedge fund. The significant variations in the classification methods used across the

---

[3]Martin [15] also argues that cluster analysis is the most applicable technique to use in style classification. His results indicate that eight distinct clusters generate the most useful results.

[4]Starting in February 2006 however, certain hedge fund advisors have to register with the SEC.

[5]We use hedge funds to refer to all funds reported in the CISDM, although the CISDM does not classify CTA/futures funds as hedge funds.

[6]Fund manager name, instead of the management company name, is reported for CTA/Futures funds.

[7]Unlike mutual funds that are heavily regulated under the Investment Company Act of 1940, hedge funds are not required to file fund information with the SEC.

available databases make it very difficult to conduct careful analysis of the performance of the various hedge fund strategies.

Exhibit 1 provides a complete list of hedge fund strategies and the number of funds within each strategy found in the CISDM database. Exhibit 2 provides summary statistics for the major hedge fund categories over the period January 1990 through December 2003. Mean returns, standard deviations, skewness, kurtosis and the average Sharpe Ratio for each of the strategies are estimated. It is interesting to note that the mean return column provides the most homogeneous results across hedge fund strategies. With the exception of Emerging Markets, most strategies provided a mean annual return between 9 and 14 percent. Standard deviations varied from .018 to .059. Skewness and Kurtosis varied the most and thus, it is likely that these third and fourth moments provided valuable information in our clustering process.

3. Clustering Methodology

Clustering analysis aims at sorting different objects into groups in such a way that the degree of association between two objects is maximal if they belong to the same group and minimal otherwise. This helps organize data into meaningful structures. Cluster analysis consists of a number of different methodologies for grouping objects of a similar kind into groups. Different clustering algorithms define different rules concerning how to cluster the objects into subgroups on the basis of the inter-object similarities. Our goal is to use the clustering methodology to classify funds that display small within cluster variation and large between-cluster variation. It is a data driven technique to objectively classify funds based on the monthly return characteristics of the funds.

The two most common kinds of clustering techniques are Hierarchical and Partitioning techniques. The Hierarchical method performs successive fusions or divisions of the data. Under this method, the allocation of a fund to a cluster is irrevocable. Once a fund joins a cluster it is never removed or fused with other funds belonging to some other cluster. The partitioning method, on the other hand, does not require the allocation of an object to the cluster to be irrevocable. As Dillon and Goldstein [6] show, objects may be reallocated if their initial assignments are found inaccurate and do not optimize the predefined criteria. This method breaks the observations into distinct non-overlapping groups. Different partitioning techniques differ with respect to the following criteria: 1) how clusters are initiated, and 2) how objects are allocated to clusters, 3) how already clustered objects get reallocated to other clusters.

Exhibit 1. Number of funds listed under each hedge fund strategy.

Hedge Fund Strategy	Number of Funds Listed in Strategy
Equity Hedge	527
FOF Diversified	398
Convertible Arbitrage	93
Merger Arbitrage / Risk Arbitrage	84
Global Macro	60
Event Driven Multi-Strategy	57
Distressed Securities	55
Equity Market Neutral	41
Emerging Markets: Global	36
Emerging Markets: Asia	33
FOF Equity Hedge	32
Fixed Income: Mortgage Backed	31
Fixed Income: Arbitrage	26
Sector: Technology	26
Sector: Financial	25
Sector: Healthcare/Bio Tech	25
Fixed Income: Diversified	23
Short Selling	23
FOF Equity Market Neutral	22
Emerging Markets: Latin America	21
Emerging Markets: Eastern Europe	17
Equity Non-Hedge	15
Sector: Miscellaneous	11
FOF Relative Value Multi-Strategy	10
FOF Distressed Securities	9
FOF Sector: Technology	9
Sector: Multi-Strategy	9
Fixed Income: High Yield	8
FOF Event Driven	7
Market Timing	7
Sector: Energy	7
Sector: Real Estate	7
FOF Emerging Markets	5
FOF Global Macro	4
FOF Convertible Arbitrage	3
FOF Fixed Income Arbitrage	3
FOF Short Selling	3
FOF Merger Arbitrage	2
FOF Sector: Healthcare	2
FOF Sector: Media & Communications	2
FOF Long Short Equity	1

Exhibit 2. Summary statistics and sharpe ratio for major hedge fund strategies.

Hedge Fund Categories	Mean returns (Annual)	Mean Returns (Monthly)	Standard Deviation	Skewness	Kurtosis	Sharpe Ratio
Convertible Arbitrage	12.78%	0.01065	0.02352	0.04200	9.75037	0.45281
Distressed Securities	12.91%	0.01075	0.02160	0.28020	2.78327	0.49769
Emerging Markets	22.83%	0.01902	0.05815	0.53526	4.91279	0.32709
Equity	14.57%	0.01214	0.05405	0.56866	10.60961	0.22461
Fixed Income	10.59%	0.00882	0.02160	0.10719	7.06639	0.40833
FOF Diversified	10.08%	0.00840	0.01878	0.10842	13.87208	0.44728
Global Macro	13.13%	0.01094	0.05998	0.06554	6.86377	0.18239
Merger & Risk Arbitrage	8.82%	0.00735	0.03954	0.58531	15.21462	0.18589
MF: Private Futures	11.05%	0.00921	0.05394	0.07068	5.83772	0.17075
MF: Public Futures	10.67%	0.00889	0.04942	0.78251	10.67304	0.17989
MF: Systematic	11.38%	0.00948	0.05655	0.64812	7.59567	0.16764

K-means, K-median, and K-center are a few of the methods that use partitioning techniques to cluster objects. In the following subsection, we describe the K-means clustering algorithm. The k-median and k-center techniques are similar in nature. Clustering methodology has been successfully applied to a wide range of research problems, such as in Banfield and Raftery [7], Das [8], Jiang and Zhang [9] and Marathe and Shawky [10].

3.1. K-Means Clustering

K-means is an iterative relocation algorithm in which an initial classification is modified by moving objects from one group to another such that it minimizes the with-in group sum of squares. The k-means algorithm is set up in the following way. Initial reference points, which may or may not be the centroid or mean are chosen and all the data points are assigned to clusters. K-means then uses the cluster centroids as reference points in subsequent partitioning, but the centroids are adjusted both during and after each partitioning. For data point x in cluster i, if centroid z_i is the nearest reference point, no adjustments are made and the algorithm proceeds to the next data point. However, if centroid z_j of the cluster j is closer to data point x, then x is reassigned to cluster j. The centroids of the "losing" cluster i, and that of the "gaining" cluster j are recomputed and the reference points z_i and z_j are moved to their new centroids. After each step, every one of the k reference points is a centroid or mean[8].

If the data points or objects are tightly clustered around the centroid, the centroid will be representative of all the objects in that cluster. The standard measure of the spread of a group of points about its mean is the variance, or the sum of the squares of the distance be-

tween each point and the mean. If the data points are close to the mean, the variance will be small. A generalization of the variance, in which the centroid is replaced by a reference point that may or may not be a centroid, is used to indicate the overall quality of a partitioning. Specifically, the error measure E is the sum of all the variances:

$$E = \sum_{i=1}^{k} \sum_{j=1}^{n_i} \| x_{ij} - z_i \|^2$$

where x_{ij} the jth point in the ith cluster, z_i is the reference point of the ith cluster, and n_i is the number of points in that cluster. The notation $\| x_{ij} - z_i \|$ stands for the distance between x_{ij} and z_j. Hence, the error measure E indicates the overall spread of data points about their reference points. For best results, E should be as small as possible.

The k-means method requires one to specify the number of clusters in advance. To determine the optimal number of clusters, Hartigan [11] suggested the following rule of thumb. If k is the result of k-means with k clusters and k+1 is the result of k-means with k+1 clusters, then it is justifiable to add the extra cluster when

$$\left(\frac{\sum_{i=1}^{k} ESS}{\sum_{i=1}^{k+1} ESS} - 1 \right) * (n - k - 1) > 10$$

Here ESS represents the error within sum of squares and n is the size of the data set. In our study, we use Hartigan rule of thumb to determine the optimal number of clusters.

3.2. Hierarchical Clustering

The Hierarchical approach is the other most commonly used clustering technique. It performs successive fusions or divisions of the data. One of the distinguishing features of Hierarchical clustering is that once an object is

---

[8]For a detailed description of the K-means algorithm and other clustering techniques, see Faber [13], Hartigan [14], and Dillon and Goldstein [6].

assigned to a cluster, it is never removed from that cluster and fused with other clusters. Agglomerative methods form a series of fusions of the objects into groups whereas divisive methods partition the objects into finer and finer subdivisions. Hence, agglomerative methods eventually result in all objects falling in one cluster and divisive methods finally split the data so that each object forms its own cluster. In either case, the important issue is where to stop. Various agglomerative methods differ to the extent that alternative definitions of distance or similarity are used in the assignment rule. The divisive methods differ in the way initial split is carried out and how the already formed clusters are subdivided[9].

In this study we use an agglomerative method proposed by Ward [12] known as the Ward's Error Sum of Squares method. This method attempts to minimize the sum of squares of any two clusters that can be formed at each step. The clustering procedure begins by assigning each object in a separate cluster. Two of the objects are then combined to form a single cluster so that the within cluster sum of squares is minimized. At the next stage, a third object is added to the cluster or two other objects are merged into a new cluster. This process of uniting clusters or objects continues while minimizing the error sum of squares. The cluster center changes each time a new case is added. This might mean that in the end some objects are no longer in the right cluster. The solution given by k-means provides a refinement over this process since the iterative relocation algorithm dynamically minimizes the within cluster sum of squares while maximizing the between cluster variability.

4. Empirical Findings

4.1. K-Means Clustering Results

Exhibit 3 provides the clustering results for the K-means algorithm[10]. The data was clustered in three different ways: 1) both hedge funds and managed futures are included, 2) only hedge funds are included and 3) only managed futures are included in the analysis. Panel A shows the individual clusters when both hedge funds and managed futures are included. Column 1 gives the number of funds in each cluster. Column 2 shows the number of funds that belong to the dominant strategy, and column 3 gives the percentage of funds in the dominant strategy. Column 4 reports the dominant strategy in each

cluster. Columns 5, 6 and 7 provide the mean, standard deviation and skewness of the returns of each cluster[11].

The results in Exhibit 3 indicate that of the ten identified clusters, four are classified as Equity Hedge, four are classified as managed futures, one is classified as Emerging Markets and one is classified as FOF. Note that none of the other hedge fund strategies such as Convertible Arbitrage, Fixed Income, Global Macro or Merger Arbitrage appeared as independent clusters[12]. It is possible that managers in some strategies, such as Global Macro or Merger Arbitrage employ sufficiently different techniques from one another that they do not form an identifiable cluster.

While the large number of funds that belong to the Equity Hedge and the managed futures categories may contribute to the relatively large number of clusters that result for these two strategies, this fact cannot explain why we observe a unique cluster for Emerging Markets and not for Convertible Arbitrage, Merger Arbitrage or Global Macro[13]. Furthermore, the results in Panel A of Exhibit 3 shows that managed futures are quite different than hedge funds as most CTA clusters are usually dominated by CTA funds.

Panel B of Exhibit 3 presents the identified clusters for the hedge fund industry when managed futures are excluded from the sample. Interestingly, the resulting hedge fund clusters are not very different from the ones obtained before. In this case we obtain seven clusters, four are still Equity Hedge, two are FOF and one Emerging Markets. Further, Panel C provides clustering results separately for the managed futures category. Once again, we obtain four distinct clusters, two clusters classified as Public and two clusters classified as Systematic managed futures.

4.2. Hierarchical Clustering Results

We apply the Hierarchical Clustering approach not only as a viable alternative to the K-means procedure but also as a robustness test on the previously estimated clusters. The results of this approach are presented in Exhibit 4. Panel A of Exhibit 4 shows the resulting clusters when all hedge funds and managed futures are included in the procedure. Similar to the earlier results, we estimate nine clusters; six of them are classified as hedge funds and three are classified as managed futures. Of the six hedge fund clusters, three are classified as Equity Hedge, two are classified as FOF, and one is classified as Emerging Markets.

---

[9]For more detailed discussion on clustering techniques, see Dillon and Goldstein [6].

[10]We should note that in all our analysis, we eliminated clusters with less than 10 funds as being not statistically reliable or economically meaningful. Eliminating very small clusters did not have any material impact on the results.

[11]A cluster is classified based on its dominant strategy. For example, a cluster will be classified as Equity Hedge if the largest percentage of its funds is from the Equity Hedge category.

---

[12]While Brown and Goetzmann [4] report a striking similarity between the styles they identify and those that are being reported by hedge funds, our results do not show such similarity.

[13]The number of funds in the Emerging Markets strategy is less than the number of funds in Convertible Arbitrage, Merger Arbitrage or Global Macro.

Exhibit 3. Individual cluster characteristics using K-Means Clustering.

# of Funds in Cluster	# of Funds in Strategy	% of Strategy to total funds	Dominant Strategy	Cluster Characteristics		
				Mean	STD	Skew
Panel A. All hegde funds and CTA's included in clustering						
125	42	33.60%	EH	0.0134	0.0441	0.4409
37	21	56.76%	EH	0.0174	0.0745	2.1621
30	16	53.33%	EH	0.0118	0.0748	0.2568
49	18	36.73%	EH	0.0154	0.0529	0.0057
26	22	84.62%	EM	0.0136	0.0623	0.0456
179	90	50.28%	FOFD	0.0084	0.0269	0.4530
146	145	99.32%	CTA	0.0129	0.0699	0.1964
441	117	26.53%	CTA	0.0092	0.0808	0.5337
58	58	100.00%	CTA	0.0062	0.0298	0.3757
72	71	98.61%	CTA	0.0072	0.0438	0.2416
Panel B. Only hedge funds included in clustering						
33	26	78.79%	EH	0.0168	0.0709	1.9429
35	26	74.29%	EH	0.0101	0.0977	0.4477
60	36	60.00%	EH	0.0127	0.0484	0.2628
21	16	76.19%	EH	0.0172	0.0863	0.2287
26	16	61.54%	EM	0.0204	0.0742	0.9700
356	107	30.06%	FOFD	0.0091	0.0177	0.1416
210	98	46.67%	FOFD	0.0100	0.0356	0.9020
Panel C. Only CTA's included in clustering						
119	36	30.25%	Public	0.00684	0.03396	0.42472
104	33	31.73%	Public	0.00654	0.03025	0.43880
62	22	35.48%	Systematic	0.01225	0.07034	0.09632
117	35	29.91%	Systematic	0.00732	0.04264	0.14448

Panel B of Exhibit 4 presents the clustering results when we exclude managed futures and only include hedge funds in the analysis. Once again, we obtain six clusters, three are classified as Equity Hedge, two are classified as FOF and one is classified as Emerging Markets. It is important to note the consistency of these results at two different levels. First, within the Hierarchical Clustering procedure, the clusters obtained with and without Managed Futures are essentially identical. Second, across both the clustering procedures, we obtain remarkably similar number of clusters and almost identical classifications when the entire hedge fund database is considered.

Finally, Panel C of Exhibit 4 provides clustering results when managed futures are examined separately. Similar to the K-means results, we obtain four distinct clusters for managed futures. Of these four clusters, two

are classified as Public Futures, one is classified as Private Futures, and one is classified as Systematic Futures. Once again, these results are very consistent with earlier results and provide further support for the notion that managed futures funds may be viewed as four distinct categories based on the four major asset classes on which futures contracts are usually traded.

5. Interpretation of Results

5.1. Why Do We Observe Three to Four Equity Hedge Clusters?

It is quite plausible to suspect that the three Equity Hedge Fund clusters represent the range of different strategies, approaches and specialties characteristic of equity hedge fund managers. Some managers add value through knowledge of special asset markets, others through trading skills, and yet others through superior asset pricing models[14]. Alternatively, the three clusters

---

[14]Fung and Hsieh [2] characterize hedge fund returns as being determined by three key factors; the returns from the assets held, their trading strategies, and their use of leverage.

Exhibit 4. Individual cluster characteristics using hierarchal clustering.

# of Funds in Cluster	# of Funds in Strategy	% of Strategy to total funds	Dominant Strategy	Cluster Characteristics		
				Mean	STD	Skew
Panel A. All hegde funds and CTA's included in clustering						
98	39	39.80%	EH	0.011	0.069	0.401
231	78	33.77%	EH	0.012	0.042	1.219
32	22	68.75%	EH	0.012	0.078	1.661
16	13	81.25%	EM	0.033	0.102	0.726
509	117	22.99%	FOF	0.008	0.013	0.211
231	85	36.80%	FOF	0.009	0.029	1.047
167	165	98.80%	CTA	0.010	0.070	0.303
133	114	85.71%	CTA	0.006	0.045	0.417
509	124	24.36%	CTA	0.007	0.032	0.277
Panel B. Only hedge funds included in clustering						
57	31	54.39%	EH	0.011	0.096	0.569
26	14	53.85%	EH	0.015	0.081	0.275
262	102	38.93%	EH	0.012	0.048	1.270
10	8	80.00%	EM	0.040	0.111	1.078
424	123	29.01%	FOF	0.008	0.014	0.213
262	96	36.64%	FOF	0.009	0.032	1.057
Panel C. Only CTA's included in clustering						
97	30	30.93%	PUB	0.012	0.063	0.221
120	36	30.00%	PUB	0.007	0.032	0.212
51	15	29.41%	PRI	0.007	0.068	0.286
124	37	29.84%	SYS	0.006	0.047	0.147

may reflect the three broad strategies utilized by equity funds. The three broad strategies are the macro funds, the funds that attempt to uncover undervalued asset opportunities, and the market-neutral relative value arbitrage funds. The macro style funds are the most directional and employ a top-down macro view to take advantage of the expected returns of various asset classes. This class of funds may represent the cluster with the highest level of risk as measured by the high levels of standard deviation and skewness[15]. The second strategy represents funds that aim to uncover undervalued asset opportunities in debt or equity markets without necessarily being market neutral. This class of funds is characterized by a middle of the range level of risk as measured by the standard deviation and skewness in Exhibits 3 and 4. The third category of funds represents the market-neutral relative

value arbitrage funds that aim to exploit temporary price anomalies between related assets, in equities or fixed income markets. This category is likely to be represented by the cluster with the lowest risk among the three Equity Hedge funds clusters.

5.2. Why Do We Observe Two FOF Clusters?

The results in Exhibit 4 with respect to the FOF clusters are very striking. In both Panel A and Panel B, the FOF clusters have comparable mean returns but their stadard-deviation and skewness are vastly different. These results strongly suggest that while FOF is supposed to be diversified across all hedge fund strategies, they seem to organize in two significantly different clusters with respect to risk. Evidently, specialization and philosophy within the FOF category appears to prevail, with one cluster perhaps representing the more risky directional strategies and the other cluster representing market-neutral, and more diversified strategies.

---

[15]Brown and Goetzmann [3] suggest that an appropriate criterion for evaluating style classifications is the extent to which these classifications can explain cross sectional differences in future year returns.

5.3. Why Do We Observe Four Managed Futures Clusters?

The observed four distinct clusters for managed futures are consistent with trading volume data for futures contracts[16]. Of the approximately total of $8 billion worth of futures and options contracts traded in 2005, $3 billion were on Equity Indices, $2 billion were Interest Rate futures, $1.8 billion in Individual Equities (mostly options), $300 million in Agricultural Commodities, $200 million in Energy, $120 million in currencies and about $100 million in Precious and Non-Precious metals. It is thus quite reasonable to expect that the four clusters we identified correspond to Equity index futures, Fixed Income futures, Options on Individual Equities and Commodity futures. Futures contracts on these four categories are likely to behave quite differently based on the characteristics of their respective underlying assets.

6. Summaries and Conclusions

This paper uses an objective clustering method for style identification of hedge funds. Monthly return data on individual hedge is used to provide a consistent classification of hedge funds. The data driven framework employed in this paper can provide better comparisons among fund categories and may help service providers, fund administrators and investors in identifying common factors that can lead to better diversification strategies. The CISDM database of the University of Massachusetts is used for this application. Our sample included 2397 live funds and covered the period January 1990 through December 2003.

We first estimated hedge fund clusters using the K-means approach. In a three stage procedure, we estimated clusters with and without managed futures, and then separately for managed futures. Of the ten independent clusters estimated with managed futures included, four are classified as Equity Hedge, four are classified as managed futures, and one is classified as Emerging Markets and one as FOF. None of the other hedge fund classifications such as Convertible Arbitrage, Fixed Income, Global Macro or Merger Arbitrage appeared as independent clusters. It is possible that managers in some strategies, such as Global Macro or Merger Arbitrage employ sufficiently different techniques from one another that they do not form an identifiable cluster.

When managed futures were removed from the clustering process, the resulting hedge fund clusters were not very different than before. We identify seven clusters, four are still Equity Hedge, and two are FOF and one Emerging Markets. Furthermore, the results obtained by separately clustering the managed futures category, indicate the presence of four distinct clusters, two of the clusters are classified as Public and the other two clusters are classified as Systematic Managed Futures.

We apply the Hierarchical Clustering procedure to check the sensitivity of the classification provided by the k-means technique. The results of this approach are very similar to the results of the k-means method, which suggests that the classification of funds is robust across different clustering methods. We estimate nine clusters; six of these clusters are classified as hedge funds and three are classified as managed futures. Of the six hedge fund clusters, three are classified as Equity Hedge, two as Fund of Hedge Funds, and one is classified as Emerging Markets. When we exclude managed futures, we obtain six clusters, three are classified as Equity Hedge, and two as Fund of Hedge Funds and one is classified as Emerging Markets. Similar to the K-means results, we obtain four distinct clusters for managed futures. These results provide support for the notion that the futures market may be viewed as four distinct categories based on the four major asset classes on which futures contracts are commonly traded.

The resulting clusters provide important insight as to the characteristics and structure of the hedge fund industry. We surmise that in spite of the very large number of hedge fund classifications within any given database, the strategies may be characteristically described by a rather few broad strategies. Our results indicate that hedge funds can be uniquely categorized into Equity, Managed Futures, Emerging Markets and FOF. Within Equity Hedge, there are three strategies, Macro, Opportunistic and Market-neutral. Managed Futures can also be categorized into four unique classes; Equity index futures, Fixed Income futures, Options on Individual Equities and Commodity futures.

5. References

[1]   W. F. Sharpe, "Asset allocation: Management style and performance measurement," Journal of Portfolio Management, Vol. 18, pp. 7–19, 1992.

[2]   W. Fung and D. A. Hsieh, "Empirical characteristics of dynamic trading strategies: the case of hedge funds," Review of Financial Studies, Vol. 10, No. 2, 1997.

[3]   S. J. Brown and W. N. Goetzmann, "Mutual fund styles," Journal of Financial Economics, Vol. 43, pp. 373–399, 1997.

[4]   S. J. Brown and W. N. Goetzmann, "Hedge funds with style," Journal of Portfolio Management, Vol. 29 (2, winter), pp. 101–112, 2003.

[5]   B. Liang, "On the performance of alternative investments: CTAs, hedge funds and funds-of-funds," Journal of Alternative Investment Management, 2004.

[6]   W. R. Dillon and M. Goldstein, "Multivariate analysis methods and applications," John Wiley and Sons Inc.,

---

[16]Data on Futures Trading Volume is obtained from the Futures Industry Association Website.

1984.

[7] J. D. Banfield and A. E. Raftery, "Ice floe identification in satellite images using mathematical morphology and clustering about principal curves," Journal of American Statistical Association, Vol. 87, pp. 7–16, 1992.

[8] N. Das, "Hedge fund classification using K-means Clustering method," International Conference in Computing in Economics and Finance, depts.washington.edu/sce2003/Papers/284.pdf, 2003

[9] D. Jiang, C. Tang, and A. Zhang, "Cluster analysis for gene expression data: A survey," IEEE Transactions on Knowledge and Data Engineering, Vol. 16, No. 11, pp. 1370–1386, 2004.

[10] A. Marathe and H. Shawky, "Categorizing mutual funds using clusters," Advances in Quantitative Analysis of Finance and Accounting, Vol. 7, pp. 199–211, 1999.

[11] J. A. Hartigan, "Clustering algorithms," New York: John Wiley and Sons Inc., 1975.

[12] J. Ward, "Hierarchical grouping to optimize an objective function," Journal of American Statistical Association, Vol. 58, pp. 236–244, 1963.

[13] V. Faber, "Clustering and the continuous k-means algorithm," Los Alamos Science, Los Alamos National Laboratory, 1984.

[14] J. A. Hartigan, "Clustering algorithms," New York: John Wiley & Sons, Inc, 1975.

[15] G.Martin, "Making sense of hedge fund returns: What matters and what doesn't," Derivative Strategy, 2000

2

The Cubrix, an Integral Framework for Managing Performance Improvement and Organisational Development

Marcel van Marrewijk

Research to Improve, Trusting Companies International and Virtu et Fortuna, Vlaardingen, Netherland

Abstract

Marcel van Marrewijk, academic director of Research to Improve, has developed an integral, multi-level, multi-disciplinary and multi-stakeholder management framework, based on a phase-wise development approach as described by Clare Graves' Levels of Existence Theory, Ken Wilber's Four Quadrant Theory and the author's Global Excellence Model. This conceptual framework is coined, the Cubrix.

This paper shortly introduces the three original concepts and shows how these models have been merged into the Cubrix. In part two the author demonstrates how Research to Improve designed various surveys, scans, monitors and assessments, all based on this framework. Furthermore, the Cubrix has also been supportive in designing the Performance Improvement Cycle and offer input for developing roadmaps for transitions in organization development.

Keywords: Value Systems, Spiral Dynamics, GEM, Cubrix, Transition Matrix, Research Framework, Sustainable Performance, Organisation Development, Transformations, High Performance Organisations

1. Introduction

2001, Van Marrewijk, in collaboration with Erasmus University Rotterdam, launched an international research project in response to an EC-assignment to develop an integral model for Corporate Social Responsibility, CSR. More than two years later, a consortium of experts delivered the European Corporate Sustainability Framework (ECSF) to the European Commission. It was a new generation management framework, demonstrating company responsible ways of doing business while achieving higher performance levels as sustainable operating organizations, carefully aligning their particular development level(s) with their major challenges [1–3].

The ECSF-research project succeeded in identifying various ways of interpreting Corporate Sustainability and Responsibility (CS-R) and aligning specific ambitions with respect to CS-R and with adequate ways of implementing it. The generic definition of CS-R is the corporate inclusion of social and environmental concerns into business operations and in interactions with stakeholders. Van Marrewijk [4] concluded that corporate responsibility (CR) expresses the corporation's willingness to be accountable for the impact of their doing to stakeholders

(Communion) and relates to phenomena such as transparency, stakeholder dialogue and sustainability reporting. On the other hand, corporate sustainability (CS) is manifested as the organization's capacity (Agency) to improve value creation with respect to the triple bottom line (people, planet & profit), due to for instance environmental friendly production systems, waste reduction policies, recycling, human potential development programs, fair trade, green energy and many more ways to improve multiple performances.

The ECSF framework hosts traditional ways of doing business, such as compliance-driven and profit-driven approaches. It also includes business approaches that have emerged only recently, such as more care-driven and synergy-driven ways of organizational behaviour [5]. Each respective approach characterizes a specific development level, transcending and including the former ones and each supported by particular value systems and management paradigms, demonstrated in coherent sets of institutional structures [6]. Business phenomena such as CS-R can thus be interpreted by each of these systems, taking different manifestations per development level [4,5]:

1) Compliance-driven: CS-R at this level consists of

providing welfare to society, within the limits of regulations from the rightful authorities. In addition, organizations might respond to charity and stewardship considerations. The motivation for CS-R is that CS-R is perceived as a duty and obligation, or correct behavior.

2) Profit-driven: CS-R at this level consists of the integration of social, ethical and ecological aspects into business operations and decision-making, provided it contributes to the financial bottom line. The motivation for CS-R is a business case: CS-R is promoted if profitable, for example because of an improved reputation in various markets (customers/employees/shareholders).

3) Care-driven: CS-R consists of balancing economic, social and ecological concerns, which are all three important in themselves. CS-R initiatives go beyond legal compliance and beyond profit considerations. The motivation for CS is that human potential, social responsibility and care for the planet are as such important.

4) Synergy-driven: CS-R consists of a search for well-balanced, functional solutions creating value in the economic, social and ecological realms of corporate performance, in a synergistic, win-together approach with all relevant stakeholders. The motivation for CS is that sustainability is crucial as it is recognized as being the inevitable direction progress takes.

5) Holistic-driven: CS-R is fully integrated and embedded in every aspect of the organization, aimed at contributing to the quality and continuation of life of every being and entity, now and in the future. The motivation for CS is that sustainability is the only alternative since all beings and phenomena are mutually interdependent. Each person or organization therefore has a universal responsibility towards all other beings.

Too often confronted with pretentious and manipulative CS-R communication (green washing), Van Marrewijk concluded that building cultures of trust within organisations was the first practical and effective step in achieving authentic corporate sustainability and responsibility. He became director Great Place to Work® Institute Netherlands, engaged primarily with transforming workplaces through research, and 'naming and faming' best practices in various award activities [2].

In 2005 he was member of an EC-research project, coordinated by Esade Business School, analysing Great Place to Work® data gathered from over 1,000 European companies. The data showed a pattern in which the best Scandinavian workplaces outperformed the ones in the Mediterranean countries. The GPTW® model is not able to explain such patterns. Once more, Van Marrewijk turned to Spiral Dynamics and Wilber's Four Quadrant (SDI) to develop a sequence of macro-economic systems, running from self sufficiency, pre-capitalist and various classical economies, capitalist (Anglo-Saxon) and socialist market (Rhineland) economies and the emerging interdependent economy [7]. Again, each economic system transcends and includes the less complex ones. Therefore the socialist market economy, predominantly present in northern continental Europe, show plenty reminiscents of former systems, such as excessive rewarding practices for CEO's.

From 2000 on, Van Marrewijk remained board member of the Dutch branch of the European Federation for Quality Management, the EFQM. The ECSF consortium of international researchers[2] was mainly drawn from an international network of quality experts. Its outcome, the ECSF framework was placed within the quality management tradition, as it regarded complex interpretations of CS-R as integral part of business improvement and organizational excellence.

Despite its elegance in framing management attention areas, the EFQM model, officially named the European Model for Business Excellence, is 'as flat as a pancake', in other words, it lacks depth to generate adequate understanding of complex organisations. In order to align the EFQM model within the ECSF framework, Van [8] adapted the EFQM model, by introducing depth and providing various contexts to business excellence, thus creating a multi-level, a multi-disciplinary and multi-stakeholder Global Excellence Model (GEM). In this paper, while discussing the GEM, the author will further elaborate on this topic.

Van Marrewijk remained enthusiastic with his multilevel approach applied to corporate sustainability and business excellence. He developed it into an even more sophisticated framework, which he coined the 'Cubrix', a cubical framework based on three dimensions: development levels (Spiral Dynamics Integral), management attention areas or disciplines, and stakeholders (both Global Excellence Model), the topic of this paper.

In practice, van Marrewijk remained preoccupied with the introduction of the rather one-dimensional Great Place to Work Concept in the Netherlands. In providing feedback to companies on the quality of their workplaces, van Marrewijk noticed that the human resource management approach is often dominant, jeopardizing the transformation towards more promising approaches. Again, the 'flat pancake' syndrome was bothering corporate development as many people managers seemed to be 'arrested' in their constrained and limited set of policies and practices. He felt the time was ready to apply new concepts to corporate research, aligning it with learning and performance improvement. He left Great Place to Work Institute Nederland to his successors and founded a new research institute, Research to Improve and started anew.

This paper elaborates on the content and structure of the Cubrix and demonstrates its use in the development of new research tools. It also deals with some derivatives from the Cubrix such as the Performance Improvement Cycle and the way to design roadmaps for organisation development and performance improvement.

1.1. Structure of This Paper

Paragraph two starts with a short introduction of Spiral Dynamics Integral, as developed by Clare W. Graves, his successors Don Beck and Chris Cowan [9], and Ken Wilber [9]. Also the second fundament underlying the Cubrix, the Global Excellence Model, will be introduced. Paragraph three describes the Cubrix. Paragraph four deals with research tools based on the Cubrix and paragraph five introduces derivatives from the Cubrix, with impact on change management and the design of a roadmap for organization development and performance improvement.

2. Supportive Structures of the Cubrix: Contexts

2.1. The Gravesian Approach to Development

Clare W. Graves, professor psychology at Union College, New York, teaching sections on psychological approaches of Freud and Jung, Watson and Skinner, Maslow and others, was confronted by his students: "OK, Dr. Graves, which one is right?" Graves recognized that all the theories had elements of truth, as well as holes. It led him on a thirty-year quest to better understand the emerging nature of psychologically healthy human beings. It placed him among scientists that try to structure evolutionary aspects of development. See Table 1.

In the 1950s throughout the early 1970s, professor Graves performed extensive empirical research on value systems. He coined his model: the Emergent, Cyclical, Double-Helix Model of Adult BioPsychoSocial Systems Development or, for short, Emerging Cyclical Level of Existence Theory (ECLET). As an introduction to his framework each qualification will be briefly summarized.

2.1.1. Emergent
With respect to 'emergent', Graves concluded that mankind has gradually developed eight levels of existence or core value systems, so far. A value system is a way of conceptualizing reality and encompasses a consistent set of values, beliefs and corresponding behaviour and can be found in individual persons, as well as in companies and societies [9]. With these statements, Graves confronted Maslow's 'Hierarchy of Needs'. He agreed to the ranking of the needs, but the image of a pyramid cannot express the emerging capacities of human beings in meeting higher levels of complexity, thus creating different manifestations of personal and collective self-actualisation. Graves' successors, Beck & Cowan, created the image of a spiral, emphasising the open ended and ever expanding nature of their approach.

Human development is an emergent, oscillating proc-

Table 1. Evolutionary aspects.

Line	Life's question	Typical researcher
Aesthetic	What is attractive to me?	Housen
Cognitive	What am I aware of?	Piaget, Kean
Emotional	How do I feel about this?	Goleman
Interpersonal	How should we interact?	Selman, Perry
Kinesthetic	How should I physically do this?	Gardner
Moral	What should I do?	Kohlberg
Needs	What do I need?	Maslow
Self	Who am I?	Loevinger
Spiritual	What is of ultimate concern?	Fowler
Values	What is significant to me?	Graves, Spiral Dynamics

ess that subordinates older, less complex ways of thinking/being to newer, more expansive, more complex ones. Older systems do not disappear, but are subsumed within the more elaborate ones and can be reactivated when older problems resurface. Each new emerging system 'transcends and includes' the previous ones [10].

A second notion regarding emergence lies in the intangible aspects 'below the surface' that influence human behaviour. The core question according to Beck and Cowan is "how does the mind process reality". The framework structures thinking systems within people, not types of people. Each value system is associated with a specific 'world view', thus generating multiple 'truths'.

2.1.2. Cyclical
The development of value systems occurs in a fixed order. The value systems can be tagged as follows: Survival; Security; Energy & Power; Order; Success; Community, Synergy and Holistic Life System. These systems brighten or dim along with changing life conditions and one's capacities. Each new value system includes and transcends the previous ones, thus forming a natural hierarchy (or holarchy).

The value systems alternate between I-oriented and we-oriented systems, with a respective focus to changing the world outside and coming to peace with the world inside.

2.1.3. Double Helix
Value systems develop in reaction to specific environmental challenges and threats: the systems brighten or dim when life conditions change. These Life Conditions (LC) consists of historic Times, geographic Place, existential Problems and societal Circumstances. As with the double helix in a DNA-string, Graves' model distinguishes LC as one of the two determining factors that cause the existence of prevailing and emerging contexts. The other one is Mind Capacities [MC's]. Their interactions produce the thinking systems, mentioned above.

Transformations to more complex contexts actually occur when life conditions have build up a sufficient level of urgency among entities to leave behind their proven pa-

Table 2. A developmental approach to values.

Development Label	Compliance-driven Order (Blue)	Profit-driven Success (Orange)	Care-driven Community (Green)	Systemic-driven Synergy (Yellow)
Environment LC	Ordered relationships requiring legitimization in order to ensure stability and security for the future	Many viable alternatives for progress, prosperity and material gain since change is the nature of things	The gap between people and their (material) possibilities has become disproportionately large	Complex problems that cannot be solved within the current systems as awareness of broad interconnections grows.
Values examples	Duty, obedience, loyalty, guilt, discipline, stability, clarity, justice, one truth	Productivity, personal esteem, image, reward, satisfaction, competition	Harmony, equality, consensus, honesty, openness, trust	Insights, tolerance, long term orientation, systems-thinking

tterns of behaviour and challenge their world view. They have to experience that current solutions are no longer adequate. In order to cope with the new life conditions, entities must have a supportive mind capacity to be able to match the new challenges life conditions offer and generate new adequate behavior and subsequent institutional arrangements.

Entities such as people and organizations will eventually have to meet the challenges their context provides or risk the danger of oblivion or even extinction. If for instance societal circumstances change, inviting corporations to respond and consequently reconsider their role within society, it implies that corporations have to re-align their value systems and all their business institutions (such as mission, vision, policy deployment, decision-making, reporting, corporate affairs, etcetera) to these new circumstances.

2.1.4. Adult

Graves restricted the outcomes of his theory to 'healthy adults' only. In practice one can observe that Spiral Dynamic thinking can also be applied to the development of children, all be it with some adjustments. As a third generation researcher, with Graves being the first and Beck and Cowan the second generation, van Marrewijk applies the theory also to groups, organisations and even societies and economic systems, as this paper will demonstrate.

2.1.5. Biopsychlogicalsocial

People tend to change their biopsychlogicalsocial beings as their Conditions of Existence change. With respect to the biological appearances, it obviously applies to the pre-historic Cro Magnon, the Pygmies, Inuits and Bedouins, as well as contemporary Salarymen. Over time mankind was able to alter his DNA information to adjust to changing circumstances and support new generations with a better constitution to cope with prevailing circumstances. Also psychologically and socially people change along with their life conditions, creating new cultural patterns and institutional arrangements that facilitate adequate behaviour.

Psychologically, people alternate between an inner locus of control with a focus on changing and controlling the world outside (the I-systems) and an outer locus of control with a focus on coming to peace with the world inside (we-systems).

Due to the ability to match MC with LC, people centralized in a value system are psychosocially congruent with components of that system. On the other hand, a person may not be equipped to move to a more complex system, even if the Conditions of Existence demand it. Psychologically, these people remain 'arrested' towards future needs or even 'closed' to less complex value systems that, naturally, should have been included in their repertoire.

Individuals and groups develop and apply values and supporting institutional structures, in order to cope with the prevailing challenges. A person may stabilize at one or at a combination of value systems if the Conditions of Existence are stable. When LC warrants, a person or group may regress to a previous value system. As with an uphill ride, people back shift to a lower gear to get more power.

2.1.6. Systems Development

Each value system includes a range of positive and negative characteristics and behaviours, adaptive and maladaptive elements. A system can become healthy and unhealthy, supportive and destructive, energizing and frustrating, sowing the seeds of change. It offers linkages to change management, what to do in order to improve performance.

It is important to understand that NO value system is inherently "better" or "worse" than another. It is all about adequateness or appropriateness to the milieu and conditions of existence. As higher value systems normally include the previous contexts, a higher system is not simply better; it offers more grades of freedom to match particular challenges. If a response can be made adequately in a basic context, there is no need to do it more sophistically and waste time and efforts. Moreover, complex value systems are much more vulnerable, or more difficult to sustain.

The actual introduction to the various levels of existence will be dealt with in the next paragraph.

2.2. Wilberian Approach to Development

In Sex, Ecology and Spirituality, Ken Wilber [10] made a large contribution to evolutionary developments. He supports Graves when stating: "Evolution proceeds irreversibly in the direction of increasing differentiation/integration, increasing organization and increasing complexity"[1]. This "growth occurs in stages, and stages are ranked in both a logical and chronological order. The more holistic patterns appear later in development because they have to wait the emergence of the parts that they will then integrate or unify[2]. This ranking refers to normal hierarchies (or holarchies) converting "heaps into wholes, disjointed fragments into networks of mutual interconnection[3]"

As the natural orientations emerged, they clearly show an increase of integratedness and complexity, each stage including and transcending the previous ones.

From evolutionary literature, Wilber concludes twenty "patterns of existence" or "tendencies of evolution" which are summarized below: reality is not composed of things or processes; it is not composed of wholes nor does it have any parts. Rather it is composed of whole/parts, or holons[4]. This is true of the physical sphere (atoms), as well as of the biological (cells) and psychological (concepts and ideas) sphere, or simply said, apply to matter, body, mind and spirit. Atoms or processes are first and foremost holons, long before any 'particular characteristics' are singled out by us.

Holons display four fundamental capacities: self-preservation, self-adaptation, self-transcendence and self-dissolution. Its agency—its self-asserting, self-preserving tendencies—expresses its wholeness, its relative autonomy; whereas its communion—its participatory, bonding, joining tendencies—expresses its partness, its relationship to something larger. Both capacities are crucial: any slight imbalance will either destroy the holon or make it turn into a pathological agency (alienation and repression) or a pathological communion (fusion and dissociation). Self-transcendence (or self-transformation) is the system's capacity to reach beyond the given, pushing evolution further, creating new forms of agency and communion. Holons can also break down and do so along the same vertical sequence in which they were built up.

These four capacities or 'forces' are in constant tension: the more intensely a holon preserves its own individuality, preserves it wholeness, the less it serves its communions or its partness in larger and wider wholes and vice versa. This tension can be manifested, for instance in the conflict between rights (agency) and responsibilities (communions), individuality and membership and autonomy and heteronomy.

If holons stop functioning, all the higher holons in the

---

[1]Wilber, K., *Sex, Ecology and Spirituality*, Shambhala, second edition. 2000, 1995 (page 19, 74).
[2]Wilber, K. *SES* (page 28) italics by Wilber.
[3]Wlber, K. *SES* (page 26).
[4]Koestler:" a holon is a whole in one context and simultaneously a part in an other".

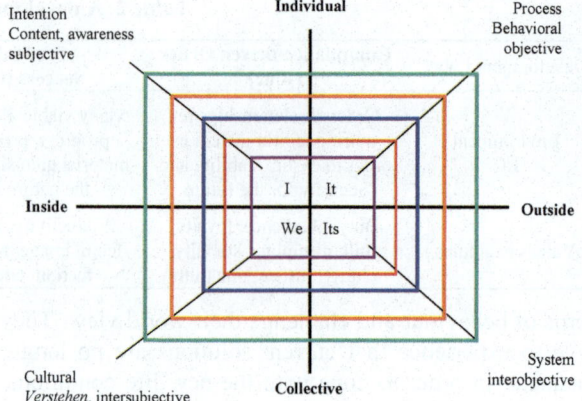

Figure 1. Wilber's all quadrant model, slightly adapted.

sequence are also destroyed, because those higher wholes depend upon the lower as constituent parts. We might say that Wilber as well as Graves, Beck & Cowan have created an almost identical phase wise orientation to reality however based on different lines of reasoning.

Wilber's rich analysis of science and (eastern) religion has culminated in a four-quadrant perspective towards Reality. The upper quadrants represent individual holons, the lower half of the diagram, social or communal holons. The left side is the interior and the right side the exterior form or structure of holons.

The upper-right quadrant represents the objective, empirical observations of holon behaviour, such as atoms, gases, fish or humans. The upper-left quadrant stands for the I-world: the interior form of an individual holon: subjective intentions and awareness. Characteristic sciences focused on this quadrant are psychoanalysis, phenomenology and mathematics. The lower-right quadrant represents the 'its-world'. With reference to humans, it shows the exterior forms of social systems such as the development from kinships to nations-states, but also tools and technology, architectural styles, forces of production, concrete institutions and even written material. The lower-left quadrant corresponds with the we-perspective of Reality, the Cultural dimension. Weber introduced an intersubjective sociologist approach, Verstehen, that characterizes this quadrant. It is the realm of relational exchange creating collective values, consciousness, worldviews and common meaning and interpretations.

The upper quadrants coincide with Graves' Biopsychosocial features of the Mind Capacity and the lower ones with Life Conditions. In both concepts, the quadrants are aligned: Each point in any of these quadrants correlate with a specific set of points in the other quadrants, such as Figure 1 above demonstrates. The Four Quadrant Model includes Graves' Levels of Existence as Table 3 shows.

Woodsmall has labeled the right quadrants as Process and System. It aligns better with the intention to apply the Quadrants Model to corporate dynamics.

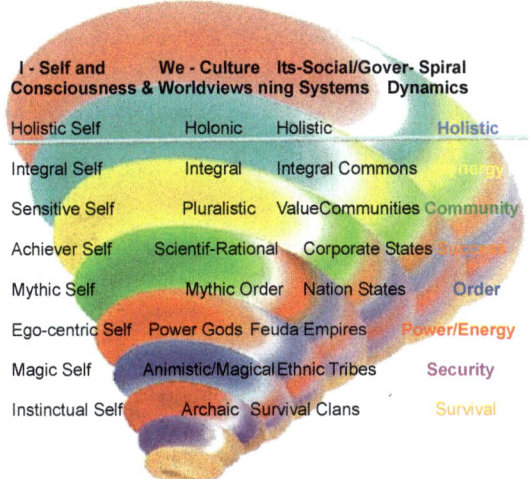

Table 3. Quadrants as process and system.

2.3. Application to Corporate Dynamics

Organizations and employees can be recognized easily as holons, as they are mutually dependent, as strikes and absenteeism clearly show. In terms of Wilber, organizations tend to support their employees (vertical relationship), creating value as an (horizontal) agency, in constant exchange with its stakeholders (horizontal communion).

Challenged by changing circumstances and provoked by new opportunities, individuals, organizations and societies develop adequate solutions that might be new sublimations, creating synergy and adding value at a higher level of complexity. Since instability increases at higher complexity levels, entities can shift to lower levels should circumstances turn unfavorable or should competences fail to meet the required specifications.

Figure 2 represents a phase-wise development of corporations, as complexity increases thus requiring additional degrees of freedom to find more adequate solutions to prevailing circumstances. Along with the evolutionary development of corporations their awareness, their culture, their behavior and their structures/systems change.

Clusters of values facilitate these institutional changes and manifestations. Evolutionary development has reveal-

ed a sequence of multiple levels or development stages. From now on we will refer to these as the contexts of organizations. In order to be able to draft ideal type organizations, aligned with specific contexts, we need to go deeper and explore the disciplines that are active within organizations. We need to elaborate on the various manifestations disciplines can take in various contexts. We therefore introduce the Global Excellence Model.

3. Supportive Structures of the Cubrix: Disciplines

3.1 Global Excellence Model

The European Model for Business Excellence (EFQM model) [11], developed in 1991, was a breakthrough in management and quality improvement, and has been applied successfully among thousands of companies, mainly all over Europe. Over time such initiatives become rigid, as they appear to be unable to include new developments in their conceptual thinking and business appliances. Their failure to include a phase-wise approach caused us to develop the Global Excellence Model (GEM). However, the resemblances are much more important, than the differences. See www.efqm.org for further information.

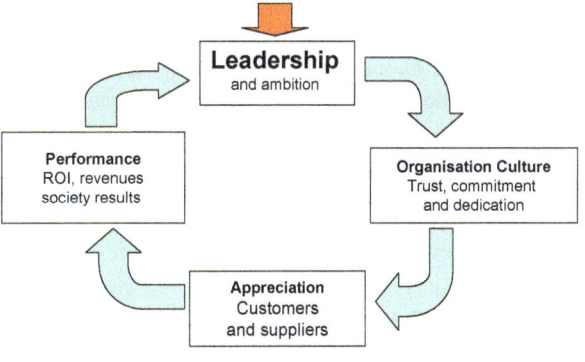

Figure 3. Linkage research by brooks & whiley' 96.

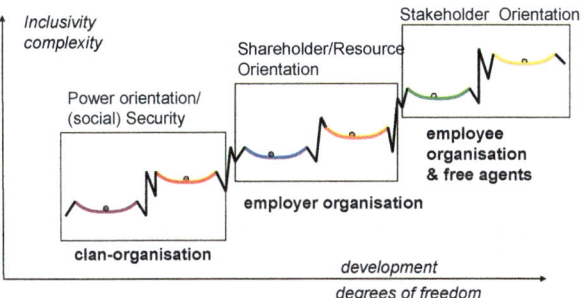

Figure 2. Phase wise orientation to business development.

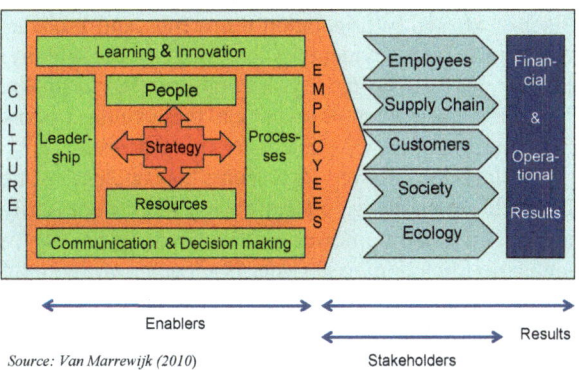

Figure 4. Global excellence model(GEM).

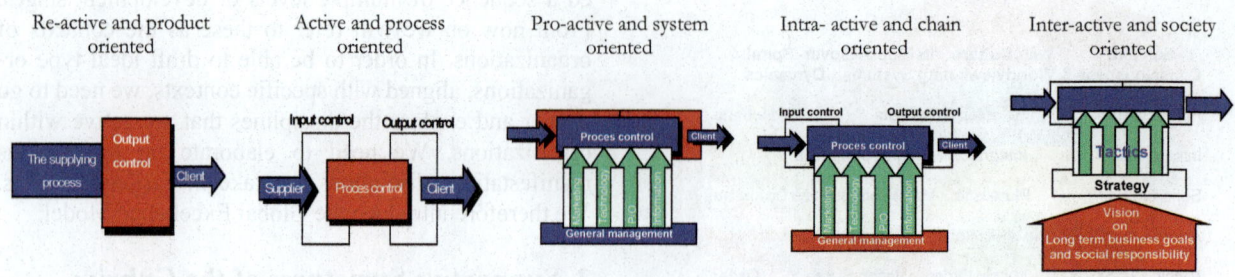

Re-active and product oriented   Active and process oriented   Pro-active and system oriented   Intra- active and chain oriented   Inter-active and society oriented

Figure 5. INK quality orientations.

The GEM as well as the EFQM model is non-prescriptive frameworks that recognizes that there are many approaches to achieving sustainable excellence. Due to their focus on excellence, the EFQM model is centred on process management. We prefer to align the GEM with Brooks and Whiley's conclusions based on Linkage Research (1996) and to focus on the impact of leadership and culture. It is people who bring passion, loyalty, entrepreneurship, trust and dedication to the work floor. Without these, processes would never achieve the expected levels of output. As Wilber taught us, it is all about balancing and consistency in order to deliver adequate solutions to prevailing circumstances.

A group of people create, plan, deploy, lead, implement, improve, execute, learn, enjoy, what ever that needs to be done, in order to achieve the desired results. These results can only come about when stakeholders appreciate the fruits of their doing. Thus, the enabler criteria cover what an organization does, while the results criteria cover what an organization achieves. See Figure 4.

The major distinction between the GEM en the EFQM model is the GEM's ability to generate multiple levels of quality development, both with respect to contexts as well as situations.

This issue of multi-levelledness was firstly challenged by the Netherlands Quality Institute (INK), already in 1993, when they introduced five quality orientations for assessment purposes: activity (or output), process, organization (or system), chain and society.

Each next quality orientation transcends and includes the previous ones, evidently increasing its complexity. The issue here is "do quality orientations align with the Grave-sian development levels or can these value systems (or contexts) support various quality orientations."

In Table 4, Van Marrewijk presents his conclusions: he INK quality complexity phases do not align necessarily with the Gravesian framework of development levels. An organization functioning in Order is adequate with output control (X), and has abilities with respect to managing processes (x). Organizations that are strong in Success are better able to manage their processes (X) and have abilities to define and apply quality in systemic terms (x). Less complex contexts might have limited abilities or none at

all to produce more complex quality orientations (O).

In order to support an organization wide approach to quality, processes and systems need to be complemented by, firstly, a culture that creates unity, trust and supports co-operation and, secondly, an approach that generates (personal) alignment of the stakeholders involved.

In trying to improve quality it makes quite a difference if a shift to a next quality orientation can be achieved within the same context, or that a transformation to a more complex value system is necessary. We believe that many advisors in quality improvement have failed in making this distinction and taking proper precautions.

Van Marrewijk therefore suggests defining quality orientations as 'situations' within a context, at the same time acknowledging the developmental aspects of qualitystating that specific orientations can be best imple more straight-forward than in organizations supported by the value system Success. Managers and advisors alike have often questioned the lack of simplicity in our approach. There is lots of evidence in the failure of numerous quality

Table 4. The quality matrix.

Contexts/Quality Orientations	Order	Success	Community	Synergy
Output	X	x	x	x
Process	x	X	x	x
Organisation	-	x	X	x
Chain	o	-	x	X

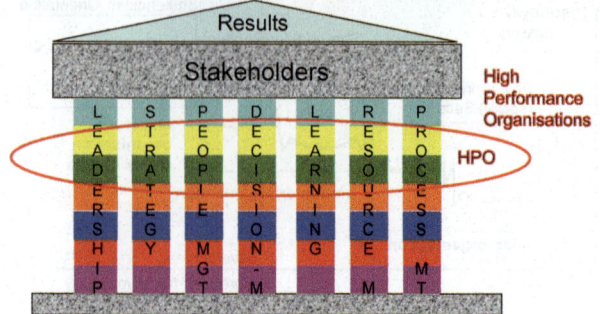

Figure 6. Global excellence model (GEM) and SDI phases.

improvements projects. People have to get used to it that managing complex organizations requires large skills and good theories, better than we ones they used to apply. In elaborating on the performance cycle, we will further deal with this topic.

In developing the GEM, we have assigned the various quality orientations as subsequent manifestations of process management, one of the seven enablers within organizations. We applied the same approach to all seven enablers, thus providing the image of a temple with seven pillars, see Figure 6, each consisting of a set of subsequent paradigms.

In Subsection 4.2 we will demonstrate how these 'pillars' support specific research tools and related implementation and learning activities.

3.2 The Cubrix

The Cubrix, as well as its supportive concepts, emphasize the relationship between performance and organization development. With a single focus on management areas, companies do make progression when they succeed in aligning various enablers into an integral business approach, but often they fail in sustaining their performance growth due to rigidness with respect to organizational development. Once organizational development also becomes a variable in improvement activities, sustainable progress is possible. In discussing High Performance Organizations we will further elaborate on this topic.

The Cubrix shows the three dimensions: Organization Development (levels), Disciplines (Management Areas, enablers) and Stakeholder Performances (or Triple Bottom Line: People, Profit, Planet). Each of the cells within the Cubrix can be highlighted and made specific. The result is the so-called Transition Matrix. The appendix shows a summarized version of this matrix.

In the next chapter, Van Marrewijk will demonstrate some of the research tools based upon the Cubrix.

4. The Cubrix: Supporting Research

4.1. Research to Improve

Successful organizations have long stopped running on just processes, numbers and systems. Their measurement systems also include organizational culture and employee intentions. Driven by values and ambitions and challenged by competition, organizations look for the right blend of 'hard' and 'soft' measures in order to continuously improve corporate performance and successfully implement a carefully drafted road map for organizational development.

Research to Improve's surveys, monitors, scans and assessments provide a deep understanding of dynamic and complex topics within organizations. The research tools

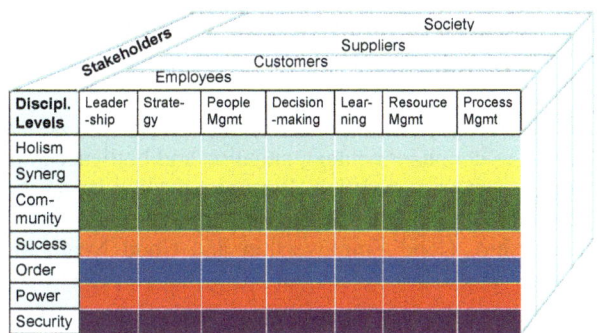

Figure 7. The cubrix.

generate results, which give an insight into what people do, how and why they do so and what steps managers and employees can take in order to achieve goals, overcome bottlenecks and enhance performance.

Each development phase has a specific culture and values, ambitions, set of characteristic institutions and related change strategies. Research to Improve has developed research tools for every development phase and within every phase, for each management criteria. By means of generic surveys and dedicated scans, Research to Improve tries to investigate the dominant contexts within an organization. Sophisticated research, strengthened with conceptual and practical expertise, generates a proper diagnosis. This should blend with the internal experiences through dialogues and 'good conversations' discussing and interpreting the contemporary contexts and situations, challenges and bottlenecks. This is the input for drafting the best way to move ahead.

The outcomes of generic surveys are presented in feedback reports and graphs based upon Spiral Dynamics, 4 Q model and the GEM. Which policies and business topics are managed best and appreciated most? Are the four quadrants consistently developed?

In the next paragraph we will introduce examples of research tools, such as the RTI Survey, the Leadership Monitor and the People Management Monitor.

Figure 8. Research to improve model (Cubrix).

4.2. Research to Improve Basic Employee Perception Survey

The RTI Survey identifies the management areas of the GEM, the dominant context, situation and bottlenecks in management and operation. It reports the results on the three most prominent performance criteria: Good Entrepreneurship, Good Employership and Good Neighborship.

The feedback report generates the opinions and perceptions of stakeholders-mostly employees-with respect to:

- The quality of leadership
- The guidance of the strategy
- The effectiveness of communication and decision-making.
- People management
- The way learning, collaboration and innovation takes place
- The support of resources and opportunities
- The quality of the processes
  As well as cultures and the development levels

The RTI Survey emphasizes the importance of trust, as trust includes and transcends employee satisfaction, motivation and commitment.

As custom-made adjustments we can include the core values of the clients' organization and report if the desired behavior not only meet the requirements, but also whether it matches the intrinsic values of the employees, and if it is sufficiently supported by their culture, by leadership behavior, and by the policies and procedures provided by the organization itself.

The RTI survey links to organizational performance to organization development, so that long-term aspirations can be made specific to day-to-day operations. Also the gap between 'what is' (ist) and 'should be' (soll) can be better understood. Combined, one can design a roadmap, by distinguishing a sequence of steps, priorities and interventions. See also Subsection 5.1.

In 2009, Research to Improve developed an innovative research tool for another stakeholder group, hospital patients by once more applying spiral dynamics thinking into the monitoring of vital processes in hospital management: the patient trust survey, we were able, among others, to distinguish levels of patients' wellbeing, their loyalty, quality perceptions from patients' perspective and various ways how medical and nursing professionals behaved towards the patients.

4.3. Leadership and People Management

The Cubrix suggests seven leadership styles, each associated with a specific development level (Figure 9). Per style, experts of the Rotterdam School of Management, Erasmus University, especially dr. Dirk van Dierendonck,

dr. Daan Stam and dr. Inge Nuijten, selected leadership qualities. The statements defining these qualities are validated via scientific methods.

An effective leader, let us say one with a natural gift in servant leadership, should firstly align with the context and challenges the organisation is facing and secondly, include the qualities of the previous leadership profiles. In addition to the congruency of leadership competences, the monitor is able to measure the contextual effectiveness of specific leaders. In the end we do not want to have an entrepreneur responsible for accountancy or a bookkeeper for an R&D department. The situational effectiveness of leaders is determined by the strategic orientation of the organization. See also Subsection 4.4.

The People Management Monitor is developed in order to provide in-depth understanding of the effectiveness of an organisation's people management practices and policies. Based on the Cubrix, Research to Improve distinguished five ambition levels in people management policies:

1) Creating a safe, vitalizing and physically and emotionally healthy community (building the foundation for a culture of trust);

2) A clear and fair salary payment system, employee benefits, and working conditions (Personnel Administration Department);

3) Employee fit in a functional perspective, especially the recruitment, career development and employee turnover, as well as work pressure and absenteeism (Human Resource Management);

4) Investing in employees' professional and personal development (Human Talent Management), by attracting and attaching employees;

Holism	**Spiritual leader:** Vulnerable, leading the mission; inspiring
Synergy	**Emergent Leader:** visionary, communicative, challenging, long term orientation
Community	**Servant Leader:** supportive, caring, personal growth, forgiving, coaching, emphatic
Success	**Entrepreneur:** courage, rewarding, result oriented, accountability
Order	**Manager:** facilitator, purposeful, monitoring, planning & control
Power-energy	**Baas:** authoritarian, decisive, competitive, corrective
Security	**Founder:** role model, mediator, story teller, Pater Familias

Figure 9. Value driven leadership styles and qualities.

Synergy	**Human Capital:** alignment, balancing intrinsic and eccentric values (*trust*)
Community	**Human Potential:** talent development; evaluation & feedback, organization development (*motivation, engagement*)
Success	**Human Resources:** recruit; retain; rouse; absenteeism (*satisfaction*)
Order	**Personal Department:** administrative, compliance driven; working conditions (*loyalty*)
Power Security	**Community Building:** a healthy and vital, non-discriminatory workplace (*cameraderie*)

Figure 10. Value driven people management policies.

5) Fine-tuning personal drives and qualities and collective ambitions, for daily operational fit, cultural alignment as well as matching individual and collective learning needs (Human Capital Management). These instruments provide a sense of consistency: "what will be the results when we stick to an authoritarian leadership style, with our business attracting more and more educated and independent employees?" "How can we support employees' dedication, engagement and motivation, as these are one of the most important success factors for High Performance Organisations?"

With a better understanding of contexts, values, challenges and organization development, companies can select more effective interventions and improvement activities.

4.4. High Performance Organizations—HPO

Jim Collins, co-author of Build to Last [12] and author of Good to Great [13], has revealed how good, mediocre and even bad companies achieve enduring greatness, and sustain their success over time by 'engineering' growth and continuous improvement into the DNA of an enterprise. Measured according the number of copies sold, the books were a huge success, but only a few companies seem to be able to apply the findings in practice.

Dr. André de Waal, a Dutch scientist and business consultant, performed a five-year study to grasp the discriminating factors for High Performance Organisations (2008). He defined five pillars:

- High quality of management
- High quality of professionals
- Long term orientation
- Open and action oriented
- Continuous Improvement

The specific qualities of leadership relate to what we called servant and emergent leadership, the green and yellow realms of organization development (see Figure 6). The same applies to professionals: they flourish in cultures of trust. If fully enabled, respectfully challenged and endowed with opportunities to take responsibility, professionals can become highly resilient, dedicated, and profoundly more productive than employees working in

Table 5. The strategy matrix.

Contexts/Strategic orientations	Order	Success	Community	Synergy
Effectiveness	x	**X**	x	x
Efficiency	**X**	x	x	x
Flexibility	x	x	**X**	x
Creativity	x	x	x	**X**

X = dominant
x = applicable

organizations offering mediocre conditions.

The GEM adds two additional criteria and combined with its phase-wise orientation, Research to Improve is quite able to measure HPO and identifying the intermediate steps in order to enter a new level of performance and ultimately becoming a HPO.

The next tool, the strategy scan, developed by Marcel van Marrewijk and Prof.dr Teun Hardjono, shows how this can be done.

4.5. The Strategy Matrix

The first step in drafting a roadmap towards sustainable performance improvement and organisation development is finding out one's position. What are the current constraints, challenges and risks? What are the dominant value systems within the organisation? In short, what (strategic) situation and context are most adequate to face current strengths and weaknesses, opportunities and threads?

In 2003 Van Marrewijk and Hardjono developed the Strategy Scan, based on the Strategy Matrix. This online scan supports the strategic dialogue, the exchange of facts and experts opinions, and gives a direction to strategy development. One can conduct the Strategic Scan in board of directors, management teams, among staff members, and as a vertical dialogue deeper into the organisation as well as outside, even with all stakeholders.

The first part of the scan focuses on strategic situations, which ultimately determine the main direction or strategic orientation of the organisation. Examples of such aspects are the consumer needs and the current bottleneck obstructing organisational performance. The result is a focus and a set of ideal type interventions. See also Van Marrewijk [7].

The second part surveys the nature and complexity of the (external) environment and the disciplinary developments (or paradigms) regarding the management criteria such as leadership, people -, resource - and process management. The Strategy Scan indicates the organisation's most dominant development phase, its favourite level of existence.

A Strategy Matrix can be drawn with all situations and contexts. In contradiction to the quality situations, all strategy situations are relevant to all contexts, but in each context a situation is manifested differently. The large X indicates the natural combinations. Efficiency can be performed adequately in Order, while Effectiveness aligns best in Success, etcetera.

Each combination provides the researchers and corporate experts a set of specific interventions and key performance indicators, which forms a major input for drafting a roadmap for performance improvement, aligned with the dominant value systems of the organisation.

The Strategic Sustainability Scan is an extended version including sustainability issues. The Sustainability Scan generates an adequate meaning of corporate sustainability and responsibility, an ideal type reference on which an organization can develop its own touch and approach. This way one can link strategy with CS/CR-policies and interventions.

5. The Cubrix Supporting Change Management

From the sheer construction of the Cubrix, in other words, through distinguishing contexts (value systems), aspects (disciplines) and situations (quality or strategic orientations) one have to conclude that all management principles, models and even hypes have their value, but often only in a certain combination of situation, aspect and/or context. Or put differently: each cell within the Cubrix will have a list of do's and don'ts, with effective approaches, tools and policies, and ones that do not apply to this particular context-situation.

Due to changing circumstances both outside as well as inside organizations, in the case of corporate dynamics, models, tools and certainly hypes have limited applicability and tenability over time. The Cubrix is therefore able to function as a framework for structuring tools, policies, models and management literature.

The multi-level approach underlying the Cubrix also revealed a set of distinctive complexity levels in change management. Furthermore, it offers a conceptual basis for the so-called Performance Improvement Cycle from which one can deduct a roadmap for sustainable business improvement and organisation development. It is the topic for our next paragraph.

5.1 The Performance Cycle

The Cubrix helped us in structuring change management into four distinctive hierarchical complexity levels: (1) vitalising, (2) optimising, (3) shifting and (4) transforming. These four dimensions of change management are explained below.

5.1.1. Vitalizing
Often the performance can be improved by enhancing the fundamental skills, structures and procedures of including contexts; these interventions are relatively simple as we have a lot of experience in managing these aspects, but being involved in more complex value systems, we tend to neglect basic competences although they can jeopardize current performance potential.

Vitalization programs ought to touch all four quadrants, or at least restore the balance between them.

5.1.2. Optimizing
Once a sound fundament has been realized, further im-

provement can occur we organizations enhance the effectiveness of the characteristic institutions within the dominant context. Try to find out and apply best practices, work smarter and excel in what needs to be done.

5.1.3. Shifting
If including and current contexts are functioning well, further improvement can be established by fine-tuning the strategic situation. Within a context, organizations must focus their business towards the most adequate situations, aligning their interventions accordingly.

5.1.4. Transforming
When the previous three change management dimensions can no longer sustain corporate performance, organizations should adopt new ways of organizing by transforming to a more complex context, adopting emerging value systems and all institutions aligned with it. Transformations are complex phenomena, especially if managed as an improvement project.

Each value system has a supporting institutional structure that consistently arranges ways of doing. As more value systems appear parallel, or nested, within organizations, these structures are reasonably flexible to comprehend elements from various value systems. Elements of emerging systems can be developed within the current structures. It needs to have a critical mass of people who can support these values and corresponding awareness and behaviour. Once these values are triggered by challenges or intrinsic motives, their full potential can become manifest causing new institutional arrangements, encompassing previous ones. These transformations are far from simple. Changing life conditions boost a sense of urgency, building up a dissonance, a pressure to move, a necessity to change, and requires commitment to change at the top of the organization. These necessary conditions can be concerted into a successful transition to a more complex level of existence. Despite its difficulty, some organisations are very good at it [14].

Having identified the four dimensions of change management, we adapted the Performance Improvement Cycle. See Figure 11. It is structured according to Deming's Plan–Do–Check–Improve sequence.

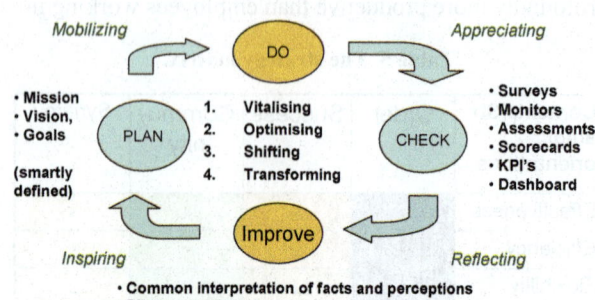

Figure 11. Performance improve cycle, based on deming's PDCA.

The Performance Improvement Cycle suggests various ways to check the impact of the implementation process. Employee perception tools, such as surveys, monitors and assessments, as well as quality management, business operation and accounting tools generate data which via business intelligence services are provided to the board of directors, to management and professionals. Together they interpret the data and determine the progress made. Easy adaptation and fine-tuning is implemented directly, but larger alterations can be tried as experiments and pilots on a small-scale basis, or postponed until they fit the next strategic orientation.

5.2. A Roadmap towards Sustainable Performance

Deducting a roadmap for performance improvement and organizational development can be difficult as each organisation is unique. Many aspects can play a role and not all of them can be foreseen. Still it makes sense to have an idea about the path of change. What can we expect? What level of complexity? Do we have the necessary competences? Do we have the right people on the bus?

Each organisation must provide its own answers, but at least, by applying the Strategy Scan, the Strategy Matrix and the Performance Improvement Cycle, one can grasp its position, its strategic focus, a set of adequate interventions in order to lift the organisation's bottlenecks and enhance its basic competences, and its dominant context to 'colour' the interventions into fitting change activities.

Good surveys can provide management information from which one can tell if vitalisation or optimisation is most effective to enhance corporate performance. Frequently held strategic analyses can provide arguments to remain focused or shift to a next strategic orientation, prioritising a new set of interventions. Strategies can shift permanently within one context. This is relatively simple, but challenging enough.

6. Building up Experiences

Since 2000, Van Marrewijk is engaged in building an integral, multi-level management framework. Now it is in operation. Several research methods have been based upon the Cubrix and consultancy firms are currently applying the new understanding in change management, performance improvement and organisation development.

Supported by our state-of-the art research platform we are able to enable researchers worldwide with our techniques, software and research methods. This will boost our experience and further development of our methods and understanding. This is an invitation to join our efforts in trying to build better businesses and a better society.

7. References

[1] M. van Marrewijk, "European corporate sustainability framework," In International Journal of Business Performance Measurement, Vol. 5, Nos. 2/3, pp. 213–222, 2003.

[2] M. van Marrewijk, "The social dimension of organizations: Recent experiences with great place to work® assessment practices," In Journal of Business Ethics, Vol. 55, No. 2, pp. 135–146, December 2004.

[3] "Excelleren in de weerbarstige praktijk: Knelpuntenonderzoek toepassing INK-managementmodel," ERBS BV/Erasmus University, 2001.

[4] M. van Marrewijk, "Concepts and definitions of corporate sustainability," In Journal of Business Ethics, Vol. 44, No. 2 and 3, pp. 95–105, May 2003.

[5] M. van Marrewijk and M. Werre, "Multiple levels of corporate sustainability," In Journal of Business Ethics, Vol. 44, No. 2 and 3, pp. 107–119, May 2003.

[6] M. van Marrewijk, "A value based approach to organization types: Towards a coherent set of stakeholder-oriented management tools," In Journal of Business Ethics, Vol. 55, No. 2, pp. 147–158, December 2004.

[7] M. van Marrewijk and T.W. Hardjono, "The social dimensions of business excellence," In Corporate Environmental Strategy, Vol. 8, No. 4, 2001.

[8] M. van Marrewijk, I. Wuisman, W. de Cleyn, J. Timmers, V. Panapanaan and L. Linnanen, "A phase-wise development approach to business excellence: Towards an innovative, stakeholder-oriented assessment tool for organizational excellence and CSR," In Journal of Business Ethics, Vol. 55, No. 2, pp. 83–98, December 2004.

[9] D. Beck, and C. Cowan, "Mastering values, leadership and change," Spiral Dynamic, Blackwell Publishers ltd., Cornwall, 1996.

[10] K. Wilber, "Sex, ecology, spirituality: the spirit of evolution," Shambhala, Boston, 1995.

[11] "European foundation for quality management," At http://www.efqm.org.

[12] J. C. Collins and J. I. Porras, "Successful habits of visionary companies," Built to Last, Century, London, 1994.

[13] J. C. Collins, "Why some companies make the leap and other don't," Good to Great, Harper Business, New York, 2001.

[14] M. van Marrewijk, and H. M. Becker, "The hidden hand of cultural governance: The transformation process of humanities, a care-driven organization providing cure, care, housing and well-being to elderly people," In Journal of Business Ethics, Vol. 55, No. 2, pp. 205–214, December 2004.

Appendix

Development labels → Enablers :	Compliance-driven Order (Blue)	Profit-driven Success (Orange)	Care-driven Community (Green)	Systemic-driven Synergy (Yellow)
Transition Matrix Labels based on Spiral Dynamics and Global Excellence Model				
Leadership	Manager	Entrepreneur	Servant Leader	Emergent Leader
Strategy	Dominance through hierarchies	Autonomous growth due to competitive qualities	Stakeholder engagement; Chain oriented	Society oriented; seeking breakthroughs
Communication & Decision making	Top down; Directive; Legal procedures	Still cascading, with room for negotiations; good info from the bottom is always welcome	Bottom-up; group decides; Consensus based	Top-down and bottom-up balance; Holacracy; Consent based
People Management	Personnel & Administration; Working conditions	Human Resource Management	Human Talent Management	Human Capital Management
Learning & Innovation	Incremental (product) innovations; knowledge and competence management	Process innovation, and product diversification; professionalization through MD-training	Social Innovations; developing supportive structures for organizational learning	System innovations, based on in-depth understanding of corporate dynamics, sustainability and needs
Resource Management	Procedural supply relations based on strict pricing policies	Maintenance on process indicators	Outsourcing with strong relationships, peer audits	Co-creating; together- win; Sustainable Purchasing
Process Management	Activity Orientation	Process Orientation	System Orientation	Chain and Society Orientation

Notes

1) The ECSF is a European-wide research project, financed under Article 6 of the European Social Fund Regulation. It has the aim to design Corporate Sustainable and Corporate Responsible (CS-R) ways of doing business. Within the project, a basic conceptual framework is developed, integrating several proven theories, in order for organizations to address and interpret CS-R. The EFQM model is one of the founding models of ECSF. Contact: marcel@vanmarrewijk.nl or +31.6.8 1953 777

2) The consortium members where (academics); Erasmus University Rotterdam, Vrije Universiteit Amsterdam/IVM, Helsinki University of Technology, Triple P Initiative; (Consultants): Virtu et Fortuna, SCS Consulting (Quality Organizations) KDI, European Organization for Quality, VCK, Excellence Ireland, Centre of Excellence Finland

3) For further reading, please read "a value based approach to ideal type organizations" in this edition, Spiral Dynamics (Beck and Cowan, 1996) and the website of the Spiral Dynamics Organization (NVC consulting and partners) at http://www.spiraldynamics.org.

4) See Van Marrewijk and Werre's article "Multiple Levels of Corporate Sustainability" in JoBE May 2003 on DBR's Value Audit (www.dbr.nl).

Abbreviations

4Q   Four Quadrants Model (Wilber)
BE   Business Excellence
CS   Corporate Sustainability
CSR   Corporate Social Responsibility
CS-R   Corporate Sustainability and Corporate Responsibility
ECSF   European Corporate Sustainability Framework
EFQM   European Foundation for Quality Management
EC   European Commission

EU   European Union
GEM   Global Excellence Model
GPTW   Great Place to Work®
HPO   High Performance Organizations
RSM   Rotterdam School of Management
RTI   Research to Improve
SDI   Spiral Dynamics Integral
TQM   Total Quality Management

3

A Literature Review on the Studies of Internet Retailing Management

Tao Zhang, Guijun Zhuang, Yuanyuan Huang
School of Management, Xi'an Jiaotong University, Xi'an, China

Abstract

This paper reviewed the studies of Internet retailing management. It found that, in general, most of the papers on the topic took focus on Internet retailing strategy and online merchandise management. Specifically, it drawn following conclusions: First, there were six major incentives for firms to adopt Internet retailing, including improving internal communication, improving operational efficiency, facing competition, enhancing customer services, reaching out to a wider audience, and improving relations with suppliers. Second, cost of Internet trading and consumer preference were negatively, while status of Internet retailing strategy, technology capability, Internet communication preference, Internet marketplace, and market development opportunity were positively, affect firms to adopt Internet retailing. Third, market positioning, business model, estimation of the market size, Internet-based innovative application, and strong brand of website were the key factors for the success of an online retailing website. Fourth, cross-channel conflict might be reduced by reconstructing the business process or adjusting the pricing strategy, while Internet retailing inventory might be improved by firms' zero inventory policy, in-stock inventory policy, and dynamic inventory policy. Finally, a firm's quality of logistics and delivery could be increased by high-value-package strategy and emergency transshipments. Implications of these conclusions were suggested.

Keywords: Internet Retailing, Internet Retailing Strategy, Online Merchandise Management, Online Store Management

1. Introduction

Retailing is the set of business activities that adds value to the products and services sold to consumers for their personal or family use [1]. Internet retailing is the retailing business on the Internet [2]. That is to say, on one side, providers sell products or provide services on their online website; on the other side, consumers buy products or services by accessing such website via connected computers (i.e., Internet). Digital products will be delivered to customers by Internet directly and non-digital products will be delivered by logistics.

Doherty and Ellis-Chadwick classified the studies of Internet retailing into three categories [3]. The first category is the studies from customer perspective, taking the focus on customer online purchasing behavior and psychology. The second category is the studies from retailer (i.e., company) perspective, taking the focus on the re-

tailing management, such as business model design and online store management. The third category is those from technology perspective, taking the focus on the innovation of emerging IT for the online retailing management. For example, Flash can be used to enhance the display of products.

This paper will review the studies of the second category for two reasons. Firstly, Internet retailing is developing rapidly, and research on Internet retailing management has important theoretical and practical significance [4]. In the market, failed and successful websites coexists. What factors affect the failures and successes of running Internet retailing? How should a firm design their business model and evaluate it? Studies on these questions are far from enough. Therefore, a review on the studies about these questions will expand the retailing theory in the cyber world and guide the management practice of Internet retailing. Secondly, no detailed review on Internet retailing management has been found in the literature. A detailed review on the studies of Internet consumer behavior, the first category, has been done by

The financial support of a NSF program (No. 70972102) from National Natural Science Foundation of China is gratefully notified.

Cheung, Chan and Limayem [5]. Although Doherty and Ellis-Chadwick [3] have reviewed the studies of Internet retailing (the second category) as a whole, their review for the studies of Internet retailing management is lack of details. To guide the future studies of Internet retailing management, it is necessary to review the studies on the topic in more depth and with more details.

The paper is organized as follows: Section 1 is a framework to summarize the papers. Section 2 reviews the papers on Internet retailing strategy. Section 3 reviews the papers on online merchandise management. Section 4 reviews the papers on online store management. Conclusions and implications are given at the final section.

2. Paper Selection and Classification

We used the term "Internet retailing" and "e-tailing" to search the papers in the EBSCO, Proquest and Science-Direct. 125 papers with full text were found. Among those papers, 86 in the perspective of consumer behavior and technology were weeded out, and 39 in the retailer perspective left, ranging from 1996 to 2007. We didn't use the term "B2C" to search because it is a general concept which refers to all the business activity between buyers and sellers in the cyber world, such as retailing, intermediary, and infomediary.

There are three areas for retailing research, namely retailing strategy, merchandise management, and store management [1]. The retailing strategy is the basis of merchandise and store management, while merchandise and store management are the implementation of retailing strategy. Internet changes the way of retailing, but does not change the retailing itself [6]. So, we use this framework to organize the papers we selected. As shown in Table 1, Internet retailing strategy received more attention, and then online merchandise management. Few studies have been found exploring the issues on online store management.

3. Internet Retailing Strategy

Most of the early studies in this area were descriptive or assumptive. Many researchers believed that, by taking advantage of Internet such as 24 × 7 online and buying at home, Internet retailing is superior to traditional retailing. They predicted Internet retailing would replace traditional retailing [7–9]. However, this was wrong. Doherty *et al.* reported that few companies had set up their own online retailing website in 1999 [10]. Hart, Doherty, Kotzab, Madlberger and Ellis-Chadwick found that Internet usage among companies was at the early stage, i.e., firms' websites were more for the informational purpose than for the trade function [11,12]. Chen and Leteney found that many traditional retailers had run both online and offline shops at the same time [13]. In brief, Internet retailing didn't flourish and traditional retailing was not replaced by Internet retailing.

As a result, researchers began to pay close attention to the following four questions: what are the incentives for a firm to adopt Internet? What factors affect a firm's Internet adoption? How a firm should design its business model and marketing strategy based on Internet? How a firm should manage the online shop and offline shop at the same time?

3.1. Incentives for Adopting Internet

Seven papers about this sub-topic were identified from the three databases (see Table 1). These papers proposed and tested two internal and four external incentives.

Two internal incentives were found to have positive impact on firms' intention of Internet adoption. The first is improving internal communication [13,14]. In daily work, employees have to communicate frequently to coordinate their works with others. Internet is capable of transmitting all kinds of information such as instant informal messages, formal documents, sound, and video at the same time with one integrated computer-based platform. Therefore, if a company wants to improve its internal communication, the tools of Internet-based communication will be the first choice. The second internal incentive is improving operational efficiency [15]. Internet-based information system (i.e., information system, such as ERP, Lotus Notes) is powerful for enhancing work efficiency, reducing cost, and simplifying workflow. It can be used to replace manual operations in daily work. Therefore, if the headquarter of a company wants to improve the operational efficiency, it is likely to adopt Internet-based information system.

Four external incentives were found to have positive impact on firms' intention of Internet adoption. The first is facing competition, i.e., a firm feels a threat from competitor's website [10,15,16]. In the competitive market, every company would try its best to gain competitive advantage. If a company have taken the advantage of Internet (e.g., setting up websites or adopting MIS), others are likely to feel a threat and follow the "me too" strategy to avoid falling behind. The second incentive is enhancing customer services [11,12,15]. Winning customers is one of the most important goals for a company. Internet-based website can play a role in winning customers. Specifically, customers may use website to search products, get related information, complain, and communicate with others. These activities are all helpful for a company to win customers by engaging in Internet retailing. The third incentive is reaching out to a wider audience [10,16]. Internet is an open system. It eliminates the borders of physical regions. With search engine

Table 1. Paper summary.

Areas	Focal questions	Number of Papers	Methodology	Conclusions
Internet retailing strategy	Incentives for adopting Internet	8	Quantity analysis based on statistics.	Six incentives, i.e. improving internal communication, improving operational efficiency, facing competition, enhancing customer services, reaching out to a wider audience and improving relations with suppliers, have positive impact on the intention of adopting Internet.
	Factors affecting the Internet adoption	6	Quantity analysis based on statistics and quality study based on case.	Two factors, i.e. cost of Internet trading and consumer preference, have negative impact on Internet retailing adoption. Five factors, i.e. status of Internet retailing strategy, technology capability, Internet communication preference, Internet marketplace and market development opportunity, have positive impact on Internet retailing adoption.
	Online business model and marketing strategy	6	Case study and paper research.	Five factors, i.e. market positioning, business model, estimation of the market size, Internet-based innovative application and strong brand of website, are the key for a successful online retailing website. And the business model and marketing strategy should be designed according to product purchasing frequency, product tangible or intangible and product differentiation.
	Multi-channel management	7	Game models.	Cross-channel conflict can be reduced in two ways. One is "integration" perception, which is aimed at reconstructing the business process; the other is "adjustment" perception, which is aimed at adjusting the pricing strategy of the two retailing channels.
Online merchandise management	Merchandise inventory strategy	4	Game models.	Zero inventory policy, in-stock inventory policy and dynamic inventory policy, are able to reduce Internet retailing inventory cost effectively.
	Merchandise logistics	4	Quantity statistics and game models.	High-value-package strategy and emergency transshipments are able to enhance the quality of logistics and delivery effectively.
Online store management	No focal questions	4	Paper research	No focus explicitly formed.

(e.g., Google or Yahoo) or catalog, it is easier for a customer to search things that he wants. Internet-based web site can help companies to win greater amount of and more remote customers. The fourth incentive is improving relations with suppliers [15,17]. It is very important for a company to keep close relationships with its suppliers given the importance of the supply chain in firm success. Many MIS (e.g., ERP, MRPII) are design to meet such needs. Therefore, those who want to improve relations with their suppliers will have higher intention to adopt Internet-based information system.

3.2. Factors Affecting the Internet Retailing Adoption

Six papers about this topic were found in the three databases, proposing and testing even factors related to the

aspects of company, customer and cyber world (see Table 1).

Three company factors, identified by previous studies, were found having different impact on firms' adoption of Internet retailing. Cost of Internet trading is negatively, status of Internet retailing strategy and technology capability are positively, related to firms' adoption of Internet retailing. If the costs of Internet trading such as logistics cost, organization expense, and operation cost are so high that the adoption of Internet retailing will reduce a company's profit, the company will loss it's enthusiasm for the adoption [18]. Status of Internet retailing strategy refers to the support from headquarters (i.e., general manager or chairman of the board) [18,19]. A headquarter has the right of using the resources such as money and technician in a company. If the headquarter supports the Internet retailing, it will provide the resources necessary for the Internet retailing adoption. The Internet retailing adoption will go smoothly and deeply. Technology capability of a firm will affect firm's web page quality, speed of accessing, and online security [18–20]. In other words, the higher a company's technology capability, the higher the website quality is, and the better the Internet retailing adoption.

Of the two customer factors identified by previous studies, consumer preference for traditional offline shopping was found having a negative, while Internet communication preference was found having a positive, impact on firms' adoption of Internet retailing [18]. Many consumers may think Internet retailing is lack of touching products, so they prefer offline shopping to online shopping. This will discourage a firm to adopt Internet retailing. Internet communication are more preferred as more and more people are living with Internet [18]. Word-of-mouth is more effective for Internet retailing than for other tools of communication. These will help a firm to adopt Internet retailing.

Two cyber world factors have positive impact on the Internet retailing adoption. The first is Internet marketplace, i.e. market management and market rules [18,19]. Good cyber market management and rules are able to create a good cyber trading environment. A good environment is helpful for a company to run a retailing website efficiently, making it more likely to adopt Internet retailing. The second is market development opportunity i.e., the sales that a firm can archive through Internet retailing [16,18]. The more sales and profit a company can get through Internet retailing, the more likely and to higher degree that the company would adopt Internet retailing.

3.3. Online Business Model and Marketing Strategy

Online business model and marketing strategy refers to the following three questions, i.e., what to sell, whom to sell, and how to sell online. Six papers on these questions were found in the databases (see Table 1).

Some researchers tried to figure out the key points of successful online retailing websites. Ring and Tigert suggested that market positioning, business model, and estimation of the market size are the three key factors for a successful online retailing website [21]. These factors can be used by a company to obtain competitive advantage and survive in the market. Kotha found that the Internet-based innovative application such as online Flash games and strong brand of website are effective for attracting consumers [22]. Therefore, applying new techniques and building a good website reputation are key factors for a successful online retailing website.

Other researchers studied the business model and marketing strategy. For example, Peterson et al. pro-

posed that business model and marketing strategy should be designed according to the three aspects of products, i.e. purchasing frequency, tangible or intangible, and differentiation [23]. For instance, a firm should choose a strategy of online retailing, high price, and steep price cuts for electronic fashion magazine (the frequently purchased, intangible, and high differentiation products), while for gold bar (the infrequently purchased, tangible, and low differentiation products), the firm should try a strategy of offline retailing with advertising online and stable price.

3.4. Multi-Channel Management

Multi-channel means a company runs online and offline retailing channel at the same time, i.e., clicks-bricks [13,24,25]. As shown in Table 1, seven papers on this topic were found. These papers focused on how to reduce the cross-channel conflict, including Internet and traditional retailing contesting for money and equipment inside and for markets and suppliers outside [13,24,26].

Some researchers adopted the perception of "integration". They tried to reconstruct the business process to reduce the conflict. For example, Chen, Enders, Jelassi and Leteney [13,24] analyzed the business process of Internet retailing and traditional retailing respectively from the perspective of merchandise transferring. They found that the supply, purvey of information, communication, logistics, and transaction processes can be combined or partially combined. For instance, the supply of Internet retailing and traditional retailing, the advertisements and part of information purvey process, can be combined into one. This will reduce the conflict between a firm's Internet and traditional retailing.

Other researchers adopted the perception of "adjustment". They tried to reduce conflict through adjusting the pricing strategy of the two retailing channels. Generally, the online price is 14% lower than the offline price, so it is believed to be the origin of the cross-channel conflict [27]. Yao and Liu [6,26] analyzed the conflict by modeling with game theory. They found an equilibrium price exists between two retailing channels. This price is close to the offline price, but much higher than the online price. It will increase the traditional retailing sales but reduce the Internet retailing sales. However, the increase will be greater than the reduction, so the total sales will be greater.

3.5. Summary

To sum four conclusions can be drawn from the above review. Firstly, there are six incentives for firms' intention of adopting Internet retailing, i.e., improving internal communication, improving operational efficiency, facing competition, enhancing customer services, reaching out to a wider audience, and improving relations with suppliers. Secondly, two factors, namely Internet trading cost and consumer preference for offline shopping, have negative impact on Internet retailing adoption. Five factors, i.e., status of Internet retailing strategy, technology capability, Internet communication preference, Internet marketplace, and market development opportunity, have positive impact on Internet retailing adoption. Thirdly, market positioning, business model, estimation of the market size, Internet-based innovative application, and strong brand of website are the key factors for a successful online retailing website, and business model and marketing strategy should be designed according to product purchasing frequency, product tangible or intangible, and product differentiation. Fourthly, cross-channel conflict can be reduced in two ways, i.e., "integration" perception which is aimed at reconstructing the business process and "adjustment" perception which is aimed at adjusting the pricing strategy of the two retailing channels.

4. Online Merchandise Management

Traditional merchandise management is the process by which a company attempts to offer the right quantity of the right merchandise in the right place at the right time in order to achieve the company's financial goals [1]. Online merchandise management, similar to that of traditional retailing, is a management process of merchandise purchasing, sorting, and transporting. Eight papers were found on this topic (see Table 1), taking focus on inventory management and logistics or delivery management.

Researchers found that redesigning inventory policy for Internet retailing is able to reduce inventory cost effectively. Combining the zero inventory policy with the in-stock inventory policy, Bailey and Rabinovich proposed a dynamic inventory policy by applying a feature of Internet retailing and the asynchrony of goods payment and procurement [28]. Zhao and Cao studied the situations under which the zero inventory policy and in-stock inventory policy should be applied [29]. They found that the zero-inventory policy were preferred under a positive relationship between reservation price and impatience for delivery, whereas the positive-inventory policy is preferred when these two variables are independent of each other. Furthermore, a more rapid expansion of market is a favorable condition for the zero inventory policy [29].

Other researchers found that some new strategies are able to enhance the quality of logistics and delivery. Rabinovich and Bailey split the quality of logistics and delivery into three dimensions, namely availability, timeliness, and reliability [30]. They proposed that, because more attention is paid to high value package, increasing the value of package is able to ensure the quality of lo-

gistics and delivery from above three dimensions [30]. Elliot found that emergency transshipments could improve the quality of logistics and delivery [31]. Du et al. [32] developed a three-phase solution strategy (i.e., initial-routes formation, inter-routes improvement, and intra-route improvement) to ensure the quality of logistics and delivery. The three-phase solution strategy was found being significantly better than conventional strategy in travel distance and delivery time.

In summary, inventory policies such as zero inventory policy, in-stock inventory policy, and dynamic inventory policy, are able to reduce Internet retailing inventory cost effectively. Some strategies such as high-value-package strategy, and emergency transshipments, are able to enhance the quality of logistics and delivery effectively.

5. Online Store Management

Traditional store management is aimed at enhancing utilization of the fixed assets and work efficiency [1]. Similarly, Internet retailing store management is aimed at enhancing the hits of web pages and work efficiency [33,34]. As shown in Table 1, four papers were found on this sub-topic.

Katerattanakul and Keng [33] proposed a framework for developing web pages, mapping the 27 factors of online store image on the physical store image. For example, the website response time is mapped on the aisle placement and width of physical shop. King and Liou [34] proposed a framework for evaluating the performance of retailing website. The framework consists of two facets of indicators, the user facet and the business facet. The user facet is made up with availability, customer loyalty, etc. And the business facet is made up with strategic position, complementarities, etc. Moreover, Alexis, Noreen, and Jiang [35,36] reviewed the extant IT, such as PC, PDA, and mobile phone. They predicted that more and more new IT will be introduced into Internet retailing. For example, the virtual reality is in prospect, giving customers a better shopping experience.

6. Conclusions and Implications

This paper reviewed the studies of Internet retailing management. We found that most of the papers focused on Internet retailing strategy management and online merchandise management. Following conclusions may be drawn. Firstly, there are six incentives for firms' intention of adopting Internet retailing, i.e., improving internal communication, improving operational efficiency, facing competition, enhancing customer services, reaching out to a wider audience, and improving relations with suppliers. Secondly, two factors (cost of Internet trading and consumer preference) have negative impact on Internet retailing adoption while five factors (status of

Internet retailing strategy, Internet communication preference, etc.) have positive impact on Internet retailing adoption. Thirdly, five factors (market positioning, Internet-based innovative application, etc.) are the key for a successful online retailing website, and online business model and marketing strategy should be designed according to product purchasing frequency, product tangible or intangible, and product differentiation. Fourthly, the cross- channel conflict may be reduced effectively by reconstructing the business process or adjusting the pricing strategy. Fifthly, zero inventory policy, in-stock inventory policy, and dynamic inventory policy are able to reduce Internet retailing inventory cost. Finally, high-value-package strategy and emergency transshipments are able to enhance the quality of logistics and delivery.

These conclusions have useful implications for companies. Firstly, obtaining as much attention as possible from its headquarter, lowering the trading cost, and improving Internet retailing related technology are the silver bullets for a firm to adopt and improve its Internet retailing. Secondly, the Internet retailing business model and marketing strategy should be designed by the characteristics of products. Reconstructing the business process and adjusting the pricing strategy are the two ways to reduce the cross-channel conflict. Thirdly, in order to reduce the cost of inventory and guarantee the quality of logistics and delivery, a company should adopt new inventory policy and logistics strategy such as dynamic inventory policy and high-value-package strategy according to the environment and situations.

7. References

[1]   M. Levy and B. A. Weitz, "Retailing management," Richard D. Irwin, Inc. Massachusetts, 2006.

[2]   B. Rosenbloom, "Marketing channels: A management view," 6th edition, The Dryden Press. New York, 1999.

[3]   N. F. Doherty and F. E. Ellis-Chadwick, "New perspectives in Internet retailing: A review and strategic critique of the field," In International Journal of Retail & Distribution Management, Vol. 34, No. 4–5, pp. 411–428, 2006.

[4]   D. Grewal, G. R. Iyer and M. Levy, "Internet retailing: Enablers, limiters and market consequences," In Journal of Business Research, Vol. 57, No. 7, pp. 703–713, 2004.

[5]   M. K. C. Cheung, W. W. G. Chan and M. Limayem, "A critical review of online consumer behavior: Empirical research," In Journal of Electronic Commerce in Organizations, Vol. 3, No. 4, pp. 1–19, 2005.

[6]   D.-Q. Yao and J. J. Liu, "Channel redistribution with direct selling," In European Journal of Operational Research, Vol. 144, No. 3, pp. 646–658, 2003.

[7]   W. R. Swinyard, "Retailing trends in the USA: Competition, consumers, technology and the economy," In International Journal of Retail & Distribution Management, Vol. 25, No. 8–9, pp. 244–256, 1997.

[8]   K. T. Rosen and A. L. Howard, "E-retail: Gold rush or fool's gold?" In California Management Review, Vol. 42, No. 3, pp. 72–100, 2000.

[9]   J. Drennan and J. R. McColl-Kennedy, "The relationship between Internet use and perceived performance in retail and professional service firms," In Journal of Services Marketing, Vol. 17, No. 3, pp. 295–311, 2003.

[10] N. F. Doherty, F. Ellis-Chadwick and C. A. Hart, "Cyber retailing in the UK: The potential of the Internet as a retail channel," In International Journal of Retail & Distribution Management, Vol. 27, No. 1, pp. 22–36, 1999.

[11] C. Hart, N. Doherty and F. Ellis-Chadwick, "Retailer adoption of the Internet: Implications for retail marketing," In European Journal of Marketing, Vol. 34, No. 8, pp. 954–974, 2000.

[12] H. Kotzab and M. Madlberger, "European retailing in e-transition?" In International Journal of Physical Distribution & Logistics Management, Vol. 31, No. 6, pp. 440–462, 2001.

[13] S. Chen and F. Leteney, "Get real! Managing the next stage of Internet retail," In European Management Journal, Vol. 18, No. 5, pp. 519–528, 2000.

[14] J. A. A. Sillince, S. Macdonald, B. Lefang and B. Frost, "Email adoption, diffusion, use and impact within small," In International Journal of Information Management, Vol. 18, No. 4, pp. 231–243, 1998.

[15] M. D. Elizabeth and J. G. David, "An exploratory comparison of electronic commerce adoption in large and small enterprises," In Journal of Information Technology, Vol. 17, No. 3, pp. 133–147, 2002.

[16] N. Whittaker, "Why marketing, not technology, drives net retail," In Marketing, 26, 1999.

[17] N. M. Levenburg, "Delivering customer value online: An analysis of practices, applications, and performance," In Journal of Retailing and Consumer Services, Vol. 12, No. 5, pp. 319–331, 2005.

[18] N. Doherty, F. Ellis-Chadwick and C. Hart, "An analysis of the factors affecting the adoption of the Internet in the UK retail sector," In Journal of Business Research, Vol. 56, No. 11, pp. 887–897, 2003.

[19] M. K. O. Lee and C. M. K. Cheung, "Internet retailing adoption by small-to-medium sized enterprises (SMEs): A multiple-case study," In Information Systems Frontiers, Vol. 6, No. 4, pp. 385–397, 2004.

[20] D. Pavitt, "Retailing and the super high street: The future of the electronic home shopping industry," In International Journal of Retail & Distribution Management, Vol. 25, No. 1, pp. 38–43, 1997.

[21] J. R. Lawrence and J. T. Douglas, "Viewpoint: The decline and fall of Internet grocery retailers," In International Journal of Retail & Distribution Management, Vol. 29, No. 6–7, pp. 266–273, 2001.

[22] S. Kotha, "Competing on the Internet: The case of Amazon.com," In European Management Journal, Vol. 16, No. 2, pp. 212–222, 1998.

[23] A. R. Peterson, S. Balasubramanian, and B. J. Bronnenberg, "Exploring the implications of the Internet for con-

sumer marketing," In Journal of the Academy of Marketing Science, Vol. 25, No. 4, pp. 329–346, 1997.

[24] A. Enders and T. Jelassi, "The converging business models of Internet and bricks-and-mortar retailers," In European Management Journal, Vol. 18, No. 5, pp. 542–550, 2000.

[25] L. P. A. Simons, C. Steinfield and H. Bouwman, "Strategic positioning of the Web in a multichannel market approach," In Internet Research, Vol. 12, No. 4, pp. 339–347, 2002.

[26] D.-Q. Yao and J. J. Liu, "Competitive pricing of mixed retail and e-tail distribution channels," In Omega, Vol. 33, No. 3, pp. 235–247, 2005.

[27] F.-F. Tang and X. Xing, "Will the growth of multi-channel retailing diminish the pricing efficiency of the web?" In Journal of Retailing, Vol. 77, No. 3, pp. 319–333, 2001.

[28] J. P. Bailey and E. Rabinovich, "Internet book retailing and supply chain management: An analytical study of inventory location speculation and postponement," In Transportation Research Part E: Logistics and Transportation Review, Vol. 41, No. 3, pp. 159–177, 2005.

[29] H. Zhao and Y. Cao, "The role of e-tailer inventory policy on e-tailer pricing and profitability," In Journal of Retailing, Vol. 80, No. 3, pp. 207–219, 2004.

[30] E. Rabinovich and J. P. Bailey, "Physical distribution service quality in Internet retailing: Service pricing, transaction attributes, and firm attributes," In Journal of Operations Management, Vol. 21, No. 6, pp. 651–672, 2004.

[31] E. Rabinovich, "Consumer direct fulfillment performance in Internet retailing: Emergency transshipments and demand dispersion," In Journal of Business Logistics, Vol. 26, No. 1, pp. 79–112, 2005.

[32] T. C. Du, E. Y. Li and D. Chou, "Dynamic vehicle routing for online B2C delivery," In Omega, Vol. 33, No. 1, pp. 33–45, 2005

[33] P. Katerattanakul and K. Siau, "Creating a virtual store image," In Communications of the ACM, Vol. 46, No. 12, pp. 226–232, 2003.

[34] S. F. King and J.-S. Liou, "A framework for Internet channel evaluation," In International Journal of Information Management, Vol. 24, No. 6, pp. 473–488, 2004.

[35] A. K. J. Barlow, N. Q. Siddiqui and M. Mannion, "Developments in information and communication technologies for retail marketing channels," In International Journal of Retail & Distribution Management, Vol. 32, No. 2–3, pp. 157–163, 2004.

[36] Z. Jiang, W. Wang and I. Benbasat, "Multi-media-based interactive advising technology for online consumer decision support," In Communications of the ACM, Vol. 48, No. 9, pp. 92–98, 2005.

4

A Value-Based and Multi-Level Model of Macro Economies

Marcel van Marrewijk

Van Linden van den Heuvellsingel 7, Vlaardingen, the Netherlands

Abstract

There is sufficient evidence that performance levels of various economic systems differ. All systems seem to have particular benefits, but all of them are adequately aligned with the dynamics and complexity of contemporary societies. In this paper, the author introduces a sequence of ideal type economic systems, based on Spiral Dynamics, a theory explaining levels of existence within people, groups of people, organizations and societies. Per type the author elaborates on the underlying value systems and relating institutional structures, such as leadership style, governance and measurement format.

Keywords: Value Systems, Economic Systems, Spiral Dynamics, Plan Economies, Capitalist Economies, Social Market Economies, Interdependent Economies

1. A "Multiple Level-View" on European Economies

Since the conclusion of the Lisbon European Council of 2000, one of the challenges for the European Union has been "to become the most competitive and dynamic knowledge-based economy in the world, capable of sustaining economic growth, with more and better jobs, and greater social cohesion". This ambition challenge Europeans to seek a convergence between competitiveness and the quality of working life for employees, as the basis for promoting employee commitment, unleashing of organizational initiatives and the development of personal potential.

The actual breakthrough in formulating this challenge lies in the conceptual notion of economic development: thinking in terms of "and" in stead of "or". Not seeking economic growth at the expense of people and planet, but striving to create a synergy by enhancing the quality of jobs and launching social innovations in order to support economic growth. Labor has become an asset, not just a resource.

The European Commission's Directorate General (DG) for Employment, Social Affairs & Equal Opportunities launched the European Union (EU) Work Climate project to stimulate co-operative research and to promote the exchange of opinions and experiences between the parties actively involved in industrial relations, about:

- Working conditions in Europe from a comparative perspective based on the results of a study commissioned by the EU.
- How European workers compare their employment conditions in the companies were they work.
- European wide trends and single out benchmarks for different models of employment relations
- Whether there is a link between quality of work and productivity? If improvements in work climate and working conditions, increase the quality and efficiency of investment in human capital and does it translates into productivity gains?

The DG regards this social dialogue as the driving force behind successful economic and social reforms.

The DG granted this EU Work Climate project to the Institute of Labor Studies (IEL) at ESADE Business School. The fundamental aim of this project is to conduct a comparative analysis amongst 14 member countries based on standardized data pertaining to employment conditions supplied by Great Place to Work® Institute Europe. The latter has developed over the years a methodology (standardized instruments and sampling procedures) for data collection enabling them to choose the "best company to work for" in each country. The data bank includes information provided by employees and managers in over 2,500 companies in 14 EU member states in three consecutive years (2003-2005). The IEL gathered an international team of experts specialized in secondary data analyses of the Great Place to Work® data bank in order to identify trends and benchmark cases. Please kindly refer to the references for further information on this research and background on the Great Place to Work® model.

The Work Climate project revealed European trends on

the quality of work, showing differences between member states that could not be expressed in a single parameter. The first explanation is due to the nature of the concept of quality: it is multidimensional and built on a wide range of components which interact with one another (intrinsic job quality, skills, lifelong learning and career development, gender equality, health and safety at work, flexibility and security, inclusion and access to the labor market, work organization and work life balance, social dialogue and worker involvement, diversity and non-discrimination and overall work performance).

The second explanation, and topic of this paper, is the multi-leveled-ness of the European Work Climate. One of the outcomes of the study is the robustness and equality of the model structure, throughout the dataset. However, different levels of perception appeared through the different countries, showing clear and consistent countries typologies. The data suggested three categories: the leading Scandinavian countries, the lagging Mediterranean countries and a mixed group in between.

The outcome was embarrassing for Great Place to Work® Institutes since they claim that its model can be applied worldwide without cultural biases and in different economic contexts. True, Great Places to Work® are found everywhere, in 30 countries worldwide and in any economic sector. As the model is highly focused on the quality of management (Are they credible? Do they behave respectfully and fairly to employees?) And with data highly sensitive toward this factor, companies can become a great place to work® despite their economic environment. This is great news for managers who want to establish an employer of choice status, but it provides no clue in explaining the multi-levelled ness of European economies.

The author, member of the EU Work Climate project group, suggested to apply an explicit phase wise development approach he successfully used in the development of the EU sponsored European Corporate Sustainability Framework.

In 2003, van Marrewijk et al. introduced a multiple level approach to Corporate Sustainability and Corporate Responsibility (CS-R). They "colored" a generic definition of CS-R into a sequence of more specific definitions matching the development, awareness and ambition levels of people and organizations: CS-R was either oriented to compliance; success and entrepreneurship; community or synergy. Each emerging orientation included and transcended the previous ones. These definitions of CS-R were framed in a more generic phase-wise development pattern, based upon the Graves' Level of Existence theory or Spiral Dynamics as it has been coined by Cowan and Beck (1996).

In 2004, in a Journal of Business Ethics publication, van Marrewijk described ideal type organizations, based upon four core value systems defined by professor Clare W. Graves. Per ideal type various organizational aspects

were described briefly, such as the leadership style, governance and decision making issues and measurement format. As a summary, he developed the Transition Matrix, indicating the paradigm shifts per management discipline, as they have developed in each of the ideal type organization models.

Formulating the EU ambitions towards 2010 by itself emphasized the stretch between current (or traditional) and espoused business practices. The majority of companies seems to be traditionally oriented at managing their (human) resources, i.e. seeking optimum returns on their investments while focusing on efficiency and cost control, while pioneering and leading organizations are practicing with emerging stakeholder oriented business concepts.

This situation pointed us to the following questions: What type of economy has supported the more traditional approach to economic growth? What are the limits to such economies? Why should and how can companies and economic systems transform to more complex systems? And what type of economies is more adequate in achieving the goals of the European Union? One way or the other, the multilevel and multidimensional nature ensure that the diversity across the European Union can be fully taken into account.

Understanding the dynamics between and within economic systems is essential for European policy making, both at the supra and national level.

This paper introduces the Spiral Dynamics Theory and presents five ideal type economic systems. The last chapter discusses the consequences for international economic policy making.

2. Ideal-Type Economic Systems Based on Spiral Dynamics

Clare W. Graves' is the founder of the Emergent Cyclical Levels of Existence Theory. His successors, Beck and Cowan, renamed it "Spiral Dynamics" and successfully introduced Graves' academic achievements to a wider audience. As professor in psychology and a contemporary of Maslow, Graves was interested in the question how the mind (thus people and groups of people) processes reality. Based on extensive empirical research Graves concluded that mankind has gradually developed eight core value systems or "worldviews", so far. Each level of existence – constructed around a core value system-provide its own hierarchy of needs. Values are considered as coping mechanisms to meet specific challenges and to structure institutions in order to influence behavior. A value system is a way of conceptualizing reality and encompasses a consistent set of values, beliefs and corresponding behavior and can be found in individual persons, as well as in companies and societies. A value system develops mainly as a reaction to specific environmental challenges and threats: the systems brighten or dim as life conditions (consisting of historic Times, geographic Place, existential Problems and societal Circumstances) change.

All entities-including organizations and economic systems-will eventually have to meet the challenges their context provides or risk the danger of oblivion or even extinction. If for instance societal circumstances change, inviting corporations to respond and consequently reconsider their role within society, it implies that corporations have to re-align their value systems and all their business institutions (such as mission, vision, policy deployment, decision-making, reporting, corporate affairs, etcetera) to these new circumstances. The quest to create an adequate response to specific life conditions results in a wide variety of survival strategies, each founded on a specific set of value assumptions and demonstrated in related institutions and behavior.

The development of value systems occurs in a fixed order: Survival; Security; Energy & Power; Order; Success; Community, Synergy and Holistic life system. Each new value system includes and transcends the previous ones, thus forming a natural hierarchy (or holarchy). Please refer to Table 1, especially the first six rows, for an introduction on the Spiral Dynamic theory.

Having discussed the issue with both Christopher Cowan and Don Beck, the co-authors of Spiral Dynamics, the author has chosen for a pairing of value systems as fundaments of economic systems:

1) Pre-capitalist systems, based on Security and Power (purple and red)

2) Classical economic systems, based on Power and Order (red and blue)

3) Capitalist economic systems, based on Order and Success/Entrepreneurship (blue and orange)

4) Social Economic Systems, based on Success/Entrepreneurship and Community (orange and green)

5) Interdependent Economic System, based on Community and Synergy (green and yellow)

Ideal types 2 and 3 are resource oriented systems and ideal types 4 and 5 are stakeholder or multiple-focus, oriented systems.

Each emerging system transcends and includes the previous ones. More complex economic systems include elements of less complex systems. Comparing economic systems should never become a model contest—which one is the prettiest?—or a black and white discussion. It is more sensible to discuss why capitalism experiences difficulties in accepting the values of a social market economy. Or, what elements of capitalism should a market economy cherish and preserve in order to sustain its system.

Each presentation of an ideal type economic system briefly touches upon the underlying value systems, the dominant worldviews and related, often psychological explanations of its agents, which brings forth supporting institutional arrangements and policies.

2.1. Pre-Capitalist Economic Systems, Based on Security and Power & Energy

2.1.1. Introduction of its Value Systems
The first three levels of existence mankind experienced are characterized as Survival, Security (bonding order) and Energy & Power (powerful self).

Historically, loose tribes evolved to clans, seeking refuge in kinships, rituals, holy ancestors and mystical nature. The value system supporting Security can also be observed in the mother and child relationship, deep feelings of belonging, but also pride and attachment to the group identity. It color code is Purple.

Table 1. Summary of spiral dynamics.

Main Themes	Security (Purple)	Energy & Power (Red)	Order (Blue)	Success & Entrepreneurship (Orange)	Community (Green)	Synergy (Yellow)	Holistic life system (Turquoise)
Environment	A frightening world	Limitless challenges about boundaries of the territory and to be dominant over self and others within the territory	Ordered relationships requiring legitimization in order to ensure stability and security for the future	Many viable alternatives for progress, prosperity and material gain since change is the nature of things	The gap between people and their (material) possibilities has become disproportionately large	Complex problems that cannot be solved within the current systems as awareness of broad interconnections grows	The consequences of human actions threaten the planet's living systems and demand coordinated effort
Drive	Safety-driven	Exploitation-driven	Compliance-driven	Profit-driven	Care-driven	Systemic-driven	Holistic-driven
Life force	Physical and social safety and security	Conquering domination	Belief, moral duty stewardship	Achievement, changeability	Belonging, idealism	Understanding	Interconnections
Main focus	Group/collective. Bonding Order	Individual/self, Powerful Self	Group/collective, Absolute Order	Individual/self, Enterprising Self	Group/collective, Egalitarian Order	Individual/self, Integrating Self	Group/collective, Holistic Order
Values examples	Reciprocity, respect and allegiance towards elders, mother love	Courage, vitality, strength, personal respect, personal power, rivalry, territorial, intimidation, hedonism, loyalty to persons, assertive	Clarity, discipline, one truth, responsibility, loyalty, duty, guilt, conformity, justice, obedience, orderliness, stability, clarity, one truth	Results, reward, image, quality, innovation, productivity, creativity, career advancement, enterprising, control personal esteem, image, satisfaction, competition	Consensus, conflict avoidance, teamwork, equality, participation, honesty and openness, being a decent person, harmony, trust, love	Insight, integrity, learning, long-term orientation, ability to reflect, flexibility, tolerance for uncertainty and paradoxes systems-thinking	Inspiration, interdependence, future generations, ability to forgive, wisdom, sufficiency, responsible living

Freeing themselves from kinships and family ties, people gradually experienced ways of expressing themselves guiltlessly and selfishly, so as to find immediate pleasure and avoid shame in a world of domination, threats and ego. Power & Energy-indicated with Red-can be easily recognized in feudal states, street gangs and war lords. Healthy Red can also be observed in top athletes and board of directors. It shows in perseverance when the going gets tough, in striving for victories and playing the power game. Unhealthy Red is often encountered in traffic (road rage), in large crowds (hooliganism), corporations ("rat" behavior) and among "party animals".

Red lacks the capacity for long term sequential thinking. They feel no guilt, only the need to gratify impulses and senses immediately. Individual persons tend to manifest these energies especially when they are young (set limits and they will test it!) or in adverse times (CEOs, admirals) or provoked and challenged to bring out the best they've got. These manifestations relate to an environment with limited possibilities, with a shortage of sources, provoking entities to fight in order to gain control and get their share.

2.1.2. Features of a Pre-Capitalist System

With reciprocity as one of the main characteristics of the Security system, economics in the early ages was based on barter, on the exchange of food or early division of tasks, such as carving stones or making artifacts. Slowly excess supplies among clan members and within little hamlets were exchanged at regional markets and gradually money was introduced to support the emerging trade relations. A systems of guilds supported skilled professionals and artists. However, political leaders where dominant in societies. In exchange for security pheasants were ordered to offer physical help to build roads for their armies, assist in constructing public buildings, such as cathedrals, or provide parts of their harvest to feed soldiers or replenish the stocks of the lords.

In his 20 year reign Ming emperor Zhu Di was responsible for renovating the Chinese wall and expanded it with more than 1.000 km. To feed the million workers he assigned to widen and expand a canal system to allow hard wood freighters to ship grain and rice from the south to the north, which took another million workers. The jungles of nowadays Vietnam were stripped from teak wood to build over thousand of maritime vessels and treasure ships that sailed the oceans from 1421 to 1423, and colonized both coasts of the Americas, 70 years before the Europeans did. Last but not least, Zhu Di moved his capital to Beijing and built the Forbidden City.

These huge efforts, that took extensive planning and economic power, primarily emphasized the greatness of the emperor. The wall was meant to strengthen national security (Purple), but the opening of the Forbidden City with ambassadors of all relevant empires and kingdoms present, marked the stature of Zhu Di (Red). Maintaining and opening trade relations was a way to expand the

tribute system for the emperor, not to exploit colonies for gold as the Europeans did many years later.
  Gavin Menzies (2002): 1421, the year China discovered America.

We can still observe these pre-capitalist economies in countries such as Afghanistan, with strong tribal structures, or war torn and impoverished countries such as Dafur and Malawi. Within European countries this system tends to marginalize and can still be observed when people sell homegrown vegetables from small market gardens or backyards, or products manufactured as personal hobbies. Also alternative money systems (local exchange currencies) relate to this type, supporting a time-for-time exchange of goods, but primarily services.

2.2. Classical Economic Systems, Based on Power & Energy and Absolute Order

2.2.1. Introduction of an Emerging Value System

When people learn to transcend the self, experience consequential thinking, they are able to live up to "higher ideals," find pride and fulfillment in their work and accept sacrifices now so as to obtain rewards later. New values emerged that matched a quest for order, meaning and purpose. Feudal states transformed to empires with strong bureaucracies and military power to control and stabilize societies. Nation states emerged, emphasizing their (purple) identities, icons for belonging and pride en newly won (red) energy to stand out and (blue) efforts to standardize legal system and so forth.

Christianity, communism, armies and bureaucracies represented Absolute Order, providing a master plan that puts people in their proper places. Impulses are controlled through discipline, guilt and punishments. The rightful authorities seek order and stability and succeed in making their people believe to sacrifice themselves for future rewards.

People "with a lot of blue" live by the book. They try to comply with the laws, regulations, procedures and agenda's that structure their lives. Life is relatively simple: for each problem there is a proven practice and a guidebook to help them solving it, step by step.

2.2.2. Features of a Classical Economic System

The grandeur and power of political leaders was envied by people who firstly succeeded in making fortunes in gradually growing money driven society, such as bankers, early industrialists and senior civil governors. Starting in the era of the renaissance up to today, new (business) leaders formed a new elite that purposefully arranged a political economic system that kept the "establishment" intact. As an old boys network, they took a pivotal position within society creating control functions to stabilize society and manage their economic sources in order to maintain their powerful position. When this system is dominant in society leadership is executed transparently, but when confronted with strong influences from emerging systems the powerful connections of leadership will hide under the surface, but the elite continue to safeguard their powerbase.

Leadership implies providing direction and maintaining stability. They will never themselves, nor allow others to "rock the boat!" If necessary leaders manipulate, pretend, divide and rule or play the boss. With support of sufficient blue, the behavior of leaders can be characterized as authoritarian and custodial[1].

The archetype leadership activity is "managing": formulating top-down planning schemes and policy deployment, determining control systems and budgets and designing and maintaining procedures and a clear division of tasks.

Strong governments with often inefficient bureaucracies try to control the status of each individual linking its position in the hierarchy or stratified society. Nation wide there is a strong sense of moral duty.

Taylorism and related scientific management is typically linked to Order. Their principles of standardization, specialization, maximization, concentration and centralization are features according to which business and the entire economic system is run. Various quality management concepts supporting a resource orientation are commonly applied in both business and government.

Although industrialization is rapidly increasing, trade and handicrafts remain predominant in urban life, while agriculture and fishery are the principle activities in the country side. The majority of companies is family owned, maintaining a strong purple bond. Markets are relatively undeveloped, especially markets for exchanging production factors such as labor and capital. New job positions are hardly presented transparently, as cooptation via family connections is commonly preferred for. Also life long employment schemes answer perfectly to the circumstances in this economic system. Capital markets gradually emerge as cooperatives among those with needs.

Economic thinking focuses on production systems with a strong bias towards resource and technology-oriented issues. Governments allow business to create economies of scale and vertical integration. This growth strategy supports the power base of the establishment.

Governments tend to protect their industries against foreign takeovers, and are often willing to financially support them despite proven inefficiencies. American agriculture and airspace industries, Suez Gas in France, Telefonica in Spain and British Steel are but a few examples of sectors and companies receiving (financial) support from governments.

---

[1]Davis (1967): Authoritarian refers to the authority of the leader, and the custodial (paternalistic) on the organization as a whole securing the (basic) needs of the employees.

Furthermore, this system is characterized by the existence of old boys networks and various types of corporatism or business groups. Success in Power and Order is measured in terms of personal prestige and material wealth of the few.

Performance measurement is not commonly applied; if so, apart from tax obligations, it is not shared openly.

The classical economic system comes in three varieties, all rooted in the value systems of Power and Order. These are 1) the neo-mercantile Developmental States, 2) the communist plan economies and 3) the traditional economic system from which the capitalist system gradually evolved.

Developmental States, coined by Chalmers Johnson (1986), show evidence of intensive, interdependent collaboration between government, bureaucrats and industrialists, particularly in heavy industries, and a planning rational how to gain long term national welfare. It has been successfully applied in countries such as post war Japan, the Asian tigers (South Korea, Singapore and Taiwan) and, contemporarily, the BRIC countries (Brazil, Russia, India and China).

Post War Japan was forced by allied powers to transform its old pre-war industrial conglomerates (Zaibatsu) into corporate networks (Keiretsu), in order to break the power of the pre war establishment. Under the surface of change, the old structure remained in tact. Japanese bureaucrats at the Ministry of Trade and Industry (MITI) and business leaders rejected the philosophy of laissez-faire and free trade of open markets. To them, these concepts were little more than protection for the economically powerful exporters. The strategy of Developmental States is the denial of extant hierarchy of comparative advantage. In close collaboration with industrialists, Japanese bureaucrats used economic interventions effectively to foster the technological development, capacity growth, and competitiveness of targeted industries. With export industries booming with first cheap and later quality superior products, the Japanese economy has grown rapidly up to the end of the eighties. Emerging influences in the world economy and growing complexities crumbled the old boys network and deteriorated the effectiveness of state interventions.

In Europe we have observed this neo-mercantile variety to some extent in Nazi Germany and pre-war Italy.

The Plan Economies, applied by communist regimes, differed with the former in two aspects: The apparatchiks, the party bureaucrats running the planning system, were quite dominant and worked strictly top down, while the old boys network in for instance Japan exchanged complex information between public and private sector representatives while using market intelligence and price information in their planning approach. The communist's planning system was highly detailed but not as sophisticated. Despite remarkable achievements, the communist economies were less effective, especially on the world market, and resulted in extensive inefficiencies which ultimately jeopardized their existence.

We can observe the traditional economic system in all western economies, as governments and bureaucrats are hardly part of the establishment or their collaboration is not backed up by a sophisticated planning system. In Mediterranean countries such as France, Spain, Greece and Italy, this classical/traditional economic system is still dominant. France also has institutions that relate to the neo-mercantile tradition.

A common example of applying traditional thinking in all western economies is the exhaustive rewarding of CEO's: it is not market competition, as they say, but getting what they think they deserve, being the "top dogs" of their organizations, (un)consciously imitating the grandeur of former kings and emperors.

2.3. Capitalist Economic Systems, Based on Order and Success & Entrepreneurship

2.3.1. Introduction of an Emerging Value System
With too much emphasis on values such as discipline, loyalty, duty, guilt, conformity, justice, obedience and orderliness the Order way attracts adverse effects such as:
- Limited problem solving capacity and reluctant creativity;
- Suffocating rules and procedures for companies and civilians;
- Planning and regulation is more important than the objective;
- One truth, one right way, always categorical.

When life conditions gradually changed, people boosted with Red energy could develop and adopt new competences, new ways in approaching new challenges, choosing new ambitions. Being born a "nickel" the "Enterprising Self" knows how to grow into a "dime", into something larger, gaining control over its destiny. Success is the new name of the game in an environment offering plenty opportunities to compete, win and make things better and better.

In Success multiplistic thinking evolved offering many options and choices. In Order, people compared to the standard, but with Success they benchmark themselves against competition and the number one. People centered in the value system of Success recognize change is the nature of things, creating new niches and introducing new technologies, enhancing life for many.

They work hard-preferably make others work hard for them–and risk time and money (not their life, as in Power) to achieve prosperity and material gain. They seek out the "good life" and abundance, rather than rewards hereafter. The expressions "keep up with the Joneses" and "if you can't make it, fake it" are typically Success and Entrepreneurship.

2.3.2. Features of Capitalist Economic Systems
Blue Order and Orange Success are the true fundaments of the capitalist system. It started off with Adam Smith's Wealth of Nations (1776), and was strengthened by academia such as David Ricardo (1817) and John Stuart Mill (1859). The "invisible hand" and the concepts of comparative advantages, resource allocation and "liberty" were major steps in the development of market oriented economies. With an enormous outburst of energy the capitalist approach was spread throughout economies. As with Schumpeter's "perennial gale of creative destruction" old establishments crumbled or are gradually losing their power. With disciples as Milton Friedman (Free to choose) the market economy based on free competition was presented as a new religion. It would bring prosperity to all people and countries alike. An "American dream" lies ahead for anyone who would "Go West" and put his pioneering spirit to work.

A typical description of the Success value system is the world presented with plenty of viable alternatives for progress, prosperity and material gain. People and organizations realize that change is in the nature of things and (personal) success the name of the game. Both people and organizations act in a calculated way while striving for autonomy and independence, seeking progress and success with the best solutions. If they are allowed to, they try to master nature and exploit its resources.

This description relate to a set of characteristics of the capitalist economic system or Anglo-American approach. They refer to leadership, resource allocation and governance structures.

The archetype role of leaders in a capitalist system is the Entrepreneur: discovering niches as opportunities for success, putting together new "combinations", creating and generating the necessary means and enjoying the fruit of their labor. Burton Klein's "Happy Warrior" and, again, Schumpeter's "creative destruction" are classic illustrations of the entrepreneurial drive behind capitalism.

This calculative attitude, seeking the best option among a variety of alternatives, supports the functioning of markets, allocating resources in the most efficient way. With its focus on prices, the capitalist system is very much cost oriented. Creating shareholder value is the ultimate aim. The Order fundament of Taylorism, scientific management and various (financial) control techniques have enhanced their focus on returns on investment and profit maximization (revenues versus costs) while continuously balancing costs and benefits. Their Success impulses increased their competitive competences, such as marketing and product development.

Along with enormous progress in transportation and information technology, the capitalist economic systems inevitable emerged into "globalization". In stead of organizing production capacities within a local hierarchy, companies decided to decentralize their production system to "low wage" countries or leave these activities to the market entirely. It has become a matter of tuning transaction versus productions costs.

Due to innovative developments in information and transportation technologies, companies in the US, Europe, Japan, Korea and Taiwan were able to outsource parts of their production process to low wage countries. A simple shirt might have been produced in Vietnam, made of Turkish cotton, dyed in India, has Mexican buttons and Chinese pins and packaging method. A Singapore cargo ship transported it to the port of Rotterdam and during this trip the cargo changed ownership several times. This shirt is sold cheap, but contributes to profits anyway. Unfortunately the capitalist system hardly monitors the social consequences of this production system. The local farmer received hardly enough to finance a new harvest, Indian rivers are completely polluted, the working conditions in Vietnam are awful and the little girls that were sewing the shirt hardly get a wage at all. Local cultures are washed way by the icons of the global capitalized world.

The role of government and bureaucrats is simply to enable people and companies to compete freely and prevent market failures to occur. Based on a set of Order competences, the capitalist system provided the context for a Regulatory State, creating a level playing field for free competition through clear legislation and subsequent enforcement. This legal system ought to be effective and visible (law and order) rooting out everything that compromise the market mechanism. Additionally, the public sector must remain as small as possible.

Business' role in society is more or less independent and (a minimum level of) social welfare is the exclusive responsibility of the state.

Order was already purposeful and goals oriented, but through typically Success values such as image, quality, (process) innovation, productivity, creativity and being entrepreneurial, companies have become result-oriented. It reinforced the desire to compete and to become better.

The Order-Success value system resulted in a strictly fact-oriented approach to measuring performance. Success is primarily measured in terms of shareholder value, thus in money and commercial assets. Especially market share, growth figures, payout periods and returns on investments are crucial indicators to mark the results of their achievements.

The Anglo-Amercian character of capitalism is emphasized in the clear distinction between the owners of capital and management of corporations. The executive managers' prime goal is to guarantee the highest profits and thus best return on their invested capital. Management is subordinate to the owners' interests and they can be fired when they fail to achieve the expected results, or rewarded when successful.

We can observe the capitalist system in all countries worldwide, from tiny spots in African cities, expanding zones in China to dominant positions in the UK and the USA.

2.4. Social Economic Systems, Based on Success/Entrepreneurship and Community

2.4.1. Introduction of an Emerging Value System

The success of the entrepreneurial capitalist way gave rise to a new value system as the negative effects could no longer be managed adequately. With profits gained at the expense of the weaker, the capitalist system generates dropouts. Its supportive value system tends to elitism, as Success is inattentive to a fair distribution. With a hang to quantity and profits, instead of quality and durability, Success creates "consumerism" and a huge waste stream. Capitalist societies tend to exploit and ultimately jeopardize their (natural) resources. At the personal level, striving for success often becomes compulsive, leaving orangists no time to enjoy their fruits.

The Purple reciprocity and Orange accumulation of material wealth paved the way for Green redistribution of society's resources among all. The self is once more being sacrificed, but this time in a world where care, love and belonging are paramount, where everything is relative and "truth" is a matter of context and the group's needs. The Egalitarian Order, as this value system has been labeled by Cowan, liberates humans from dogma and greed, promoting a sense of community and unity. Solidarity is felt with the weaker and dropouts, victims of a system exploiting resources and causing an unequal distribution of material wealth.

People and organizations with a lot of Community-sense try to explore the inner beings of themselves and others. They refresh spirituality and seek to bring New Harmony. Generally Community is anti-dogmatic, and since everyone is unique, anti-labeling and anti-hierarchy, but highly tolerant.

2.4.2. Features of a Social Economic System

The Dutch "Polder" approach—introduced in the White House by former Dutch Prime Minister Wim Kok—and Tony Blair's "Third Way" are strongly rooted in the values systems Success and Community. They question the outcomes of capitalist societies but remain centered in a market economy approach.

The capitalist-socialist transformation is quite dramatic, as one can observe strong resentments in the political arena discussing it. Three features of the capitalist system are subject to major change:
- The democratization of power: the old establishment has finally lost its powerful position, as decision making must include the interests of all stakeholders;
- Market failures: free competition does not necessarily generate the best outcomes to all; Governments have to intervene in markets to improve their performance;
- Resource allocation: as efficiency does not neces-

sarily include all costs, social issues are left to negotiations between social partners.

As the capitalist system focuses at managing resources and increasing shareholder value, the socialist market economy is primarily oriented at managing stakeholder interests: balancing the stakes of various groups in a market environment, of which the preconditions are set in the political arena or the negotiation table of social partners. As elites and establishments violate the sense of equality, especially regarding the distribution of wealth, and short term market arrangements jeopardize the interests of other stakeholders, such as employees, next generations and the ecological environment, new value systems emerge that inspire new institutions to make manifest a multi stakeholder approach.

In the level of development characterized as the Egalitarian Order or Community, the concept of an organization has changed. It is no longer regarded as an entity as such but as a group of people engaged in a process of organizing, of working together in trying to achieve common goals. It inevitably implies the involvement of all stakeholders, within and outside the organization. Community values, such as empathy, trust, kindliness and care, support competences enhancing the ability to involve everyone (engagement) and listen carefully (dialogue). In 2003, the author phrased it as follows: "The principle of Agency (autonomy, self-determination), the right to be and act according to ones awareness, capabilities and best understanding of its situation, is balanced by the moral obligation to be accountable for its impact on the environment. It is this principle of Communion that limits freedom when it interferes with the freedom of others."

In a socialist market economy resources are not exploited but cared for. In this system the exploitation of natural resources is counteracted with the ideology to protect and preserve ones habitat and those of other beings.

Employees are no longer considered resources and also customers are recognized as human beings. As Peter Drucker already noticed in 1952 "when hiring a worker, one gets a whole man," In addition to the physical and intellectual capacities, human beings tend to include its emotional and spiritual dimensions. These capacities allow persons to better understand one other, learn from each other, collaborate more effectively and create a two-way flow of information, turning top down telling what to do into proper conversations and dialogues with all those concerned.

The archetype leadership style in Community is "coaching"—the servant leader. The servant leader, a term coined by Robert Greenleaf, implies a state of being, not doing: the first and important choice a leader can make is the choice to serve life, without which one's capacity to lead is profoundly limited. Servant leaders enable professionals to grow and develop their talents. Instead of providing solutions (as in Order), leaders should allow employees to create the answers themselves.

With typical values such as consensus, conflict avoidance, teamwork, equality, participation, honesty, openness, being a decent person and harmony, decision making in the context of Community is an, often time consuming, group process. Once the decision is reached, the buy-in is guaranteed and implementation can be done quickly. This type of consensus oriented decision-making implies that a new type of corporate governance structure has emerged, including a new role of management, a flat organization structure and shareholder value being balanced against the interests of other legitimate stakeholders.

Corporations influenced by this value system invite representatives of various stakeholders to the negotiation table. The first example, often supported by government regulations, is the workers councils, with its members voted by their colleague employees. Ideally, management and workers discuss corporate strategies and ways to enhance workers conditions. Corporate wise or collectively per industry union representatives negotiate wage schemes and packages of labor conditions, which, after an agreement with employer associations, is made law applicable for the entire sector.

Being care driven, companies tend to take better care of the workers and professionals. Absenteeism caused by work stress and incidents or work practices causing (permanent) injuries, such as RSI, are not only a costly affairs from employers perspective, but at the personal level, cause situations that must be brought back to its absolute minimum.

The Dutch laws on labor conditions are strict, obliging for instance all organizations to monitor the wellness of its employees and take actions whenever the outcome does not match the proper norms.

A second example of the centeredness of employees is talent management and human resource development. Due to increased complexity, organizations must invest in various ways to enhance personal skills and competences. It makes sense business wise (Success), but also supports the personal growth and professional development of employees (Community). These activities also increase employee flexibility and employability, which support the functioning of the labor market.

Especially in situations of labor shortages, companies try to become "employer of choice". By practicing creating a culture of trust internally first, a company is much more authentic (and successful) in trying to create a culture of trust among suppliers and customers.

Having discussed, to some extent, the inequality of previous systems and the Rhineland ways of overcoming them, we now turn to the shortsightedness of markets and how socialist governments tend to counteract them.

In capitalist systems governments ought to support the

functioning of markets, and the smaller the governmental claim on resources and capacities the better. In social(ist) economic systems governments' primal role is to counteract the negative consequences of the market mechanism. They levy the financial outcomes of markets via taxes and social premiums and redistribute incomes to various groups who come short in maintaining decent life conditions.

Furthermore governments apply social regulations to prevent exploitation of workers as we have seen in extensive laws in enhancing labor conditions.

Governments stay at arm length when social partners, (employers - and employee associations) negotiate wages schemes, labor conditions and the functioning of markets in general. If requested governments such as in the Netherlands can lift collective agreements to law and made applicable to entire industries.

In addition to income policies and labor markets, socialist governments are inclined to influence markets that tend to favor specifics interests at the expense of others, such as natural monopolies in energy and telecom.

Redistributing up to 65% of BNP, the scale and impact of governments in social economic systems is much larger than in previous systems. The sheer size of governments has made them significant motors in their national economies. However, the adverse effects of rigid bureaucracies, has also burdened socialist governments as the cause of stagflation.

Socialist's success is measured in terms of the quantitative as well as the qualitative impact for all stakeholders involved, including groups who do not take part in economic production or distribution. The socialist dashboard is much larger and more complex than the one of the capitalist system.

"God create the earth... and the Dutch the Netherlands". This American expression refers to the century old situation of Dutchmen commonly reclaiming low-lying stretches of land from a body of water by building dikes and applying various techniques to manage the level of water within so called "polders". A typical governance structure emerged in which all stakeholder participated expressing their desired water level and their financial commitment, enabling authorities to balance the various interests and to achieve the compromised goals. The polder metaphor is used by the Dutch and foreigners alike to express decision making process based on consensus.

In the Netherlands, unions have often tempered their requests for a raise of wages to meet other social goals and prevent a frustration of long term economic perspectives. This situation was the fundament of the Dutch Miracle with respect to economic growth and the smooth transition towards a service oriented economy.

The essence of the social economic system is the ability and willingness of talking together and being collectively responsible for the choices made. The socialist system creates fora to discuss complex dilemmas such as being pragmatic or ethical, short-term profit oriented or sustainable. With all stakeholders present in the debates interests are expressed and respectively balanced, but sustainable solutions are hardly found.

We can observe this system as dominant in Continental Europe and especially the Netherlands and Scandinavian countries.

2.5. Interdependent Economic System, Based on Community and Synergy

2.5.1. Introduction of an Emerging Value System

Trying to be a nice, loving and decent person, are highly regarded qualities in Community. Conflict avoidance, however, also have negative consequences. With criticism smothered by love and judgments made relative to the situation at hand, decision-making risk non-functional and abstract outcomes.

Using each other's qualities for mutual growth, Community is able to create good learning conditions. However, the aura of an expert is badly regarded: consensus is more important than expertise and incompetence is not a reason to be laid off. With rising complexity levels, Community does no longer provide the ultimate solutions to the problems at hand. Furthermore, equality and consensus building may lead to pooling of ignorance.

Being confronted by chaos in a world at-risk, typical Community features such as the lack of leadership and expertise and the emotional and economic cost of caring are important arguments to develop new ways to cope with the ever increasing complexity of challenges.

Comprehension, understanding and connectedness are the buzzwords of Synergy. A person and organization centered in Synergy, express itself, but never at the expense of others or the earth. They will not say: "These people can't cook", but "This food is not of good taste".

In Synergy there is room for authenticy, since internal motivations matter a lot. Existentialism is strong.

People with values associated to Synergy can blend conflicting "truths", for it is able to see more colors and uses more senses at the same time. By focusing on functionality and applying competencies to get buy-in from others, Synergy is able to create win-win options and breakthrough solutions, seeking self-interest without doing harm to others and nature.

People dominantly centered in Synergy understand that the complexity of today's world cannot be solved within the current systems, as their awareness of broad interconnections grows. They recognize the inevitability of nature's flows and seek ways to accommodate "natural design". Understanding interconnectivities in all Wilberian quarters, seeking to grasp the very essence of their presence and by having created flexibility through breaking up structures into network organizations, people start to support all life in the most natural, sustainable, and fitting ways.

In order to meet its drive, to be, to learn and to discover, persons with a lot of Synergy function best in a network with a strong sense of direction, while demanding flexibility and open systems. Values such as insight, long-term orientation, ability to reflect and tolerance for uncertainty and paradoxes support the drive for self-development and boost people's ability to learn and apply knowledge. They are able to learn from any source. With a mind that quickly wanders, they have difficulty in maintaining focus.

2.5.2. Features of an Interdependent Economy

The social (ist) economic system is still rooted in capitalist practices, with political leaders mitigating its outcomes primarily through income redistribution. Due to a strong Order dominance they believe they can construct an ideal society. Dutch parliamentary history shows various examples of launching growth policies in the expectation that this will fulfill the needs of people. Unfortunately, the majority of these interventions have failed to meet its targets, fueling the capitalist propagandists and often causing a shift in parliamentary power in favor of the right wing conservatives.

Blue linear thinking can not serve as a construction philosophy, a blue print for contemporary needs. Being able to better understand the subtleties of human nature (Community) and system dynamics (Synergy), the successors of the hard core socialists create room for organic growth, by allowing nature, structures and society to unfold itself. It seeks to facilitate the emergence of a natural design.

Indeed is there a future for a socialist politician? Is there a way out in the Anglo-Saxon vs. Socialist Market economy debate? What are the pitfalls that caused failure and what values and what competences do we need to create new institutions in line with the envisaged Interdependent Economy?

Community consensus building hardly results in innovative breakthroughs and sustainable solutions. Community lacks vision, lacks leadership to match collective needs with stakeholder interests and personal ambitions. Synergy possesses these qualities. Therefore one must expect that the interdependent economic system will find ways to overcome current challenges in western social economies.

A private initiative in the Netherlands, launched by a.o. McKinsey, conducted the largest Dutch online survey ever, taking place in September/October 2006 and 2008. More than 170,000 inhabitants, being a representative sample of the Dutch society, took 21 minutes of their time to respond to current issues.

The Dutch expressed a strong desire (90%) to attain a society build on solidarity, modesty and oriented towards quality of living. There is a wide support for measures stimulating growth of prosperity and simultaneously help

achieve the desired organization of society. They strongly support new economic reforms as long as this does not increase the pressure on the environment. Examples are a more flexible labor market, working at home, accept restrictions on deducting mortgages and intensify inservice training.

Unfortunately, confidence in government's policies and the authorities' execution thereof is very low (25%). Dutch citizens are very critical to the content of political parties, as they seem to root in traditional systems, thus unable to lead the Netherlands into the new era. (www.21minuten.nl)

The Interdependent Economic System seems to aim directly at the fulfillment of needs of all people. In addition to socialist redistribution policies, the new system seek to align vision with personal commitment, balance long term interests with short term needs and harmonize ideology with pragmaticism. The life conditions that provoke Synergy to emerge are adequately matched by new ways sublimating "either - or" and "win - loose" arrangements.

Larger organizational entities are transforming - or breaking up - into network structures, demonstrating the drive behind Synergy. The Hollywood movie scene is a good example of a once highly successful oligopoly which broke up in numerous small professional clusters, who work together in a network for the duration of a project. Not far from Hollywood, in Silicon Valley, a network structure emerged bottom up, as independent professionals clustered into networks, creating the necessary competences to meet the challenges facing Synergy. Inertia transformed to flexibility, creating room for new strategies, new approaches to running economic activities resulting in improved performance levels.

Redistribution policies often resulted in pampering groups in need, stigmatizing their position as victims of the market economy. Interdependence, aligning the principles of agency and communion at a more complex level, emphasizes personal accountability or responsibility and acting accordingly. Interdependent economies educate those in need to reshape their futures. In popular terms: "when hungry, learn and enable them how to fish, instead of providing them just a fish".

The archetype leader in Yellow is the "Emergent Leader'. He or she authentically connects visionary qualities to a practical and personal approach and is able to link the various qualities of previous contexts into one effective and coherent approach. Emergent leadership lifts people, organizations and societies to levels where adequate answers can be developed to meet current challenges. It supports the sublimation, the transition of living entities to emerging levels of existence.

Leadership as defined in terms of Synergy is no longer confined to what people do, but grounded in who people are. An authentic choice to serve life increases ones capacity to lead by allowing life to unfold through you. The hierarchy between the leader and the led remains healthy: leadership is never dominating or abusing raw power. The leadership potential can be developed in everyone. It implies identifying the personal responsibility and the alignment between one's personality and ambitions with one's role within the network. Therefore, essentially, leadership is about learning how to shape the future.

Marketing as a concept is 60 years old. Human resource management became popular since the early nineties. What will be a new management discipline? "Synnovator", coined by the Center of Human Emergence, makes a good chance. This notion means to interconnect and vitalize. Companies explore new ways of cooperation and strategic partnership, both horizontally and vertically. By effectively working together with internal and external stakeholders, thus tapping into their competences and capacities, organizations find new opportunities to boost their performance. This time with respect to the triple bottom line: people, planet and profits.

Companies with a lot of Synergy tend to chose for a "people first strategy". They act as if they say: "We take care of the people. Our people take care of the business." They successfully allow professionals to be who they are and bring out the best they can. This way, highly skilled workers are able to create a sense of flow and achieve productivity levels which are unheard of in previous circumstances. According to research conducted in the USA, UK and Brazil, the very best Great Places to work®, being also listed at stock markets, score a four times higher financial growth than the average stock prices. Similar conclusions were drawn by Jim Collins in his best selling management book "Good to Great".

The Synergy value system is emerging rapidly at the personal and corporate level. Unfortunately, characteristic institutions of the interdependent economic system remain hypothetical. However, we can sketch the outlines of this approach:

- The scale of governments will decline again, as ministries no longer feel themselves being representatives of a particular stakeholder group, but act in the interest of the whole, while applying a better understanding of system dynamics;
- Bureaucracies, law enforcements and ministerial responsibility will be organized in more sophisticated manners;
- (Municipal) Authorities pro-actively support the concept of "great places to live", while collaborating with dedicated private and social institutes providing education, (health) care, safety, housing et cetera.
- Governments, social partners, individual corporations and NGO's work together intensively, exchanging information and using each others expertise to create breakthroughs in improving the quality of life for all;
- Governments and social partners should guarantee work protection in stead of job protection, empha-

sizing each others' role in taking personal responsibility in improving ones future opportunities;
- Social security systems are not focused at income distributions alone, but emphasize the inclusion of those in needs in social communities and economic systems. Kennedy's statement: "Ask yourself what you can do for your country, in stead of what your country can do for you", gets a new dimension.
- As globalization involves the whole world, supra national institutes must be initiated to meet its challenges, not to protect particular interests at the cost of others.

We can observe the early stages of this system as emerging in the Netherlands and Scandinavian countries.

3. Consequences for International Economic Policy Making

This paper described various economic systems that are aligned with their (historical) contexts, their challenges and ambitions. The models can be placed in a specific sequence of development, creating an organic flow of macro economic institutions. Figure 1 tries to summarize these models as stages of development, each model including two subsequent and dominant value systems. The color codes have been introduced in Table 1. The more complex, recently emerged systems transcend and include the less complex ones, the ones to their left, while the basic systems tend to marginalize as complexity emerges. We still tend to see the reminiscents of old systems, but their importance is decreasing.

Policy makers cannot choose from a menu card which system they like best. One cannot skip development levels. We have observed the troubles that occur when Afghani economic activities functioning at subsistence and pre-capital levels are forced into modern capitalist economies. It doesn't make much sense when Italian Mediterranean bureaucrats study Danish experiences.

Their first challenge is to transform into the next level. This is difficult enough as it is.

Even when traditional policies, approaches and economic structures fail to deliver improvements, in spite of the rising awareness that current institutions are no longer in tune with changing circumstances, it still isn't easy to adapt to new structures, new institutions, creating a new coherent model.

It helps to understand system dynamics. As a summary, Table 2 presents macro economic characteristics, structured according Spiral Dynamics.

The main questions arise, however, do political and economy leaders have the guts to move ahead, challenging the "ceilings" and collaborating with pioneering spirits.

Asking oneself if Europe's economic systems are converging to a particular level is implicitly raising the

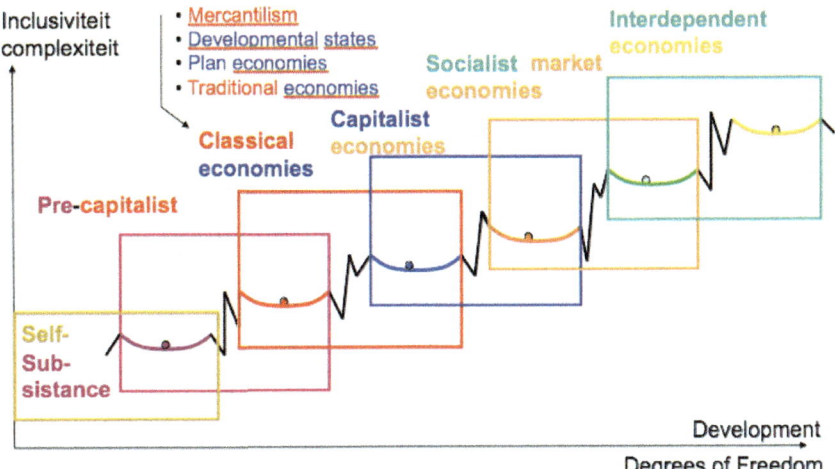

Figure 1. Phase wise development of economic systems.

Table 2. Macro characteristics inspired by spiral dynamics.

Main Themes	Security (Purple)	Energy & Power (Red)	Absolute Order (Blue)	Success & Entrepreneurship (Orange)	Community (Green)	Synergy (Yellow)	Holistic life system (Turquoise)
Scope	We are but a small and modest part of the world, given to us by the Gods, the natural spirits and our ancestors and should be left intact	The world is there to conquer, or at least control or safeguard its scares and vital resources	The world must be stabilized to maintain order (and maintain the current establishment and balance of power)	The world occurs at the local, national and globalized level, but is primarily restricted to economic parameters and opportunities	The world is one village, a brotherhood of man; has one climate and has no other place to go	The social and environ-mental degradation are inevitable when mankind is not able to act accor-ding a systemic under-standing of the whole	Interdependency. Each person or organization there-fore has a universal responsibility towards all other beings, both present and future generations
Dominant political institution	Tribes, warlords	Feudal States, Tribu-tary systems	Empires, Nation States, early de-mocracies	NATO, Security Council, Top X-Roundtable	European Union, United Nations, UNTAD	Supranational governance, e.g. International Court of Justice	Not known yet
Style of decision making	The words of the elder; the in-crowd	Authoritarian; dicta-torship	Procedural, top down decision making and policy deployment	Top down and bottom up; negotia-tions	Bottom Up; Con-sensus principle: everyone equally counts	Consent principle; anyone with a valuable contribu-tion counts	All information counts, including from spiritual entities
Criteria for decision making	The decision ought to be taken in accordance with the proper rituals	Based on personal power and status	According the proper procedures, by the proper au-thority and in line with the basic purpose	Financial criteria: Shortest 'pay out period' and highest shareholder value	Social criteria: everyone must be included and heard	Balanced, func-tional decision making, taking into account all available expertise and con-siderations	In line with and in favor of holistic interests for survival of life on the planet
Main stake-holders	Elders	Old boys networks, elite, powerful ones	Legal authorities	Finance, owners and industrialists	Civilians, employ-ees, deprived groups	All relevant stake-holders	All living creatures
Role and size of govern-ment	Emerging local authorities, around the elders	Supporting staff of the ruler and en-forcement (like the mandarins in old China)	Dedicated bureauc-racy designing and enforcing regula-tions	Public agencies, maintaining a level playing field for competition	Large bureaucracy supporting redistri-bution processes	Smaller but dedi-cated government officials conducting new societal devel-opments	Resilient network of government institu-tions supporting the needs of the whole.
Dominant strategy	Providing security for levying taxes	Supporting emerging markets and boosting economic activities	Policy deployment; the constructive society	Level playing field; supporting global-ized economies	Negotiation for a with stakeholder representatives	Creating break-thoughts in themes that endanger societies	Supporting habitats for the different needs
Example: orientation towards sustainability	Maintain what is there already, do not alter the cur-rent state	Constructing large statues, castles, cathedrals, mauso-leums and other buildings expressing the grandeur of the leaders, the capitals, etc	Sustainability implies a system of legal rules and procedures enforc-ing people how to behave and how processes should be run	Sustainability is left to market forces that will impact social, ethical and eco-logical aspects into business operations and decision-ma-king, provided it contributes to the financial bottom line	Sustainability implies the balanc-ing of economic, social and ecologi-cal concerns, in-cluding initiatives that go beyond legal compliance and profit considera-tions	Sustainability implies a search for well-balanced, functional solutions creating value in the economic, social and ecological realms of corporate performance, in a synergistic, win-together ap-proach with all relevant stake-holders	Sustainability is fully integrated and embedded in every aspect of the soci-ety, aimed at con-tributing to the quality and con-tinuation of life of every being and entity, now and in the future

question if Europe offers uniform life conditions and value patterns that would allow all economies to adapt similar approaches. Unfortunately this is not the case. Brussels and the representatives of individual economies must live with this situation and must learn to turn it into an asset. At the same time it must support the emergence of modern institutions in response to the challenges of modern day economics due to the international systemic crises, such as climate changes, food and water shortages and the economic instability.

4. Acknowledgements

I thank people who commented on earlier drafts or presentations of this paper.

- Wilbert van Leijden en Paul Zuiker, authors of "Nederland op doorbreken"
- The people attending my lecture at the Rotterdam School of Management on this subject, including prof.dr. Gerard Zwetsloot, dr. Dirk van Dierendonck and dr. Andre de Waal;
- The Rhineland workgroup in the Netherlands, including professor Matthieu Weggeman;
- Associates of the Center of Human Emergence and Synnervate, such as Peter Merry and Morel Fourman
- Co-founders of Corporate Dynamics, being experts on Value management;
- Professor John Groenewegen, my former professor on Institutional Economics and Economic Systems, Erasmus University Rotterdam.
- Guido Enthoven, director of IMI—Instituut voor Maatschappelijke Innovatie

5. References

[1]   D. Beck and C. Cowan, "Spiral dynamics," Blackwell Publishers, 1996.

[2]   T. van den Brink and F. van der Woerd, "Industry specific sustainability benchmarks: An ECSF pilot bridging corporate sustainability with social responsible investments," Journal of Business Ethics (forthcoming), 2004.

[3]   C. Johnson, "MITI and the Japanese miracle: The growth of industrial policy, 1925–1975," 1986.

[4]   J. C. Collins and J. I. Porras, "Built to last successful habits of visionary companies." New York: HarperCollins Publishers, 1997.

[5]   T. W. Hardjono, "Ritmiek en Organisatiedynamiek: Vierfasenmodel," Kluwer, 1995.

[6]   T. W. Hardjono and P. de Klein, "General introduction to the European corporate sustainability framework," Journal of Business Ethics (forthcoming), 2004.

[7]   R. S. Kaplan and N. P. David, "the Balanced scorecard: Translating strategy into action," Harvard Business School Press, 1996.

[8]   W. van Leijden and P. Zuiker, "Nederland op doorbreken: een vernieuwend perspectief voor een land in crises," Emergent Publishing, 2007.

[9]   M. van Marrewijk and T. W. Hardjono, "The social dimensions of business excellence," Corporate Environmental Strategy, Vol. 8, No. 3, 2001.

[10] M. van Marrewijk, "Concepts and definitions of corporate sustainability," Journal of Business Ethics Vol. 44, Nos. 2 and 3, May 2003.

[11] M. van Marrewijk and M. Were, "Multiple levels of corporate sustainability," Journal of Business Ethics, Vol 44, Nos. 2 and 3, May 2003.

[12] M. van Marrewijk and T. W.Hardjono, "European corporate sustainability framework for managing complexity and corporate change," Journal of Business Ethics, Vol. 44, Nos. 2 and 3, May 2003.

[13] M. van Marrewijk and Timmers, "J. human capital management," Journal of Business Ethics, Vol. 44, Nos. 2 and 3, May 2003.

[14] M. van Marrewijk, "European corporate sustainability framework," International Journal of Business Performance Measurement, Vol. 5, Nos. 2 and 3, 2003.

[15] M. van Marrewijk, W DeCleyn, I. Wuisman, et al., "A developmental approach to business excellence," Journal of Business Ethics (forthcoming), 2004.

[16] M. van Marrewijk, "The social dimension of organizations: Recent experiences with Great Place to work® assessment practices," Journal of Business Ethics (forthcoming), 2004.

[17] M. van Marrewijk and H. M. Becker, "The Hidden hand in cultural governance: the case of humanities' ten year period of transformation," Journal of Business Ethics (forthcoming), 2004.

[18] A. Maslow, "Toward a psychology of being." Van Nostrand Reinhold, 1982.

[19] J. Wempe and M. Kaptein, "The Balanced company: A theory of corporate integrity," Oxford University Press, 2002.

[20] K. Wilber, "A theory of everything: An integral vision for business, politics, science and spirituality," Shambhala, 2000.

[21] K. Wilber, "Sex, ecology, spirituality: The spirit of evolution," Shambhala, 1995.

[22] F. van der Woerd and T. van den Brink, "Feasibility of a responsive business scorecard-a pilot study," Journal of Business Ethics (forthcoming), 2004.

[23] World Business Council for Sustainable Development WBCSD Meeting Changing Expectations. Corporate Social Responsibility. New York: WBCSD, 1999.

[24] World Business Council for Sustainable Development WBCSD Corporate Social Responsibility: Making Good Business Sense. Geneva: WBCSD, 2000.

Abbreviations

CS-R	Corporate Sustainability and Responsibility	EU	European Union
ECSF	European Corporate Sustainability Framework	IEL	Institute of Labor Studies, Esade Business School
ECLET	Emerging Cyclical Levels of Existence Theory		

5

On the Ideal Duration of Entrepreneurial Resources Commitment

Panagiotis E. Petrakis
Department of Economics, Division of Economic Development,
Athens National and Kapodistrian University, Athens, Greece

Abstract

The paper proposes that the entrepreneur's perception of time in the form of average ideal duration of entrepreneurial resources commitment is an important personal trait. The entrepreneur develops a particular checking filter for the entrepreneurial involvement on which the evaluation of entrepreneurial opportunities is based. The concept of ideal time dimension of entrepreneurial engagement is crucially related to the development of structural prototype prevailing in space and time. Three main influences have been located with respect to the formation of duration on entrepreneurial commitment: microeconomic influences, long-term macro-environmental influences and short-term macro-environmental influences.

Keywords: Entrepreneurship, Time Commitment, Payback Period

1. The Traditional Treatment of Preference in the Allocation of Investment Resources

The significance of preference of time in the bibliography, which is related to the allocation of resources and investment decisions generally, has been shown in at least three different approaches: the first refers to the rate of preference of time (RTP) of the neoclassical model [1, 2]; the second refers to the payback period criterion [3]; and the third to the concept of the intrinsic time of investors [4].

In the standard literature of project evaluation the payback criterion and hurdle rates criterion are often used. Lefley [3], in a review article on the PB method, states that the PB method is an important, popular, primary and traditional method [5] and is particularly used in advanced manufacturing technology projects [6]. Wambach [7] connects payback criterion and hurdle rates with the values of waiting. The hurdle rate is (usually) based on subjective assessments and the perceived level of project risk [3], particularly in cases in which future cash flows increase with time [8].

2. Perception of Time as a Cultural and Personal Entrepreneurial Trait

According to Bird [9] the entrepreneurship engagements in the resources-time interface have at least three time elements: perception, anticipation and action. Perception refers to people who are good judges of feasibility or the potential to instigate activity [10]. Anticipation denotes the future tense and touches on the possibilities of future states. It draws upon individuals' abilities to recognise the future. Jaques [11] outlines two dimensions of time related to anticipation: succession and intuition. The latter captures the complexity of moving forward in time. The size and the value of the firm are fundamentally linked to the entrepreneur's intentions.

According to Shane and Venkataraman [12] entrepreneurship means the process by which opportunities to create future goods and services are discovered, evaluated and exploited. In the framework of a well-structured theory for tracing and developing entrepreneurial opportunities [13] two levels of analysis appear. The first includes the process of tracing and developing entrepreneurial opportunities (development, recognition, perception, discovery and evaluation) while the second includes the factors that influence this process (entrepreneurial alertness, information asymmetry and prior knowledge, discovery versus purposeful search, social networks and finally personality traits).

The individual according to his sensitivity alertness [14, 15] reacts to the information he receives and recognises the entrepreneurial opportunity. The entrepreneurial opportunities are continuously evaluated either within a formal or informal process [16]. The individual informally collects information until it takes a more formal form and particularly when the collaboration of third parties is necessary in the search for essential resources. If the result of this process is satisfactory, then a feasibility study is produced.

The entrepreneur develops his entrepreneurial alertness either on the grounds of backward or forward interpretation [17] of incoming information and only to the level that he keeps pace with his time preference. For example, he excludes from his evaluation all information (in this case preference for short-term entrepreneurship) connected to long-term entrepreneurship. Thus entrepreneurial alertness is not a complete process but a unilaterally developed sensitivity which is biased in favour of short-terms actions. Note that in cases where a long-term perception of time prevails in society, then the long-term entrepreneurial trap can arise where no immediate results in entrepreneurial activity are taking place. Thus, the time preference is a personal attitude of the entire process of opportunity tracing and development.

The final phase of the evaluation by using time discount of future inflows constitutes only part of the influence of the time preference on the process of entrepreneurship. Time preference is much more important in all previous stages of the process of opportunity, identification and development.

3. The Macro-Environment and the Perception of Time

The macro-environment of entrepreneurship includes the economic and social dimensions. Central governments policies, local government aspects and financing systems [18] influence the general economic conditions of entrepreneurship [19]. The work ethic and cultural values shape the social background of the entrepreneurial environment [20].

Regarding the macroeconomic environment and its relation to the personal process of evaluation of time, we can trace a number of factors which seem to be able to shape it:

1) An entrepreneur who lives in a richer economic environment (per capita income), as compared to a poorer one, will obviously make a different evaluation. Under these circumstances, it is logical for the future to have a higher value since the present facilitates the resolution of most current personal and social problems.

2) Moreover, in an economy with higher rates of growth, for the same reasons the future is valued higher than the present [21]. The opposite is held in an economy with low rates of growth.

3) The entrepreneur is influenced by the phase of business cycle. If he is in the exodus of the recession phase he would prefer the future to the present, and the opposite in the upward phase.

4) The nominal interest rates combined with inflation rate indicate the evaluation of time, since they theoretically express the conditions of perfect competition and equilibrium markets.

5) A factor of similar importance emanates from the political environment and generally from the conditions of political stability. The entrepreneur who is active in an area with continuous political agitations and applications such as continuous changes in the administrative machine and in the tax system etc., will give with difficulty a higher value to the future over the present.

6) An entrepreneur who lives in an unstable economic environment will obviously show a higher preference for the present over the future. We may consider variability of income as a satisfactory proxy of instability of economic environment [22]. It is, therefore, logical to assume that he puts more weight on the present than on future periods.

7) Another factor that influences the evaluation of time is public finances conditions. A non-investment budgetary deficit of central government is in itself a powerful signal, ceteris paribus, for the entire society about the preference for the present versus the future.

8) The administrative burdens created by the operation of bureaucracy in terms of cost for the operation of firms are a serious factor that influences the process of evaluation of time [23], included the corruption cost that is probably more serious in the least developed economies. The higher this type of transactions cost, the higher the preference of present versus future is.

9) The legal framework of exploitation of entrepreneurial patents is one more factor which determinates the relationship between present and future. The non-existence of such a framework makes time disappears from the process of exploitation of an entrepreneurial idea [24]. The more its exploitation is developed for the short term, the less is the risk of losing the benefits from its exploitation.

10) The conditions of the job market considerably influence the time horizon of an entrepreneurial idea. When the job market is characterised by rigidity, the entrepreneur is led to abandon the flexibility that constitutes a basic element of entrepreneurship [18].

11) We should also give a great deal of attention to the more general geo-strategic factors of the entrepreneurial environment. Thus, an entrepreneur who is active in a region where national conflicts (wars, changes of borders, exterior threats) succeed one another, is being very logical in having a powerful preference for the present over the future.

4. Cultural Entrepreneurial Idiosyncrasies and the Perception of Time

The literature [23,25–27] shows a very clear picture of the level of research concerning the role of culture in the entrepreneurship.

1) The relation of individualism vs collectivism with entrepreneurs' perception of time is difficult to determine. We will stick to the idea that societies dominated by collectivist views have negative effects on the duration of entrepreneurial activities. This is because they usually do not promote the importance of individualist action.

2) Societies that show low uncertainty avoidance usually have high confidence in the future. Geletkanycz [28], raising a point of preference between a forward-looking vs more historical perspective, considers this perception to be a fifth cultural dimension, also known as Confucian Dynamism.

3) We could also accept that societies characterised by a high tolerance of social inequality (power distance) accept higher values for entrepreneurial activities. Also they accept a higher value for the future over the present since they usually promote perceptions of future expectations.

4) Societies which are characterised by masculinity (a materialist and achievement orientation) give more value to the future. Importance is given to maximising prosperity in the present life. Consequently if this requires certain sacrifices in the short-term present, it is quite bearable as long as it this is extended into a short number of future periods.

5. The Entrepreneur's Personal Characteristics and the Specifics of the Project

Here we can specify two distinct sources which influence the entrepreneurial perception of time: personal characteristics and the microeconomics of the project. In the first category we should include: a) family situation; b) age; c) health; and d) educational level. Thus, marital status combined with personal characteristics may have mixed effects on the preference of present over the future. We may say that the higher the personal obligations, the higher the preference for the present. The same applies to the entrepreneur's health condition. A good health creates conditions of preference for the future while the younger the entrepreneur is, the higher is the preference for the future. Finally, a high level of education encourages a preference for the future since it is related to human investments, which are originally accumulated on an expectations basis.

The microeconomics of the project include:

1) The nature and the origin of the resources that are to be used. The marginal value of obtaining each additional money unit depends on the way that it comes into the entrepreneur's possession. The harder the way, the higher is its marginal value and consequently the higher is the preference for the present over the future.

2) A financial structure based on devotion to high own capital creates conditions of higher preference for the present.

3) The greater the size of the project, the greater the preference for the present. In contrast greater the size of the firm, the more confidence there will be in the future and consequently there will be greater preference for the future.

4) The sector in which the entrepreneur is working is very likely to influence his or her time preference. Entire sectors are characterised by ephemeral activities and entrepreneurs have a powerful preference for the present over the future.

6. Cognitive Factors, Entrepreneurial Motives and the Perception of Time

Following Locke [29] all entrepreneurial factors are the result of the combination or integration of cognition and motivation. The main cognitive factors are knowledge (industry, technology), skills (selling, bargaining, leadership, decision-making, planning etc.) and abilities (intelligence etc.) [30]. The possession of all the above factors develops vision. Vision may include opportunity fit, venture diagnostic and opportunity recognition. Entrepreneurial cognitions tend to be distinct from those of other business people, are universal and differ by national culture [27].

Do cognitions affect entrepreneurs' perception of time? The answer that can be given in principle is positive even though it needs a lot more research to certify the degree of interaction. Thus it is obvious that when the businessman possesses good knowledge of the industry, he knows with precision the ideal horizon of his entrepreneurial activity. He also has a great perception of time which is formed about the specific industry in which he is operating as if is influenced by the precise business cycle phase and the life cycle of the product [31].

In any case we generally accept that the more developed cognitive factors are, the more easily the entrepreneur may be willing to extend the time horizon of his entrepreneurial effort and the more he will value the future over the present.

7. The Entrepreneurial Perception of Time: A Field Research

According to the analysis a Questionnaire was formed [32] with which we addressed 420 businessmen of SMEs in the Greek analysis whose own capital was smaller than 10,000,000 Euros (EU definition of SMEs) in the period 2002–2006. The size and sectoral structure of the firms in the sample were representative of the corresponding measures in the Greek economy. It is quite difficult to formulate questions that would concern all factors in the six different groups as we have located them. This would require a much broader and cross-cultural field research. However, very few factors were excluded.

We define duration as the time interval during which he should be dedicated to a precise entrepreneurial activity and not to any other. Then, in order to count the significance of the rest of the factors, we evaluate their influence on the change of this duration.

The size and sector of the firms chosen is distributed as follows: 20% of the firms are active in industry, 44% in trade and 36% in services. The respondents' rate to the questionnaire was 32% to the total number of firms initially chosen. In 38% of the firms it became impossible to locate the entrepreneur; in 1% of cases the firms' data were not correct, 1% of the firms were subsidiaries and the refusal rate was 28%. The research was conducted with personal interviews by a professional team.

From the answers to the questionnaire we estimate that the Average Ideal Duration of Entrepreneurial Commitment (AIDEC) is 5.57 years. The AIDEC is compared to Payback Period (PB) which is 3.91. The difference between AIDEC and PB criterion is statistically significant at a 95% level of significance. The finding of the difference in statistical significance leads us to the conclusion that the entrepreneur shapes an image for the time dimension of his involvement in the entrepreneurial effort which is larger than the requirement to take back his money but is not large enough to justify his involvement in investments that require long-term involvement. This finding is, up to a point, related to the fact that we refer to SMEs that can not accurately be distinguished for the realisation of huge investments (with long-term depreciation).

Thus the entrepreneur gradually develops his entrepreneurial activity in a time horizon for each stage that varies around 5.57 years.

An important issue that arises is to what extent the AIDEC found, apart from picturing the time and geographical conditions under which the field research was conducted, is directly connected with the amount of investment referred to in the questionnaire (500,000€). Indeed, there is a question in the questionnaire that aims to reveal the relative elasticity that connects the project size and the AIDEC. So, if the project size is 2,000,000€ then the AIDEC would be 6, 31 years. The difference found in the AIDEC is statistically important at a 95% level of significance. However, if the project size rises exorbitantly, the elasticity may become irrelevant.

The answers to the questionnaire were categorized into six different groups (Categorization details are available upon request). The six groups are as follows: macro-environmental variables (Group 1); cultural entrepreneurial idiosyncrasies (Group 2); personal characteristics (Group 3); microeconomics of the project (Group 4); entrepreneurial motives (Group 5); and cognitive variables (Group 6). Since between the variables multicol-

linearity is inherited and the amount of the data used is large, we employed factor analysis (with varimax rotation) on each group as a data reduction technique to reveal the main influences on the AIDEC. The analysis (Table 2) shows that the variables of Group 1 can be reduced to two principal components: G1PC1 and G1PC2 eingen values greater than one, accounting for the 68.6% of the variation in the macro-environmental variables. The variables of Group 2 can also be reduced to two principal components G2PC1 and G2PC2 which account for the 65.4% of the variation of the cultural and entrepreneurial variables. The variables of the Group 3 can be reduced to one G3PC1 which account for the 41.7% of the variation of the personal characteristics variables. The variables of Group 4 can be reduced to two, G4PC1 and G4PC2, which account for the project. Finally the variables of Group 5 can be reduced to three, GP5C1, G5PC2 and G5PC3 which account for 77% of the variation of the entrepreneurial motives variables. The principal components are uncorrelated.

Then we employee the Stepwise regression technique with the AIDEC as an independent variable and the GjPCi as independent variables. The model with the higher adjusted R square (37.3%) includes the G4PC1, the G1PC1 and G1PC2. (Table 1)

The three principal components exercise positive influences on the AIDEC. The first includes the origin of resources, the leverage influence, the project size influence and the payback period variable. The G2PC1 includes the rate of growth-income level, the bureaucracy, corruption influences and the labour market conditions. Some might characterise interest rate fluctuations, the level of risk-return them as the long term micro-environmental factor. The third includes the influence of business circles phase, relationship and finally the geo-strategical and political condition influences. This component could be characterised as the short-term macro-environmental factor.

An interesting point for discussion emerges from the exclusion of the member factors included in Groups 2 and 4 as explanatory variables of the AIDEC. It is case 4 of cultural entrepreneurial idiosyncrasies and entre-

Table 1. Statistical significance of principle components on AIDEC.

AIDEC = 5,567+0,42G4PC1 + 0,91G1PC1 + 0,71G1PC2				
t-test	33,182	1,95	4,56	3,78	
(Sig.)	(0,00)	(0,00)	(0,00)	(0,00)	$\bar{R}^2 = 0,37$ $R^2 = 0,39$

F = 24,64

Sig. ≈ 0,00

Table 2. Principal components, variables' scores and influences on the AIDEC.

Variables	G4PC1 The microeconomics influences			G1PC1 The long-term macro-environmental influences			G1PC2 The short term macro-environmental influences		
	Rotated components scores	*Difference from AIDEC*	*T-test (Sig)*	*Rotated components scores*	*Difference from AIDEC*	*T-test (Sig)*	*Rotated components scores*	*Difference from AIDEC*	*T-test (Sig)*
The origin of resources (zero cost)	0,66	-0,6	2,011 (0,05)						
Increased leverage (financial structure)	0,80	-0,9	4,153 (0,00)						
Project size increase	0,82	+0,74	-2,830 (0,01)						
Increase payback period	0,57	-0,35	2,447 (0,02)						
Higher rate of growth-income				0,88	-1,23	5,720 (0,00)			
Reduction of bureauc-racy-corruption				0,86	-0,70	2,877 (0,01)			
Labour market improvement				0,87	-0,74	3,523 (0,02)			
Business cycles phase (recession)							0,79	1,13	-4,520 (0,00)
Interest rate increase							0,79	-0,25	0,987 (0,33)
Increased risk–return relationship							0,50	-0,31	1,170 (0,24)
Deterioration of geo-strategical, political conditions							0,80	+0,5	-1,534 (0,13)

Note: Only scores greater than 0, 4 absolute value are shown. There are all statistical significant at 5% level. See Koutsoyiannis (1977)

preurenerial motives which have been found irrelevant to the AIDEC. So, perception of time emerges as a new independent entrepreneurial trait non-dependent either on the knowledge of cultural values or on the known entre-preneurial motives. On the contrary, it has a protogenic character that could influence the rest of the entreprenrial traits. This point may also give chance for further re-search.

An important issue that should also be investigated is connected to the extent that some factors have an effect on AIDEC. The positive factors (not all of them) func-tion towards the decline of AIDEC. The negative factors function towards its increase. Thus, it seems that for the entrepreneur there is a notional time of entrepreneurial involvement that in any case would be better if it was smaller. The entrepreneur accepts for it to be lengthened only when he is forced to by external conditions. Thus, when he obtains part of his capital by a non-costing method (lottery or by state's grants), the entrepreneur

does not think that, in this case, he should have more patience to disengage from his entrepreneurial activity, but that the conditions have been created for his easier disengagement. The same happens when a) the financial leverage is increased; b) the payback period is increased; c) he lives in a wealthier economy; d) the costs of bu-reaucracy decline; and e) the conditions of the labour market improve. The opposite happens when the size of the project increases, if recession conditions prevail, and if conditions of political stability are getting worse.

There are two findings which require further comment, regarding the influence of the interest increase and the level of risk-return relationship. Here we revert to or-thodox economic behaviour. This means that declining influences are exercised on the AIDEC on the basis of the following arguments: it seems that the entrepreneur has a notional time of entrepreneurial involvement that in any case would be better if it was smaller. But when the cost of money is increased or the time of systematic risk is increased, then his notional time of entrepreneurial involvement declines. Thus when the entrepreneur is forced by external conditions that concern the whole of the economy in which he is active, he compromises and accepts a longer AIDEC.

8. Conclusions

This paper has supported the idea that perception of time which concerns the average ideal duration of entrepreneurial commitment is an important personal trait. In other words, if the entrepreneur has formed a particular checking filter for the extent of the entrepreneurial involvement, he will never check on the possibility of being involved in larger scale entrepreneurial efforts. The new point proposed by this article at the theoretical level is that the rejection of these entrepreneurial activities is not performed according to a project appraisal criterion but is at an earlier level, which is at the beginning of the search and analysis of entrepreneurial opportunities.

Consequently, the perception of the AIDEC may be on a large scale responsible for the observed phenomenon of the reproduction of light production prototypes that are observed in specific geographical districts and for a long period of time.

The article proposes six factor groups that are responsible for the formation of AIDEC: macro-environmental factors, cultural entrepreneurial idiosyncrasies, personal characteristics, the microeconomics of the project, entrepreneurial motives and cognitive factors. Each group consists of a series of partial factors.

A research was conducted to locate the average ideal duration of entrepreneurial commitment. In this it was ascertained that an AIDEC of a specific duration (5.57 years) was specified according to the time and space characteristics of the field research conducted.

In this article it has been verified that the entrepreneur has a non-one-directional behaviour towards the formation of AIDEC and the factors that form it. Factors that have positive influence on entrepreneurial commitment, and allow entrepreneurs to disengage faster, function towards the reduction of AIDEC. In contrast, external factors that form a negative entrepreneurial environment force entrepreneurs to accept a longer AIDEC. The elasticities of AIDEC with its factors of influence are small. This non-one-directional behaviour could probably be connected with the cyclical and subjective perception of time through the states of the world in which the entrepreneur is engaged. The willing entrepreneur on the one hand conceives from past experiences that his disengagement may be delayed but will eventually come. On the other hand he recognises that the activation of certain factors may shorten the AIDEC for which he is happy.

What is shown from the above analysis is an 'AIDEC trap' for the economic policy that wishes to influence the production prototype towards the investments with a long average duration of entrepreneurial commitment.

In conclusion, we may argue that the analysis reveals that the average duration of entrepreneurial commitment is formed by long-lasting influences on entrepreneurial behaviour which enter with the form either of microeconomic variables or long-term or finally short-term macro-environmental influences.

9. References

[1] L. G. Epstein and S. E Zin, "Substitution, risk aversion, and the temporal behaviour of consumption and asset returns: an empirical analysis," Journal of Political Economy, Vol. 99, pp. 269–286, 1991.

[2] P. Weil, "Nonexpected utility in macroeconomics," Quarterly Journal of Economics, Vol. 105, pp. 29–42, 1990.

[3] F. Lefley, "The payback method of investment appraisal: a review and synthesis," International Journal Production Economics, Vol. 44, pp. 207–224, 1996.

[4] E. Derman, "The perception of time, risk and return during periods of speculation," Quantitative Finance 2, pp. 282–296, 2002.

[5] D. S. Remer, S. B. Stokdyk and M. V. Driel, "Survey of project evaluation techniques currently used in industry," International Journal of Production Economics, Vol. 32, pp. 103–115, 1993.

[6] F. Lefley, "Capital investment appraisal of advanced manufacturing technology," International Journal of Production Research, Vol. 32, No. 12, pp. 2751–2776, 1994.

[7] A. Wambach, "Payback criterion, hurdle rates and the gain of waiting," International Review of Financial Analysis, Vol. 9, pp. 247–258, 2000.

[8] R. O. Chistiansen and C. Ferrell, "Survey of capital budgeting methods used by medium size manufacturing firms," Baylor Business Studies, November and December, pp. 35–43, 1980.

[9] B. J. Bird and W. Page, "G. III. Time and entrepreneurship," Entrepreneurship Theory and Practice Vol. 22, No. 2, pp. 5–136, 1997.

[10] P. Nutt and R. Backoff, "Crafting vision," Journal of Management Inquiry, Vol. 6, No. 4, pp. 308–328, 1997.

[11] E. Jaques, "Introduction to special issue on time and entrepreneurship," Entrepreneurship Theory and Practice Vol. 22, No. 2, pp. 11–12, 1997.

[12] S. Shane and S. Venkataraman, "The promise of entrepreneurship as a field or research," Academy of Management Review, Vol. 25, No. 1, pp. 217–226, 2000.

[13] A. Ardichvili, R. Cardozo and S. Ray, "A theory of entrepreneurial opportunity identification and development," Journal of Business Venturing, Vol. 18, No.1, pp. 105–123, 2003.

[14] I. M. Kirzner, "Competition and entrepreneurship." Chicago: University of Chicago Press, 1973.

[15] I. M. Kirzner, "Perception, opportunity and profit." Chicago: University of Chicago Press, 1979.

[16] J. A. Timmons, D. F. Muzyka, H. H. Stevenson, *et al.*, "Opportunity recognition: the core of entrepreneurship," N. C. Churchill et al., eds., Frontiers of Entrepreneurship Research. Wellesley, MA: Babson College, pp. 109–123, 1987.

[17] T. Fu-Lai Yu, "Entrepreneurial alertness and discovery." Review of Austrian Economics, Vol. 14, No. 1, pp. 47–63, 2001.

[18] Organization for Economic Co-Operation and Development. Fostering Entrepreneurship: The OECD Jobs Strategy. OECD. 1998.

[19] S. Lee and S. Peterson, "Culture, entrepreneurial orientation, and global competitiveness." Journal of World Business, Vol. 35, No. 4, pp. 401–416, 2000.

[20] D. C. McCleland, "the Achieving Society. Princeton," NJ: Van Nostrand, 1961.

[21] P. D. Reynolds, D. Storey and P Westhead, "Regional characteristics affecting entrepreneurship: a cross-natio nal comparison," Frontiers of Entrepreneurship Research, Wellesley, MA: Babson College, pp. 550–564, 1994.

[22] N. Majumder and D. Majumder, "Measuring income risk to promote macro markets," Journal of Policy Modelling Vol. 24, pp. 607–619, 2002.

[23] C. Baughn and K. Neupert, "Culture and nation conditions facilitating entrepreneurial start ups," Journal of International Entrepreneurship 1, pp. 313–330, 2003.

[24] Organization for Economic Co-Operation and Development. Intellectual Property, Technology Transfer and Genetic Resources: An OECD Survey of Current Practices and Policies. OECD, 1996.

[25] G. Hofstede and M. H. Bond, "The Confucius connection: from cultural roots to economic growth," Organization Dynamics Vol. 16, No. 4, pp. 4–21, 2001.

[26] J. Hayton, G. Georg and S. Zahra, "National culture and entrepreneurship: a review of behavioural research," Entrepreneurship Theory and Practice, Vol. 26, No. 4, pp. 33–52, 2002.

[27] R. Mitchell, B. Smith, E. Morse, *et al.*, "Are entrepreneurial cognitions universal? Assessing entrepreneurial cognitions across cultures," Entrepreneurship Theory and Practice, Vol. 26, No. 4, pp. 9–32, 2002.

[28] M. A. Geletkanycz, "The salience of culture's consequences: the effects of cultural values on top executive commitment to the status quo," Strategic Management Journal, Vol. 18, No. 8, pp. 615–634, 1997.

[29] E. A. Locke, "Motivation, cognition and action: an analysis of studies of task goals and knowledge," Applied Psychology: An International Review, Vol. 49, pp. 408–429, 2000.

[30] S. Shane, E. Locke and C. Collins, "Entrepreneurial motivation," Human Resource Management Review, Vol. 13, No. 2, pp. 257–279, 2003.

[31] R. Agarwall, "Survival of firms over the product life cycle." Economic Journal, Vol. 63, No. 3, pp. 571–584, 1997.

[32] URL: http://elearn.elke.uoa.gr/petrakis/appendix/

Appendix

Instructions for filling the questionnaire

1) We have chosen entrepreneurs from firms with equity up to 10,000,000€ and established the year as being after 1980.

2) The enterprises are representative of the sectoral structure of enterprises active in the Greek economy.

3) The answers must be given by the entrepreneur or 'the person in charge of the economical decisions' of the enterprise.

4) The answers are based on the following assumption: the rest of the factors that could influence the answer, apart from those involved in the question, remain stable.

Question 1

Consider that you have already planned an investment of 500,000€ in the field in which you are active or in any other field under the present circumstances. This investment is viable and profitable. For this investment any amount may be spent from your personal fund up to 500,000€. According to this investment you regain your fund in a specific period of time that you know today and which satisfies you. If you were to choose the ideal for your rate of return in a 1–10 years period of time, what would it be?

Please bear in mind that we define 'duration' as the period of time to which you are committed in any way, either by your personal work or by the commitment of your personal or external funds to a particular investment and to no other entrepreneurial activity.

Tick THE YEARS									
1	2	3	4	5	6	7	8	9	10

Question 2

In a period of 1–10 years, when do you want to take back your money for this investment?

ONE ANSWER

TICK THE YEARS									
1	2	3	4	5	6	7	8	9	10

Question 3

Now I would like you to tell me which would be the average ideal duration for this investment, in a 1–10 year period of time, if each of the following alternative conditions prevail?

	YEARS									
1. If you were active in a richer economy with higher rates of growth, low variability of income and small public deficits	1	2	3	4	5	6	7	8	9	10
2. If you were in a downturn of the economy	1	2	3	4	5	6	7	8	9	10
3. If the rates of interest were significantly increased	1	2	3	4	5	6	7	8	9	10
4. If the investment had twice the possibility of failing, but also double the rate of return	1	2	3	4	5	6	7	8	9	10
5. If the government had taken serious measures against bureaucracy, corruption and copyright piracy	1	2	3	4	5	6	7	8	9	10
6. If the government had taken measures for the improvement of labour market conditions	1	2	3	4	5	6	7	8	9	10
7. If political and geostrategical conditions were to deteriorate	1	2	3	4	5	6	7	8	9	10

Question 4

I will itemise various types of personal circumstances and I would like you to tell me about your relation to them. Please answer according to the scale from 1 to 10, where 1 signifies that this behaviour does not mean anything to you and 10 signifies that it means everything.

	Not at all									Fully
1. You take care of your personal entrepreneurial interests	1	2	3	4	5	6	7	8	9	10
2. You avoid situations of uncertainty	1	2	3	4	5	6	7	8	9	10
3. You accept economic disparity	1	2	3	4	5	6	7	8	9	10
4. You are trying to achieve the highest possible level of living	1	2	3	4	5	6	7	8	9	10

Question 5

I will itemise various types of personal circumstances and I would like you to tell me about your relation to them. Please answer according to the scale from 1 to 10, where 1 signifies that this behaviour does not mean anything to you and 10 signifies that it means everything.

	Not at all									Fully
1. You are a risk-taker	1	2	3	4	5	6	7	8	9	10
2. You are capable of controlling things	1	2	3	4	5	6	7	8	9	10
3. You wish to be independent of external interventions	1	2	3	4	5	6	7	8	9	10
4. You tolerate ambiguity	1	2	3	4	5	6	7	8	9	10
5. You are a creative person	1	2	3	4	5	6	7	8	9	10

Question 6

Now I would like you to tell me which would be the average ideal duration for this investment, in a 1–10 year period of time, if each of the following alternative conditions prevail?

	YEARS									
1. You have won all of the 500,000€ yesterday in the lottery and you use them in the investment. Generally speaking you may get this amount without cost or any kind of obligation (i.e. state free grants)	1	2	3	4	5	6	7	8	9	10
2. From the 500,000€, 100,000€ were from your own money and the 400,000€ were borrowed	1	2	3	4	5	6	7	8	9	10
3. The required investment capital was 2,000,000€ instead of 500,000€	1	2	3	4	5	6	7	8	9	10
4. If the payback period is significantly increased	1	2	3	4	5	6	7	8	9	10

DEMOGRAPHIC DATA

1. SECTOR (choose one from the list):

Industry 1
Trade 2
Services 3

2. EQUITY CAPITAL (1998–2002):

3. PERMANENT WORKING PERSONNEL OF THE FIRM:

4. FOUNDATION YEAR:

5. SALES:

6. TOTAL OF ASSETS (1998–2002):

7. PROFITS BEFORE TAX (1998–2002):

RESPONDENT'S DEMOGRAPHIC INFORMATION

8. AGE: How old are you?

9. EDUCATIONAL LEVEL: what is your highest level of education/studies?

Illiterate/not all the classes of primary school (till the second grade)	_____1
From the third grade-primary school graduate (till 12 years old)	_____2
High school graduate (3 classes) (till 15 years old)	_____3
High school graduate (6 classes) (16–18 years old)	_____4
Higher education graduate (19+ years old)	_____5

Highest education graduate (university)	_____6

10. FAMILY STATUS: You are :

Married _____ 1
Single _____ 2
Divorced or widow_____ 3

6

Hybrid Decision Models in Non-Proportional Reinsurance

Maik Wagner

Department of Business Statistics, Friedrich-Schiller-University Jena, Germany

Abstract

Over the past years, risk measurement and therewith risk measures became more and more important in economics. While in the past risk measures were already adopted at the deposit of credit and shareholders equity, the approach now generates two hybrid decision models and applies them to the reinsurance business. The two introduced models implement a convex combination of risk measures and with it provide the possibility of modelling risk attitudes. By doing that, for the two hybrid decision models on the one hand can be shown, which risk attitude leads to the acceptance of a reinsurance contract and on the other hand, a deductible of which height an insurer is willing to undertake. Hence the possibility exists to identify the risk attitude of an insurer. In return, due to the knowledge of risk attitudes, under similar conditions the possibility arises to establish recommendations about the extent of the deductible at reinsurance contracts.

Keywords: Insurance; Optimization; Risk; Decision Analysis

1. Introduction

The application of risk measures gains more and more importance. These measures can be applied on the one hand in the determination of the deposit of equity capital and on the other hand in the modelling of decision models considering the risk attitude. First of all, in Section 2 a short insight into the topic reinsurance should be given, in order to introduce subsequently the profit function of an insurer for a non-proportional reinsurance contract. In Section 3 two complementary decision principles will be introduced. These use a hybrid preference functional for the determination of the deductible. With the help of this the optimal deductible of an insurer can be determined depending on the insurers risk attitude (see Section 4). The interpretation of the results follows in Section 5 and will be completed by a prospect in Section 6. Hence the aim of the article is to show possibilities of integrating risk attitudes into the determination of deductibles.

2. Non-Proportional Reinsurance

An insurer uses a reinsurance [1–3] for risk limitation and risk diversification of its compulsory treaty indemnity with its private customer. Thereby the aim of a reinsurance is to replace a part of the assumed ambiguous costs of the losses by fixed costs. These fixed costs represent the recompense of the reinsurance, the so-called reinsurance premium. Hence the reduction of the risk charge plays a central role for the insurer.

In this process reinsurance has two fundamental tasks: First, to restrain the annual variation of the loss burden of the insurer and second, to ensure the solvency of the insurance company in the extreme event of loss. Consequently the violation of the solvency [4] is the highest risk, which the insurer wants to avoid.

Reinsurance contracts can be distinguished in the reinsurance form and hence in the limitation of the obligation or voluntariness of the acceptance of risks, but also in their type. The distribution of risk is crucial for this differentiation between the insurer and the reinsurer. The risk is divided between the parties either in a proportional or non-proportional way [5,6]. In the following the focus is only on the non-proportional reinsurance.

The non-proportional reinsurance is characterized by a liability of the reinsurer which is only influenced by the amount of loss. This implies in connection of the arrangement of the contract, that the reinsurer only contributes to the loss in case the determined limit of loss is exceeded. This limit of loss is called deductible. The loss burden undertaken by the reinsurer is called reinsurance loss. It is necessary that the reinsurance loss

$$RL(d, X) = \begin{cases} 0, & \text{for } x < d \\ X - d, & \text{for } d \le X \end{cases} = X - \min(d, X),$$

whereas d is the deductible and X the loss that evolves

from the private customer business. The loss describes a random variable with a distribution function and the corresponding density f. This density is zero for negative values, due to the non-existence of negative losses.

In return for the acquired reinsurance protection the insurer pays the reinsurance premium RP(d). The basic structure of such a premium contains the expected reinsurance loss and an additional profit mark-on. The profit mark-on can refer to the expected reinsurance loss on the one hand and to the variance or to the standard deviation on the other hand [7]. In the following the premium is applied with a profit mark-on, which is linked to the expected reinsurance loss.

Definition 1

$E(RL(d,X))$ is the expected reinsurance loss and γ the profit mark-on of the reinsurer with $\gamma \geq 0$. Then $RP(d) := (1+\gamma)\,E(RL(d,X))$ is called reinsurance premium.

Additionally to the incomes and costs from the reinsurance business the reinsurer possesses the insurance premium Pr from the private customer business minus the loss X. Additionally the insurer has the costs of operation B. Consequently the profit function of an insurer has the following form

$$G(d,X) = Pr\text{-}B\text{-}X\text{-}RP(d)+X\text{-}\min(d,X)$$
$$= Pr\text{-}B\text{-}RP(d)\text{-}\min(d,X).$$

an insurer has the choice between different decision principles. For each decision principle a preference functional, modelling its behaviour, exists. In this process the aim of an insurer is to maximize its profit function in reference to the deductible.

3. Decision Principles

A situation is identified as decision under risk [8,9] in case the possible entry scenarios as well as their entry probabilities are known. Consequently this case applies to an insurer, as the cedent knows the loss distribution from historical data and hence the insurer can estimate the possible loss as well as its probability.

In the following, two hybrid models are introduced and applied to the reinsurance problem. Both decision models represent a weighting between expected value and conditional expected value. The first preference functional uses the Conditional Value at Risk (the lower conditional expected value) and the second preference functional the upper conditional expected value of the target function.

The preference functionals have the following form

$$\Phi_{\alpha,\lambda}(G(d,X)) = \frac{1-\lambda}{1-\alpha}\,E(G(d,X))$$
$$+\frac{\lambda-\alpha}{1-\alpha}\,E(G(d,X)\,|\,G(d,X)\leq g_\alpha(d))$$

and

$$\Phi_{\beta,\delta}(G(d,X)) = \frac{1-\delta}{1-\beta}\,E(G(d,X))$$
$$+\frac{\delta-\beta}{1-\beta}\,E(G(d,X)\,|\,G(d,X)\geq g_{1-\beta}(d)),$$

whereas α and λ are the risk parameters of the first preference functional and β and δ are the risk parameters of the second preference functional with $\alpha,\beta \in [0,1[$ and $\lambda,\delta \in [0,1]$. It is necessary that $\frac{1-\lambda}{1-\alpha}+\frac{\lambda-\alpha}{1-\alpha}=1$ and $\frac{1-\delta}{1-\beta}+\frac{\delta-\beta}{1-\beta}=1$. Furthermore $g_\alpha(d)$ is the α–quantile of the profit in the first and $g_{1-\beta}(d)$ is the $(1-\beta)$– quantile of the profit in the second functional. Both preference functionals can be applied amongst others in the Newsvendor problem [10,11] with risk preferences [12,13].

In the Newsvendor model a trader wants to sell a product at the price p. However the product can only be sold within one time period. The trader buys the product at price c and in case of not selling can return it at the price of z. The analogy between the News-vendor and the reinsurance model is represented in Poser, Wagner [14].

Both preference functionals represent risk neutrality in case of equality of their risk parameters. In this case both functionals are equal the expected profit. In case $\alpha < \lambda$ the lower expected value has a positive influence on the preference functional and represents risk aversion. Analogical in the second functional the upper expected value has a positive influence for $\beta < \delta$ and conse- quently reflects risk taking. In cases $\alpha > \lambda$ and $\beta > \delta$ the lower and upper expected value is integrated nega- tively and represents risk taking for the first decision functional and risk aversion for the second one. It should be present that the complementary preference functionals have the same results.

The two following questions shall be clarified for the two introduced preference functionals:

1) At which risk attitude the insurer decides in favour of the reinsurance?

2) If the insurer decides in favour of the reinsurance, which level of the deductible is preferred?

4. Determination of the Deductible

In this section the deductible is determined with the help of two preference functionals depending on the risk attitude of a decision maker. The profit function is dependent on the loss while the lower and upper expected value comprise the profit quantile.

From Chart 1 can be noticed, that the $\alpha \cdot 100\%$ low-

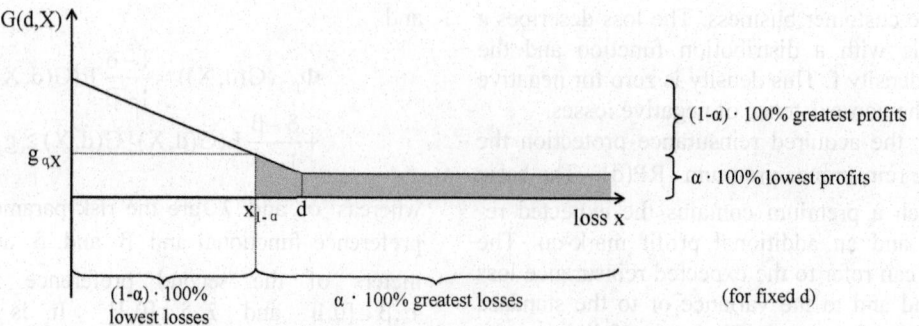

Chart 1. Profit function of the insurer with α-profit quantile.

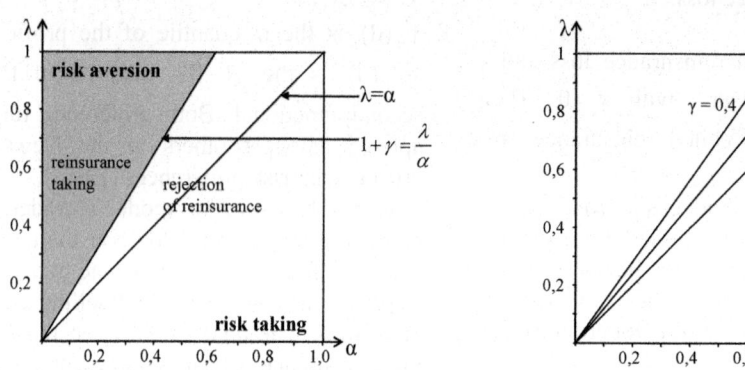

Chart 2. Risk preference space for the preference functional $\Phi_{\alpha,\lambda}(G(d,X))$.

est profits are realized with the $\alpha \cdot 100\,\%$ greatest losses. Consequently $(1-\alpha) \cdot 100\,\%$ of the losses are located below the loss quantile. Consequently it is the $(1-\alpha)$-loss quantile.

Hence the following equation applies

$$E(G(d,X)|G(d,X) \leq g_\alpha(d))=E(G(d,X)|X \geq x_{1-\alpha}),$$

whereas $x_{1-\alpha}$ indicates the loss quantile. Analogical the $\beta \cdot 100\,\%$ greatest profits[1] appear at the $\beta \cdot 100\,\%$ lowest losses. $\beta \cdot 100\,\%$ of the losses are located below the β-loss quantile. Hence the following applies

$$E(G(d,X)\,|\,G(d,X) \geq g_{1-\beta}(d)) = E(G(d,X)\,|\,X \leq x_\beta),$$

whereas x_β characterizes the β-loss quantile. Hence it is possible to maximize the two preference functionals. The two following theorems verbalize this.

Theorem 1

Let $G(d,X) = \text{Pr-}\,B\text{-}RVP(d)\text{-}\min(d,X)$ be the profit function of an insurer and

$$\Phi_{\alpha,\lambda}(G(d,X)) = \frac{1-\lambda}{1-\alpha}E(G(d,X))$$
$$+ \frac{\lambda-\alpha}{1-\alpha}\ E(G(d,X)\,|\,X \geq x_{1-\alpha})$$

its objective function. Then the maximizing problem $\max\limits_d \Phi_{\alpha,\lambda}(G(d,X))$ has the following implicit solution

$$F_X(d*(\alpha,\lambda)) = \begin{cases} 1, & \text{for} \quad 1+\gamma > \dfrac{\lambda}{\alpha} \\[2ex] \dfrac{(1-\alpha)\gamma}{(1-\alpha)(1+\gamma)-(1-\lambda)}, & \text{for} \quad 1+\gamma < \dfrac{\lambda}{\alpha} \end{cases}$$

with $\alpha \in\ ]0,1[,\ \lambda \in [0,1]$ and $\gamma \geq 0$.[2]

Theorem 2

Let $G(d,X) = \text{Pr-}\,B\text{-}RVP(d)\text{-}\min(d,X)$ be the profit function of an insurer and

$$\Phi_{\beta,\delta}(G(d,X)) = \frac{1-\delta}{1-\beta}E(G(d,X))$$
$$+ \frac{\delta-\beta}{1-\beta}E(G(d,X)\,|\,X \leq x_\beta)$$

its objective function. Then this maximizing problem $\max\limits_d \Phi_{\beta,\delta}(G(d,X))$ has the following implicit solution

$$F_X(d*(\alpha,\lambda)) = \begin{cases} 1, & \text{for} \quad 1+\gamma > \dfrac{1-\delta}{1-\beta} \\[2ex] \dfrac{\beta\gamma}{\beta(1+\gamma)-\delta}, & \text{for} \quad 1+\gamma < \dfrac{1-\delta}{1-\beta} \end{cases}$$

with $\beta \in\ ]0,1[,\ \delta \in [0,1]$ and $\gamma \geq 0$ [16].

---

[1] These are the profits lying above the $(1-\beta)$-profit quantile.
[2] The proof of theorem Theorem 1 can be found in the appendix.

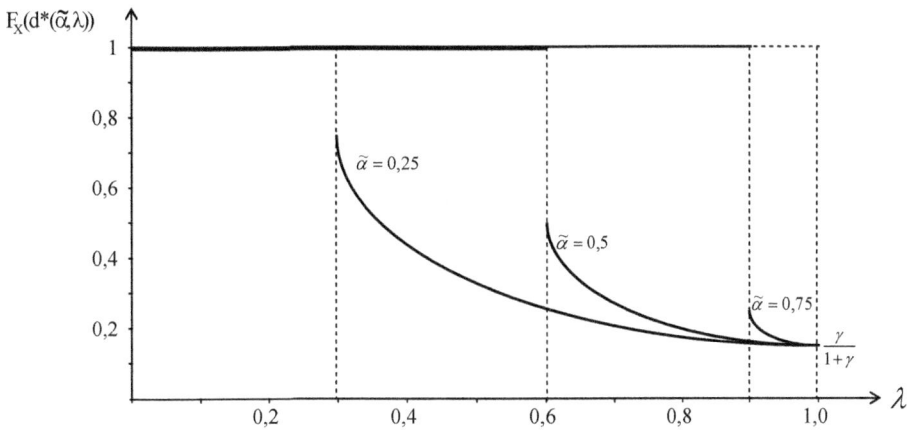

Chart 3. $F_X(d*(\alpha,\lambda))$ **for a given** $\tilde{\alpha}$.

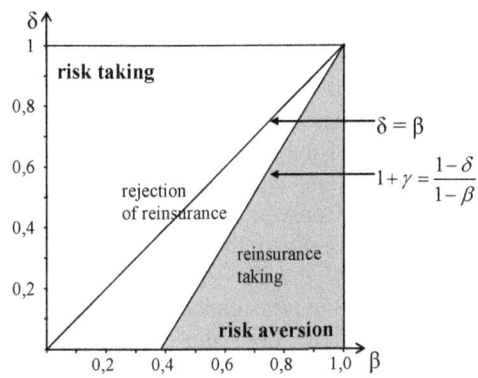
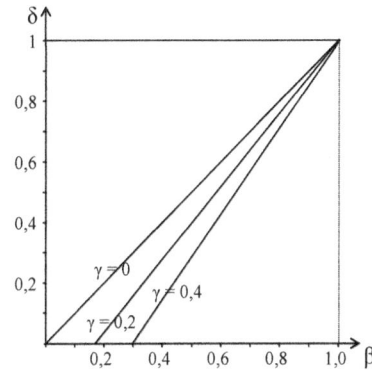

Chart 4. Risk preference space for $\Phi_{\beta,\delta}(G(d,X))$.

5. Interpretation

At first the risk preference space for the preference functional $\Phi_{\alpha,\lambda}(G(d,X))$ is examined. This one is illustrated by the left figure of the Chart 2. The space is splitted into two halves by the angle bisector. The surface above the angle bisector $(\alpha < \lambda)$ contains all $\alpha - \lambda$ - combinations for risk aversion and below $(\alpha > \lambda)$ all combinations for risk taking. The angle bisector $(\alpha = \lambda)$ itself is the combination for risk neutrality.

Furthermore within this figure appears the border between the optimal solutions $1+\gamma = \dfrac{\lambda}{\alpha}$. The value of the distribution at the optimal deductible below that border thereby is $F_X(d*(\alpha,\lambda)) = 1$ and above

$$F_X(d*(\alpha,\lambda)) = \frac{(1-\alpha)\gamma}{(1-\alpha)(1+\gamma)-(1-\lambda)}.$$

The conclusion can be drawn, that the insurer with $F_X(d*(\alpha,\lambda)) = 1$ chooses a deductible to the extent of the greatest losses. This implies, that the insurer wants to

bear every occurred loss himself. In this case the cedent rejects the reinsurance. In the case $1+\gamma < \dfrac{\lambda}{\alpha}$ the distribution of the optimal deductible fulfils

$$F_X(d*(\alpha,\lambda)) = \frac{(1-\alpha)\gamma}{(1-\alpha)(1+\gamma)-(1-\lambda)} \in [0,1-\alpha].$$

That implies, that the insurer intends to take the reinsurance. At the border $1+\gamma = \dfrac{\lambda}{\alpha}$ the insurer is indifferent between the optimal solutions.

The right figure of Chart 2 illustrates the changing of the border between contract taking and rejection depending on the profit mark-on of the reinsurer. The border moves in an area of higher risk aversion for a higher profit mark-on γ. So the insurer has to surmount this mark-on before he chooses the contract. In case, that the profit mark-on gamma is zero the risk neutrality line is the border between contract taking and rejection.

A further question is: If the insurer decides in favour of the reinsurance, which level of deductible is preferred? It can be adhered, that in case of choosing the reinsurance the value of the distribution at the optimal

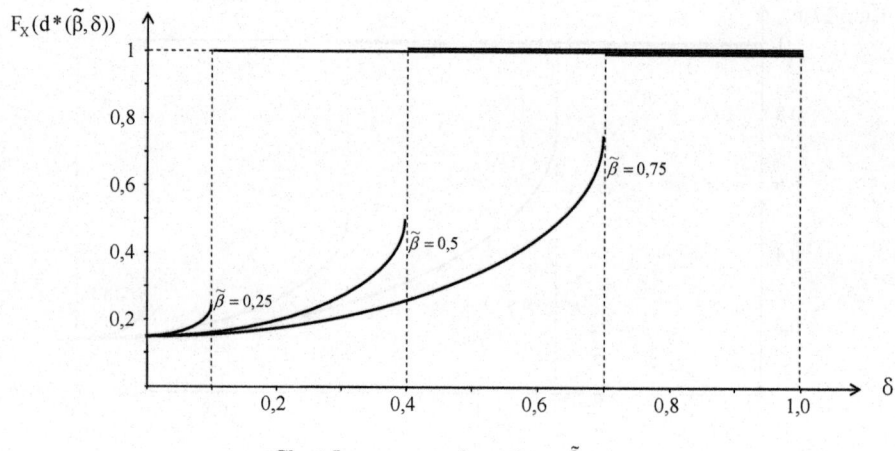

Chart 5. $F_X(d*(\beta,\delta))$ **for a given** $\tilde{\beta}$.

deductible decreases with the increase of risk aversion $(\lambda \rightarrow 1)$. That implies, that the cedent wants to release more risk to the cessionary. Chart 3 illustrates this for a given α.

At the point of the highest risk aversion $(\lambda = 1)$ the value of the distribution at the optimal deductible is $\frac{\gamma}{1+\gamma}$ and so independent of the risk parameter α. Within the chart a profit mark-on of 20 % is assumed.

Now the results of the preference functional $\Phi_{\beta,\delta}(G(d,X))$ are observed. The left figure of Chart 4 shows the risk preference of the preference functional. The space is divided into two halves by the angle bisector as well. This time the space above the angle bisector $(\beta < \delta)$ contains all β-δ-combinations for risk taking and below all combinations for risk aversion. The angle bisector itself describes the combination for risk neutrality.

Likewise the border between the optimal solutions $\left(1+\gamma = \frac{1-\delta}{1-\beta}\right)$ is illustrated in this figure. The value of the distribution at the optimal deductible above this border is $F_X(d*(\beta,\delta)) = 1$ and below

$$F_X(d*(\beta,\delta)) = \frac{\beta\gamma}{\beta(1+\gamma)-\delta}.$$

It can be concluded, that an insurer with $F_X(d*(\beta,\delta)) = 1$ chooses the deductible in the amount of the greatest possible loss and consequently rejects the reinsurance.

In the case $1+\gamma = \frac{1-\delta}{1-\beta}$ the value of the distribution at the optimal deductible fulfils

$$F_X(d*(\beta,\delta)) = \frac{\beta\gamma}{\beta(1+\gamma)-\delta} \in [0,\beta[.$$

Hence the cedent decides in favour of the reinsurance. The border between accepting and rejecting the reinsurance depending on the profit mark-on of the reinsurer, is illustrated by the right figure of Chart 4.

It likewise can be recognized, that the purchase decision of the reinsurance moves in an area of higher risk aversion with increasing profit mark-on of the reinsurer. Consequently it is necessary that the higher the profit mark-on of the reinsurer is, the greater the risk aversion of the decision maker has to be, so that he purchases the reinsurance.

Concluding this, the following question remains: Which deductible, depending on the risk attitude with the β-δ-preference functional, does the insurer choose in case of accepting the reinsurance? In this situation the value of the distribution at the optimal deductible decreases with an increase of risk aversion $(\delta \rightarrow 0)$. That means, that the insurer wants to release more risk to the reinsurer. This is illustrated by Chart 5 for a given β.

Concerning both decision principles it can be concluded, that risk taking as well as risk neutral insurers reject the reinsurance. For risk aversion in contrast, two cases can be distinguished: On the one hand the case of lower risk aversion $\left(1+\gamma > \frac{\lambda}{\alpha}\right.$ rather $\left.1+\gamma > \frac{1-\delta}{1-\beta}\right)$, where the reinsurance is rejected as well and on the other hand the case of higher risk aversion $\left(1+\gamma < \frac{\lambda}{\alpha}\right.$ rather $\left.1+\gamma < \frac{1-\delta}{1-\beta}\right)$, where the insurer decides in favour of the reinsurance. That implies that only an insurer having enough risk aversion decides to take the reinsurance. In case that the reinsurance is accepted, the deductible decreases with the increase of risk aversion. It can be stated, that the higher the risk aversion is, the more risk is transferred to the reinsurer by the cedent.

The interpretations of results are identical for both preference functionals. For this reason it is irrelevant, whether using the preference functional with the lower or with the upper expected value. It is possible to find for each α-λ-combination of the first preference funktional a β-δ-combination of the second preference funktional.

The analogy is $\alpha = 1 - \beta$ and $\lambda = 1 - \delta$.

6. Prospect

With the solutions of the optimal deductible it is possible to detect the risk preference of the insurer in case of knowing the loss distribution and the coverage limit. Furthermore the optimal deductible for a different assumed loss distribution can be calculated when knowing the risk preference of the insurer.

The introduced models only consider the maximization of the profit function in reference to the deductible. One possible prospect is the application of the hybrid decision model for the maximization of the profit function in reference to the cover or continuative the maximazation of a two dimensional model with deductible and cover.

Furthermore an investigation of the models could be made with the use of a fair premium and also the consistence to decision theories could be established.

7. References

[1] K. Gerathewohl, "Reinsurance principles and practice," Vol. 1, Verlag Versicherungswirtschaft, Karlsruhe, 1980.

[2] E. Wollan, "Handbook of reinsurance law," Aspen Publishers, New York, 2002.

[3] S. C. Bennett, "Dictionary of insurance, pearson education," Zug, 2004.

[4] E. Helland, C. R. Nysæter, "Solvency II: An Illustration, " Forfatterne, Bergen, 2006.

[5] A. Schwepcke, D. Arndt, "Reinsurance: Principles and state of the art," Verlag Versicherungswirtschaft, Karlsruhe, 2004.

[6] R. Phifer, "Reinsurance fundamentals: Treaty and facultative," John Wiley, New York, 1996.

[7] M. Kaluszka, "Optimal reinsurance under mean-variance premium principles," Insurance: Mathematics and Economics, Vol. 42, 2008.

[8] P. J. Montana, B. H. Charnov, "Management, Barron's educational series," New York, 2000.

[9] V. Torra, Y. Narukawa, "Modeling Decisions for Artificial Intelligence," Springer , 2009.

[10] G. Cachon and C. Terwiesch, "Matching supply with demand," Mc Graw-Hill, New York, 2006.

[11] S. Chopra and P. Meindl, "Supply chain management," 2. Edition, Prentice Hall, New Jersey, 2004.

[12] W. Jammernegg and P. Kischka, "A decision rule based on the conditional value at risk," Jenaer Schriften zur Wirtschaftswissenschaft, Vol. 9, 2005.

[13] W. Jammernegg and P. Kischka, "Risk-averse and risk-taking newsvendors: A conditional expected value approach," Review of Managerial Science, Vol. 1, 2007.

[14] K. Poser, M. Wagner, "Das Newsvendor Modell mit nicht-linearer Kostenfunktion und seine Anwendung bei nicht-proportionalen Rückversicherungsverträgen," Jena Research Papers in Business and Economics, Vol. 15, 2007.

[15] P. Embrechts, R. Frey, and A. J. McNeil, "Quantitative risk management: Concepts," Techniques and Tools, Princeton University Press, Oxford, 2005.

[16] M. Wagner, "Bestimmung von Deckungsgrenzen bei nicht-proportionalen Rueckversicherungsvertraegen," German Journal of Risk and Insurance, Vol. 3, 2008.

Appendix

Proof of Theorem 1:
The following applies

$$\Phi_{\alpha,\lambda}(G(d,X)) = \frac{1-\lambda}{1-\alpha}E(G(d,X))$$
$$+ \frac{\lambda-\alpha}{1-\alpha}E(G(d,X)\,|\,X \ge x_{1-\alpha})$$

The first derivation of the preference functional is generated and the following can be received

$$D_d(\Phi_{\alpha,\lambda}(G(d,X))) = \frac{1-\lambda}{1-\alpha}D_d(E(G(d,X)))$$
$$+ \frac{\lambda-\alpha}{1-\alpha}D_d(E(G(d,X)\,|\,X \ge x_{1-\alpha})).$$

At first the first differential of the expected profit and also of the conditional expected value has to be determined. For the profit function of the insurer can be assumed $G(d,X) = Pr - B - X - RP(d) + RL(d,X)$. For the expected profit can be obtained

$$E(G(d,X)) = E\left(Pr - B - X - RP(d) + \begin{cases} 0, & \text{for } X < d \\ X - d, & \text{for } d \le X \end{cases}\right)$$
$$= Pr - B - E(X) - RP(d) + \int_0^d 0\,dF_X(x) + \int_d^\infty (x-d)dF_X(x)$$
$$= Pr - B - E(X) - RP(d) + \int_d^\infty (x-d)dF_X(x) \quad ^3$$
$$= Pr - B - E(X) - RP(d) + \int_d^\infty xdF_X(x) - d\left[1 - F_X(d)\right].$$

By the use of differentiation and the main theorem of the infinitesimal calculus for the expected profit follows

$$D_d(E(G(d,X))) = -RP_d(d) - d \cdot f_X(d) - (1 - F_X(d)) + d \cdot f_X(d)$$
$$= -RP_d(d) - 1 + F_X(d)$$

In the case $F_X(d) \ge 1 - \alpha$ is for the conditional expected value essential, that

$$E(G(d,x)\,|\,X \ge x_{1-\alpha})$$
$$= \frac{1}{\alpha}[Pr - B - RP(d)][1 - (1-\alpha)] - \frac{1}{\alpha}d[1 - F_X(d)]$$

---

[3] It is necessary that

$$\int_d^\infty (x-d)dF_X(x) = \int_d^\infty xdF_X(x) - \int_d^\infty ddF_X(x) = \int_d^\infty xdF_X(x) - d\int_d^\infty dF_X(x) =$$

$$\int_d^\infty xdF_X(x) - d\left[1 - F_X(d)\right].$$

[4] It is necessary that $\frac{1-\lambda}{1-\alpha} + \frac{\lambda-\alpha}{1-\alpha}\frac{1}{\alpha} = \frac{\alpha(1-\lambda)+\lambda-\alpha}{\alpha(1-\alpha)} =$

$$\frac{\alpha - \alpha\lambda + \lambda - \alpha}{\alpha(1-\alpha)} = \frac{\lambda(1-\alpha)}{\alpha(1-\alpha)} = \frac{\lambda}{\alpha}.$$

[5] It is necessary that $RP_d(d) = (1+\gamma)[-1 + F_X(d)]$.

$$- \frac{1}{\alpha}\int_{F_X^{-1}(1-\alpha)}^d xdF_X(x)$$
$$= [Pr - B - RP(d)] - \frac{1}{\alpha}d[1 - F_X(d)]$$
$$- \frac{1}{\alpha}\int_{F_X^{-1}(1-\alpha)}^d xdF_X,$$

whereas F^{-1} is the inverse function of the loss distribution. In general, the generalized lower inverse $F^*(a)$ of the distribution function $F(x)$ is required. This has the following definition $F^*(a) := \sup(x \in IR\,|\,F(x) \le a)$, whereas $a \in [0,1]$. On the contrary, if one assumes a continuous and strictly increasing distribution function then the generalized lower inverse is equal to the inverse function F^{-1} of the loss distribution. In the following a continuous and strictly increasing distribution function should be assumed.

The first derivation of the conditional expected value is

$$D_d(E(G(d,x)\,|\,X \ge x_{1-\alpha}))$$
$$= -RP_d(d) - \frac{1}{\alpha}(1 - F_X(d)) + \frac{1}{\alpha}df_X(d) - \frac{1}{\alpha}df_X(d)$$
$$= -RP_d(d) - \frac{1}{\alpha}(1 - F_X(d))$$

and so it is essential for the first derivation of the preference functional, that

$$D_d(\Phi_{\alpha,\lambda}(G(d,X)))$$
$$= \frac{1-\lambda}{1-\alpha}[-RP_d(d) - 1 + F(d)]$$
$$+ \frac{\lambda-\alpha}{1-\alpha}\left[-RP_d(d) - \frac{1}{\alpha}(1 - F_X(d))\right]$$
$$= -RP_d(d) + \left[\frac{1-\lambda}{1-\alpha} + \frac{\lambda-\alpha}{1-\alpha}\frac{1}{\alpha}\right][-1 + F_X(d)]$$
$$= -RP_d(d) + \frac{\lambda}{\alpha}[-1 + F_X(d)] \quad ^4$$
$$= -(1+\gamma)[-1 + F_X(d)] + \frac{\lambda}{\alpha}[-1 + F_X(d)] \quad ^5$$
$$= \left[\frac{\lambda}{\alpha} - (1+\gamma)\right][-1 + F_X(d)].$$

Therefore the optimal solution $F_X(d^*) = 1$ can be obtained. For the second derivation of the preference functional follows

$$D_{dd}(\Phi_{\alpha,\lambda}(G(d,X))) = \left[\frac{\lambda}{\alpha} - (1+\gamma)\right]f_X(d).$$

It is necessary that $\left[-(1+\gamma) + \frac{\lambda}{\alpha}\right]f_X(d^*) < 0$ and

$1+\gamma > \dfrac{\lambda}{\alpha}$ because the loss density is not negative. Hence $F_X(d*(\alpha,\lambda)) = 1$ is the maximum in the case of $1+\gamma > \dfrac{\lambda}{\alpha}$.

In the case $F_X(d) < 1-\alpha$ the conditional expected value is

$E(G(d,X)\mid X \geq x_{1-\alpha})$

$= \dfrac{1}{\alpha}\displaystyle\int_{F_X^{-1}(1-\alpha)}^{\infty}[Pr-B-RP(d)-x+x-d]dF_X(x)$

$\quad - \dfrac{1}{\alpha}[Pr-B-RP(d)-d]\displaystyle\int_{F_X^{-1}(1-\alpha)}^{\infty}dF_X(x)$

$= \dfrac{1}{\alpha}[Pr-B-RP(d)-d][1-(1-\alpha)]$

$\quad - Pr-B-RP(d)-d,$

After differentiation it is necessary that $D_d(E(G(d,X)\mid X \geq x_{1-\alpha})) = -RP_d(d)-1$.

Consequently for the first derivation of the preference functional can be obtained

$D_d(\Phi_{\alpha,\lambda}(G(d,X)))$

$= \dfrac{1-\lambda}{1-\alpha}[-RP_d(d)-1+F_X(d)]+\dfrac{\lambda-\alpha}{1-\alpha}[-RP_d(d)-1]$

$= -RP_d(d)-1+\dfrac{1-\lambda}{1-\alpha}F_X(d)$

$= -(1+\gamma)[-1+F_X(d)-1+\dfrac{1-\lambda}{1-\alpha}F_X(d)$ [6]

$= \gamma+\left[-(1+\gamma)+\dfrac{1-\lambda}{1-\alpha}\right]F_X(d)$

Therefore the optimal solution is

$F_X(d*(\alpha,\lambda)) = \dfrac{(1-\alpha)\gamma}{(1-\alpha)(1+\gamma)-(1-\lambda)}.$

Now the determination of the second derivation for the identification of the type of optimum can be made. It is necessary that

$$D_{dd}(\Phi_{\alpha,\lambda}(G(d,X))) = \left[-1(1+\gamma+\dfrac{1-\lambda}{1-\alpha}\right]f_X(d).$$

As the loss density can not receive negative values, the second derivation of the preference functional is negative in case that $1+\gamma > \dfrac{1-\lambda}{1-\alpha}$. The following question arises: When does the optimum exist? At first $F_X(d*(\alpha,\lambda)) \geq 0$ is observed. This equation can be assumed, when the denominator of the solution is not negative. It is necessary, that

$$(1-\alpha)(1+\gamma)-(1-\lambda)\geq 0 \Rightarrow 1+\gamma \geq \dfrac{1-\lambda}{1-\alpha}.$$

Therefore $F_X(d*(\alpha,\lambda))$ is a maximum, for $F_X(d*(\alpha,\lambda)) \geq 0$. The second step $F_X(d*(\alpha,\lambda)) < 1-\alpha$ is observed. It is necessary, that

$$\dfrac{\gamma(1-\alpha)}{(1-\alpha)(1+\gamma)-(1-\lambda)} < 1-\alpha$$

and this is equivalent to $1+\gamma < \dfrac{\lambda}{\alpha}$, because

$\dfrac{\gamma(1-\alpha)}{(1-\alpha)(1+\gamma)-(1-\lambda)} < 1-\alpha \Rightarrow \gamma < (1-\alpha)(1+\gamma)-(1-\lambda)$

$\Rightarrow (1-\alpha)(1+\gamma)-(1+\gamma)+\lambda > 0 \Rightarrow (1-\alpha-1)(1+\gamma)+\lambda > 0$

$\Rightarrow -\alpha(1+\gamma)+\lambda > 0 \qquad \Rightarrow 1+\gamma > \dfrac{\lambda}{\alpha}$

The result is, that the maximum exists, when the other maximum $F_X(d*(\alpha,\lambda)) = 1$ does not exist.

---

[6]It is necessary that $RVP_d(d) = (1+\gamma)[-1+F_X(d)]$.

7

How to Support Innovative Behaviour?—
The Role of LMX and Satisfaction with HR Practices

Karin Sanders, Matthijs Moorkamp, Nicole Torka,
Sandra Groeneveld, Claudia Groeneveld
Department of Organizational Psychology and Human Resource Development, University of Twente,
Enschede, the Netherlands

Abstract

Innovative behaviour of employees refers to a key aspect of organizational effectiveness: the creation, introduction and application of new ideas within a group or organization in order to benefit performance. Using data from a Dutch and German survey in four technical organizations (n=272) we developed and tested two models to explain the relationships between Leader-Member-Exchange (LMX), satisfaction with HR practices (employee influence, flow, rewards and work content) and innovative behaviour. As expected both LMX and satisfaction with HR practices were positively related to innovative behaviour. Furthermore, we found evidence that satisfaction with HR practices mediates the relationship between LMX and innovative behaviour. No significant interaction effects between LMX and satisfaction with HR practices on innovative behaviour were found.

Keywords: Innovative Behaviour, Leader Member Exchange, Satisfaction with HR Practices, Technical Organizations

1. How to Support Innovative Behaviour?

For contemporary organizations, the financial attractiveness of their products and/or services is mostly not enough to guarantee sustainable survive: goods also have to be of high-quality and preferably unique [1,2]. Uniqueness refers to innovation: "the development and implementation of new ideas by people" [3]. It is claimed that innovative behaviour of employees defined as the creation, introduction and application of new ideas within a group or organization in order to benefit performance [4,5] is crucial for the long-time survival of organizations [3,6–9].

Given the importance of innovation, there is a growing interest among scholars trying to answer the question why and under which circumstances employees express innovative behaviour within their organization. To gain such critical employee contributions, scholars argue that the development and implementation of Human Resource Management (HRM) is vital [10]. In general HRM is defined as the management of people and workplace to achieve competitive advantage and involves both HR professionals and (line) management. Although a lot of research has been done in the last two decades, and strategic HRM researchers have converged in their belief that HRM is associated with organizational outcomes, the understanding of the "HRM-performance" relationship, including innovative behaviour is still open to question [11].

In stead of the written HR practices, such as selection and recruitment, performance appraisal, and pay (for performance) attention is moved to the perception of employees regarding the HR practices in a firm. Employees' perceptions of HR practices are likely to precede employee behaviour links in the causal chain: to exert their desired effect on employee behaviour, HR practices first have to be perceived and interpreted subjectively by employees in ways that will engender behavioural reactions [11,12]. And, as we know from psychology that people perceive reality differently, we can expect that employees interpret HR practices differently. In this study, we focus on employees' satisfaction with HR practices [13,14]. Because satisfaction with HR practices can be seen as a facet of job satisfaction we examine the relationship between satisfaction with HR practices and job satisfaction as well.

When including employees' satisfaction with HR practices, the role of the direct supervisor can not be underestimated. Many companies delegate operational HRM to those who lead employees directly [10] and as a result several key HR administrative tasks—hiring, performance management and compensation—have been devolved to line managers [10]. Since supervisors have some degrees of freedom in dealing with these practices, their decisions and behaviours can be seen as major antecedents of employee attitudes and behaviours. Leader-Member-Exchange (LMX) theory suggests that leaders do not use the same style in dealing with all subordinates, but develop a different relationship with each subordinate on a dyadic basis [15–18]. To date, despite agreement on the importance of the relationships employees have with their supervisor (e.g. [20]), relatively little has been done to study the relationship between LMX and innovative behaviour (see for exceptions [20–22]).

This study contributes to the filling of the knowledge gap related to innovative behaviour in three ways. First, in stead of the (formal) HR practices as described by HR managers or direct supervisors, we focus on the satisfaction employees have regarding the HR practices. Second, since it can be assumed that both employees' satisfaction with HR practices and LMX influence innovative behaviour, we consider the relationship between satisfaction with HR practices and LMX on innovative behaivour. Third, in this study we relate a single-item measurement for general job satisfaction to satisfaction with HR practices. Consequently, using survey data from 272 medium to high-educated technical employees from a Dutch and three German industrial companies, we formulated the research question as follows: How can the relationships between LMX, satisfaction with HR practices, and innovative behaviour be explained?

1.1. Satisfaction with HR Practices and Innovative Behaviour

Beer *et al.* [13] distinguished four HR practices: employee influence, human resource flow, rewards, and work systems. Employee influence refers to a process that allows employees to exercise influence over their work and the conditions under which they work. Human resource flow refers to issues of recruitment, selection, development and ending the contract of organizational members. Rewards are concerned with how employees are rewarded for their work. They include monetary rewards such as pay, bonuses and profit sharing, and non-monetary rewards such as holidays and health insurance. Work systems refer to a particular combination of job tasks, technology, skills, management style and personnel policies and practices. Given the sample of this study – technicians, we separate primary (monetary) from secondary (non-monetary) rewards and refer to work content as work systems.

Innovative behaviour refers to discretionary employee behaviour, behaviour that goes beyond prescribed role expectations and is not directly or explicitly recognized

by any formal reward system [23,24]. The link between employees' satisfaction and innovative behaviour as a discretionary behaviour can be explained by social exchange theory [25]. Reciprocity lies at the heart of the social exchange perspective [26,27]. Economic exchange refers to employment relationships where the conditions of employment are specified and "fixed quid pro quo" is the nature of exchange: a fair day's pay for a fair day's work. Social exchange refers to relationships that entail unspecified future contributions, inducements and obligations and allows parties to reciprocate through discretionary behaviours [28,29].

Employees' satisfaction can be seen as an important predictor of discretionary behaviours like innovative behaviour as theory suggests that whether employees give their efforts wholeheartedly to the organization and produce up to their potential depends to a large part on the way they feel about their job and work environment (e.g. [21,22,30]). Therefore, the norm of reciprocity is important in explaining discretionary behaviour in organizations. This line of reasoning assumes that satisfaction with HR practices is viewed by employees as organization's commitment towards them which is then reciprocated back to the organization by employees through positive behaviours, like innovative behaviour [12,14]. Hence, this means that we can formulate our first hypothesis: satisfaction with HR practices is positively related to innovative behaviour (Hypothesis 1).

1.2. Leader Member Exchange (LMX) and Innovative Behaviour

The basic premise of LMX theory is that leaders establish higher quality exchanges with some of their followers (in-group members) while with other followers leaders rely more on the terms of employment in forging exchanges (out-group members). Research suggests that the quality of the exchanges between employees and their leaders are predictive of attitudinal job outcomes. Examples of attitudinal outcomes which are related to LMX are satisfaction, leader support and organizational commitment (e.g. [17,20,31]). Sanders and Schyns [27] provide evidence that workers' perceptions of the helpfulness of their supervisor are positively related to their willingness to show discretionary behaviour like cooperative behaviours and assisting co-workers. Low- quality exchange relationships, on the other hand, are characterized by more formal, role-defined interactions that result in hierarchy-based downward influence and distance between the parties [32].

Prior research has found that LMX is related to innovative job performance [20–22]. Janssen [4] found evidence that employees responded more innovatively to higher levels of job demands when they perceived that their efforts were fairly rewarded by their leader. This means that employees who perceive a fair balance between supervisor's inducements relative to their work efforts will respond with more innovative behaviour. Referring back to social exchange theory additional arguments can be derived for a relationship between LMX and innovative behaviour. Employees personify the organization since everything an organization does, it does through human beings. Direct supervisors can act as organizational agents. Employees tend to view actions by agents of the organization as actions of the organization itself [33]. Therefore, they reward favourable supervisor treatment with desired behaviours. Hence, we can formulate our next hypothesis: LMX is positively related to innovative behaviour (Hypothesis 2).

1.3. Satisfaction with HR Practices, LMX and Innovative Behaviour

In general, two lines of reasoning related to the relationships between satisfaction with HR practices, LMX, and innovative behaviour can be found in literature. The first states that satisfaction with HR practices mediates the relationship between LMX and innovative behaviour: satisfaction with HR practices can explain the relationship between LMX and innovative behaviour [17]. The second states that the interaction between satisfaction with HR practices and LMX relates to innovative behaviour: LMX and satisfaction with HR practices stimulate each other and this leads to more innovative behaviour [12].

1.3.1. Satisfaction with HR Practices as a Mediator

Positive leader experiences and expectations appear to be associated with favourable leader behaviour towards followers such as the assignment of challenging tasks, distribution of rewards, and constructive feedback (e.g. [34,35]). Moreover, research on Leader-Member-Exchange (LMX) shows that the quality of the relationship between supervisor and subordinate strongly impacts employee perceptions concerning the quality of HR practices (e.g. [36,37]). For example, employees' satisfaction of influence will be shaped fundamentally by their personal experience with their supervisor. Furthermore, LMX is related to the job satisfaction of employees [17]. Given that members in high quality dyads perceive more favourable treatment than members in low quality dyads it is not surprisingly that the former have been found to be more satisfied with their jobs than the latter. This means that we can expect that LMX is positively related with satisfaction with HR practices and satisfaction with HR practices are positively related to innovative behaviour. Hence we formulate the following hypothesis: satisfaction with HR practices mediates the relationship between LMX and innovative behaviour (Hypothesis 3).

1.3.2. Interaction between Satisfaction with HR Practices and LMX [47]

Bowen and Ostroff [12] suggest that leadership behaviour and HR practices, in terms of a high HR system, can stimulate each other and increase the willingness to show discretionary behaviour. Thus, the quality of HR practices as perceived by the employees is not necessarily perceived as a consequence of line management behaviour or responsibility. In this way satisfaction with HR practices is regarded as a context within which individuals function. In commenting on contextualization in organizational behaviour research Rousseau and Fried argue that the explicit addressing of contextual factors is necessary for enhancing the comprehensiveness and creativity of research findings [47]. In terms of LMX and satisfaction with HR practices this means that satisfaction with HR practices can be seen as a context in which the relationship between LMX and innovative behaviour is embedded. We can also provide an alternative argument for this interaction effect of satisfaction with HR practices and LMX. Not all direct supervisors have responsibilities and power on the HR practices of their subordinates. In such a situation, HR practices are shaped outside the leader-member relationship [38]. Hence we formulate the following hypothesis: the interaction between satisfaction with HR practices and LMX is positively related to innovative behaviour (Hypothesis 4).

2. Method

2.1. Sample

The survey included 272 employees in four Dutch and German technical organizations (response rate for the four organizations varies between 42 to of 66%). Participation was voluntary for all employees, and confidentiality was assured. Respondents with supervisory tasks were excluded from this sample.

Of these 272 respondents 200 are men (74%). 75 Employees (52%) are between 25 and 35 years old and 45 employees (31%) between 35 and 45 years old. 89 respondents (62%) worked less than 5 years within the organization, 29 respondents (20%) between 5 and 10 years and 26 respondents (18%) worked ten years or longer in the organization. Finally, 73 respondents (27%) finished their secondary vocational education. 76 respondents (28%) finished their higher vocational education and 41 (15%) achieved their university degree.

The four organizations differ in the number of respondents (between 32 and 135) and in terms of the age of the employees (F (3, 265) = 19.92, p<.01), education (F(3,265) = 4.74; p<.01) and tenure within the organization (F(3,265) = 18.88, p<.01). The organizations did not differ in terms of sex distribution within the organization ($\chi^2(3) = 2.37$, n.s.)

2.2. Procedure

All employees had access to computers. Employees received an e-mail with a link to the questionnaire. The e-mail contained supplementary information about the subjects that the questionnaire contained and the utmost confidence in which respondent answers are treated. Respondents had a week time to fill out the questionnaires. The introduction letter of the questionnaire contained supplementary information to motivate and inform the respondent about the questionnaire.

2.3. Measurements

Following Janssen [4] innovative behaviour is measured by a nine-item scale, an example being "How often does it occur that you create new ideas for difficult issues?" Respondents were asked on a five-point-scale ranging from 1 "never" till 5 "always" to give their opinion. Given the high inter-correlations between the idea generation, idea promotion, and idea realization subscales (all above .82) these subscales were conceived to combine additively to create an overall scale of innovative work behaviour. The scale was found reliable (Cronbach's α = .92).

Leader-Member-Exchange was measured using the twelve-item scale of Grean et al. [34]. Examples of this scale are "My supervisor would come to my defence if I were 'attacked' by other", and "My supervisor is a lot of fun to work with". The response format was a five-point scale ranging from 1 "disagree completely" till 5 "agree completely". The scale was found reliable (Cronbach's α = .92).

For the different aspect of satisfaction with HR practices we combined previous scales from Torka [38], and Van den Heuvel. For all items of the HR practices the response formats ranged from 1 "very dissatisfied" till 5 "very satisfied". For measuring satisfaction with employee influence two sub-dimensions were distinguished: employee voice (an example: "How satisfied are you with the extent to which your opinion is sought regarding (changes in) your job?") and participation in decision making (an example: "How satisfied are you with the extent to which you can co-decide on (changes in) your job?"). Each dimension was measured with three items. Although these two sub-dimensions are theoretically fundamental different, given the high inter-correlations between these two sub dimensions, they are taken together. Moreover the different items of the two sub-dimensions loaded on one factor. The scale turned out to be sufficient (Cronbach's α = .93).

Satisfaction with HR flow was measured using a five item-scale excluding outflow issues. An example of this scale is: "How satisfied are you with the guidance you were given during the first six months of your employ-ment at this organization?" The scale turned out to be sufficient (Cronbach's α = .76). Satisfaction with primary rewards was measured using a nine item-scale. An example of this scale is: "How satisfied are you with your salary". The scale turned out to be sufficient (Cronbach's α = .95). Satisfaction with secondary rewards was measured using a five item-scale. An example of this scale is: "How satisfied are you with the wide-ranging package of secondary terms of employment". The scale turned out to be sufficient (Cronbach's α = .94). Satisfaction with work content was measured using an eight item-scale. An example of this scale is: "How satisfied are you with the variation offered by your job?" The scale turned out to be sufficient (Cronbach's α = .86).

Furthermore the respondents were asked to give a score (1 till 10) for their job satisfaction in general. The average of this score is 7.08 (SD = 2.05).

2.4. Analyses

To control for the possibility that socio-demographic differences in the predictor and outcome variables might lead to spurious relationships, gender (0 = male, 1 = female), age (year of birth was recoded), educational qualifications (1 = secondary education, 2 = higher education, and 3 = university), and tenure in the organization (number of years) were entered as control variables in the analysis. Moreover, we controlled for country (location of the organization) and for nationality of the employees (1 = German, 2 = Dutch, and 3 = other). Because these variables did not have a significant effect, nor did they influence the other effects these effects are not presented in the Tables.

Because all variables in this study were based on self reports and collected at a single point in time, Harman's one factor test was used to investigate the potential influence of common method variance. Therefore, the items of the dependent and independent variables were submitted to a principal components analysis with oblique rotation. The results show seven factors (innovative behaviour, LMX, and satisfaction with five HR practices) with an "eigenvalue" greater than 1, accounting for 49.38 percent of the variance. Each item "loaded" on its appropriate factor, with primary loadings exceeding .40 and cross-loadings lower than .25. This strongly suggests that the measures of the predictors are independent of the dependent variable and that common method bias is likely to have a very limited effect.

Given our mean interest to explain employee-to-employee difference in innovative behaviour we decided to test the hypotheses with an ordinary regression analyses on individual level and not to use multi level analyses, although the data is nested within four organizations. Moreover the intra class correlation of innovative behaviour is low: .02, meaning that only two percent of the variance of innovative behaviour can be explained by differences between the four organizations (in other terms: 98 percent of the variance of innovative behaviour occurs within organizations). Moreover, both LMX and satisfaction with HR practices can be seen as individual characteristic in nature.

To test the mediating effect (H3), in reference to the method of Baron and Kenny, we first checked whether the effect of LMX on satisfaction with HR practices was significant (first part of Table 3), and furthermore if the effect of LMX on innovative behaviour is significant and decreased or disappeared when adding the mediator (satisfaction with HR practices) to the model (second part of Table 3). To test the interaction-effect of satisfaction with HR practices and LMX (H4) the Aiken and West and Cohen *et al.* method was used (Table 3).

3. Results

3.1. Descriptive Statistics and Correlations

Table 1 presents means and standard deviations, and zero-order Pearson correlations for the variables investigated in this study. Regarding the satisfaction with the HR practices, the respondents are more satisfied with work content than with the other HR practices (influence: $t(244) = 12.25$, p<.01; flow ($t(260) = 8.340$; p<.01), primary rewards: $t(257) = 17.02$; p<.01; and second rewards: $t(243) = 6.62$, p<.01). In addition, employees are more satisfied with influence and flow than with rewards ($t(243) = 7.95$, p<.01; $t(246) = 7.97$; p<.01).

Innovative behaviour is positively related to LMX ($r = .25$, p<.01), satisfaction with work content ($r = .26$, p<.01), and satisfaction with influence ($r = .30$; p<.01). Moreover innovative behaviour is positively related with level of education ($r = .16$, p<.01). LMX is positively related to all forms of satisfaction with HR practices except secondary rewards: influence ($r = .47$, p<.01), flow ($r = .30$, p<.01), primary rewards ($r = .28$, p<.01) and work content ($r = .42$, p<.01). Furthermore, LMX is negatively related to age ($r = -.21$, p<.01) and tenure ($r = -.34$, p<.01). All of the different forms of satisfaction with HR practices are positively interrelated to each other, and to the overall measurement of job satisfaction.

3.2. Facet and Global Measures of Satisfaction

To examine the relationship between the satisfaction with the HR practices and the overall job satisfaction we conducted a regression analysis with the overall job satisfaction as dependent variable and the control variables in the first model and satisfaction with the HR practices as the independent variables in the second model (see Table 2). While age is positively related to the overall

job satisfaction ($\beta = .24$, p<.01), tenure and education level are negatively related to the overall job satisfaction (respectively $\beta = -.19$; p<.05; $\beta = -.15$, p<.05). All significant effects disappeared however when satisfaction with the HR practices were added to the model, meaning that satisfaction with HR practices mediates the relationship between characteristics of the employees and overall satisfaction. Related to the satisfaction with HR practices the results show that especially satisfaction with work content ($\beta = .60$; p<.01), and to a lesser extent satisfaction with flow ($\beta = .13$; p<.05) and primary rewards ($\beta = .13$, p<05) are related to the overall job satisfaction. The individual characteristics and the satisfaction with the HR practices explain 55 percent of the total variance of the overall job satisfaction.

3.2.1. Test of the Hypothesized Models

The results of the regression analysis to test the different hypotheses are reported in Table 3. In the first model the individual variables are added (Step 1). Sex is negative related to innovative behaviour (men report more innovative behaviour; $\beta = -.20$; p<.01), and education level is positive related to innovative behaviour ($\beta = .17$; p<.01). H1 predicted a positive relationship between LMX and innovative behaviour. Given the beta of LMX in Model 2 (second part of the Table, Step 2; $\beta = .19$, p<.01), H1 can be confirmed.

H2 predicted a positive relationship between satisfaction with the HR practices and innovative behaviour. In line with this hypothesis positive relationships are found for satisfaction with influence ($\beta = .27$; p<.01), and work content ($\beta = .20$, p<.01). Contrary to the hypothesis satisfaction with primary rewards show a negative relationship with innovative behaviour ($\beta = -.19$; p<.01). No significant effects were found for satisfaction with flow and secondary rewards. This means that H2 can be confirmed for satisfaction with influence and work content yet have to be rejected for satisfaction with primary rewards, and can not be confirmed for satisfaction with flow and secondary rewards.

To test the mediating effect of satisfaction with HR practices in the relationship between LMX and innovative behaviour (H3) first the relationship between LMX on the satisfaction with HR practices are examined (first part of Table 3). Although the effect of LMX on satisfaction with secondary rewards is only marginal ($\beta = .12$; p<.10) the results show that LMX is positive related to the HR practices, meaning that the first part of the mediating effect can be confirmed. Furthermore, the effects for the individual characteristics differ for the forms of satisfaction. While women are more satisfied with the primary rewards, men are more satisfied with the work content. And while education level is positively related to satisfaction with flow, it is negatively related to satisfaction with primary rewards and work content. In ge-

Table 1. Means, Standard deviations and zero order Pearson Correlations for the variables used in our analysis.

	M	SD	1.	2.	3.	4.	5.	6.	7.	8.	9.	10.	11.
1. Innovative behaviour	3.15	.75											
2. LMX	3.67	.73	.25**										
Satisfaction HR practices													
3. Influence	3.20	.68	.30**	.47**									
4. Flow	3.38	.77	.09	.30**	.57**								
5. Primary Rewards	2.79	.80	-.06	.28**	.44**	.29**							
6. Secondary Rewards	2.78	.88	.08	.12	.28*	.14*	.30**						
7. Content	3.71	.67	.26**	.42**	.55**	.57**	.32**	.15**					
8. *Job satisfaction*	7.08	2.05	.17*	.31**	.48**	.54**	.38**	.20**	.69**				
9. Sex	.26	.44	-.08	.16**	.16**	.06	.17**	-.06	-.10*	.03			
10. Tenure	2.27	1.27	-.05	-.34**	-.15**	-.16	-.13*	-.05	-.12*	-.04	-.11		
11. Age	2.38	1.02	.07	-.21**	-.09	-.08	.04	.07	.09	.07	-.11	.65**	
12. Education	1.88	.64	.16**	.09	-.09	-.06	.14*	.05	-.04	.09	.18**	-.06	.11

Table 2. Results of a regression analysis with job satisfaction as dependent variable and satisfaction with the HR practices as independent variables.

Variables	Model 1	Model 2
Control variables		
Sex	.08	.07
Tenure	-.19*	.08
Age	.24**	-.02
Education	-.15*	-.06
Satisfaction with HR practices		
Influence		.01
Flow		.13*
Primary rewards		.13*
Secondary rewards		.08+
Work content		.60**
Explained variance	.04	.55

Table 3. Results of regression analysis with innovative behaviour as dependent variables.

	Influence	Flow	Primary rewards	Sec. rewards	Content	Step 1	Step 2	Step 3	Step 4	Step 5
Control variables										
Sex	.10	.02	.16**	-.07	-.16**	-.20**	-.16*	-.06	-.07	-.07
Tenure	-.17*	-.07	-.23**	-.14	-.14**	-.09	-.06	-.05	-.05	-.05
Age	.29**	.04	.29**	.19*	.27**	.26	.22*	.05	.17*	.19**
Education	-.01	.13*	-.12*	.04	-.12*	.17*	.16*	.14*	.13	.13
LMX	.45**	.29**	.24**	.12+	.47**		.19**		.11	.07
Satisfaction with										
Influence								.27**	.19**	.17**
Flow								-.10	-.06	-.07
Primary Rewards								-.19**	-.22**	-.22**
Sec Rewards								.07	.07	.07
Work content								.20*	.18*	.17*
Interaction LMX – Satisfaction with										
Influence										-.19+
Flow										-.07
Primary Rewards										.03
Sec Rewards										.13
Content										.08
Adjusted R²	.27	.10	.16	.04	.25	.05	.11	.15	.22	.23
R² change	.17	.08	.06	.02	.20		.06	.10	.17	.01

**= p≤.01; *=p≤.05;

neral, tenure is negatively related, and age is positively related to satisfaction with the HR practices.

To test if satisfaction with HR practices mediates the relationship between LMX and innovative behaviour, satisfaction with the HR practices is added to Step 2 (see Step 4; second part of the Table). The results show that the significant effect of LMX disappeared (from β = .19, p<.01 to β = .11, *n.s.*), while some of the HR practices show a significant effect (influence: β = .19; p<.01; primary rewards: β = -.22, p<.01, and work content: β = .20, p<.01). This means that we can confirm H3: satisfaction with HR practices mediates the relationship between LMX and innovative behaviour.

In addition we test if LMX mediates the relationship between satisfaction with HR practices and innovative behaviour. Comparing Step 4 with Step 3 no significant effect of the satisfaction with HR practices disappeared when LMX is added, nor did LMX show a significant effect.

To test H4 the interaction effects between LMX and satisfaction with HR practices were added to the model (Step 5). None of interaction effects were found significant. This means that H4 can not be confirmed.

4. Discussions

The aim of this article was to answer the question if satisfaction with HR practices and Leader-Member-Exchange (LMX) can explain innovative behaviour, and, if so, to examine how satisfaction with HR practices and LMX are related to innovative behaviour. To clarify these relationships we used data from employees working in technical organizations in the Netherlands and Germany. The results of this survey study lead to the following conclusions. First, satisfaction with HR practices, especially satisfaction with influence and work content are positively related to innovative behaviour; satisfaction with primary rewards is however negatively related to innovative behaviour. Second, LMX is positively related to innovative behaviour. Third, in stead of an interaction effect between satisfaction with HR practices and LMX, satisfaction with HR practices mediates the relationship between LMX and innovative behaviour. Furthermore, we found that satisfaction with influence, primary rewards and especially work content are positively related to general job satisfaction.

Next to the conclusions the results demand answers for two issues: the effect of satisfaction with primary rewards on innovative behaviour and the relationship between the HR practices and general job satisfaction. First, in contrast to our hypotheses we found a negative effect of satisfaction with primary rewards to innovative behaviour: the more employees are satisfied with their salary the less innovative behaviour they show. Moreover, satisfaction with primary rewards was positively

related to the overall job satisfaction. In other words, satisfaction with pay influences discretionary behaviours negatively, but employees' general satisfaction positively.

One explanation might be related to our measurements. Tremblay *et al.* [41] conclude that the use of a general pay satisfaction measure could influence conclusions on pay satisfaction and its correlates. We measured overall pay satisfaction composed of the three pay satisfaction dimensions. The authors suggest to differentiate between three dimensions: 1) compensation amount—satisfaction with the amount of individual compensation considering work done and effort put in; 2) compensation comparison—satisfaction with individual compensation relative to other people and other jobs (distributive justice concerning pay or pay equity; [39,40]) and compensation practices—satisfaction with compensation increase policies and the criteria employed in determining compensation structure. Research shows that distributive justice perceptions play a more important role for employees' attitudes than procedural justice in job satisfaction and satisfaction with the organization [41]. Therefore, we assume that social comparisons (distributive justice) concerning pay may predict innovative behaviour better than self-comparisons and general measures of pay satisfaction.

We can present two alternative explanations for the negative relationship between pay satisfaction and innovative behaviour. First, pay can not replace good management. In other words, when employees are satisfied with pay, but other organization inducements lack such as job characteristics tailored to employee needs, management does not offer the motivators necessary for discretionary behaviour. Second and related to Herzberg's theory, Deci suggests that compensation may only influence performance strongly for those individuals who have high endorsement of money ethic. In contrast, extrinsic rewards such as money may also undermine people's intrinsic motivation to a task [42]. Considering the last-mentioned explanation, the sample of our study consists of medium to high educated technicians, often referred to as knowledge workers. Several authors argue that for knowledge workers the work content is most important in work life [43,44] and our results show that for this occupational group the work content is one of the two HR practices important for innovative behaviour. Thus, knowledge workers are foremost intrinsically motivated and for them (over) compensation may poison the willingness for discretionary behaviour turning their preliminary relational psychological contract into a transactional contract braking extra-role behaviour [28].

The other HR practice important for technical employees' innovative behaviour is influence or *voice*: a process that allows employees to exercise influence over their work and the conditions under which they work. Since our results show that not all HR practices influence medium to high-educated employees in their innovative behaviour, we assume that for them voice concerning different HR practices is not equal important. The results suggest that voice concerning the work content is most important. Therefore, future research on HR practices should include employees' opportunities for voice taking into account different practices as well as include different occupational groups in general [14].

Earlier studies collected data from single respondents in each firm—mostly HR managers or other top managers—and were related to written HR practices within a firm. This approach has been widely criticized because of its subjectively character, and of its focus on intended in stead of espoused HR practices as perceived by employees: one of the explanations for the inconclusive results of studies on the HRM-performance link in general (e.g. [45]). We can assume that employee attitudes are influenced not so much by the way these HR practices are intended to operate as by the way they are actually implemented by line managers on a day-to-day basis [14]. Therefore in this study we focused on the employees' experience of the HR practices because we know that behaviour is mostly driven by employee interpretations in stead of practices as described by managers.

Our data showed that general job satisfaction is not in the same way related to the HR practices: general job satisfaction is related to satisfaction with influence and with primary rewards and is especially related to satisfaction with work content. The results show that it makes sense to separate the different HR practices. After all, researchers and managers want to gain insight in the impact of different facets of HRM on general job satisfaction. Given our results it can be expected that satisfaction of HR practices and job satisfaction differ in their antecedents and in their consequences. More research is needed to the different facets of job satisfaction and their interrelationships.

The practical implication of this study is that in order to improve employees' innovative behaviour within technical organizations attention should be paid to the managers and the relationships they have with the subordinates. This study shows that LMX is positively related to satisfaction with HR practices, and satisfaction with HR practices is positively related to innovative behaviour. The relationships managers have with their employees can be improved by providing a formal and informal training for managers to improve their leadership qualities, and by making them aware of the impact of their relationship with the employees. Research shows that leaders with different backgrounds need other kinds of training to become effective [46].

On the other hand, research shows that the perception of employees of the leadership is not only influenced by the manager yet is influenced by characteristics of the employees as well [27]. For instance, the more the employee and the manager are alike in terms of personality, the higher the relationship between employee and manager is qualified by the employees. This means that attention can be paid to the similarity between managers and subordinates when employees are hired and teams are created. Furthermore employees can become aware that they can influence their perception of and their relationship with the manager.

This study has limitations and strengths. First we have to make a causality remark due to the cross-sectional limitations. Future research could be extended but also deepened by a qualitative part: collecting in-depth information on HR practices as perceived by top-managers, supervisors and different subordinates. Second a social desirability in the answers of the respondents should be taking into account as a possible limitation. Furthermore, research shows that the career commitment of knowledge workers moderates the relationship between company practices and organizational commitment as well as turnover intention. Therefore, further research should include commitment to work, career and commitment to the organization into account and should examine the relationships between commitment and innovative behaviour [20].

Strength of this study is that we focused on LMX and satisfaction with HR practices, and how these are related to innovative behaviour. It appeared that LMX and satisfaction with work content and with influence had the strongest influence in explaining innovative behaviour. Furthermore, the results show that satisfaction with HR practices mediates the relationship between LMX and innovative behaviour, meaning that the relationships the supervisor have with his or her subordinates have, via satisfaction with HR practices, an impact on innovative behaviour of employees.

5. Acknowledgements

The authors would like to thank Suzanne Siep, Thomas Kowalewski, Britta Lange, Britta Ruschoff and Maria Demir (master students of psychology; University of Twente, the Netherlands) for part of the data collection.

6. References

[1] P. T. Bolwijn and T. Kumpe, "Manufacturing in the 1990s—productivity, flexibility and innovation," Long Range Planning, Vol. 23, pp. 44–57, 1990.

[2] L. J. Harrison-Walker, "The measurement of word-of-mouth communication and an investigation of service quality and customer commitment as potential antecedents," Journal of Service Research, Vol. 4, pp. 60–75, 2001.

[3] J. L. Pierce and A. L. Delbecq, "Organization structure, individual attitudes and innovation," Academy of Man-

agement Review, Vol. 2, pp. 27–37, 1977.

[4]   O. Janssen, "Job demands, perceptions of effort-reward fairness and innovative work behaviour," Journal of Occupational and Organizational Psychology, Vol. 73, pp. 287–302, 2000.

[5]   T. Amabile, "A model of creativity and innovation in organizations," In: B. M. Staw and L. L. Cummings. (Eds.) Research in organization behaviour. Greenwich, CT: JAI Press, pp. 187–209, 1988.

[6]   R. Kanter, "When a thousand flowers bloom," In: B. M. Staw and L. L. Cummings (Eds.). Research in organization behaviour. Greenwich, CT: JAI Press, pp. 169–211, 1988.

[7]   M. A. West and J. L. Farr, "Innovation at work: Psychological perspectives," Social Behaviour, Vol. 4, pp. 15–30, 1989.

[8]   G. R. Oldham and A. Cummings, "Employee creativity: Personal and contextual factors at work," Academy of Management Journal, Vol. 39, pp. 607–634, 1996.

[9]   A. H. Van de Ven, "Central problems in the management of innovation," Management Science, Vol. 32, pp. 590–607, 1986.

[10] D. E. Guest, "Human resource management and industrial relations," Journal of Management Studies, Vol. 24, pp. 503–521, 1987.

[11] L. H. Nishii, D. P. Lepak, and B. Schneider, "Employee attributions of the 'why' of HR practices: Their effects on employee attitudes and behaviours, and customer satisfaction," Personnel Psychology, Vol. 61, pp. 503–545, 2008.

[12] D. E. Bowen and C. Ostroff, "Understanding HRM-firm performance linkages: The role of the 'strength' of the HRM system," Academy of Management Review, Vol. 29, pp. 203–221, 2004.

[13] M. Beer, B. Spector, P. R. Lawrence, D. Q. Mills, and R. E. Walton, "Managing human assets," New York: The Free Press, 1984.

[14] N. Kinnie, S. Hutchinson, J. Purcell, B. Rayton, and J. Swart, "Satisfaction with HR practices and commitment to the organization: Why one size does not fit all," Human Resource Management Journal, Vol. 15, pp. 9–29, 2005.

[15] G. B. Graen, R. C. Liden, and W. Hoel, "Role of leadership in the employee withdrawal process," Journal of Applied Psychology, Vol. 67, pp. 686–872, 1982.

[16] G. B. Graen and T. A. Scandura, "Toward a psychology of dyadic organizing," Organizational Behaviour, Vol. 9, pp. 175–208, 1987.

[17] C. R. Gerstner and D. V. Day, "Meta-analytic review of Leader-Member-Exchange theory: Correlates and construct issues," Journal of Applied Psychology, Vol. 82, pp. 827–844, 1997.

[18] G. B. Graen and M. Uhl-Bien. "Relationship-based approach to leadership: Development of Leader-Member-Exchange (LMX) theory of leadership over 25 years: Applying a multi-level multi-domain perspective," Leadership Quarterly, Vol. 6, pp. 219–247, 1995.

[19] T. Elkins and R. T. Keller, "Leadership in research and development organizations: A literature review and conceptual framework," The Leadership Quarterly, Vol. 14, pp. 587–606, 2004.

[20] R. Basu and S. G. Green, "Leader-Member-Exchange and transformational leadership: An empirical examination of innovative behaviours in leader-member dyads," Journal of Applied Social Psychology, Vol. 27, pp. 477–499, 1997.

[21] S. G. Scott and R. A. Bruce, "Determinants of innovative behaviour: A path model of individual innovation in the workplace," Academy of Management Journal, Vol. 37, pp. 580–607, 1994.

[22] S. G. Scott and R. A. Bruce, "Innovation and the LMX connection: Getting a foothold on relationships that work," IEEE Journal, Vol. 17, pp. 10–11, 1994.

[23] T. S. Bateman and D. W. Organ, "Job satisfaction and the good soldier: The relationship between affect and employee citizenship," Academy of Management Journal, Vol. 26, pp. 587–595, 1983.

[24] D. W. Organ, "Organizational citizenship behaviour: It's construct clean-up time," Human Performance, Vol. 10, pp. 85–97, 1997.

[25] P. Blau, "Exchange and power in social life," New York: Wiley, 1964.

[26] A. W. Gouldner, "The norm of reciprocity: A preliminary statement," American Sociological Review, Vol. 25, pp. 161–178, 1960.

[27] B. Schyns and K. Sanders, "In the eyes of the beholder: Personality and the perception of leadership," Journal of Applied Social Psychology, Vol. 37, pp. 2345–2363, 2007.

[28] D. M. Rousseau, "Psychological contracts in organizations: understanding written and unwritten agreements," Newbury Park, CA: Sage Publications, 1995.

[29] A. S. Tsui, J. L. Pearce, L. W. Porter, and A. M. Tripoli, "Alternative approaches to the employee-organization relationship: Does investment in employees pay off?" Academy of Management Journal, Vol. 40, pp. 1089–1121, 1997.

[30] A. A. Nerkar, R. G. McGrath and I. C. MacMillan, "Three facets of satisfaction and their influence on the performance of innovation teams," Journal of Business Venturing, Vol. 11, pp. 167–188, 1996.

[31] D. Duchon, S. G. Green, and T. D. Taber, "Vertical dyad linkage: A longitudinal assessment of antecedents, measures and consequences," Journal of Applied Psychology, Vol. 71, pp. 56–60, 1986.

[32] O. Janssen and N. W. Van Yperen, "Employees' goal orientations, the quality of Leader-Member-Exchange, and the outcomes of job performance and job satisfaction," Academy of Management Journal, Vol. 47, pp. 368–384, 2004.

[33] R. Eisenberger, R. Huntington, S. Hutchinson, and D. Sowa, "Perceived organizational support," Journal of Applied Psychology, Vol. 71, pp. 500–507, 1986.

[34] G. Graen, J. B Orris., and T. W. Johnson, "Role assimila-

tion processes in a complex organization," Journal of Vocational Behaviour, Vol. 3, pp. 395–420, 1973.

[35] C. R. Leana, "Predictors and consequences of delegation," Academy of Management Journal, Vol. 29, pp. 754–774, 1986.

[36] L. M. Lapierre, R. D. Hackett, and S. Taggar, "A test of the links between family interference with work, job enrichment and Leader-Member-Exchange," Applied Psychology: An International Review, Vol. 55, pp. 489–511, 2006.

[37] H. K. S. Laschinger, N. Purdy, and J. Almos, "The impact of Leader-Member-Exchange quality, empowerment, and core self-evaluation on nurse manager's job satisfaction," Journal of Nursing Administration, Vol. 37, pp. 221–229, 2007.

[38] N. Torka, M. Van Riemsdijk, and J. C. Looise, "Werkgeversbetrokkenheid," [Employers commitment] Tijdschrift voor Arbeidsvraagstukken, Vol. 23, pp. 45–59, 2007.

[39] J. S. Adams, "Toward an understanding of inequity," Journal of Abnormal and Social Psychology, Vol. 67, pp. 422–436, 1963.

[40] J. S. Adams, "Inequity in social exchange," In L. Berkowitz (Ed.), Advances in experimental social psychology, New York: Academic Press, Vol. 2, pp. 267–299, 1965.

[41] M. Tremblay, B. Sire and D. B. Balkin, "The role of organizational justice in pay and employee benefit satisfaction, and its effects on work attitudes," Group and Organization Management, Vol. 25, pp. 269–290, 2000.

[42] E. L. Deci, "Effects of externally mediated rewards on intrinsic motivation," Journal of Personality and Social Psychology, Vol. 18, pp. 105–115, 1971.

[43] B. L. Rosenbaum, "Leading today's technical professional," Training and Development, Vol. 45, pp. 55–66, 1991.

[44] S. R. Barley, "Technicians in the workplace: Ethnographic evidence for bringing work into organization studies," Administrative Science Quarterly, Vol. 41, pp. 404–441, 1996

[45] D. Guest, "HRM: The workers' verdict," Human Resource Management Journal, Vol. 9, pp. 5–25, 1999.

[46] A. N. Garman and P. W. Corrigan, "Developing effective team leaders," New directions for Mental Health Services, Vol. 79, pp. 45–54, 1998.

[47] D. M. Rousseau and Y. Fried, "Location, location, location: Contextualizing organization research." Journal of Organizational Behaviour, Vol. 22, pp. 1–13, 2001.

8

Strategic Orientations: Multiple Ways for Implementing Sustainable Performance

Marcel Van Marrewijk

Van Linden van den Heuvellsingel 7, Vlaardingen, Netherlands

Abstract

The Four Phase Model®, created by prof. dr. Teun W. Hardjono [1] in 1995, distinguishes four ideal type strategic orientations and shows that these strategies brighten and dim in a specific sequence, adding the most required competences to the organization, and creating a natural rhythm to corporate dynamics. By applying this theory one can understand the nature and whereabouts of the organization's systemic constraints, revealing the basic features for creating a roadmap towards sustainable performance improvement and competence development. The model generates the top priorities, selects the most adequate (ideal type) interventions and key performance indicators. Combining strategic "situations" as indicated by the Four Phase Model and phase-wise "contexts" as introduced by Spiral Dynamics [2], provides a conceptual synergy with four innovative outcomes: Firstly, aligned with specific contexts, the strategic interventions and KPI's can be made more specific and practical, thus creating a roadmap for performance improvement and organizational development. Secondly, it structures change management into four distinctive hierarchical complexity levels: 1) enhancing fundamental skills, structures and procedures (vitalizing); 2) improving contemporary levels, aligned with the dominant value system (optimizing); 3) new re-orientations while continuing within current systems (shifting) and 4) a transformation to a more complex context or emerging value system (transforming). Thirdly, powered with the combined understanding of above concepts, one can deduct the specific context and situation for each intervention, instrument or approach to be applied effectively. Fourthly, the combination provided the bases for the so-called Strategy Scan and Strategic Sustainability Scan.

Keywords: Spiral Dynamics, Four Phase Model, Hardjono, Flexibility, Creativity, Effectiveness, Efficiency, Sustainability Scan, CSR, Corporate Sustainability

1. Introduction

The rising public expectations, the increasing social and environmental problems both locally and globally and the continuous strive for quality improvements and innovations are challenging corporations to choose new ambitions and aspire for higher performance levels with respect to corporate sustainability. They need to chart a course with respect to corporate sustainability and responsibility (CS/CR) within an increasing complex and dynamic environment.

In other publications, Van Marrewijk [3,4] presented a set of definitions of CS/CR differentiated for various development phases (or contexts, or levels of existence). Companies can initiate activities or approaches supporting sustainability, which aligns their institutional structure, values systems and ambition levels. True, traditional capitalist structures hardly enhance sustainable development, but these first small steps are essential in – eventually-moving into a worldwide transition towards structures which support a sustainable way of living, working, producing and consuming.

The more corporations recognize that CS/CR activities might increase their success, support their branding and reduce theirs risks, the more they will invest in these activities. Stated in another "worldview": the more companies accept their role in contributing to solving societal problems, to bridging the gaps between rich and poor and stop environmental degradation which are jeopardizing ecosystems, the more companies will create new product concepts and processes which include improvements to all objectives, for people, planet and profits. [5]

Each company needs to position itself within the CS/CR debate. What definition aligns their context and situation best? Which CS activities-among the numerous CS-initiatives already taken-make sense with respect to their fundamental objectives? What rate of progress do they need to take in order to stay ahead of competition? In the Journal of Business Ethics, Van Marrewijk and Hardjono [6] listed a set of the basic questions that stemmed from their SqEME approach: What does the organization want? Who are allowed to take part in this decision process? Which factors will influence the new ambitions? Which actions are most effective? And how can the espoused progress be measured and shown to the stakeholders?

This paper can support companies formulating strategies towards implementing corporate sustainability and responsibility by introducing the factors that influence the most adequate strategic orientation and the factors that indicate the developmental level at which companies need to act. Combining these outcomes will result in a sequence of strategic steps, which are placed in a context aligning the organization' value systems and institutional structures. Depending the company's ambition, the sequence of strategic steps can lead to performance improvement, a shift to new corporate orientations or set out a transition to new ways of doing business in a more sustainable way.

Paragraph two summarizes the Four Phase Model®, created in 1995 by Dr. Teun W. Hardjono, professor on Quality Management at the Erasmus University Rotterdam [1]. Paragraph three focuses on the integration of the Four Phase Model and Spiral Dynamics [2], combining the two dimensions mentioned above. Paragraph four will briefly summarize the possible sustainability interventions that can be implemented at different combinations. Paragraph five elaborates on the consequences with regard to corporate dynamics and the final chapter introduces an online strategy scan which is able to support a strategic dialogue.

2. Four Phase Model

Teun W. Hardjono presented his Four Phase Model® as a PhD thesis in 1995 [1], capturing 20 years of experiences in corporate strategy and organizational change as a senior consultant at one of the Netherlands' most renowned management consultancies. In practice, the Four Phase Model® has appeared an effective model for managers and management consultants to analyze the present state of organizations and to determine the most likely strategy to further improve their organizations. The model structures various organizational performance indicators and possible interventions and is able to provide guidelines for a program of organizational change.

2.1. Core Assets

The Four Phase Model's basic assumption is the recognition that organizations are striving to increase the sum of four essential assets, in a continuous process of exchanging one asset for another. These assets relate to basic organizational competences. These assets/competences are the:

o Material asset: the ability to increase, maintain and optimally utilize the tangible resources of an organization. Its worth is reflected-more or less-in the balance sheet.
o Commercial asset: the ability to have access to and to act on markets and the skills to execute commercial transactions.
o Socialization asset: the ability to inspire people and create supporting structures in order to achieve the common, corporate objectives.
o Intellectual asset: the learning capability of organizations, the ability to (pro-actively) adapt to changing circumstances and the creative capacity, which is based on the collective intellect and creativity of the members of organizations.

These core assets or basic competences also relate psychologically to the core drivers and professional ambitions of people and therefore also organizations. See **Table 1.**

Employees bring their best talents, skills, relationships and personality to the workplace and in return expect fair rewards, not only in financial terms, but also career opportunities, chances to grow their professional skills, challenging tasks to boost their experience, et cetera. Companies could make use of the relationships between corporate and personal drivers by for instance linking their reward schemes and employees' personal developments plans in line with their core strategies. But first, lets elaborate some more on the core assets.

Tabel 1. Basic assets at organizational and individual level (Hardjono), [1].

	Organizational level		Individual level	
	Cost	Revenue	Input	Output
Material asset	Money, products	Revenue, profits	P.M.	Wage
Commercial asset	Relations	Market share	Network	Customers
Socialisation asset	Workplace	Commitment	Behaviour	Colleagues
Intellectual asset	Talent development	Knowledge	Intelligence	Experience

Maximizing, for instance, the material assets at the expense of the other assets will ultimately lead to poor results. It is a myth that doing business is only focused at making profits. We all know what happened when a business unit manager shows double-digit growth figures, shortly after the CEO passionately requested for performance improvement on the shortest term possible. Having stripped research and development, postponed marketing campaigns, cut back conference trips and training possibilities, cancelled the annual day out while demanding overtime from his workers producing stocks, of course his financial figures improved. Soon his unit will be in dismay and he ought to be fired for that.

Healthy, sustainable organizations have learned to optimize the mix of the four essential competences: the abilities to create wealth, engage in transactions, enhance employee commitment, dedication and trust and the ability to adapt or proactively respond to changing circumstances.

Creating an optimal mix of the assets, companies exchange one asset for the other; For instance, invest money/ material assets for increasing the company's commercial abilities. As long as the marginal revenues exceed the marginal costs, companies will invest in enhancing their assets in order to meet their corporate objectives. In creating an optimal mix, the organization is gaining more ability to protect and improve its future.

For creating an optimal mix of basic assets, organizations need adequate strategies. The following questions are relevant: What is the constraint in increasing corporate performance? What single factor will impact performance improvement most? What extra competences should be prioritized? What is the organization's greatest risk? What kind of needs do our customers have? What are the needs of the other stakeholders? Is our organization fit to meet these requests? Although these questions seem to have different natures, the answers tend to come together nicely, as abundant case studies based upon the Four Phase Model have shown.

The Four Phase Model suggests organizations to focus on either internal or external issues and-at the same time-focus on control or change. Both pairs are dichotomies: although each side of these dichotomies are relevant, in a specific situation only one site contains the whereabouts of the constraint (inside or outside) or the key to the solution (via control or allowing change). The result can be presented in a so-called Harvard Diagram, presented in **Figure 1**. The diagram shows four concentric circles, representing the core assets, the diagram, representing the basic dichotomies, and the resulting four ideal type strategies, or strategic orientations.

These strategic orientations are:

- Effectiveness: A market-driven orientation which is directed towards increasing the effectiveness of an organization;

- Efficiency: A productivity orientation in order to enhance the efficiency of an organization;
- Flexibility: A people oriented strategy to increase the flexibility of an organization;
- Creativity: An innovation (and adaptedness)-driven orientation in order to increase the creativity of an organization.

Each strategic orientation contributes to all assets, but enhances one basic competence in particular. Effectiveness primarily boosts the commercial abilities; Efficiency focuses mainly on increasing the material assets; a strategy aimed at Flexibility has its most impact on the socialization competence and Creativity improves the intellectual capacity and the company's adaptedness to changes in the environment.

The next paragraph will elaborate on the basic interventions, structured according the Four Phase Model.

2.2. The Basic Orientations

Ideal type interventions can be plotted in the basic graph of the Four Phase Model: four assets, four quadrants (result areas) and two dichotomies (orientations) makes 32 interventions.

We will now demonstrate the Effectiveness Quadrant, (top left) in **Table 2**:

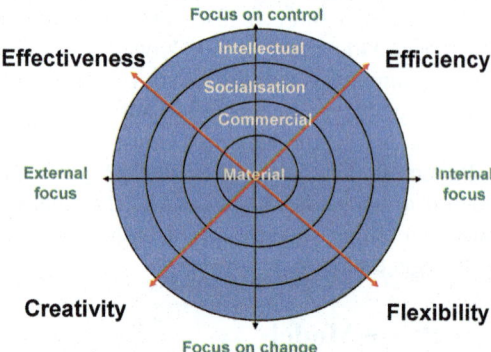

Figure 1. The core assets, dichotomies, and strategic orientations (source: T.W. Hardjono) [1].

Table 2. The Effectiveness Quadrant (Hardjono) [1].

	External Focus	Result: Effectiveness	Focus on Control
Material asset	Produce	Cash flow	Be profitable
Commercial asset	Generate supply and demand	Market share	Plan and order
Socialisation asset	Anticipate the social environment	Direction	Structure
Intellectual asset	Anticipate the societal environment	Plans	Explain and predict

It reads as follows:

- Production, or adding value in general, generates products and services. These are positively appreciated on the balance sheets, but once sold to customers it delivers a cash flow and, given its cost structure, it might be profitable.
- By carefully planning and organizing marketing, sales, supply chain and distribution, thus generating supply and demand, and competing on the market, resulting in a specific market share.
- By structuring the organisation and setting targets to all employees, organisations proved a sense of direction and a specific customer orientation. Employees engage into social networks thus stimulating the organisation's effectiveness.
- By anticipating and grasping the changing life conditions and societal circumstances, generating intelligence and understanding which will be used as inputs in new plans.

The appendix includes the full matrix of ideal type interventions.

The items in the overview are fairly basic-no rocket science here-stocks turn to revenues, to cash flow, to profits etcetera. It is the elegancy of the model providing a coherent image of complex organisations summarized in 32 activities. The model needed a fourth layer to acquire a level of sophistication in order to better meet the complexity of real life. Having defined the four basic assets, the diagram with the four quadrants based on the two dichotomies, and the four strategic orientations, the fourth level is formed by the various aspects of dynamics, which brought a specific sequence and rhythm to the model.

3. The Dynamics of the Four Phase Model

3.1. Balancing Reverse Effects

The model offers a few arguments that bring balance, sequence and rhythm to the model. The first one introduced here is "too much of anything will inevitably have a reverse effect". Too much Efficiency results in a rigid bureaucratic organisation. Too much focus on Change and Flexibility will end up in chaos and anarchy. Too much room for Creativity leads to amateurism and too much focus on the market Effectiveness causes an oversensitive, segregated organisation.

One may conclude that balance needs a temporarily focus, as a continuous focus ultimately results in adverse effects. **Figure 2** could therefore be read as follows: *"Our main focus is on Efficiency, there we can make our biggest impact on our organisation and achieve our goals, but in order to prevent our largest risk to occur— rigidness and bureaucratic tendencies—management must already prepare the roads for our next strategy and*

focus on Flexibility."

To prevent reverse effects to happen, organizations should turn to the "next" strategy that happens to include the competency that can prevent this effect to occur. More Flexibility will lift the fear for bureaucracies and Effectiveness soon turns hobbyism into successful marketing and sales campaigns. Taken from a risk perspective, having invested in improving creativity the largest risk is developing new products the market doesn't want. Having successfully boosted marketing and sales, the organization needs to improve corporate efficiency to see to it that gained market shares leads to profits. Efficiency activities can turn organizations into control-driven bureaucracies and "lean and mean" entities that have lost employees' commitment to give something extra at customers' requests. Having successfully created supporting structures and gained employees' dedication and trust, companies intend to expect creative and adaptive achievements, which ought to meet the customers' perceptions, etcetera.

3.2. Prioritising Interventions

A second argument supporting balance is the fact that all four quadrants, and all 32 basic interventions are important, but not at the same time. Suppose an organisation has a focus internally and a focus on control, as **Figure 2** presents. Its strategic orientation is thus aimed at Efficiency. The more impact-in both time, efforts and means-is spend on this strategy the more powers are building up on the other end of the dichotomies. Reverse effects will occur, forcing the system to move on to the next strategy.

A metaphor can explain this in more detail: a top indoor cyclist engaged in a sprint duel can be forced to a stand still—sur place—as he does not want to take lead position. In cycling this is a strategic option. It takes great skills to remain on one spot, but he cannot stay

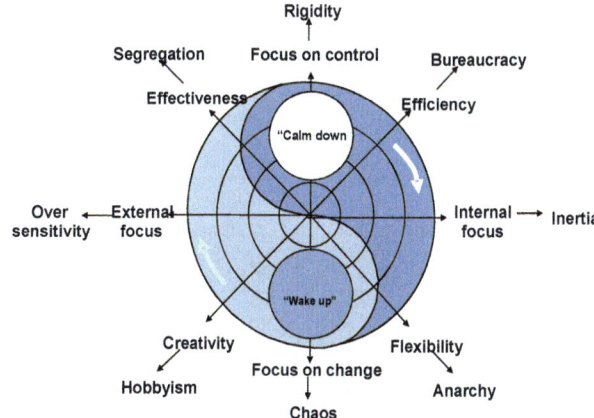

Figure 2. Dynamics of the Four Phase Model© (Hardjono) [1].

there forever. Inevitably, in order to prevent from tumbling when his skills are fading or when his adversary was finally forced to take the lead, he moves his cycle downward while building up speed, heading for the finish line.

The next quadrant represents the organisation's greatest challenge. For instance: Becoming more efficient while maintaining flexibility. If you fail, the organisation turns rigid and bureaucratic. Or, creating innovations, which promise a boost in sales. Without this market orientation creativity might lead to hobbyism. **Figure 2** therefore shows a "wake up", a position currently out of focus, but it needs extra attention in the near future to prevent large risks to occur.

As said before, all interventions are relevant but-strategically-not at the same time. Ideally, half the number of basic interventions can be adequately addressed. As **Figure 2** shows, "half" does not represent just two quadrants: the intellectual asset moves ahead, as represented in the outer circle, creating a yin-yang shape. In total 16 interventions are relevant. The dark shades in **Figure 2**: Three times four interventions aligned with internal focus, Efficiency and focus on control, three lagging interventions on Effectiveness (material, commercial and socialisation) and a leading one on Flexibility (intellectual). In the shaded area there are no conflicting interventions.

In conducting surveys among clients, we have often applied this model while structuring the employee answers to open questions such as "what can be improved in order to become a *great place to work* or a *high performance organisation*". All employee arguments can be counted and represented in **Figure 3**. Collectively employees suggest to focus internally and especially on Flexibility. The best suggestion however would be to focus first on Efficiency and implement all improvement that will have impact within short notice. Then move on to focus on Flexibility. After a while management should start preparing the issues in Creativity that needs (strategic) attention.

3.3. System Constraints

Implementing strategic interventions covered in the dark

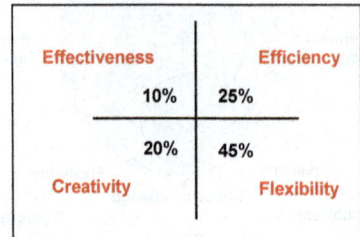

Figure 3. Results of an empirical analyses on employee arguments by Van Marrewijk

shape is supposed to enhance the necessary competences and ultimately contribute to obtaining the espoused performance results. The "yin-yang" shape indicates a dynamic process. Indeed, the Four Phase Model is a dynamic model suggesting a specific rhythm of shifting from one strategic orientation to the next, adding, each time, new improvements and competences. Ahead always lie new objectives to be met and new competences to be gained. The previous section discussed strategic risk management, with the organisation's largest challenge represented in the next phase or quadrant, and reverse effects that occur when organisations become rigid. Trying to prevent them to occur was presented as the first factor that causes dynamic effects within organisations.

This paragraph will elaborate on the system constraint, the organisation's bottleneck in improving corporate performance. Eli Goldratt elegantly proved in 'the Goal' (1984), his introduction to his Theory of Constraints, that in the end one factor obstructs the performance of an entire system. The investments that are able to lift this constraint by improving its quality or capacity will yield the highest productivity. The question is: where lies the constraint? On what factor should we target?

In terms of the Four Phase Model: 1) The constraint lies internally or externally and 2) the competences needed to lift the constraint are the material, commercial, socialisation or intellectual assets. In a strategic dialogue-within the board of directors, among experts, deep within the organisation or with various stakeholders-one must find out the whereabouts of the constraint. The following strategic issues might deliver the final clue:

Customer profile

Strategies developed with the Four Phase model apply to product/market combinations. Therefore market saturation levels, customer profiles, rate of progress et cetera are highly relevant. Our model distinguishes four ideal type profiles for customer needs. The organisation should focus on:

- Latent needs of customers. Surprise them with new, innovative products and services that where unheard off but are recognizes has attractive (Creativity).
- The customer must choose among a wide range of products, he does not fully comprehend. The traditional portfolio of marketing techniques is developed for this type of customer needs (Effectiveness).
- The customer is fully aware of all alternatives and seeks the lowest price (Efficiency).
- The customer is sensitive for the quality of services, which requires a flexible approach of the organisation (Flexibility).

Each specific customer profile can be serviced best by one of the strategic orientations mentioned between brackets. Customer needs can change over time, forcing the organisation to respond likewise. In many maturity models and life cycle approaches one can observe a sequence of these consumer types.

Although important, the strategic orientation will be influenced by more aspects than customer profile alone. We will provide an extra example:

Major risk

What is the major risk of your organisation?

- We have to prevent growing into an over-bureaucratic, inert organisation, no longer able to respond adequately to customer needs for dedicated services.
- Myopia due to conflicting kingdoms existing in the organisation, and the unbalance between customer focus and cost control might bring us in jeopardy.
- In offering ample room and insufficient focus, our employees invest too much time in their hobby's and personal interests.
- Our continuous attention for employee needs might turn into informalities and anarchy. Further more our service oriented, customer friendliness attitude might cost more than it generates.

Suppose the first option is recognised as the largest risk within the organisation, forcing it to shift to Flexibility in order to meet the needs for dedicated services while allowing human relations and corresponding socialisation ample room to balance existing rules and procedures.

With a wide spectrum of strategic aspects raised it is possible that not all answers align, but in practise these outcomes tend to match one other nicely, thus reinforcing a specific strategic orientation.

3.3. Maturity

Hardjono also dealt with the concept of maturity within his Four Phase model, especially the start up situation. See **Figure 4**. Any company starts with a good idea (Creativity). The pioneer enters the market, quickly turning to Efficiency in order to collect financial means, attracting employees and integrating them into the core processes. They need to respond to customers' remarks thus adapting the products and services and probably expanding the

scale and internal procedures (again Creativity). A new cycle starts. As a start up cycles pass quickly, and with gaining maturity they slow down. The best rhythm is a matter of flow: a balance between external and internal developments. Whenever an organisation fails to meet this flow it jeopardizes its existence.

My criticisms lies in the fact that being on the path of gaining maturity most organisations enter new levels of existence which influence the way strategies are implemented. Each level of existence is characterised by specific institutional arrangements: the dominant leadership style, the policies according which people and processes are managed, the way the organisation is structured, how decision making takes place, the relationship with partners et cetera. All these aspects relate with one and other and reinforce each other.

The nature of the interventions-as suggested by the Four Phase model-remain the same, however the context or value system that appear to be dominant highly impacts the way a specific intervention is implemented. I therefore prefer to apply strategic orientations as situations shifting from one to the next phase within a specific context, or "level of existence" as Clare Graves has put it. The next chapter will reveal an attractive effect once the Four Phase model is combined with Spiral Dynamics.

4. Combining Four Phase Model with Spiral Dynamics

4.1. Spiral Dynamics

Van Marrewijk introduced Spiral Dynamics in several previous publications [3,4,6-8]. Readers, not familiar with Spiral Dynamics, should first turn to this text before continuing with this chapter. We now summarize its features.

Clare W. Graves is the founder of the Emergent Cyclical Levels of Existence Theory. His successors, Don Beck and Chris Cowan, renamed it "Spiral Dynamics" and successfully introduced Graves' academic achievements to a wider audience [2]. Based on extensive empirical research Graves, who was professor in psychology and a contemporary of Maslow, concluded that mankind has gradually developed eight core value systems so far. Each level of existence-constructed around such a core value system-provides its own hierarchy of needs. Values are considered as coping mechanisms to meet specific challenges and to structure institutions in order to influence behaviour. A value system is a way of conceptualizing reality and encompasses a consistent set of values, beliefs and corresponding behaviour and can be found in individual persons, as well as in companies and societies. The core question that summarises this theory is: *how does the mind process reality?* Spiral Dynamics does not "label" people and organisations, but it

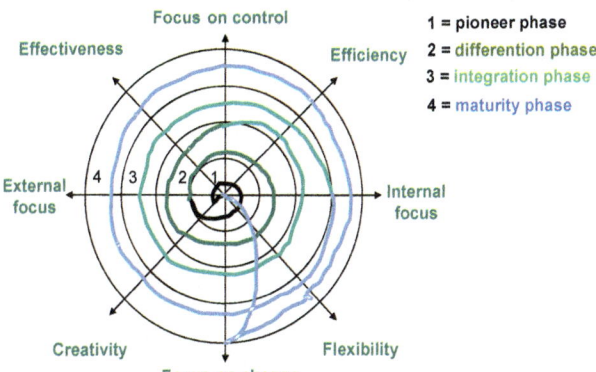

Figure 4. A start up situation gaining maturity.

structures thinking systems within entities. It reveals the fundaments of our behaviour that are covered below the surface.

A value system develops mainly as a reaction to specific environmental challenges and threats: the systems brighten or dim as life conditions (consisting of historic Times, geographic Place, existential Problems and societal Circumstances) change.

All entities-including organizations-will eventually have to meet the challenges their situation provides or risk the danger of oblivion or even extinction. If for instance societal circumstances change, inviting corporations to respond and consequently reconsider their role within society, it implies that corporations have to re-align their value systems and all their business institutions (such as mission, vision, policy deployment, decision-making, reporting, corporate affairs, etcetera) to these new circumstances. The quest to create an adequate response to specific life conditions results in a wide variety of survival strategies, each founded on a specific set of value assumptions and demonstrated in related institutions and behaviour. Evidently, the strategies introduced above also adopt the influence of specific value systems and show different approaches and alternative interventions.

The development of value systems occurs in a fixed order: Survival; Security; Energy and Power; Order; Success; Community, Synergy and Holistic life system. Each new value system includes and transcends the previous ones, thus forming a natural hierarchy (or holarchy) [9, 10]. Despite the recognition of specific levels, reality is a continuum of developments including transition zones between the levels. These transition phases are highly interesting but are left out in these analyses, leaving ideal type development phases or contexts.

4.2. Dominant Challenges

In determining the strategic orientation we also elaborate on the major challenges that occur within the organisation. We distinguish the following options:

• We need to manage all our operations efficiently in order to protect our margins (Efficiency).

• We need to transform good ideas and innovations into saleable products and services (Effectiveness).

• We need to enhance the dedication and resilience of our people, which are crucial to the success of our organisation, especially since customers demand dedicated services with respect to speed, flexibility and quality (Flexibility).

• We need to gain a better understanding of under surroundings, *i.e.* the life conditions that impact our organisation, such as the market and technological developments, trends in society and changes in people's needs. We have to improve our ability to change along with

these trends or-better-cause the changes to occur through the impact of our breakthroughs, innovations and new approach to design, produce and market our products and services (Creativity).

These options have been linked to strategic situations - as indicated between the brackets-but they also relate to contexts: Efficiency can be best implemented in Order, Effectiveness in Success, Flexibility in Community and Creativity in Synergy. However, in practice *and* theory one can observe all four strategic options in each context. In each context one strategic option can be considered dominant with all other options in a more supportive role.

The issue now arising is that for instance Effectiveness can take different appearances in various contexts. Depending how an organisation interprets one's business environment and its ambition, values and capabilities, it will adopt the characteristic way of a particular context while implementing a specific set of interventions, associated to a selected strategic orientation.

We here summarize the core appearances of Effectiveness for the various contexts:

• *Order*: Organisations produce for stock and sell what is available against well-calculated prices;

• *Success*: A wide spectrum of marketing tools and communication techniques (including packaging) is applied to inform and influence customers to buy products;

• *Community*: Customers are recognised as human beings, with particular needs. Product qualities align with customer needs. Mass production systems are adapted to small batches with diversified products;

• *Synergy*: Customers are involved in the early stages of product design. People oriented marketing approaches change the industry. Product qualities align with societal needs.

The effects of contexts on implementing strategic orientations can be acquired via Van Marrewijk, since it can not be dealt within the context of this paper. One can observe that the interventions suggested in the Four Phase model have gained practical use when combined with Spiral Dynamics: the strategic interventions and KPI's can be made more specific and practical.

In some industries you can see organisations shifting their strategies in a rapid sequence. More often one can observe particular strategies being quite persistent over time, such as a focus on low costs and Efficiency. Here we can see the mixed effects of contexts and situations. Suppose a particular industry can function adequately in Order. Rules and procedures would influence all strategies implemented within Order: Efficiency would be executed in a "blue" way, as well as Flexibility, Creativity and Effectiveness. Companies in Order cannot survive when they maintain their focus strictly on Efficiency. They have to shift their strategy to enhance the other core competences, all be it for a relative short period. Now and than, companies adapt their procedures to include new methods in order to cut costs. The challenge for these organizations remains to keep the prevailing structures from turning into rigid organizations generating reverse effects.

4.3. The Strategy Matrix

With four ideal type strategies and four selected contexts a grid can be made with sixteen combinations of specific situations and contexts. This is the Strategy Matrix, showed in **Table 3**.

This matrix offers a several distinctive benefits:

1) It expresses a basic philosophy behind the Four Phase model as well as Spiral Dynamics: all management principles, models and even hypes have their value, but often only in a certain situation/context combination. Or put differently: Due to changing circumstances both outside as well as inside organizations, models, tools and certainly hypes have limited applicability and tenability over time.

2) The matrix is therefore able to function as a framework for structuring for instance academic literature on business strategies and related policies. Also, all strategy models and tools mentioned above can be structured according this matrix.

3) The matrix implies four distinctive hierarchical complexity levels in change management: a) vitalising, b) optimising, c) shifting and d) transforming.

4) The matrix offers the conceptual basis for the Strategy Scan, which can generate the most adequate strategic situation and context of organisations, or their product/market combinations.

5) The matrix also offers a conceptual basis for performance cycle from which one can deduct a roadmap for sustainable business improvement and organisation development.

4.4. Four Dimensions of Change Management

By combining the dynamics of the Four Phase model and Spiral Dynamics, in other words: by combining strategic

"situations" and phase-wise "contexts", we were able to structure change management into four distinctive hierarchical complexity levels: a) vitalising, b) optimising, c) shifting and d) transforming. These four dimensions of change management are explained below.

Vitalising
Often the performance can be improved by enhancing the fundamental skills, structures and procedures of including contexts; These interventions are relatively simple as we have a lot of experience in managing these aspects, but being involved in more complex value systems, we tend to neglect basic competences although they jeopardise current performance potential.

Optimising
Once a sound fundament has been realised, further improvement can occur when organisations enhance the effectiveness of the characteristic institutions within the dominant context. Try to find out and apply best practices, work smarter and excel in what needs to be done.

Shifting
If including and current contexts are functioning well, further improvement can be established by fine-tuning the strategic situation. Within a context, organisations must focus their business towards the most adequate situation, aligning their interventions accordingly.

Transforming
When challenged by more complex conditions, which cannot be met by prevailing work procedures, organisations have to transform into an emerging context in order to sustain their corporate performance. Organisations should adopt new ways of organising by transforming to a more complex context, adopting emerging value systems and all institutions aligned with it. Transformations are complex phenomena, especially if managed as an improvement project.

Having identified the four dimensions of change management, we adapted the Performance Cycle (**Figure 5**). It is structured according Deming's Plan-Do-Check-Improve sequence. The related activities, provided by professor Wessel Ganzevoort, are "mobilizing, appreciating, reflecting and inspiring".

Table 3. The strategy matrix (Hardjono and van Marrewijk) [6].

Contexts/Strategic	Order	Success	Community	Synergy
Effectiveness	x	**X**	x	x
Efficiency	**X**	x	x	x
Flexibility	x	x	**X**	x
Creativity	x	x	x	**X**

X = dominant
x = applicable

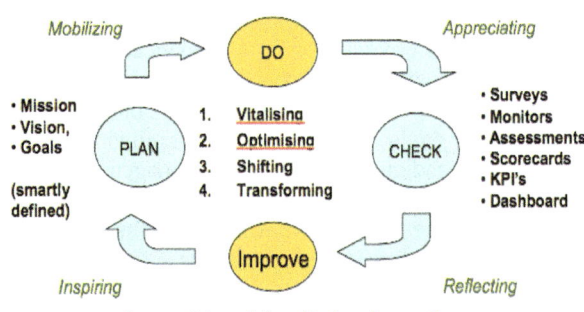

Figure 5. Performance improvement cycle, inspired by Deming and Ganzevoort.

The performance cycle suggests various ways to check the impact of the implementation process. Employee perception tools, such as surveys, monitors and assessments, as well as quality management, business operation and accounting tools generate data which via business intelligence services are provided to the board of directors, to management and professionals. Together they interpret the data and determine the progress made. Easy adaptations and fine-tuning are implemented directly, but larger alterations can be tried as experiments and pilots on a small-scale basis, or postponed until they fit the next strategic orientation.

4.5. Strategy Scan

The first step in drafting a roadmap towards sustainable performance improvement and organisation development is finding out one's position: what are the current constraints, challenges and risks; what are the dominant value systems within the organisation. In short, what (strategic) situation and context are most adequate to face current strengths and weaknesses, opportunities and threads?

In 2003 Van Marrewijk and Hardjono developed the Strategy Scan, based on the Strategy Matrix.

This online scan supports the strategic dialogue, the exchange of facts and experts opinions, and gives a direction to strategy development.

The Strategy Scan is a powerful online instrument, which takes stock of opinions, ideas and perceptions of those directly involved in the company's strategy formulation process. One can conduct the Strategic Scan in board of directors, management teams, among staff members, and as a vertical dialogue deeper into the organisation as well as outside, even with all stakeholders.

The Strategy Scan supports the strategy dialogue and gives an insight into your organisation's strategic positioning and context within which the strategy ought to be executed.

The first part of the scan focuses on strategic aspects, which ultimately determine the main direction or strategic orientation of the organisation. Examples of such aspects are the consumer needs and the current bottleneck obstructing organisational performance. The result is a focus and a set of ideal type interventions.

The second part surveys the nature and complexity of the (external) environment and the disciplinary developments (or paradigms) regarding the management criteria such as leadership, people-, resource-and process management. The Strategy Scan indicates the organisation's most dominant development phase, its favourite level of existence. Combined with the strategic orientation, the researchers and corporate experts can indicate specific interventions and sketch a roadmap for development, aligned with the dominant value systems of the organisation.

The feedback report gives an insight into shared opinions, priorities and most important differences among the responders. The first direct effect refers to the quality of the strategic dialogue with discussions focusing on the topics with a relative high level of variation. In focus groups or a workshop setting with representatives of the different views, one can try to tighten the strategy's selection and formulation. Furthermore, the Strategy Scan's result offers a solid base for an implementation plan and selecting key performance indicators.

The Strategy Scan is offered by Research to Improve. They also developed the Strategic Sustainability Scan, an extended version including additional sustainability issues. The Sustainability Scan generates an adequate meaning of corporate sustainability and-responsibility, an ideal type reference on which an organization can develop its own touch and approach. This way one can link strategy with CS/CR-policies and interventions.

5. A Roadmap towards Sustainable Performance

Deducting a roadmap for performance improvement and organizational development can be difficult as each organisation is unique. Many aspects can play a role and not all of them can be foreseen. Still it makes sense to have an idea about the path of change. What can we expect? What level of complexity? Do we have the necessary competences? The right people?

Each organisations must provide its own answers, but at least-by applying the Strategy Scan, the Strategy Matrix and the Performance Cycle-one can grasp its position, its strategic focus, a set of adequate interventions in order to lift the organisation's bottlenecks and enhance its basic competences, and its dominant context to 'colour' the interventions into fitting change activities.

Good surveys can provide management information from which one can tell if vitalisation or optimisation is most effective to enhance corporate performance. Frequently held strategic analyses can provide arguments to remain focused or shift to a next strategic orientation, prioritising a new set of interventions. Strategies can shift permanently within one context. This is relatively simple, but challenging enough.

Changing life conditions can force organisations to gain maturity by transforming into emerging value systems, thus creating new contexts. Strategies will than not only shift to a next phase, but also transform into a new context. Logically, the starting point of the transformation lies in the Creativity phase: adapting to new circumstances have forced the organisation to move its boundaries, to create adaptations "out of the box", introducing new ways of doing things. Leaving Order, a company will start adopting Effectiveness in a more entrepreneurial, profit-driven way. Marketing and leadership will be the pioneers in adopting a Success-driven approach, with People-and Process Management quickly catching up. After a while, Learning and Innovation and Communication and Decision-Making could be the two enablers, which will face the next performance constraint. When functioning within Success seems no longer adequate anymore, the need to sustain performance improvement will force the organisation to transform once more, this time into Community. It will support the need to learn, collaborate, engage and meet with society needs.

Strategic orientations (phases) as well as levels of existence (contexts) brighten and dim as responses to changing environmental circumstances and internal considerations, such as organizational structures and intrinsic motivations. We now elaborate on two developments situations: times of crises and a performance gap.

Crises

Ideally, strategies develop 'clockwise' in a natural sequence, creating additional competences and adding to the organization's total sum of assets. Especially in economic downturns, one can observe sudden shifts backwards! From for instance Efficiency back to Effectiveness, thus remaining in a control mode and ignoring the need to become more flexible and socialisation oriented. Due to such shifts specific competences are lost, expectations shattered and total sum of assets diminishes. But these shifts-for better or worse-can also support the organization's survival.

Due to changing life conditions organizations can also choose to shift to less complex value systems. The more complex ones are more vulnerable and difficult to sustain when times are hard. Eventually, tides will turn and organizations, as well as individuals and societies, will try again the more complex value systems in order to escape the limitations of the former ones.

Performance gap

Especially when centred in Success, organisations like to benchmark. Certain benchmarks such as the very best Great Places to Work® [11] and High Performance Organisations (HPO's) [12] have average scores of 85% to 90%, while ordinary organisations only score for instance 50%. These benchmarks provide a high performance level but do not provide intermediate 'stepping stones'. A target aimed at a 10% increase doesn't make much sense. The point is what should an organisation do and try to accomplish with the least effort and with maximum effect: first focus and than select the nature of the intervention and determine in what context the best contribution can be made.

In trying to bridge the performance gap, organisations often need intermediate goals. With the matrix and cycle introduced above, one is now able to design a development path with the intermediate goals as stepping goals towards the ultimate result. Both children and top athletes take the same approach in trying to establish espoused performance levels.

In designing a roadmap for change and performance improvement it is important to be aware of the complexities at hand. In a stable world one can predict the best approach and establish the expected results much easier. Prof. Ralph Stacey [13] defined this realm as 'rules'. In Spiral Dynamics it coincides best with Order. If one is uncertain of the impact of interventions, complexity increases, ultimately reaching the level of chaos. See **Figure 6**. Strategies are aimed at bringing down the level of complexity in order to be better able to predict and manage, preferably control, the outcome of one's activities.

Van Marrewijk presents Spiral Dynamics' levels of existence as 'local' equilibriums [14], offering adequate solutions to prevailing circumstances. See **Figure 7**. At each local equilibrium a specific set of values 'rules' and determines the institutional structures and patterns of behaviour, with which people and organisations are able to cope with prevailing circumstances. The moment entities become aware that current behaviour is no longer adequate to meet new challenges, periods of chaos emerge. Facing increasing complexity, people and organisations have to transform into new value systems. Each transition contains elements of chaos, due to people's resistance for the unknown, leaving behind old patters of behaviour and trying to get accustomed to new institutions, to new ways of working and new competences.

Once people and organisations feel aligned with a new context, a new level of existence, they can apply their newly acquired competences to deliver adequate solutions

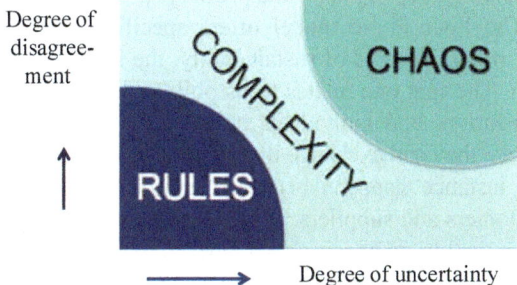

Figure 6. Reality according Prof. R. Stacey.

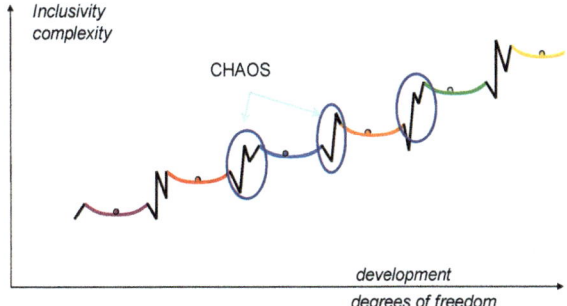

Figure 7. Phasewise orientation according Graves, (representation by van Marrewijk).

to prevailing challenges. They are able to match a higher level of complexity, as if complexity has been transformed into the realm of Stacey's rules.

Turning back to the issue of bridging performance gaps, one can observe in Western economies that successful workplaces and HPO's are often centred in Success /Community/Synergy, while the majority of organisations seem to function within Order/Success and still, quite a lot are in Power/Order.

A 40% performance gap can statistically be overcome by an average performance improvement of 4% for 10 years in a row. In practice it could imply a transition from a power-oriented organisation, via a shareholder, control- and profit-driven organisation to a stakeholder-oriented organisation. This is not an easy task, certainly not in 10 years time.

6. Corporate Sustainability (CS)

In this chapter we focus on sustainable performance, the ability to sustain organisational performance over time. Through shifting strategic orientations 'clockwise', thus building up basic competences that match the challenges and bottlenecks occurring in business operations, organisations remain fit, flexible and balanced, thus securing the best performance possible.

The philosophy behind the Four Phase model does have added value in understanding a second interpretation of corporate sustainability. One that is related to balancing people, planet and profits [5].

The Four Phase model offers specific contributions regarding the topic of sustainability, the latter interpretation. The first one relates to its philosophy: Since all organizations and individuals have the same set of basic assets, they can exchange their assets among one other as for instance happens between organizations and their customers and suppliers. In Order and Success organisations tend to emphasis shareholder value, through focusing on control and resource management. Apart from the basic exchange of assets with customers, these organisations tend to enhance their total sum of assets mainly through internal activities. Inevitably, this approach reaches its boundaries, forcing companies to seek new opportunities to grow their assets and sustain their performance. The limits of growth can be overcome by transforming into new emerging contexts, thus facing a period of change and chaos due to learning new ways of doing business (**Figure 6**).

In the process of sustaining corporate performance- thus enhancing corporate sustainability in both interpre-

tations-organizations learn to involve their stakeholders in corporate decision-making and business practices. Organisations demonstrating Community and Synergy learn from one other, theoretically spoken they exchange intellectual assets with stakeholder inside (employees) and outside (customers, neighbourhood, etc). Involving customers in for instance product design impacts the innovation process of new product formats that include added values for various stakeholders. Therefore, Corporate Sustainability[1], ultimately, means totalling the sum of assets, not only of the company, but of a much wider group of entities, eventually including the whole planet. In this latter context, CS implies that the material assets include the planet's resources (natural capital). Depletion or exploitation of these resources is at best a zero sum game, which is no longer an attractive business objective.

Functioning in Synergy implies that organizations operate in an open system surrounded by other open systems. The interaction between these systems will lead to new and unexpected opportunities. By forming coalitions these possibilities can be explored and exploited in a way that they create added value for everyone concerned, generating added value not only in a material/financial way, but also in a commercial, social and intellectual way.

Managing the complexity of thinking and working in an environment of open systems, full of coalitions, offering great variety and diversity, opens the way to introducing "basic rules". Only when you have mastered complexity, simplicity might work. Basic rules can be understood as the principles by which complex systems function. Paradoxes and dilemmas are seen as effects and sources of inspiration, often leading to new insights, new ideas, new concepts and new learning experiences.

The second contribution of the Four Phase model lies in aligning the strategic orientations with specific sustainability activities associated with the Triple Bottom Line. In stead of implementing CS-R activities as 'add-ons' to business operations, it will generate much more impact when out of many potential CS-R activities those ones are selected which will reinforce the effect of selected strategic interventions.

The two concepts described in this chapter, the strategic phases and development contexts, are distinct notions. The contexts are broader, psychological stages in evolutionary development, while the phases are more instrumental, structuring the interventions for strategy implementations.

The Strategy Matrix-integrating both concepts-presented above can help executives and business consultants to understand organization dynamics in general and facilitate them in plotting a course for organizational change, shifts or transformation, whenever they want to implement a more ambitious approach towards CS and CR, or corporate improvement in general.

---

[1]Corporate responsibility, in this sense, means being accountable for working in such a way the total sum of assets will increase for direct or indirect stakeholders, now and in the future.

7. References

[1]   T. W. Hardjono, "Ritmiek en Organisatiedynamiek: Vier-fasenmodel," Kluwer, 1995.

[2]   D. Beck and C. Cowan, "Mastering Values, Leadership and Change," *Spiral Dynamics*, Blackwell Publishers, 1996.

[3]   M. van Marrewijk, "Concepts and Definitions of Corporate Sustainability," *Journal of Business Ethics*, Vol. 44, No. 2-3, May 2003, pp. 95-105.

[4]   M. van Marrewijk and M. Werre, "Multiple Levels of Corporate Sustainability," *Journal of Business Ethics*, Vol. 44, No. 2-3, May 2003, pp. 107-119.

[5]   J. Elkington, "Cannibals with Forks: The Triple Bottom Line of 21st Century Business," Capstone Publishing Ltd., Oxford, 1997.

[6]   M. van Marrewijk and T. W. Hardjono, "European Corporate Sustainability Framework for managing Complexity and Corporate Change," *Journal of Business Ethics*, Vol. 44, No. 2-3, May 2003, pp. 121-132.

[7]   M. van Marrewijk, "European Corporate Sustainability Framework," *International Journal of Business Perform-ance Measurement*, Vol. 5, No. 2-3, 2003, pp.95-105.

[8]   M. van Marrewijk, "A Value Based Approach to Organisation Types: Towards a Coherent Set of Stakeholder Oriented Management Tools," *Journal of Business Ethics*, Vol. 55, No. 6, December 2004, pp. 147-158.

[9]   K. Wilber, "Sex, Ecology, Spirituality: The Spirit of Evolution," Shambala Publications, 1995.

[10] K. Wilber, "A Theory of Everything: An integral vision for Business, Politics, Science and Spirituality," Shambala Publications, 2000.

[11] M. van Marrewijk, "The Social Dimension of Organizations: Recent Experiences with Great Place to Work® assessment practices," *Journal of Business Ethics*, Vol. 55, No. 2, December 2004, pp. 135-146.

[12] J. C. Collins, "Good to Great," Harper Collins Publishers, New York, 2001.

[13] R. Stacey, "Strategic Management and Orgnisational Dynamics," 5th Edition, Prentice Hall, 2007.

[14] M. van Marrewijk, "The Cubrix, an Integral Framework for Managing Performance Improvement and Organisational Development," *Journal of Technology and Investment*, Vol. 1, No. 1, 2010, pp. 1-13.

Abbreviations

CEO	Chief Executive Officer
CS	Corporate Sustainability
CR	Corporate Responsibility
CSR	Corporate Social Responsibility
ECSF	European Corporate Sustainability Framework
ECLET	Emerging Cyclical Levels of Existence Theory
EU	European Union
HPO	High Performance Organizations
KPI	Key Performance Indicator

9

Environmental Policies and Firm Behavior with Endogenous Investment in R & D

Emanuela Giusi Gaeta

University of Rome "Tor Vergata", Rome, Italy

Abstract

This paper investigates upon the optimal amount of oil usage in an economy characterized by competitive firms and by a monopolistic innovator. It is close in spirit to Denicolo 1999 and Parry 2003. There are two alternative oil saving technologies: the conventional one is promptly available to firms while the advanced one, providing more efficiency in oil saving, must be paid to the monopolistic innovator. By assuming that innovation follows a Poisson process, whose arrival rate depends on the amount of resources invested in R & D, we show that central authority provides higher level of social welfare than market instruments.

Keywords: Environmental Policies, Technological Change, Energy Saving, Welfare Analysis

1. Introduction

During the last years, several authors have included R & D into the analysis of environmental policy incentives, giving life to a new research branch. This literature can be divided in two strands. The first one is characterized by the microeconomic approach, making use of the game theory in order to study the strategic behavior in equilibrium. The major parts of these models are characterized by a partial equilibrium approach, which can be static [1] or quasidynamic, where each actor-firm, regulator and innovator-chooses in a sequential way [2]. This literature captures several aspect, such as market conditions, uncertainty about the R & D success and the environmental damage. The second research strand follows the endogenous growth approach [3,4]. We concentrate the attention on the first case, where innovation is mainly firm specific and depends on the total amount of R & D needed to developing energy saving technologies.

In this kind of models, where innovation is a private good, the literature investigates upon the optimal policy instrument to develop and diffuse the new technology. There are two alternative strategies to do so: the ex ante and the ex post policy. Several authors assume that in the former there is only one innovator [5,6] or several identical firms, engaging in a patent race: in the latter just one innovator prevails in the market, gaining market power. This innovator can sell or license to the other firms which choose for adoption or not. For this reason it becomes crucial the commitment and the timing of poli-cies, which can make the difference in terms of welfare results [7].

Denicolo was the first at explicitly comparing ex ante and ex post regulation both for emission taxes and tradable permits in a model with an upstream monopolistic R & D firm and many polluting downstream firms [4]. In this model the degree of emissions reduction depends on R & D investment and he finds that taxes and permits give the same results for ex post regulation. However, if the regulator adopts the ex ante policy, the first best equilibrium doesn't exist, since both the instruments lead to underinvestment in R & D. The author shows an alternative solution, where the regulator can commit to the second-best optimal level of the instruments, but the choice depends on the social cost of pollution and there is no certainty about the effectiveness of taxes and permits.

Unlike most of other contributions, in Parry [8] there is free entry on both markets, and he shows that a higher tax rate produces a double effect: it involves a smaller number of polluting firms but we know that the firms with the highest willingness to pay for the new technology stay in the market, so a higher tax also induces a higher license fee. Parry [7] introduced some variations to his model and he investigated upon the magnitude of welfare gain coming from abatement cost reducing innovation, relative to the welfare gain induced by optimal pollution control over time. He found that this magnitude depends on three factors: the initially optimal abatement level, the speed at which innovation reduces future abatement costs (on the optimal innovation path) and the social discount rate. This factor plays a key role in the determinants controlling the welfare gain from innovation and pollution control. Parry shows that there are several scenarios where the welfare gains from innovation are smaller than those which come from the pollution control. In many cases the R & D investment decided by regulator does not coincide with the market decision. This result seems to contradict the earlier assertion by economist who supported the welfare gain from innovation.

Our paper is close in spirit to Denicolo [5] and Parry [6] and represents a further refinement of Gaeta [2], which analyzes how market instruments are able to mimic optimal social choice in driving the adoption of advanced oil saving technologies. In that paper the advanced technology was exogenously available to investing firms. This paper analyzes the case where the advanced technology comes from an innovating monopolistic firm investing in R & D. Main result is that, with endogenous R & D, the social planner provides Pareto optimal solution that market is not able to mimic. These results are in line with the cited literature, although our analysis involves a different microeconomic setup. Under this point of view our results confirm that market instruments provide sub-optimal oil usage amount in the economy. Even when we want to measure social welfare by means of the amount of R & D, as some authors point out, the central policy provides always higher level of investment than the free market.

2. The Model: Firms Behaviour and Market Instruments

We are going to assume an economy characterized by two sectors: manufacturing and R & D. In the manufacturing sector there are n firms acting in a competitive way. Production uses oil only. Oil is costly and polluting. Government wants to reduce oil usage in the economy by means of suitable policies. As in [1], there are two alternative oil saving technologies; conventional and advanced. The first one is promptly available free of charge; the second one involves a lump sum cost. Firms act by choosing optimal oil using; in a free market, without central policy, firms choose the maximum amount of oil, O_{Max}. With centralized policies, firms change their optimal plan; we are going to take into account how alternative oil saving policies (tax, permits and command and control) affect firms behaviour.

2.1. Taxation

When firms are charged with a tax on the amount of oil usage O, profits are given by:

$$\pi_0 = Q(O_0) - (P_0 + \tau)O_0 - C_0(O_0) \qquad (1)$$

$$\pi_1 = Q(O_1) - (P_0 + \tau)O_1 - C_1(O_1) - P_R \qquad (2)$$

where 0 means that the firm is not adopting the advanced technology and 1 the opposite. Functional assumptions are as usual: $Q(O) > 0$, $Q'(O) > 0, Q''(O) < 0$ and $O \in [0, O_{Max}]$ C is the oil saving cost related to the chosen technology. As usual we are going to assume convexity in $C, C(O) > 0$, $C'(O) > 0, C''(O) > 0$. P_O is the exogenous oil price and τ the tax rate. Moreover we assume that the advanced technology is more efficient in oil saving, thanks to research and development m. Efficiency is given by the r coefficient that depends on m, i.e. $C_1 = (1 - r(m))C_0$ with $r(m) \in [0,1]$, $r'(m) > 0$. P_R is the patent price paid by firms adopting the advanced technology.

Firms maximize profits (Equations (1) and (2)) with respect to the oil usage O_0 and O_1, given τ, P_R and m. The optimal oil usage is implicitly given by the following first order conditions.

$$Max \ \pi \to O_0^*(\tau \,|\, P_0) \quad O_1^*(\tau, P_R, m \,|\, P_0)$$

Whenever $\pi_1 > \pi_0$ all firms are induced to adopt the advanced technology and so $n_1 = n$ Otherwise if $\pi_1 = \pi_0$, n_1 is not determined.

A single firm must choose which technology is going to adopt. This is done by comparing profits in both situations:

$$\Delta \pi = \pi_1 - \pi_0 \to \Delta \pi(\tau, P_R, m \,|\, P_0, k) \qquad (3)$$

R & D is performed by a single monopolistic firm. It invests m in R & D and obtains the new technology with probability $p(m)$, that follows a Poisson process with cumulative distribution function $(1 - e^{-\phi m})$. The R & D cost for unit of research is k so that the innovating firm produces a quantity of R & D that makes equal the expected profit to the actual cost of investing in R & D (this is standard in the neo-shumpeterian approach). The arbitrage equation is

$$p(m)n_1 P_R = km \qquad (4)$$

We can solve this equation in order to get P_R $(m, n_1 \,|\, k)$ and then we substitute in the Equation (3). By doing so, we have $\Delta \pi(\tau, m, n_1 \,|\, P_0, k, P_0)$.

In the decentralized economy τ and n_1 are exogenous to the firm, so firm behaviour in adopting or not the advanced technology depends on $\Delta \pi(m, |\, \tau, n_1, P_0, k, P_0)$, where m depends on the R & D firm.

With partial adoption $\Delta \pi = 0$ and this leads to $m(n_1 \,|\, \tau, P_0, k, P_0)$. The main goal is to investigate upon this relationship and on the general equilibrium of the economy.

With full adoption $n_1 = 1$ and $\Delta\pi > 0$. In such a case the R & D firm chooses m in order to induce $\Delta\pi > 0$ but, once more, nothing assures that such equilibrium does exist and more analytical work must be developed.

2.2. Partial Adoption

Let us assume that the cost reduction function follows:

$$C_0 = \frac{\alpha}{2}(O_M - O_0)^2$$

$$C_1 = (1 - r(m))\frac{\alpha}{2}(O_M - O_1)^2$$

Profit maximization leads to:

$$O_0^*(\tau) = Q'^{-1}\left(P_0 + \tau + C_0'(O_0)\right)$$

$$O_1^*(\tau, m) = Q'^{-1}\left(P_0 + \tau + C_1'(O_1) + P_R\right)$$

where Q'^{-1} is the inverse first order derivative. When partial adoption is at work we have $\Delta\pi(\tau, P_R, m \mid k, P_0) = 0$. Equilibrium is determined by closing the model through the R & D equation $p(m)n_1 P_R(\tau, m) = km$. Nonetheless the left hand side is characterized by a strong non-linearity and in general not much can be said on the amount of R & D $m(\tau, n_1)$ characterizing the equilibrium. For further investigation, we are going to assume homothetic production function, $Q = \log(O)$ and that probabilities of new discovery follows a Poisson law $p(m) = 1 - e^{-\phi m}$. At the same time we are going to assume $r(m) = 1 - e^{-\lambda m}$.

Let us investigate upon the first order conditions. Profit maximization leads to:

$$\frac{1}{O_0} - P_0 + \alpha(O_M - O_0) = \tau \qquad (5)$$

$$\frac{1}{O_1} - P_0 + \alpha(1 - r(m))(O_M - O_1) = \tau \qquad (6)$$

First order conditions mean that firms uses oil until marginal profit is equal to the usage cost given by the tax rate. Solving Equations (5) and (6) provides optimal oil usage conditioned on the tax rate. Following lemma holds:

Lemma 1 *First order conditions imply*

$$O_1^* < O_0^* \in (0, O_{Max}).$$

Proof. When $O = O_{Max}$ we have $O_1^* = O_0^* = O_{Max} = \frac{1}{P_0 + \tau}$. Being $(1 - r(m)) < 1$ Equation (6) lies everywhere under Equation (5). (end of proof).

Equation (6) links O_1 to the amount of R & D via $r(m)$. The relationship is linear-concave in r, being O_1 a quadratic function. Following lemma holds:

Lemma 2 O_1^* *is decreasing in m.*

Proof. By normalizing $\alpha = 1$, from Equation (6) we have:

$$\lim_{r \to 0} O_1^* = \chi \quad \text{with}$$

$$\chi = 5 + 0.5\left(\sqrt{(P_0 + \tau)^2 - 20(P_0 + \tau) + 104} - (P_0 + \tau)\right) > 0$$

$$\lim_{r \to 1} O_1^* = \chi_2 \quad \text{with}$$

$$\chi_2 = 5 + 50\left(\sqrt{(P_0 + \tau)^2 - 0.20(P_0 + \tau) + 0.05} - (P_0 + \tau)\right) < \chi$$

Given the linear concavity of O_1 w.r.t. r and being $\frac{\partial r}{\partial m} > 0$ the lemma holds. (end of proof).

The lemma underlines the oil saving feature of R & D; more investment in new technologies has a positive effect in the economy as reduces the optimal amount of oil usage per firm.

Once the optimal oil usage $O_1^*(\tau) O_0^*(\tau)$ is carried out, Equation (2) provides the patent price P_R given the perfect market condition $\pi_1 = \pi_0$.

$$P_R(m \mid \tau) = \log(O_1) - (P_0 + \tau)O_1 - \frac{\alpha}{2}(1 - r(m))(O_M - O_1)^2 \qquad (7)$$
$$- [\log(O_0) - (P_0 + \tau)O_0 - \frac{\alpha}{2}(O_M - O_1)^2]$$

The Equation (7) sets the patent price that firms are allowed to pay for using the new technology. It depends on the optimal amount of R & D that the monopolistic firm is investing. The relationship is strongly non linear in m. The equation can be rearranged in the following way:

$$P_R(m \mid \tau) = a(O_0^*) + b(m) + c(m) \qquad (8)$$

with $a(O_0^*) = \left[\log(O_0) - (P_0 + \tau)O_0 - \frac{\alpha}{2}(O_M - O_0)^2\right]$,

$$b(m) = \log(O_1) - (P_0 + \tau)O_1 - \frac{\alpha}{2}(O_M - O_1)^2$$

and

$$c(m) = \frac{\alpha}{2} r(m)(O_M - O_1(m))^2.$$

Following lemma holds:

Lemma 3 P_R *is increasing in m. Nevertheless second order derivative can not be signed unambiguously.*

Proof. By deriving Equation (8) with respect to m we obtain:

$$\frac{\partial b(m)}{\partial m} = \left(\frac{1}{O_1} + \alpha(O_M - O_1) - (P_0 + \tau)\right)\frac{\partial O_1}{\partial m}.$$

We are going to assume that the term in brackets is

negative and so, by Lemma 2, $\frac{\partial b(m)}{\partial m} > 0$. Moreover:

$$\frac{\partial c(m)}{\partial m} = \frac{\alpha}{2} \frac{\partial r}{m} (O_M - O_1(m))^2 - \alpha r(m)(O_M - O_1(m))^2$$

$$\frac{\partial O_1}{\partial m} = \alpha(O_M - O_1(m))^2 \left[\frac{1}{2} \frac{\partial r}{\partial m} - r(m) \frac{\partial O_1}{\partial m} \right] > 0$$

However, second order derivatives are not unambiguously determined and so convexity and concavity of the function can alternatively be viable. (end of proof).

The model is closed by analyzing how the monopolistic firm chooses the price P_R according to Equation (4).

Following lemma holds:

Lemma 4 *The supply curve for* P_R *is monotonically increasing in m.*

Proof. Let us rewrite Equation (4) in the following way:

$$P_R = \frac{k}{n_1} \frac{m}{(1 - e^{-\phi m})}$$

In a decentralized economy, n_1 does not depend on m. Hence:

$$\frac{\partial P_R}{\partial m} = \frac{k}{n_1} \frac{((1 - e^{-\phi m}) - m\phi e^{-\phi m})}{(1 - e^{-\phi m})^2}$$

and so:

$$\lim_{m \to 0} \frac{\partial P_R}{\partial m} = \frac{1}{2} \frac{k}{n_1} > 0$$

$$\lim_{m \to \infty} \frac{\partial P_R}{\partial m} = \infty$$

Moreover first derivative is zero only when $m = 0$. (end of proof).

General equilibrium comes from comparing P_R by Lemmas 3 and 4, *i.e.* by crossing supply and demand for m. By Lemma 3, multiple equilibria are viable results. Nevertheless stable equilibrium requires that Brouwer's assumptions for fixed point are satisfied. In general, number and stability of equilibrium depend on parameters. Moreover, the general equilibrium depends on τ and is not possible to asses how taxation affects market equilibrium. For such a reason the model will be numerically analyzed by normalizing $\alpha = \phi = \lambda = 1$.

Following **Figure 1** shows the equilibrium relationship in such a case.

Although we are working in a static context, some equilibria are unstable and so not robust at the bargaining process involved by P_R. Stability of Brouwer fixed point theorem requires that first derivative be less than one in the neighborhood of the crossing point between demand and supply; this leaves just one single stable equilibrium. Since we are going to analyze the model by

through some numerical investigations the unstable equilibria are ruled out from the analysis.

Table 1 sums up some numerical exercises (deep parameters $\alpha = \phi = \lambda = 1$).

Main findings are the strict non linearity of the functions; τ is defined on a subset only of the feasible domain $[0,1]$ according to the number of adopting firms. What is relevant is the monotonicity of m w.r.t. τ; an increase in taxation, all other things equal, leads firms to reduce remarkably the oil usage in both technology. This induces the R & D firm to invest more and to charge a higher price (or conversely). This means that taxation matters for the amount of R & D in the economy. However it is hard to establish a hierarchy of equilibrium. With $n_1 = 0.25$ the tax rate is high; this drives firms to reduce remarkably oil usage; nonetheless the maximum investment in R & D is obtained with $n_1 = 0.75$. This warns us on the government objective function: as the literature remarks, by adopting the maximum investment in R & D or the lowest level of oil usage as the government objective function is not neutral for results. The first target involves lower level of taxation and conversely.

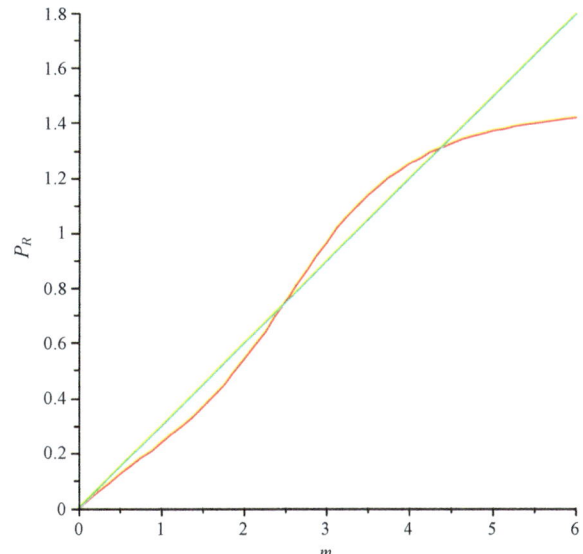

Figure 1. Multiple equilibria.

Table 1. Taxation outcome.

τ	0.80	0.9	τ	0.2	0.3	0.4	τ	0.2	0.30	0.4
O_0	9.25	9.15	O_0	9.64	9.55	9.21	O_0	9.65	9.12	9.55
O_1	1.44	1.17	O_1	9.17	8.83	7.89	O_1	8.15	4.11	2.36
m	4.38	5.30	m	1.57	1.84	2.04	m	2.95	4.83	8.65
P_R	5.32	6.4	P_R	2.16	2.32	4.41	P_R	1.34	1.86	3.66
$n_1 = 0.25, \tau \in (0.8,1)$			$n_1 = 0.50, \tau \in (0.2,0.4)$				$n_1 = 0.75, \tau \in (0.1,0.5)$			

2.3. Full Adoption

When $\Delta\pi(\tau, P_R, m \mid k, P_0) > 0$ every firm invests in the advanced technology and $n_1 = 1$. Profits are:

$$\pi_1 = Q(O_1) - (P_0 + \tau)O_1 - C_1(O_1) - P_R$$

maximization leads to $O_1^*(\tau, P_R, m \mid P_0)$. In such a case the solution is quite simple; once solved for O_1^*, the optimal amount of R & D can be carried out by Equation (4).

3. Permits

Before analyzing the social planner problem, it is useful to compare results obtained in the tax case with alternative market based instruments. Let us start from permits. In such a case firms are permitted to use oil in a given amount. According to literature, we are going to distinguish between costly, auctioned and free permits (grandfathering). When firms are charged with a price P_p per unit of oil usage, results are not different from taxation. In fact, each firm acts in a price-taker environment, taking P_p as the tax rate, i.e. $P_p = \tau$ and Equations (1) and (2) are unchanged.

$$\pi_0 = Q(O_0) - (P_0 + P_p)O_0 - C_0(O_0) \qquad (9)$$

$$\pi_1 = Q(O_1) - (P_0 + P_p)O_1 - C_1(O_1) - P_R \qquad (10)$$

With auctioned permits results are different. Let us assume that L permits are exogenously issued by central authority and P_p be the market clearing price. Unlike costly permits, when partial adoption is at work, the following constraint must be satisfied:

$$L = n_1 O_1 + (n - n_1)O_0$$

where oil usage comes from firm first order conditions. This means that n_1 is not a free parameter but depends on L:

$$n_1 = \frac{nO_0 - L}{O_0 - O_1}$$

By replying simulations by taking into account such a constraint leads to **Table 2**.

By comparing results with the ones obtained with the tax rate, we can conclude that auctioned permits confirm the monotonicity of m w.r.t. the cost of oil usage related to permits; an increase in P_p, all other things equal, leads firms to reduce remarkably the oil usage in both technologies and to increase the investment in R & D, m. Nevertheless, auctioned permits allow less oil saving than non-auctioned permits (or taxation) and involve consequently a lower level of investment in R & D. As literature shows, taxation provides more incentive to firm

Table 2. Permits outcome.

P_p	0.75	0.80	0.95	P_p	0.2	0.30	0.50	P_p	0.2	0.30	0.45
O_0	9.30	9.25	9.1	O_0	9.85	9.75	9.55	O_0	9.85	9.75	9.60
O_1	1.96	1.44	1.08	O_1	9.57	9.03	2.14	O_1	8.55	4.31	2.24
m	3.51	4.38	5.7	m	1.51	1.63	5.50	m	2.86	4.43	7.63
P_R	4.34	5.32	6.86	P_R	1.16	1.21	3.31	P_R	1.21	1.79	3.05
L	7.46	7.30	7.10	L	9.71	9.39	5.84	L	8.87	5.67	4.08

$n_1 = 0.25$ $n_1 = 0.50$ $n_1 = 0.75$

in reducing oil usage.

The last case we are going to analyze is free permits (grandfathering); in such a case each firm is endowed with the permits of using a given oil quantity O_p. However, since advanced technology allows firms to save out of oil, investor firms can trade their permits to not-adopting ones. Partial adoption means that firms are indifferent and the following constraint must hold:

$$Q(O_0) - (P_0)O_0 - C_0(O_0) - P_p(O_0 - O_p)$$
$$= Q(O_1) - (P_0)O_1 - C_1(O_1) - P_R + P_p(O_p - O_1)$$

given that $P_p O_p$ cancels out in both sides we obtain Equations (9) and (10). So incentive to adopt the new technology is the same under free or costly permits.

We can sum up results in the following proposition:

Proposition 5 *Non auctioned and free permits allows same results in terms of oil saving and investment in R & D than auctioned permits.*

4. Command and Control

This last section is devoted to the so called "command and control" policy; in such a case a firm is not allowed to use more than O^* units of oil. Firms are indifferent when the following condition is satisfied:

$$Q(O^*) - C_0(O^*) = Q(O^*) - C_1(O^*) - P_R$$

since $C_0(O^*) > C_1(O^*)$ the above equation is decreasing in O^*; in other words, the relaxing of the constraint on oil usage reduces the incentive to adopt the new technology. This means that for $O > O^*$ no firms will adopt the new technology and vice versa.

5. The Centralized Economy

In this section we are going to compare market equilibrium with the one chosen by a central authority. The central planner has to maximize the social welfare given by the private firm profit net of environmental damage,

$$D(O_o, O_1) = (n_1 O_1 + (n - n_1) O_0)^2 \;:$$

$$V = \underset{n_1}{Max}[n_1 \pi_1 + (n - n_1)\pi_0 - (n_1 O_1 + (n - n_1)O_0)^2] \qquad (11)$$

$$s.t : O_1, O_0 \in [0, O_{Max}]$$

The government chooses the optimal oil usage, the optimal number of adopting firms and leaves the optimal size of R & D to the monopolistic firm. The lagrangian function does not allow a closed form solution. We have to solve for:

$$O_0^* : \frac{\partial \pi_0}{\partial O_0} = 2(n_1 O_1 + (n - n_1)O_0) \qquad (12)$$

$$O_1^* : \frac{\partial \pi_1}{\partial O_1} = 2(n_1 O_1 + (n - n_1)O_0) \qquad (13)$$

Equations (12) and (13) mean that the private marginal profit must be equal to the marginal social cost; in the decentralized economy these must be equal to the tax rate.

The model is closed by:

$$n_1^* : \pi_1 - \pi_0 = 2(n_1 O_1 + (n - n_1)O_0)(O_1 - O_0) \qquad (14)$$

with:

$$\pi_1 - \pi_0 > 0 \rightarrow n_1 = 1$$

$$\pi_1 - \pi_0 < 0 \rightarrow n_1 = 0$$

$$\pi_1 - \pi_0 = 0 \rightarrow n_1 O_1 = (n - n_1)O_0$$

The R & D is still determined by Equation (4) once that oil usage and market size are optimally chosen.

Basically the model uses a fixed point argument to find social optimum; Equations (12) and (13) provide $O_0(n_1, \mathrm{Pr}, m)$ and $O_1(n_1, \mathrm{Pr}, m)$. These results plugged in 14 provide solution for n_1 and finally Equation (4) provides the optimal R & D.

Unfortunately the algebra can not be managed in an easy way. However, assumptions on functional form assure that an equilibrium do exist. **Figure 2** shows Equation (14); as can be seen, it does exist $n_1 \in [0,1]$ that satisfies the $\Delta\pi = 0$ constraint.

For analyzing the model, a numerical routine in Maple V has been written down. The routine follows a fixed point algorithm with a backward induction; by starting from a prior on m and P_R the optimal values for n_1, O_1 and O_0 are calculated through Equations (12), (13) and (14). Then the prior is updated with Equation (4) and the routine goes on, until the fixed point is achieved.

By using $\alpha = \phi = \lambda = 1$, the numerical simulation brings to this optimal value for oil usage and the consequent size of R & D.

The optimal number of adopting firms is $n_1 = 0.6$; what is striking is the very low level of oil usage chosen

by the central authority. The relative high demand for advanced technology pushes up the price of patents, which in turn induces the R & D firm to invest more. By comparing this solution to the ones obtained in the market analysis with $n_1 = 0.6$, the social planner chooses always the lowest level of oil. This is summarized in the following proposition.

Proposition 6 *In the centralized economy, 60% of manufacturing firms uses the advanced technology for oil saving. This induces a very low level of oil usage per firm. By comparing such a result with market based instruments, the central economy provides the lowest level of oil usage with respect to the market equilibrium.*

The difference between social and market equilibrium comes from the more complex relationship entailed by the social question. By comparing first order conditions in both situations, we have that, in the decentralized economy, the marginal profit is equal to the market instrument (tax or permits) which is exogenously given by the government. In the decentralized economy, first order conditions lead to:

$$Q'(O_i(m, P_R)) - P_0 - C''(O_i(m, P_R)) = \tau \qquad i = 0, 1 \quad (15)$$

while in the centralized economy we have:

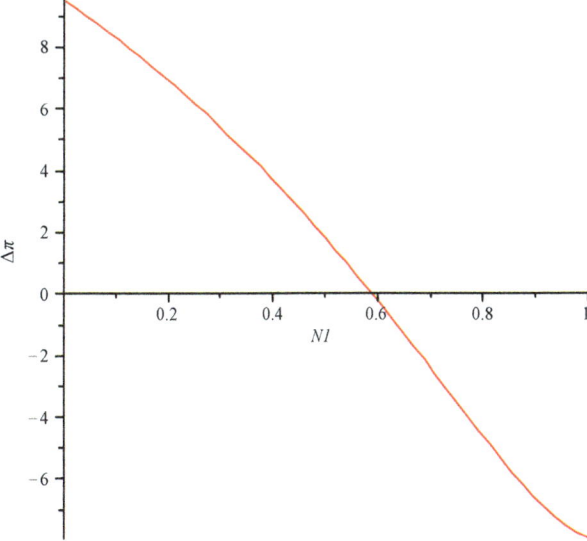

Figure 2. Partial adoption.

Table 3. Centralized economy.

O_0	5.03
O_1	0.20
m	11.5
P_R	14
n_1	0.6

$$Q'(O_i(m, P_R)) - P_o - C'(O_i(m, P_R))$$
$$= 2(n_1 O_1(m, P_R) + (n - n_1)O_0(m, P_R)) \quad i = 0,1$$

In the last equation both sides depend on the amount of R & D which responds to the amount of oil usage in the economy. Such a situation is completely different from the decentralized solution where tax can be exogenously adjusted in order to satisfy Equation (15).

This result is new in the literature; Parry 2003 achieves the opposite result in the context of pollution control. He finds that market based instrument provides higher pollution abatement than the social planner and in general the positive effect on the amount of R & D is small. In our case there is a strong effect on the optimal amount of investment in new technology. Had we assumed technological spillover, we would have added a positive effect to the development of economy, as in [9].

Similar result are instead shown in Denicolo, where tax and permits are not able to reach the first best optimal solution in an economy very close to the one we assumed. In his paper, the author makes a rank market instruments according to the incentive to innovate. Following Denicolo, we compute the welfare function W by using the different oil usage quantity arisen from different policies. **Tables 4-6** sum up the previous findings adding the calculated welfare function V in the three policies: taxation, auctioned permits and social planner.

Table 4. Taxation.

τ	0.80	0.9	τ	0.2	0.3	0.4	τ	0.2	0.30	0.4
O_0	9.25	9.15	O_0	9.85	9.75	9.65	O_0	9.85	9.75	9.65
O_1	1.44	1.17	O_1	9.57	9.03	7.89	O_1	8.55	4.31	2.56
m	4.38	5.30	m	1.51	1.63	2.04	m	2.86	4.43	6.65
P_R	5.32	6.4	P_R	1.16	1.21	1.41	P_R	1.21	1.79	2.66
V	50	52	V	10	16	25	V	27	40	87

$n_1 = 0.25$ $n_1 = 0.50$ $n_1 = 0.75$

Table 5. Auctioned Permits.

P_p	0.75	0.80	0.95	P_p	0.2	0.30	0.50	P_p	0.2	0.30	0.45
O_0	9.30	9.25	9.1	O_0	9.85	9.75	9.55	O_0	9.85	9.75	9.60
O_1	1.96	1.44	1.08	O_1	9.57	9.03	2.14	O_1	8.55	4.31	2.24
m	3.51	4.38	5.7	m	1.51	1.63	5.50	m	2.86	4.43	7.63
P_R	4.34	5.32	6.86	P_R	1.16	1.21	3.31	P_R	1.21	1.79	3.05
L	7.46	7.30	7.10	L	9.71	9.39	5.84	L	8.87	5.67	4.08

$n_1 = 0.25$ $n_1 = 0.50$ $n_1 = 0.75$

Table 6. Social Planner.

O_0	5.03
O_1	0.20
m	11.5
P_R	14
n_1	0.6
V	91

As results show, the highest value for V is obtained with the centralized solution. The picture is more fuzzy when we compare taxation and auctioned permits; it is not possible to find a strict hierarchy; V depends both on n_1 and tax rate or permits price.

Finally, a last word on the number of adopting firm. Being the optimal number of adopting firm less than one (0.61 in our simulation) one can wonder how central authority can effectively implement this number in the economy. The same question arose in Gaeta [1], and it can be managed in same way, *i.e.* adopting a "multistage game with observed actions in a perfect information context" [10]. Nevertheless, this case can easily be managed by a command a control policy, where central authority commits both on the number of adopting firms (*e.g.* throughout permissions) and on the amount of oil usage. Results confirm that such a policy is successfully when R & D is endogenous.

6. Conclusions and Further Refinements

This paper analyzes the strong interplay between investment in R & D and firm behaviour in reducing oil usage. We show that market instruments are not able to mimic central authority. This is basically induced by the endogeneity of the R & D process. The result is similar to Denicolo, although under different assumptions. However, unlike this author, it is not possible to rank instruments on a Pareto ladder. There is a strong non-linearity in the behavioral equation and this reduces the relevant domain of existence. In general it is not possible to establish which instrument performs better. However it is true that higher taxation induces more investment in R & D, as in Parry and Denicolo.

This paper must be considered a first approach to the problem; however several refinements are possible. First of all, numerical simulations should call for some calibration to "stylized fact". Unfortunately is very hard to find microdata on such phenomena; despite our efforts to get in touch with international agency we were not able to fill the gap. Second, we should analyze the case where central authority chooses the optimal amount of R & D, instead of leaving such decision to an external firm. This would be very close to Parry 1998.

7. References

[1] T. Requate, "Dynamic Incentives by Environmental Policy Instruments—A Survey," *Ecological Economics*, Vol. 54, No. 2, 2005, pp. 175-195.

[2] E. G. Gaeta, "Environmental Policy and Firm Investment Behavior When Energy Saving Technologies are Available," Mimeo, 2008.

[3] G. Barlevy, "On the Cyclicality of Research and Development," Working paper, Federal Reserve Bank of Chicago, 2006.

[4] Y. Tsur and A. Zemel, "Scarcity, Growth and R & D," *Journal of Environmental Economics and Management*, Vol. 49, No. 3, 2005, pp. 484-499.

[5] V. Denicolo, "Pollution-Reducing Innovations under Taxes or Permits," *Oxford Economic Papers*, Vol. 51, No. 1, 1999, pp. 184-199.

[6] C. Fisher, I. Parry and W. Pizer, "Instrument Choice for Environmental Protection When Technological Innovation is Endogenous," *Journal of Environmental Economics and Management*, Vol. 45, No. 3, 2003, pp. 523-545.

[7] I. W. H. Parry, W. A. Pizer and C. Fischer, "How Large are the Welfare Gains from Technological Innovation Induced by Environmental Policies?" *Journal of Regulatory Economics*, Vol. 23, No. 3, 2003, pp. 237-255.

[8] I. Parry, "Optimal Pollution Taxes and Endogenous Technological Progress," *Resource and Energy Economics*, Vol. 17, No. 1, 1995, pp. 69-85.

[9] I. Parry, "Pollution Regulation and the Efficiency Gains from Technological Innovation," *Journal of Regulatory Economics*, Vol. 14, No. 3, 1998, pp. 229-254.

[10] D. Fudenberg and J. Tirole, "Game Theory," MIT Press, 7th Edition, 2000.

Petrochemical Industry: Assessment and Planning Using Multicriteria Decision Aid Methods

Carlos E. Escobar Toledo[1], Claudia Garcia Aranda[1], Bertrand Mareschal[2]
[1]*Faculty of Chemistry, National University of Mexico, Mexico City, Mexico*
[2]*Solvay School of Business Administration, Université Libre de Bruxelles, Brussels, Belgium*

Abstract

A methodology to solve a large and complex problem is proposed. OR methods as Multilevel Planning, Network Techniques, Multicriteria Decision Aid (MCDA) and Mixed Integer Linear Programming (MILP) were used to structure the methodology. One of the principal objectives of this work is reduce the complexity of a large problem and solve it to find the better solution for the decision makers. The methodology is applied to a petrochemical industry of Mexico, which is structured in a network, having different alternative routes of production; each of them having also a different technology. This network begins from the crude oil as raw material in order to produce the basic petrochemicals until finals ones. It has been considered that basic petrochemicals will be produced through a set of Refineries with a high production of basic petrochemicals yield, searching the best configuration among it, according with the needs of basic petrochemicals coming from the final's and its best route selected.

Keywords: Multiple Criteria Analysis, Multilevel Planning, Network Flows, Linear and Integer Programming, Petrochemical Industry Assessment

1. Main Objectives and Goals: Description of the Work

The targets to be reached in this work are:

a) To reduce the complexity of a large system using a model of coordination in a framework of decentralized multilevel planning with a lot of interrelated subsystems.

b) To structure a methodology with different operational research (OR) tools, as Network Techniques, MCDA (PROMETHEE II and V methods) and MILP, according with the problem stated.

c) To apply the methodology to the Mexican petrochemical industry as a case study, with a horizon planning starting in 2003 until 2025 and taking into account the demand of each final petrochemical as an exogenous variable.

As particular objectives:

d) Considering that the model must start with the crude oil as raw material and end with the final petrochemicals, the methodology will be able to choose the best technology process alternative from a set of them to produce final petrochemicals.

e) Another part of the model will be developed in order to show the final petrochemicals production from crude oil, is at least equally competitive than the exportation of it. The value of the Mexican crude oil exportation will be the reference of comparison.

f) The feasibility to produce petrochemicals with more added value than exporting only crude oil will be showed.

2. Mathematical Tools to be Utilized in the Methodology

2.1. Coordination Models

A lot of work have been done in this field; see references as [1-3,5,14,15,17,18,22, 24-26,36,38].

2.2. Network Approach

Chavez has used PASCAL to build a graphical linked data structure, with the nodes representing the chemicals and processes [13], and arcs indicating the relations between them. Then, through recursive programming, the procedure could traverse the graph both up-and downstream to observe the affects of any perturbations. In this manner it is possible to examine the process individually, within the context of the industry, rather than observing all of the process as a single unit. This removes the tendency (found in LP formulations) to operate one section of the industry sub optimally in order to improve some industry-wide objective function. For the Mexican Petrochemical Industry, Escobar and Rodriguez have used the same approach, focusing it to increment the added value along the chain of production [16].

The "traversing the arcs" algorithm can be expressed mathematically as the Generalized Network Problem (GNP) [37]:

From GNP, we will only use the following constraints:

Let x_{ij} = the amount of flow over arc (i, j) during the planning horizon.

Then a generalized network model is:

$$\sum_{j=1}^{p} x_{kj} - \sum_{i=1}^{p} x_{ik} = T_k \quad for \ each \ int \ ermediary \ node \ "k"$$

(1)

where: T_k is the flow value at each node k.

We will consider as S_i the production capacity of a petrochemical plants i, $(i = 1,2,...m)$ and there are n different final products whose annual demand is known as D_j for each product j $(j = 1,2,...n)$. For different petrochemical plants and a_{ij} indicates the corresponding relative production efficiencies (input/output), i.e. the real stoichiometric coefficients of chemical reactions described in the network.

Then we have the following additional constraints:

$$\sum_{j=1}^{n} x_{ij} \leq S_i \quad for \ i = 1,2,...,m$$

(2)

and,

$$\sum_{i=1}^{m} a_{ij} x_{ij} \geq D_j \quad for \ j = 1,2,...,n$$

(3)

$$x_{ij} > 0 \quad for \ all \ i \ and \ j$$

(4)

Constraint (3) is the driven force for this network, because it induces the production of any product in the network trough the exogenous demand.

2.3. MCDA Methods

We don't discuss here the importance of Multicriteria Methods; a lot of bibliography is available to the interested lector. See: [6,7,9-13,27, 29-32,36] among others.

One of the more important methods of this kind is the PROMETHEE family. [6,8]

The PROMETHEE II complete ranking is based on net flow $\phi(a)$ that is computed from the pair wise compari-

son.

PROMETHEE V will be used to determine the production of the refinery, and to choice the better configuration.

The followed steps will be used to apply PROMETHEE V:

Step 1: The multicriteria problem is considered first, without constraints. In our case, we have utilized PROMETHEE II results; the rankings are obtained and the net flows for the best technological routes for each final petrochemical have been computed as also the subset of the best final petrochemicals, using the same criteria to choose the technological routes.

Step 2: The following mixed integer linear program could be considered in order to take into account additional constraints.

$$Max \sum_{i=1}^{k} \phi(a_i) x_i$$

$$s.t.: \sum \lambda_{p,i} x_i \ \{=,\geq,\leq\} \ \beta_p \qquad p = 1,2,...,P$$

$$x_i \in (0,1); \qquad i = 1,...,n$$

(5)

where $\lambda_{p,i}$ and β_p are coefficients and right hand sides associated to the constraints.

The coefficients of the objective function are the net outranking flows.

3. A Technology Evaluation Model

The model is supported by Ackoff's interactive planning theory [39,40] and by Rudd and Watson [33] with the multilevel attack on very large problems.

Nevertheless, the evaluation model is completed using MCDA, network and mixed integer linear (MILP) techniques, in order to choose the better alternatives of a large and complex problem. The case study is a complex problem considering different combinations in order to produce a final product.

This model serves as a focus for bringing together the results of the formulation of the mess and ends planning with technology choice as it relates to various activities along of the whole industry's added value chains. [19,23]

Figure 1 show a simple example of a complex problem, which is characterized by two levels (upper and lower) of coordination. In the lower level are the different subsystems linked with both, another subsystem and with the upper level, who is the coordinator. It is clear that should have a flow of data among some coordination variables in order to make the better decisions to solve the problem jointly. It looks like simple but it does not.

It is important define that each:
·   local decision unit represent a set of processes to

produce a final product from a set of raw materials,

· process is structured for a sequence of intermediate process or chains of production or process' routes,

· chain of production is a technology to be assessed.

Also,

· The raw material for each process unit is transformed to intermediate product; which is the new raw material for next process and;

· Each final product has been selected by a marketing study being its demand an exogenous var-

iable of the problem.

In consequence, the complexity of the problem is increased. Nevertheless, using a mixed methodology, the problem can be solved. This methodology is divided in three large steps, taking them as iterations. See **Figure 2**.

The first and the second iteration represent the upper and lower level of coordination showed in **Figure 1**; in **Figure 2** are represented by steps 1 to 6. Once the results are obtained from the first and second iteration, step 7 is performed and step 8 (MILP model) is developed. The results are then sent to the central unit in order to make the better decision.

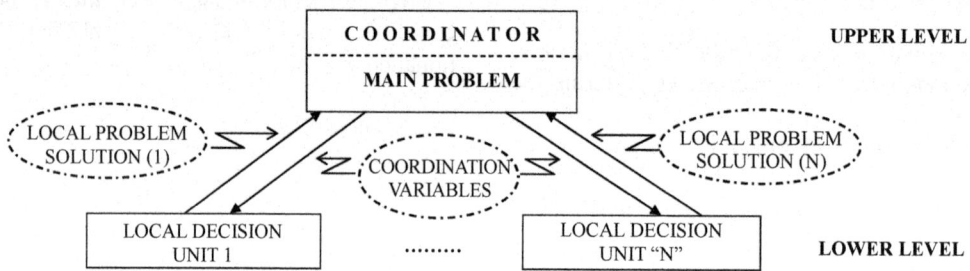

Figure 1. A two level attack structure.

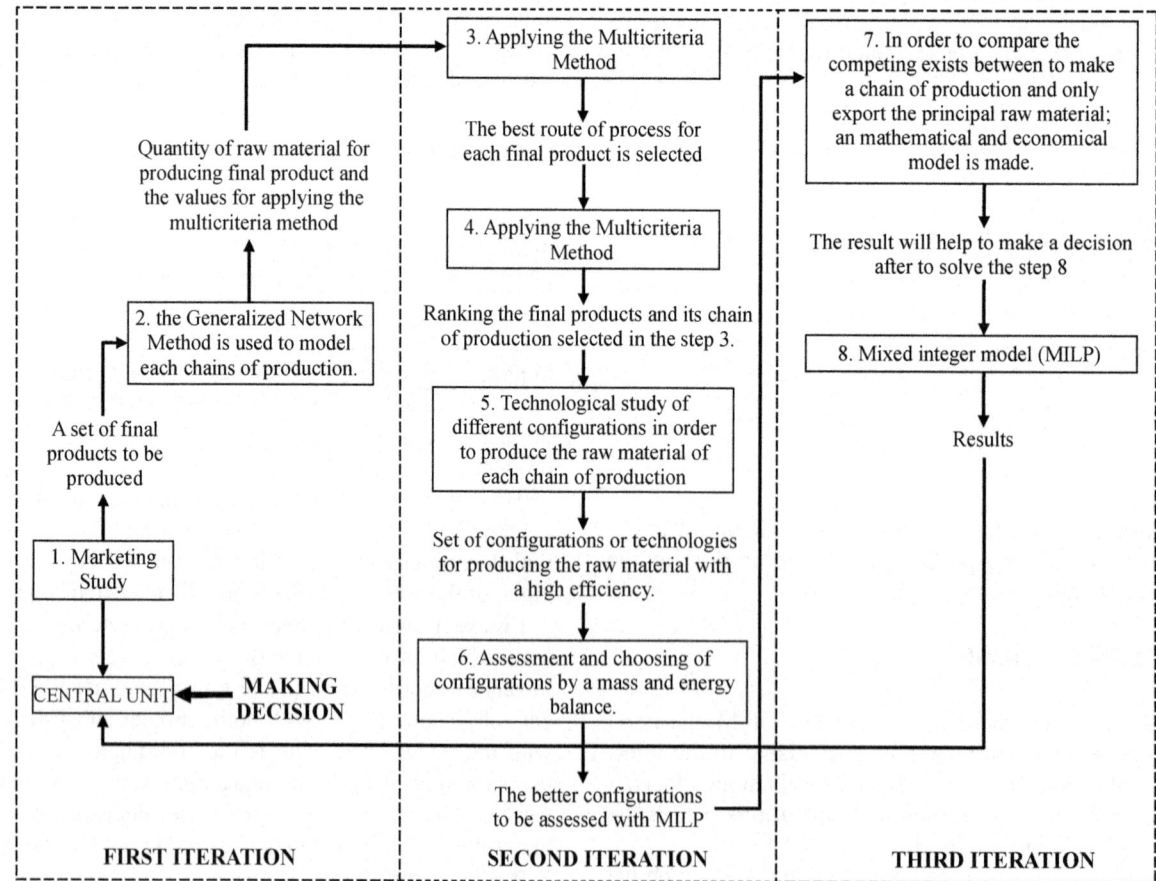

Figure 2. Generalized methodology proposed.

4. Case Study: Introduction to the Petrochemical Industry

The hierarchical multilevel model planning, to be developed in this paper, to be well understood, requires a brief presentation of the Petrochemical Industry. This important Industry is a huge of network of processes and products.

The petrochemical industry system is a large, complex, and constantly changing industry. There are more than 8000 different compounds in commercial production derived from petroleum and natural gas. It is capital and energy intensive. It has also structured in an oligopoly. The petrochemical products multiply their value along the chain of production until their final destination. For example: p-xylene increments 170 times in a shirt, PVC increments 40 times in a tennis ball and the acrylonytrile increments 150 times in a sweater.

The Petrochemical Industry is based upon the production of chemicals from petroleum and natural gas. This industry also deals with chemicals manufactured from the by-products of petroleum refining. Also included, are chemicals produced from natural gas liquids.

Those raw feed stocks, petroleum and natural gas, are found at the beginning of the production chain. From these feed stocks it can be produced a relatively small number of important building blocks. These building blocks include the lower olefins and aromatics: ethylene, propylene, butylenes, butadiene, benzene, toluene and xylenes.

These building blocks are then converted into a complex array of thousands of intermediate and final chemicals, considering of course, their technology processes. The final products of the petrochemical industry are generally not consumed directly, but are used by other industries to manufacture consumer goods. Such versatility, adaptability and dynamic nature are three of the important features of the modern petrochemical industry.

The structure of the petrochemical industry is extremely complex. It is severely cross-linked, with the products of one process being the feedstock of many others. For most chemicals, the production route from feed stocks to final products is not unique, it includes many possible alternatives. As complicated, as it may seen, this structure is however comprehensible, at least in a general form [4,34]. In fact, there is a multitude of production routes available for most chemicals which are produced by more than one technology. The classification and description of petrochemical end products is not an easy task, because petrochemicals find their way into such a broad diversity of products and frequently a particular product will fall into more than one category. However, it is generally agreed that the main end products are in the form of polymers and copolymers: as plastics, but also elastomers, fertilizers and fibbers. Other products are solvents, detergents, paints, coatings, pigments, dyes, cosmetics, pharmaceutical forms, and food uses.

When the oil crises and embargoes came, the environment in which the international petrochemical industry operates suddenly changed. No longer were feedstock supplies and costs steady and predictable, nor was energy consumption a minor consideration.

In 90's decade, the three critical factors in the changing international industry face were: severe cycles in profits, globalization and continuing and substantial industry learning curve effects.

4.1. Mexico's Petrochemical Industry

Petrochemical industry was one of the largest Mexico's industries. Up 35% of Mexican industries required petrochemicals in their operations at the moment of this industry was at its best level of production (1950-1990).

The Mexican politician decision makers, have took the decision to sell the entire infrastructure and go, briefly speaking, to sell more crude oil abroad the country, considering that it could be an interesting business. Mexico lost in that moment the opportunity to increase the added value along the production chain of crude oil exported. In all these decisions the country lost the possibility of real industrialization, producing more petrochemicals for the internal market and to then develop the manufacturing industry still more.

Then, the three critical factors described above and the industrial flexibility has not taken into account in Mexico's Petrochemical Industry planning and consequently, it lost both; the dynamic growth and the possibility to add value to their products.

5. Applying the Methodology to the Case Study

In this section we propose a model to assess technologies within a set of petrochemicals chains as case study, in order to promote the industrial development and then their added value.

The system can be viewed in its general form in the **Figure 3**.

From left to right, in the "*t*" period of planning horizon, the **Figure 3** shows the sequence of the problem; it starts with the crude oil availability as raw material of a refinery to produce basic petrochemicals using a ad-hoc technological configuration and then, use those basic petrochemicals to produce intermediate and finals depending of the exogenous demand of the later.

From right to left, in the same figure, the situation becomes more complex, *i.e.*, with the exogenous demand coming from the manufacturing industry, the production

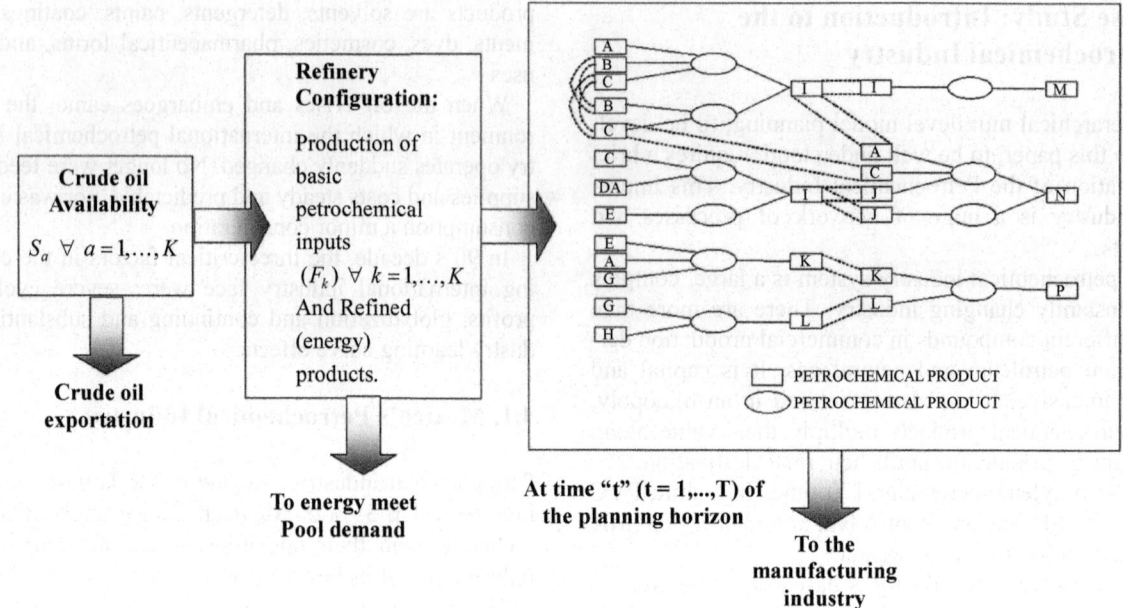

Figure 3. Intermediate and final petrochemical industry.

of final petrochemicals should be defined using network analysis; select the best routes of production considering different criteria (MCDA) and then choose the final demanded products using the same criteria. The productions of intermediate and basic petrochemicals are then induced depending on the route chosen. A mixed-integer linear programming model is built in order to choose the best refinery configuration and to define the production of the basic petrochemicals and the size of the chosen refinery configuration.

Then, the exogenous demand-coming by the manufacturing industry-defines which the final petrochemicals candidates for production are. The network analysis induce de intermediate and basic petrochemicals, generating alternatives, meanwhile MCDA is used to select the best routes of production for final petrochemicals, defining the intermediate's and basic's. Also, MCDA is used to select the final petrochemicals to be produced and the integer linear programming to schedule and size the better refinery configuration, among a subset of technological configurations available. In order to know if the best solution is obtained, it is utilized a multilevel planning decentralization procedure to be sure that the solution converges.

This methodology will be discussed in subsection 5.3.

Therefore, the following data are needed to develop the methodology:

1) Value of every petrochemical product (VP) (total costs-excluding the cost of intermediate and final products-plus i% Return on Investment); i = rate of return.

2) Value of every petrochemical product (VP) (total costs-excluding the cost of intermediate and final products-plus i% Return on Investment); i = rate of return.

3) Total costs of production and investments for all the petrochemical processes.

In the case of investments, a source of economic and technical data, were 3 different production capacities for each one of all products/technologies in the network, considering the Process Economic Program information published by Stanford Research Institute. Then, we have needed a function to find a correlation between those 3 capacities, considering economies of scale, in order to interpolate o extrapolate other capacity:

$$\log(Inv) = \log(\alpha) + \beta \log(Cap)$$
$$Inv = \alpha * Cap^{\beta}, \quad 0 \le \beta \le 1 \tag{6}$$

Where: α and β are constants to be calculated by a regression; Inv = Investment and Cap = Production capacity.

4) To calculate the added value into the whole petrochemical system. This amount is: (VP) variable costs, for each petrochemical product.

5) To search a set of technological configurations for a Refinery with interesting basic petrochemicals yields. This search was one of the most important contributions in the chemical engineering field [20].

6) To search indexes of damage to the environment and to human health in every chemical produced along the petrochemical chains.

It is important to leave clear, that it was searched the best Refinery's configurations among a lot of possibilities. At that point, we have dressed a technology intelligence system in order to have sufficient alternatives about those configurations. We have got a reduced number of refinery configurations and then, we design them.

To have confidence of those configurations, a process simulation program was used to be sure that all of them will operate with the necessary yields, obtaining the basic petrochemicals needed. With those designs, the investment and operating costs were calculated.

5.1. Network Model Representation of the Petrochemical Industry

The network structure processes and products linked by "chains of production" in a production route are shown in **Figure 4**. As it can be seen, there are five important elements on this network. The first, on the left hand side are a few "basic" products (coming from a petroleum refinery production). On the contrary, there is a huge quantity of "intermediate products" in the network being these products one hundred times more than the basic products. The final of the network there also are a few "final products". Second, the intermediate products can be shared to produce the final products, beginning always with any one or more of basics. Third, in order to traverse the arcs, one should know (exogenously) which final products are needed to be produced. Fourth, it exits always at least one associated process of production for a product. Fifth, it is necessary to choose the technological route to take, in order to know the inputs of the final products, needed to be produce.

The algorithm constructed utilizes the Equations (1) to

(4) and was constructed by Sevilla [35]. Then for "traversing the arcs" of the network composed by final products with an exogenous demand, intermediate and basic products, we "induced" the demand required meeting the final's products. Once the arcs are traversed and the demands of intermediate and basic products are calculated, we will utilize a multicriteria method in order to focus on the best route of production and reduce the dimension of the complexity due to the combinatorial problem.

5.2. Multicriteria Decision Analysis (MCDA)

To evaluate the best petrochemical chain for a given final petrochemical, we have utilized multicriteria decision analysis.

The criteria used are:

1) Maximization of the added value along the petrochemical chains (routes) in order to produce the final petrochemical "p_i";

2) Minimization of investments required trough the petrochemical chains to produce the final petrochemical product "p_i";

3) Minimization of the real quantity of energy needed by different process/products along the petrochemical chains to produce the final petrochemical "p_i";

4) Minimization of the risk of damage the environment by any of the products along the petrochemical chains for producing the final product "p_i".

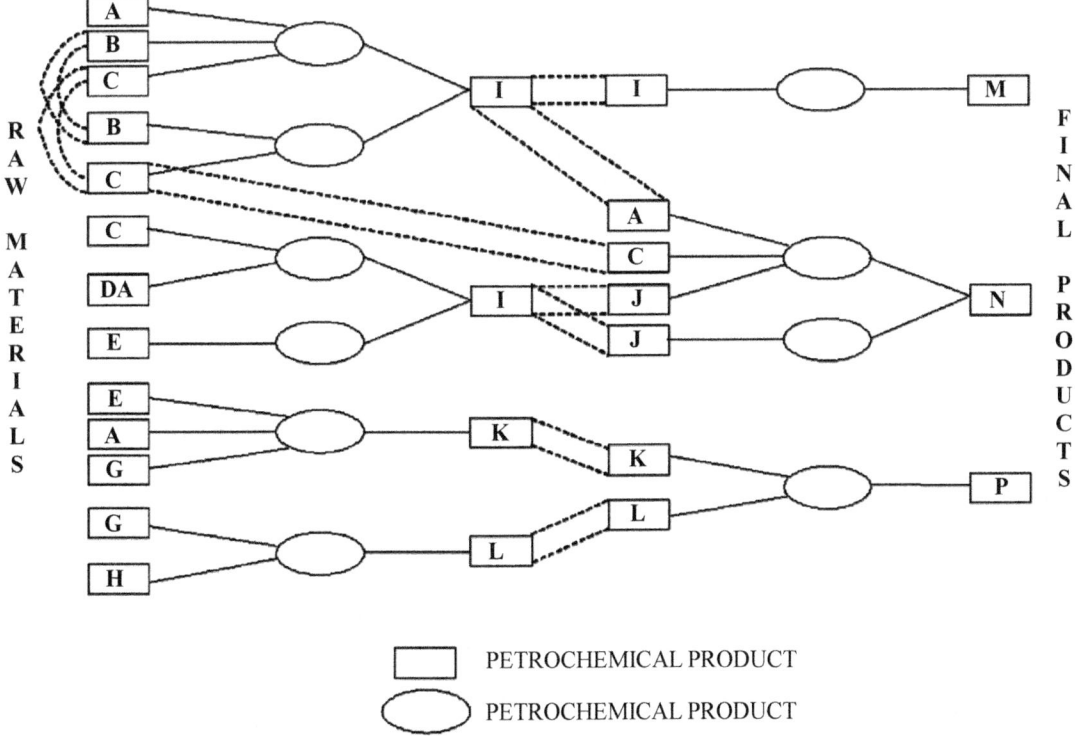

◻ PETROCHEMICAL PRODUCT

⬭ PETROCHEMICAL PRODUCT

Figure 4. Graphical representation of petrochemical processes and products.

5.3. Multilevel Planning

The three steps to coordinate the decision making will be:

Consider a hierarchy of three levels, the first level, represents the Central Unit that receives information from "the market". The market demands of some final petrochemicals, a time "t" ($t = 1,...,T$). This information came from econometric and prospective models, exogenously performed. The information (the calculated demand for one "t" of the horizon planning), is transmitted the "Central Unit", which is a strategic planning centre. This Central Unit also coordinates the levels below it. See **Figure 5**.

The Central Unit (CU) will then transmit the information to the next two lower levels, named "The Refinery" and the "Final and intermediate petrochemicals' Producers". At the same time the CU, is transmitting the information to decentralize the decisions. At the second level, the Refinery knows the conditions under which it can use crude oil to produce petrochemicals. This is considered as the first iteration.

Of course all the levels have the information about the "induced" demands of intermediate and basic petrochemicals.

The coordination variables under the control of the CU are the market demands of final petrochemicals and the four criteria to choose the best technological chains utilizing multicriteria decision making.

In the second iteration of the lower levels decentralization procedure, the final petrochemical producers will select the best chain of production taking into account a multicriteria analysis. This information is returned to the CU. On the other hand these petrochemicals producers will induce the demand of basic petrochemicals. The information is communicated to the Refinery with the product values. The Refinery will inform to the CU how are the values of those petrochemicals that will be equivalent to a certain price of the crude oil. The CU will inform to the market if it is possible to produce all the products (production = demand) or not: production is lower than demand.

If the final demand is not satisfied, the CU can take the decision of import the necessary quantity to meet the final demand. But the CU, ask the producers to take a multicriteria decision making with the same criteria, but now in order to know which final products can be really considered, ordered in a hierarchy, ranking process. With this information, it will be possible to know which products are outranked to others. This valuable information serves to solve a linear programming problem to know the refinery's assignment and scheduling solution. So, the Refinery will search their own best technological configurations with high yields of basic petrochemicals, and the petrochemical's producers will rank the final products for each one of the final products demanded.

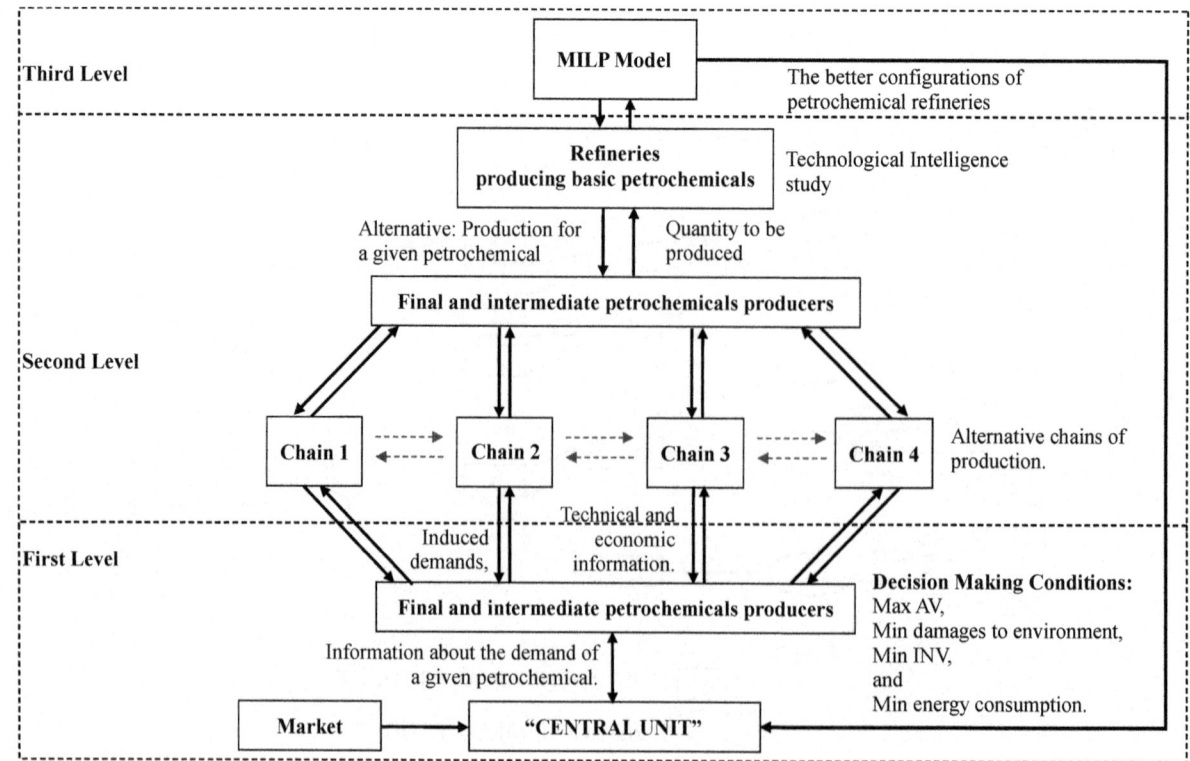

Figure 5. Graphical representation of the problem.

This information is taken for the Refinery decision makers to select finally the basic petrochemicals to be produced taking into consideration the quantity of crude oil allowed and the technical configurations. This is the third and last iteration if the solutions converge in a feasible technical solution.

The CU gives the order to the Refinery to solve jointly with the petrochemical's producers, a MILP model, using as general idea the procedure of PROMETHEE V. This model is explained in the next section.

Finally, this information is taken for the Refinery decision makers to select the basic petrochemicals to be produced taking into consideration the whole added value of the chains of production and also its own. The iterative process has finished.

5.4. The MILP Model and the Equivalence of Crude Oil

Considering the choice of the best technological routes for every final petrochemical product in the network, was solved utilizing PROMETHEE II (complete ranking), we are going to purpose a new approach considering as a framework the procedure of PROMETHEE V, in order to solve the refinery's problem. The refinery's problem consists in choosing a mix of the best technological configurations of refineries, and then obtaining the schedule of production of basic petrochemicals to meet the demand of finals, through the routes ranked, using multicriteria techniques as it was pointed out in previous sections. To do it, the objective function, will use the values of the net flows obtained by PROMETHEE II in the case of ranked final petrochemicals.

We will define the constraints needed in our case to treat the Refinery's problem: The total crude to be processed to obtain petrochemicals for all periods of the Horizon Period (HP) will be an allowed quantity of crude oil in "t" period.

For other periods of HP, it is possible to increment the capacity of processing crude oil until a maximum of a fixed quantity.

The Planning Horizon will be taken by periods of 3 years each one until we reach the last year of the HP ($t = 1..., T$).

We will call [$REUTCRU_{k,t}$] the set of constraints that:

$$PQCRU_{k,t} \leq \left(\#_t\right) \qquad \forall \ k; \ \forall t \tag{7}$$

where # is the quantity of crude oil assigned by the Central Unit for each technology; and $PQCRU_{k,t}$ is the quantity of crude oil allowed to the basic petrochemical production and being "k", the possible refinery's configuration.

Because we should choose the better production program among six refinery configurations, we will use in-

teger variables in order the model can decide which configurations are best than others and also to know how many refineries will be needed of each configuration, replacing Equation (7) as follows:

$$[REUTCRU_{k,\ t}]: \ XPQCRU_{k,\ t}\text{-}\#*K_k = 0; \tag{7a}$$

where: K_k is an integer.

The total balance [TOTAL] for all refineries can be chosen is, then:

$$\sum_{k=1}^{k} XPQCRU_{k,t} \leq \text{Total crude oil available, in each period "}t\text{"} \tag{7b}$$

The refinery's LP problem is then transformed to a Mixed Integer Linear Programming (MILP).

The production of basic petrochemicals [$PRBPQ_{i,t}$] for configuration k is as follows:

For all "t"; $t = 1,...,T$

$$Ethylene: \sum_{k=1}^{K} ce_{k,t} PQCRU_{k,t} - PRETL_t = 0$$

$$Pr\,opylene: \sum_{k=1}^{K} cp_{k,t} PQCRU_{k,t} - PRPRL_t = 0$$

$$Mixed\ Butadiene: \sum_{k=1}^{K} cm_{k,t} PQCRU_{k,t} - PRBUT_t = 0$$

$$Benzene: \sum_{k=1}^{K} cb_{k,t} PQCRU_{k,t} - PRBEN_t = 0 \tag{8}$$

$$Toluene: \sum_{k=1}^{K} ct_{k,t} PQCRU_{k,t} - PRTOL_t = 0$$

$$Xylenes: \sum_{k=1}^{K} cx_{k,t} PQCRU_{k,t} - PRXIL_t = 0$$

$$Gasoline: \sum_{k=1}^{K} cg_{k,t} PQCRU_{k,t} - PRGASOL_t = 0$$

$$Fuel: \sum_{k=1}^{K} cc_{k,t} PQCRU_{k,t} - PRCOMB_t = 0$$

Being $PRBPQ_{i,t} = \{PRETL, PRPRL, PRBUT, PRBEN, PRTOL, PRXIL, PRGASOL, PRCOMB\}$.

The coefficients

$$cip_{q,k,t} = \left\{ce_{k,t},\ cp_{k,t},\ cb_{k,t},\ ct_{k,t},\ cox_{k,t},\ cpx_{k,t}, cg_{k,t},\ cg_{k,t},\ cc_{k,t}\right\}$$

are the yields in weight % of each product (ethylene, propylene, mixed butadiene, benzene, and toluene, xylenes, gasoline and fuel). These yields could be different for each "k" configuration in the period "t" of the PH.

$$\alpha_{i,l*\in L,t} = \frac{Ton\ of\ basic\ petrochemical}{Ton\ of\ final\ petrochemical\ (l* \in L)}$$

$$and: \quad PRFPQ_{i,l*\in L} = all\ final\ petrochemical. \tag{9}$$

$$\therefore \qquad \alpha_{i,l*\in L} PRFPQ_{i,l*\in L} - PRBPQ_{i,t} = 0$$

where $PRFPQ_{i,l^* \in L}$ denotes the final petrochemicals production resulting from MCDA selection and describes all better technological chain which has outranked all others, and $l^* \in L$ for all final products and for all "t" ($t = 1, ..., T$).

On the other hand for each period "t", the demand constraints [$DEMANDFPQ$] for all final petrochemical, are:

$$PRFPQ_{i,l^* \in L,t} \leq Demand_{i,l^* \in L,t} \qquad \forall\, i \in l^* \in L, t \qquad (10)$$

where $Demand_{i,l^* \in L,t}$ was calculated by an econometric model and a prospective approach.

Additionally, we have modelled another constraint to take into account that the offer of the Refineries is not necessarily equal to the final petrochemicals demand. This constraint is called [$PROFIT$]. We can write:

$$\sum_k \sum_i pqb_{i,k} * cip_{i,k} * PQCRU_{k,t} -$$
$$\sum_k \sum_i pqb_{i,k} * \alpha_{i,l^* \in L,k} * PRFPQ_{i,l^* \in L,k,t} - \qquad (11)$$
$$\sum_k \cos top_k * PQCRU_{k,t} - SPROFIT = 0 \qquad \forall\, "t"$$

where: $pqb_{i,k}$ is the market price of the basic petrochemicals "i" from "k" configuration, $\cos top_k$ is the operation cost of the "k" configuration and $SPROFIT$ is the refineries' margin profit.

Of course all variables are greater or equal to zero.
The objective function is then:

$$Max \sum_{i \in L} \phi_{i,l^* \in L,t} \left(PRFPQ_{i,l^* \in L,t} \right) \qquad \forall\, t \qquad (12)$$

Being $\phi_{i,l^* \in L,t}$ the net outranking flows came from PROMETHEE II, for each final petrochemical ($PRFPQ_{i,l^* \in L,t}$) at period "t".

5.5. Crude Oil Equivalence Value of One Ton of Versus the Final Petrochemical's Product Value

The problem here is to answer the following question: which is the marginal rate of substitution of petrochemicals for crude oil exportation. In others words it should be answer the following question: Which is the equilibrium price that equals the crude oil price with the product value of basic petrochemicals?

To answer to this question, we present a procedure below.

$$VP_i = d_j + 0.25\, I_{0,j} \qquad (13)$$

$$d_j = d_1 + d_c \qquad (14)$$

$$d_c = p_c q_c \qquad (15)$$

$$VP_i = d_1 + p_c q_c + 0.25 I_{0,j} \qquad (16)$$

All terms in Equation (16) are annualized (F), where F is $\sum_{t=1}^{n} \dfrac{1}{(1+i)^n} = \left[\dfrac{(1+i)^n - 1}{i(1+i)^n} \right] = F$.

Being "i" the rate of return.

$$VP_i * F = d_1 * F + p_c \left(q_c * n \right) + 0.25\frac{I_{0,j}}{F} \qquad (17)$$

Then p_c is:

$$p_c = \frac{VP_i * F - d_1 * F - 0.25\dfrac{I_{0,j}}{F}}{q_c * n} \qquad (18)$$

where:

VP_i = Product value of petrochemical "I" through the chain of production (US$)

$I_{0,j}$ = Annualized investment of the "j" ($j=1, ..., 6$) Refinery configuration (US$)

d_1 = Total costs of production but not considering the crude oil (US$)

d_c = Cost of the crude oil (raw material) (US$)

p_c = Crude oil market price (US$/Ton)

q_c = Demanded quantity of crude oil being utilized by the Refinery (Ton)

$0.25_{0,j}$ = 25%, is the rate of return on investment (ROI)

n = Number of years in the horizon planning (HP).

6. Results Obtained

In order to have a reference framework to present the results obtained in this work, we will present in **Figure 6** a generalized flow sheet of the proposed methodology and then, following with that description, the results have been obtained.

6.1. Flow Sheet of the Proposed Methodology

Figure 6 shows the flow sheet of the proposed methodology for the case study. This figure has been taken from the Section 3 and adapted for the purpose of the case study.

6.2. The Case Study

We will use a case study a part of Mexico's Petrochemical Industry. For doing that, we need to define the final petrochemicals for planning their better way of production, taking into account the several technological routes.

The CU receives information about the market requirements in form of demands considering $t = 1$ as 2009, the first year of the HP $t = T$, the end of the HP as 2025. **Table 1**, gives an overview of the market needs.

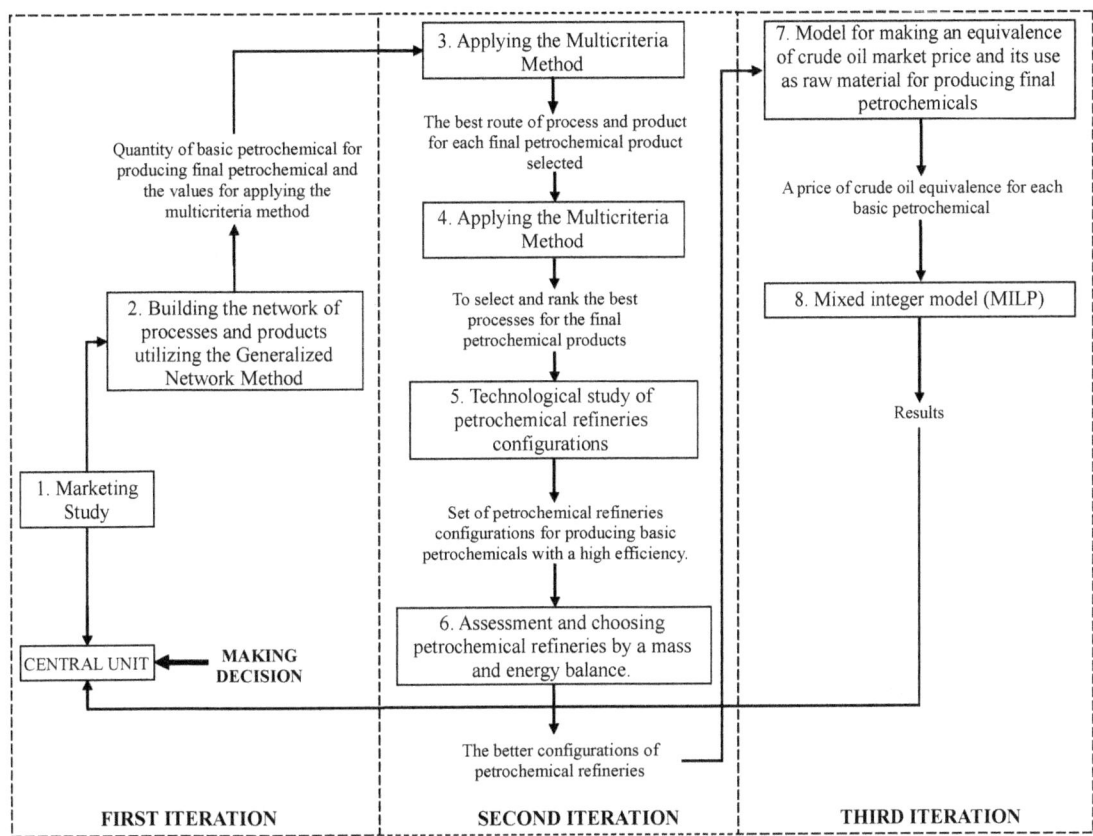

Figure 6. Applying the methodology to the case study.

Table 1. Demand overview for some final petrochemicals.

YEAR	2009	2025
PRODUCT **(10^3 Ton/year)**		
Polystyrene (normal and expanded)	545	2,800
Polyurethane	220	556
Polyester fibbers	366	2,283
Polyethylene Terephthalate resins and films (PET)	1,704	2,972
High density Polyethylene (HDPE)	1,040	3,900
Low density Polyethylene (LDPE)	1,061	2,600
Linear low density Polyethylene (LLDE)	305	728
Polypropylene	1,158	407
Styrene/Butadiene Rubber (SBR)	279	430
Styrene Latex	15	31
Acrylonytrile/Butadiene/styrene (ABS) and Styrene Acrylonytrile (SAN) resins	529	887
Phtalic Anhydride	86	105
Polybutilen Terephthalate (PBT)	220	349

With this information, the CU sends it to the petrochemical producers and also to Refinery decision makers. The petrochemical's producers (intermediate and final), will build their alternative chains of production.

They proceed to make the selection of the best technological routes (chains) using multicriteria decision analysis with PROMETHEE II, having as criteria:

1) Maximization of the added value along the petrochemical chains (routes) in order to produce the final petrochemical "p_i"(Weight: 4.8).

2) Minimization of investments required trough the petrochemical chains to produce the final petrochemical product "p_i"(Weight: 2.0).

3) Minimization of the real quantity of energy needed by different process/products along the petrochemical chains to produce the final petrochemical "p_i"(Weight: 1.7).

4) Minimization of the risk of damage the environment by any of the products along the petrochemical chains for producing the final product "p_i" (Weight: 1.5).

The results from PROMETHEE II are presented in the **Table 2**.

As an example of how PROMETHEE II is applied, in **Figure 7** is presented the case of polyester fibbers.

From this figure, whose results have been obtained from Decision-Lab software, it is possible to conclude that the best technological route for the polyester fibbers is the number 1, taking into account the four above mentioned criteria.

Considering this "best" technological routes to produce the final petrochemical, the second step is to make compete products considering the technological route chosen. We also utilized PROMETHEE II. With the same 4 criteria, same weights and same threshold function. **Table 3**, shows the data for this competition.

With these results the Petrochemical producers communicates to the CU which route is the best for each final product. The CU asks to the final producers to make a selection of the best final products, but considering the best technological route have been chosen previously. The results, coming from data in Tables 2 and 3, are presented in **Table 4**.

The CU makes an exploration taking into account the quantities of basic petrochemicals needed to be produced, consulting the Refinery's decision makers.

These last decision makers look for an appropriate configuration to produce those basic petrochemicals. The first outcome is considered that all the final and intermediate petrochemicals are derivatives from benzene, toluene, orthoxylene, and paraxylene and also from ethylene, propylene and butadiene. They will search the alternative refineries configurations. The results are as follows [21].

It was found 6 configurations having as characteristic that more petrochemicals yield they have more investment and operations costs are put into consideration. See **Table 5**.

For the whole solution of the problem, it is necessary now to solve the MILP model having as objective function the values of the net flows obtained for PROMETHEE II, when the final products have ranked.

The results obtained will tell the decision makers how much of the final petrochemicals could be produced and also whose refinery's configurations or a mixed of them could be possible to operate. On the other hand these results will compare the marginal value of use a ton of crude oil for producing petrochemicals instead of export it, when the marginal benefit is about 60 $/barrel.

At the end the Refinery communicates to the CU how much crude oil can be put in operation to produce the demanded petrochemicals and also communicates to the petrochemical producers how much basic petrochemicals could be produced.

Table 2. First step: competition among chains.

Final Petrochemical Product	Number of Alternative Chains
Phtalic Anhydride	2
Polyester Fibbers	9
Styrene/Butadiene Rubber	14
High Density Polyethylene(HDPE)	4
Low Density Polyethylene (LDPE)	2
Linear Low Density Polyethylene (LLDPE)	4
Polybutilen Terephthalate (PBT)	14
Polystyrene (normal and expanded)	14
Polypropylene (PP)	4
Polyurethane	8
Acrylonytrile/Butadiene/styrene (ABS) and Styrene Acrylonytrile (SAN) resins	14
Polyethylene Terephthalate Resins and Films (PET)	9

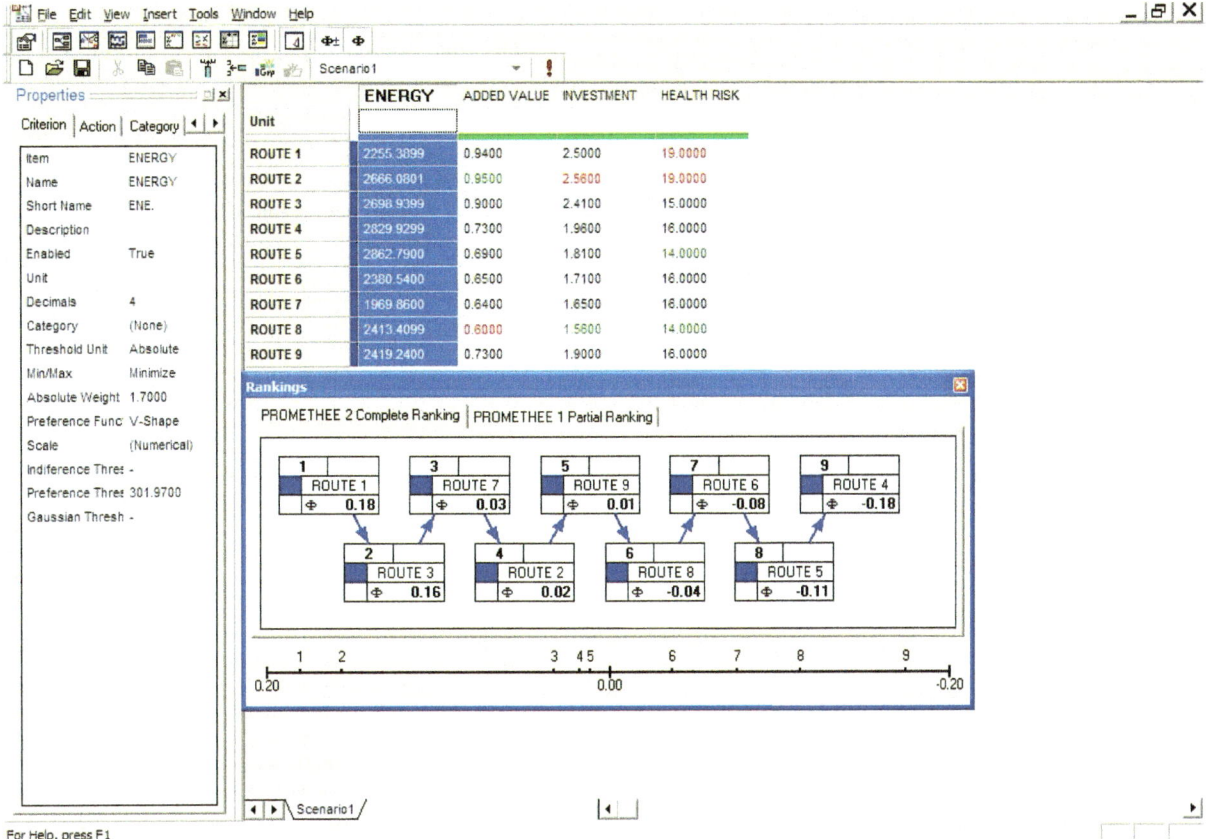

Figure 7. Choosing of process' route for polyester fibbers using PROMETHEE II.

Table 3. Data to select final petrochemical products.

Final selected petrochemical from technological chains	Min: Energy 10^6 kcal/kg	Max: Added Value 10^6 US\$/kg	Min: Investment 10^6 US\$/kg	Min: Environmental Damages Index
Phtalic Anhydride	167.214	0.243	0.700	10
ABS Resins	1081.006	0.385	0.908	22
High density Polyethylene	294.394	0.117	0.252	13
Low density Polyethylene	771.097	0.168	0.413	10
Linear low density Polyethylene.	213.598	0.156	0.311	13
PET resins	1932.450	0.579	1.740	18
PBT resins	2569.233	1.487	3.690	17
Polyester Fibbers	2255.389	0.938	2.501	19
Polyurethane	4774.572	1.802	3.862	50
Polypropylene	138.215	0.101	0.151	11
Styrene-Butadiene Rubber	2002.784	0.649	1.388	19
Polystyrene	2179.858	0.387	1.156	17

6.3. Refinery's LP Solution

The solution of LP model (set of Equations (7) to (11)), solved with the" LINGO" 10" SOFTWARE, is as follows:

1) The solution had a global optimal.

2) The solution considers the exploitation of 300,000 b/day of crude oil (15 millions ton/year), using the six technical refinery configurations at its upper limit of the availability.

3) The final and basic petrochemical products considered in the solution are as follows (see **Table 6**).

Table 4. Final petrochemicals in competition. Results.

Final Petrochemical	Values of ϕ for final petrochemicals in competition
Phtalic Anhydride	0.0974
Polyester Fibbers	0.0245
Styrene Butadiene Rubber	0.0075
High Density Polyethylene	0.0021
Low Density Polyethylene	0.0285
Linear Low Density Polyethylene	0.0285
Poly Butylen Terephthalate	0.1063
Polystyrene	−0.1568
Polypropylene	0.0463
Polyurethane	−0.037
Abs-San Resins	−0.0944
PET Resins	−0.0527

Table 5. Technical and economical data for Refinery's configurations.

Refinery Configuration Weight, %	1	2	3	4	5	6
Ethylene	8.7	16.1	18.3	18.9	22.5	26.0
Propylene	4.6	9.1	11.0	12.9	12.8	15.0
Butadiene	1.5	2.8	3.4	3.1	3.9	4.6
Aromatics	4.9	8.2	9.7	14.4	12.0	13.9
Total basic petrochemicals	19.7	36.2	42.4	49.3	51.2	59.5
Gasoline	2.3	3.9	4.7	8.4	5.6	6.4
Other products	69.8	47.6	38.3	22.6	25.5	12.6
Total Investment (10^6 US\$)	346.5	450.4	517.4	570.6	595.9	686.1
Process Cost (US\$/Ton of crude oil)	56.64	76.70	90.18	95.55	103.17	118.00
(US\$/bbl of crude oil)	7.76	10.50	12.35	13.09	14.13	16.19

Table 6. Production of final petrochemicals.

Final Petrochemical	Production Ton/year	Demand Ton/year	Unsatisfied demand Ton/year
Polyester Fibbers	192,855	366,000	173,145
Styrene-Butadiene Rubber	294,000	294,000	
High Density Polyethylene	1,040,000	1,040,000	
Low Density Polyethylene	1,061,000	1,061,000	
Linear Low Density Polyethylene	305,000	305,000	
Polybutilen Terephthalate	220,000	220,000	
Phtalic Anhydride	86,000	86,000	
Polypropylene	1,158,000	1,158,000	

4) The following data has been taken from the optimal solution; it concerns the basic petrochemicals to be produced to obtain the quantity of final petrochemicals and the quantities put on the free market to be sold (See **Table 7**).

The dual of the problem has some significance: The reduced costs as well as the dual prices express that no final products will be produced if the Φ's have a negative value; nevertheless an important set of dual variables, are then associated to the upper level of crude oil quantity allowed for each refinery configuration (see **Table 8**). For example the more important configuration are the forth. That configuration has a dual variable many times greater than the other five, as follows:

As an experiment to prove that configuration 4 is the better, we put 6 times a module of this configuration, *i.e.*

$PQCRU_4 \leq 2.5 \times 10^6$ Ton/year, 6 times. We have obtained better results: the objective function has increased from 0.1334227 to 0.1376648, because it has produced the total demand of the Polyester fibbers, from 192,855 Ton to 366,000 Ton. The rest of the solution was the same reported in **Table 6**. Other interesting results from the dual problem were that if some final products had positive values in the objective function (*i.e.* their flows had been able to be positives), the production of ABS resins, were incremented the value of objective function (reduced cost).

5) Other results about the properties of the solution are as follows:

In the **Table 9**, all the values correspond to the petrochemicals chains from basic to finals and do not include nor the Refinery's expenses as operations costs does

Table 7. Production of basic petrochemicals.

Basic Petrochemicals (Ton/year)	Production (Ton/year)	Used to produce petrochemical finals (Ton/year)	Send to external market (Ton/year)
Ethylene	2,797,000	2,556,070	241,930
Propylene	1,665,500	1.204,323	461,177
Benzene	612,100	59,432	552,668
Toluene	516,000	0	516,000
Xylenes (o and p)	342,000	342,000	0

Table 8. Shadow price comparison.

Refinery Configuration	Number of times that the shadow price of Configuration 4 is greater than:
1	6.50
2	3.61
3	2.95
5	2.50
6	2.17

Table 9. Product values, added values, investment and energy consumed (Millions).

Final Petrochemicals	Product value US $/year	Added value US $/Year	Investment $US	Energy kcal/year
Polyester Fibbers	428.02	180.97	428.30	434.96
Styrene-Butadiene Rubber	426.46	190.91	408.02	588.82
High Density Polyethylene	192.6	122.18	261.87	306.17
Low Density Polyethylene	266.28	178.21	438.72	818.13
Linear Low Density Polyethylene	76.80	47.51	94.96	65.15
Polybutilen Terephthalate	528.26	327.23	811.82	565.52
Polypropylene	404.66	117.39	174.91	160.05
Phtalic Anhydride	29.75	20.87	60.24	14.38
Total of final petrochemicals	2,352.83	1,185.27	2678.84	2953.18
Refinery's Investment			3164.0	
Total (Investment)			5,896.84	

Table 10. Equivalence of final petrochemicals to one barrel of crude oil (US $/bbl).

Refinery Configuration	1	2	3	4	5	6	TOTAL BY FINAL PRODUCT
Polyester Fibbers	26	39	44	47	53	58	267
Styrene Butadiene Rubber	51	86	99	100	120	133	589
High Density Polyethylene	5	6	6	6	6	6	35
Low Density Polyethylene	5	6	6	6	6	7	36
Linear Low Density Polyethylene	5	6	6	6	6	7	36
Polybutilen Terephthalate	6	7	7	10	7	8	45
Polypropylene	5	6	6	6	6	6	35
Phtalic Anhydride	5	5	5	6	6	6	33

neither the energy use.

The total investment, considering the Refinery's is about 5, 897 millions US $. With this last figure, it is possible to express and 1US $, gives an added value of 0.20 US $, much better than nothing if the only exportation of crude is take into account.

On the other hand, if it is added the sales income for the basic petrochemicals sold to the external market, the product value of 2,353 millions US $ is risen to 4,014 millions US $. This figure can be considered as an income and then, a benefit/cost relationship is about 70%. These figures do not take into account the gasoline, fuel oil and other products produced by the refineries, to be sold in the free market.

6) Equivalence of crude oil price for the petrochemicals produced: The marginal rate of substitution.

Considering that one of the objectives of this work, was to compare the equivalence of the petrochemical's chains with one barrel of crude oil to be exported at least at $ US 65 per barrel, in the following table (**Table 10**), it is dressed the values in terms of their crude oil equivalence. It is important to consider that these values are calculated for the whole chains, using the Equations (12) to (17).

The difference between the refinery's configurations is due both, to the complexity of them and also to the fact of more complex are the refinery more basic petrochemicals products can be obtained. One can also see that with these total values for the petrochemical chains of US$/bbl 1,076 can paid more than16.5 times the exportation price of the same barrel of crude oil, *i.e.* US $ 65/bbl.

7. Conclusions

1) We have successfully finished with a new characterized model to coordinate decision makers at different levels of a decentralized hierarchy, considering a mix of operational research tools as the generalized net work technique jointly with multicriteria decision aid methods and mixed integer linear programming.

2) We have reduced the complexity of the combinatory decision making to select more efficiently the final petrochemicals chains.

3) In the case study, we have shown the petrochemical products give more added value comparing those values with the only crude oil exportation. A multiplier of the investment of about 0.20 US$, has a great significance. On the other hand a relationship of 70% of benefice/cost is very attractive one.

4) We have found the dual of the MILP problem. From it, we have been able to select the better of technological configurations of the Refineries.

5) We have also been able to experiment with a "natural ranking" of the Refineries trough the shadow prices of the dual problem, whose value help us to improve the first 'optimal' solution found.

6) We can also show that the equivalence of the petrochemicals compared with only exportation of crude oil is well paid. It is important to mention then, that use crude oil as petrochemical raw material instead of export it is a good business and will serve to develop the industrialization of the country.

7) All the values coming from the whole methodology does not have the concept of real "optimal solutions" as a mathematical programming model has, but these solutions are the 'best' can be obtained considering the decision maker's preferences.

8. Acknowledgements

We want to acknowledge Mr. Sevilla, whose aid was very important in discussing a lot of parts of this work but overall, for the construction of the software "traversing the arcs".

9. References

[1] R. Armand, "La dècentralisation des décisions par les prix," *Metra*, Vol. 7, No. 3, 1968.

[2] K. J. Arrow and L. Hurwicz, "Decentralization and Com-

putation in Resource Allocation," *Mathematical Methods in the Social Sciences*, University of North Carolina Press, 1960, pp. 34-104.

[3] J. P. Aubin, "Multigames and Decentralization in Management," In: Cochrane, J. Ed., *Multiple criteria decision making*, University of South Carolina, Columbia, 1973.

[4] J. T. Bell, "Modeling of the Global Petrochemical Industry," Ph. D. Thesis, *Department of Chemical Engineering*, University of Wisconsin-Madison, Madison, 1990.

[5] A. Bensoussan, "Decentralization in Management," European Institute for Advance Studies in Management, Bruxelles, 1972.

[6] J. P. Brans, "The Space of Freedom of the Decision Maker Modeling the Human Brain," *European Journal of Operational Research*, Vol. 92, No. 3, 1996, pp. 593-602.

[7] J. P. Brans and P. Vincke, "A Preference Ranking Organization Method: The PROMETHEE Method for MCDM," *Management Science*, Vol. 31, No. 6, 1985, pp. 647-656.

[8] J. P. Brans and B. Mareschal, "PROMCALC & GAIA: A New Decision Support System for Multicriteria Decision Aid," *Decision Support Systems*, Vol. 12, No. 4-5, 1994, pp. 297-310.

[9] J. P. Brans and B. Mareschal, "Promethee-V: MCDM Problems with Segmentation Constraints," Vol. 30, No. 2, 1992, pp. 85-96.

[10] J. P. Brans and B. Mareschal, "The PROMETHEE VI Procedure, How to Differentiate Hard from Soft Multicriteria Problems," *Journal of Decision Systems*, Vol. 4, 1995, pp. 213-223.

[11] J. P. Brans, B. Mareschal and P. Vincke, "PROMETHEE: A new Family of Outranking Methods in MCDM," In: Brans, J. P. Ed., *Operational Research'84 (IFORS'84)*, Amsterdam, 1984, pp. 477-490.

[12] J. P. Brans, "L'ingéniérie de la décision. Elaboration d'instruments d'aide à la decision," Méthode PROMETHEE. Université Laval, Quebec, Canada, 1982.

[13] O. E. Chavez, "Structural Simulation in the Analysis of the Chemical Industry," Ph. D. Thesis, University of Wisconsin-Madison, Madison, 1986.

[14] G. B. Dantzig and P. Wolfe, "Decomposition Principle for Linear Programs," *Operations Research*, 1960, Vol. 8, No. 1, pp. 101-111.

[15] T. C. Escobar, Modèles de décentralisation, prix de transfert et coordonnabilité dans les systèmes de Raffinage et la Planification du Gaz naturel. Thèse de doctorat en Calcul économique et Analyse de Système, Groupe de Recherche en Analyse de Système et Calcul Economique (ERA-CNRS No 640), Université d'Aix-Marseille, Belgium, 1979.

[16] C. Escobar and F. Rodríguez, Metodología para la Evaluación de Tecnologías y su Aplicación en el Cálculo del Valor Agregado en Cadenas Petroquímicas. Revista del Instituto Mexicano de Ingenieros Químicos IMIQ, Vol. 4, 1994.

[17] C. Escobar and R. Trémoliéres, Dècentralisation, Prix de transfert et Contrôle de gestion dans les Raffineries.

Aix-en-Provence: IAE (Institut d'Administration des Entreprises), 1978.

[18] C. Escobar, Descentralización y Coordinación de un Sistema Jerárquico de Oferta de Productos Petrolíferos y Petroquímicos. En: Memoria de Simposio: Modelos Matemáticos para la Planeación Energética. Universidad Nacional Autónoma de México y Consejo Nacional de Ciencia y Tecnología, 1983. pp. 85-112.

[19] D. Ford, "Develop Your Technology Strategy," *Long range planning*, Vol. 21, No. 1, 1988, pp 85-95.

[20] C. Garcia, Documento de examen predoctoral en Ingeniería (Ingeniería Química). Ciudad Universitaria (UNAM), México, 2006a.

[21] C. Garcia, Refinería petroquímica. En: C. Escobar Toledo Ed., Recuperación del Valor Agregado y de la Productividad en la Industria Petroquímica Mexicana. Ciudad Universitaria, México, 2006b, pp. 1-44.

[22] A. Geoffrion, "MElements of Large-Scale Mathematical Programming," *Management Science*, Vol. 16, No. 11, 1970, pp. 652-691.

[23] W. F. Hamilton, "The Dynamics of Technology and Strategy," *European Journal of Operational Research*, Vol. 47, No. 2, 1990, pp. 141-152.

[24] J. Kornai, "Thoughts on Multilevel Planning Systems," In: Goreux, L. M. and Manne, A. S. Eds., *Multilevel Planning*, Cases Studies in Mexico, North-Holland Publishing Company, Amsterdam, 1973, pp. 201-214.

[25] J. Kornai and T. Liptak, "Two-Level Planning," *Econometrica*, Vol. 33, 1965, pp. 141-169.

[26] J. Kornai, "Multilevel Programming—A First Report on the Model and on the Experimental Computation," *European Economic Review*, Vol. 1, No. 1, 1969, pp. 134-191.

[27] C. Macharis, J. P. Brans and B. Mareschal, "The GDSS PROMETHEE Procedure (A PROMETHEE-GAIA Based Procedure for Group Decision Support)," *Journal of Decision Systems*, Vol. 7, 1998, pp. 283-307.

[28] E. Malinvaud, "Decentralized Procedures for Planning," In: Malinvaud, E. and Bacharach, M. O. L. Eds., *Activity Analysis in the Theory of Growth and Planning*, Macmillan, London, 1967, pp. 170-208.

[29] B. Mareschal, "Weight Stability Intervals in Multicriteria Decision Aid," *European Journal of Operational Research*, Vol. 33, 1988, pp. 54-64.

[30] B. Mareschal, "Aide à la décision multicritère: développements récents des méthodes PROMETHEE," *Cahiers du, C.E.R.O.*, Vol. 29, 1987, pp. 175-214.

[31] B. Roy, "Analyse et choix multicritère," *Informatique et Gestion*, Vol. 57, 1974, pp. 21-27.

[32] B. Roy and P. Vincke, "Multicriteria Analysis: Survey and New Directions," *European Journal of Operational Resarch*, Invited Review, Vol. 8, No. 3, 1981, pp. 207-218.

[33] D. F. Rudd and C. C. Watson, "Strategy of Process Engineering," Wiley Internacional Edition, New York, 1968.

[34] D. F. Rudd, S. Fathi-Afshar, A. A. Treviño and M. A. Stadtherr, "Petrochemical Technology Assessment," Wil-

ey-Interscience, New York, 1981.

[35] E. Sevilla, De los petroquímicos finales a los básicos: Algoritmo de recorrido y métodos multicriterio. En: C. Escobar Toledo (Ed.), Recuperación del Valor Agregado y de la Productividad en la Industria Petroquímica Mexicana. Ciudad Universitaria (UNAM), México, 2006, pp. 1-25.

[36] D. Vanderpooten and P. Vincke, "Description and Analysis of Some Representative Interactive Multicriteria Procedures," *Mathematical and Computer Modelling*, Vol.

12, No. 3, 1989, pp. 1121-1238.

[37] H. M. Wagner, "Principles of Operations Research," Prentice-Hall, Englewood Cliffs, 1970.

[38] L. Walras, "Elements of Pure Economics," *On the theory of Social Wealth*, George Allen, London, 1954.

[39] R. L. Ackoff, "Creating the Corporate Future," John Wiley & Sons, Inc., New York, 1981.

[40] R. L. Ackoff, "Mission Statements," *Planning Review*, Vol. 15, No. 4, 1987, pp. 30-31.

11

A Typology of Institutional Frameworks for Organizations

Marcel Van Marrewijk
Van Linden van den Heuvellsingel 7, Vlaardingen, Netherlands

Abstract

Inspired by Dr. Clare Graves' research on evolutionary developments in value systems and levels of existence, this paper introduces an integral business framework—a sequence of ideal type organizations—each characterized by specific institutional arrangements. A table—the transition matrix—summarizes the specific features of each type. It is an update of former version based upon an international EU-financed ECSF research project [1].

Keywords: Value Systems, Organization Types, Responsive Scorecard, Organization Framework, Order, Success, Community, Synergy, Spiral Dynamics

1. Introduction

With Spiral Dynamics, based on the research of Clare Graves [2], summarized in paragraph two, this paper presents ideal type organizations structured according the Gravesian holarchy of value systems. Each type is showing a coherent set of ambitions, relating institutional structures and corresponding business practices, demonstrating different levels of corporate performance and manifestations of for instance sustainability.

In the final paragraph the author presents the Transition Matrix, published earlier in the Journal of Business Ethics [3]. It was the first step in a development that created a more sophisticated integral management framework—coined the Cubrix [4], introduced in the previous edition of this journal.

2. Value Systems

2.1. Graves' Value Systems Model

In the 1950s through 1970s Professor Clare W. Graves performed extensive empirical research regarding values and levels of existence (value systems). The focus of his research—*how does the mind process reality*—resulted in a overall framework for "healthy adult behavior" which he coined the "Emergent, Cyclical, Double-Helix Model of Adult BioPsychoSocial Systems Development". He rarely published his findings. In 1996, his successors, Don Beck and Chris Cowan, introduced Graves' Emerging Cyclical Level of Existence Theory—the shorter title of his model—as Spiral Dynamics [2].

Based on Graves' research they concluded that mankind has gradually developed eight core value systems so far. A value system is a way of conceptualizing reality and encompasses a consistent set of values, beliefs and corresponding behavior and can be found in individual persons, as well as in companies and societies.

The development of value systems occurs in a fixed order. These can be tagged as follows: Survival; Security; Energy and Power; Order; Success; Community, Synergy and Holistic life system. Each new value system includes and transcends the previous ones, thus forming a natural hierarchy (or holarchy).

In most occasions, a value system develops in reaction to specific environmental challenges and threats: the systems brighten or dim when life conditions (consisting of historic *Times*, geographic *Place*, existential *Problems* and societal *Circumstances*) change. Transformations, that is shifts of contexts, actually occurs when life conditions (LC) have build up a sufficient level of urgency among entities to leave behind their proven patterns of behavior. Secondly, these entities must have a supportive mind capacity (MC) to be able to match the new challenges life conditions offer and generate new adequate behavior and subsequent institutional arrangements.

It is all about balancing MC and LC. Psychologically, people might not be able to match changes in the environment, so they remain "arrested" towards future needs or even "closed" to less complex value systems that, naturally—should have been included in their repertoire.

Entities such as people and organizations will eventually have to meet the challenges their situation provides or risk the danger of oblivion or even extinction. If for instance societal circumstances change, inviting corporations to respond and consequently reconsider their role within society, it implies that corporations have to re-align their value systems and all their business institutions (such as mission, vision, policy deployment, decision-making, reporting, corporate affairs, etcetera) to these new circumstances.

The quest to create an adequate response to specific life conditions results in a wide variety of survival strategies, each founded on a specific set of value assumptions and demonstrated in related institutions and behavior.

Out of the eight core Gravesian value systems, we are only taking the six most recent ones as these are most relevant in the context of corporate sustainability. The same color codes as introduced by Beck and Cowan [2] are used to label the value systems, respectively red, blue, orange, green, yellow and turquoise. In **Table 1** a short description of each value system is given, in relation to (the perceptions of) the environment (life conditions), which induce the value system.

3. Organization Types

3.1. Thinking Systems

It is absolutely essential to understand that Gravesian value systems are distinguishing types of thinking *in* people and not types *of* people. It is about the intentions and awareness of people and their actual thinking systems to match the issue at hand. *A person is not "Blue". No, a Blue way of thinking is dominant within this person.*

When the coping possibilities a value system offers are no longer sufficient to provide an appropriate response to the existing circumstances, there is an incentive to move on to the next value system. The awareness that a current pattern of behavior or a certain institution is no longer adequate to tackle a problem can propel a change in the perception of reality. Increasing complexity requires more complexity of the value systems in coping with the situation. More complex value systems allow more degrees of freedom to act in accordance with the environment.

The question is often posed: "Is a more complex value system better than a basic one? In general, the answer is no. When the life conditions are adequately dealt with in less complex value system there is no need to aim for a higher value system. However, in highly complex environments, Yellow can provide a more adequate response to outside challenges than Blue because it offers more degrees of freedom to act appropriately under varied circumstances. The real issue therefore is "adequateness", the ability to provide a balance between Life Conditions and Mind Capacity.

The gradual move to a new value system facilitates new patterns of behavior and the creation of new institutions in line with the emerging value system. In other words, challenged by changing circumstances and provoked by new opportunities, individuals, organizations and societies develop adequate solutions, creating synergy and adding value at a higher level of complexity. Since instability increases at higher complexity levels,

Tabel 1. Development of human and organizational value systems, inspired by Graves and Spiral Dynamics [2].

Main Themes-Labels	Energy & Power (Red)	Order (Blue)	Success (Orange)	Community (Green)	Synergy (Yellow)	Holistic life System (Turquoise)
Environment: Life Conditions	Limitless challenges about boundaries of the territory and to be dominant over self and others within the territory.	Ordered relationships requiring legitimization in order to ensure stability and security for the future	Many viable alternatives for progress, prosperity and material gain since change is the nature of things	The gap between people and their (material) Possibilities has become disproportionately large	Complex problems that cannot be solved within the current systems as awareness of broad interconnections grows.	The consequences of human actions threaten the planet's living systems and demand coordinated effort.
Life Force	Conquering Domination	Belief	Achievement Changeability	Belonging	Understanding	Interconnections
Main Focus	Individual/self	Group/collective	Individual/self	Group/collective	Individual/self	Group/collective
Thinking System: Mind Capacity	Egocentric/cunning	Absolutistic/linear (consequential)	Multiplistic/calculating	Sociocentric/affiliative	Systemic/existential	Holistic/experimental
Typical Values	Courage, vitality, strength, respect, personal power, rivalry, territorial, intimidation, hedonism, loyalty to persons	Clarity, discipline, one truth, loyalty, duty, guilt, justice, conformity, obedience, orderliness, quality, craftman-ship	Results, reward, entrepreneurial, image, career advancement, productivity, guts, creativity, control, satisfaction	Consensus, conflict avoidance, team-work, equality, participation, honesty and openness, being a decent person, harmony	Insight, integrity, learning, long-term orientation, ability to reflect, flexibility, tolerance for uncertainty and paradoxes	Inspiration, interdependence, future generations, ability to forgive, wisdom, sufficiency, responsible living

entities can shift to lower levels if circumstances turn unfavorable or if competences fail to meet the required specifications. Charles Darwin once concluded: "It is not the strongest of the species that survive, nor the most intelligent, but the one most responsive to change".

When one studies particular expressions (e.g. certain behavior) within an organization one should not deduct automatically that the related value system is functioning. Since a particular value system includes and transcends previous ones, a basic expression can be found in all contexts. For example rules and regulations will be found in every organization, not only in organizations with a dominant Blue value system. The key question when certain behavior is displayed is: "Why is it important for you to do this?" In the example of rules and regulations, in the case of a Blue value system, the answer to this question could be: "Because rules provide me with the desired order and stability; rules are important by themselves and must be followed". In an Orange value system the answer might be: "Because the rules we use ensure smooth functioning and lead to success and high profit; rules can be followed as long as they help us in achieving our goals (and can be bent when not)".

In presenting ideal type organizations we will focus on the institutional structures and arrangements of four core value systems, for which we use the color codes, introduced by Christopher Cowan, the co-author of Spiral Dynamics. The selected systems are Order, Success, Community and Synergy, *i.e.* blue, orange, green and yellow. The transition zones between core value systems are also not included in the analyses. Each context is introduced by the underlying value system, its dominant worldview and related, often psychological explanations, which brings forth supporting institutional arrangements and structures.

3.2. Compliance-Driven, Based on Order (Absolute Order: Blue)

Introduction of the value system

Before mankind experienced Order, it was able to function at three previous levels of existence characterized by the Survival, Security (bonding order) and 'Energy and Power (powerful self)'. Historically, loose tribes evolved to clans, seeking refuge in kinships, rituals, holy ancestors and mystical nature. The value system supporting Security can also be observed in the mother and child relationship, in feelings of pride and belonging and in the identity of organizations. Its color code is Purple.

Freeing themselves from kinships and family ties, people gradually experienced ways of expressing themselves guiltlessly and selfishly, so as to find immediate pleasure and avoid shame in a world of domination, threats and ego. Power and Energy—indicated with Red—can be easily recognized in feudal states, in perseverance when the going gets tough and in negative manifestations such as

in traffic (road rage), hooliganism and "party animals". Red lacks the capacity for long-term sequential thinking. They feel no guilt, only the need to gratify impulses and senses immediately. Individual persons tend to manifest these energies especially when they are young (set limits and they will test it!) or in adverse times (CEOs, admirals). These manifestations relate to an environment with limited possibilities, with a shortage of sources, provoking entities to fight in order to gain control and get their share.

When people learn to transcend the self, experience consequential thinking, they are able to live up to "higher ideals", find pride and fulfillment in their work and accept sacrifices now so as to obtain rewards later. New values emerged that matched a quest for order, meaning and purpose. History has shown empires transcending the feudal states. Christianity, communism, armies and bureaucracies represented absolute order, providing a master plan that puts people in their proper places. Impulses are controlled through discipline, guilt and punishments. The rightful authorities seek order and stability and succeed in making their people believe to sacrifice themselves for future rewards.

People "with a lot of blue" live by the book. They try to comply with the laws, regulations, procedures and agenda's that structure their lives. Life is relatively simple: for each problem there is a proven practice and a guidebook to help them solving it, step by step.

Organizational features associated with Order

Organizations grounded in Order have a clear purpose, often explicitly or implicitly founded on principles, which often find their background in history and religion. Organization-wide there is a strong sense of moral duty.

These organizations are structured in strict bureaucracies, with the status of each individual linked to its position in the hierarchy. The archetype leadership style is "manager": formulating top-down planning schemes and policy deployment, determining control systems and budgets and designing and maintaining procedures and a clear division of tasks.

Taylorism is an approach typically linked to Order. Taylor's principles of standardization, specialization, maximization, concentration and centralization are typical features according to which business is run. Furthermore, the Deming's Quality Circle and other traditional quality tools as well as optimizing techniques and resource allocation are applied in order to economize on costs and expenditures.

Focusing on the various departments within an organization, one can observe that the production system is based on internal priorities and mainly technology-oriented in order to create economies of scale and vertical integration. They often dominate or try to include the supply chain within the hierarchy. Innovations are often of incremental nature and mainly apply to product development.

The people department is mainly an administrative unit, with employees fulfilling their tasks provided by line managers. Corporate behavior can often be characterized as authoritarian and custodial[1]. The market strategy is primarily a supply push approach, charging consumers a price based on integral costs plus a justifiable margin.

It is a goal-oriented system, with a focus on assigned tasks, not on persons.

Progress in Order is measured in terms of material wealth. The traditional scorecard format, relating to Order, is the annual financial report organizations have to show to Tax Authorities, the Chamber of Commerce or the Stock Exchange, in case the organization is publicly listed. The format is determined by law and carefully described by accountancy boards, such as the ACCA.

Organizations in Order expect governments to provide clear legislation and subsequent enforcement, which is effective and visible (law and order). Business' role in society is more or less independent and social welfare is the exclusive responsibility of the state.

The "license to operate" is applicable to organizations that are compliance-driven, thus matching Order.

Certain things are best done in the "blue way", such as maintenance, bookkeeping, chemistry, refineries, energy production and transport. The banking system, court's practices, the judge and jury, are all embedded in Absolute Order. Also private companies rely on a basic blue fundament: "a deal is a deal". Contracts are important ways to conclude arrangements between people and organizations.

Furthermore, many public services flourish within a hierarchical environment, but fail once these services are privatized and left to compete within a market environment.

With too much emphasis on linear thinking and values such as discipline, one truth, loyalty, duty, guilt, conformity, justice, obedience and orderliness the blue way attracts adverse effects such as:

- Limited problem solving capacity and reluctant creativity;
- Suffocating rules and procedures for employees and customers;
- Planning and regulation is more important than the objective;
- One truth, one right way, always categorical.

These omissions created the seeds for a new value system to emerge. It awaited the right circumstances to change paradigms once more. Instead of being what you are meant to be, more and more people longed to be who they could become. What kind of organization supports this new attitude?

---

[1]Davis (1967): Authoritarian refers to the authority of the CEO (or minister), and the custodial (paternalistic) on the organization as a whole securing the (basic) needs of the employees. [5]

3.3. Profit-Driven Based on Success and Entrepreneurship (the Enterprising Self: Orange)

<u>Introduction of the Value System</u>

In a world with plenty of viable alternatives for progress, prosperity and material gain, people and organizations with a sufficient level of Orange realize that change is in the nature of things and (personal) success within reach of anyone with talents and guts. When you are born a "dime" the "Enterprising Self" knows how to grow into something larger and gain control over its destiny. Success is the new name of the game in an environment offering plenty opportunities to compete, win and make things better and better.

In Success multiplistic thinking evolved offering many options and choices. In Order, people compared to the standard, but here they benchmark themselves against competition and the number one. People with a lot of Orange recognize change is the nature of things, creating new niches and introducing new technologies, enhancing life for many.

They work hard—preferably make others work hard for them—and risk time and money (not their life, as in Red) to achieve prosperity and material gain. They seek out the "good life" and abundance, rather than rewards hereafter. The expression "keep up with the Joneses" is typically Orange. Both people and organizations act in a calculated way while striving for autonomy and independence, seeking for progress and success with the best solutions. If they are allowed to, they try to master nature and exploit its resources.

<u>Organizational features associated with Success and Entrepreneurship</u>

Organizations with a dominant level of Orange make use of an active hierarchy, with informal and pragmatic lines of communication. The matrix and business unit structure are Orange varieties to open up and loosen the hierarchies, while maintaining a firm grip on business processes.

Through typically Orange values such as image, productivity, creativity, career advancement, entrepreneurship and control companies are result-oriented through (gradual and continuous) improvement, stimulating a desire to compete and to become better.

The archetype role of leaders is the Entrepreneur: discovering niches as opportunities for success, putting together new "combinations", creating the necessary means and enjoying the fruit of their labor. Burton Klein's "*Happy Warrior*" and Schumpeter's "*perennial gale of creative destruction*" are classic illustrations of the entrepreneurial drive behind capitalism.

Success in this context is primarily measured in terms of money and commercial assets. Organizations, having already established a sound-Blue-production system tend to focus on marketing efforts in trying to gain market share. Related practices such as communication, and advertising are also important activities in Success, with often pretending and "make believe" as its underlying intentions. "Window dressing" is invented in Orange!

Organizations engage with suppliers in a market environment, with contracts primarily based on prices and secondly, on specific quality requirements. Product development takes place, especially diversification, moreover Orange gained the competences to enhance process innovations and apply them in the context of quality management.

Human Resource Management treats employees as full time equivalents, as resources, and as costs, carefully selecting where each employee fits best. Employee satisfaction is the crucial standard for HR-performance measurement. HR managers might support its employees with bonuses, various benefits, training facilities and alike, when they are convinced it will lead to higher revenues, lower (turnover) costs and corporate success. In the same way, CS/CSR is accepted only as an opportunity to gain success, significantly reduce risks or enhance reputation, image, prestige and personal esteem. Thus, companies tend to embrace CS/CSR, the moment CS/CSR activities are supported with business case evidence.

A commonly applied measuring format, typically matching Success and Entrepreneurship, is the Business Balanced Scorecard, introduced by Kaplan and Norton. Its anchor point remains the financial position of the organization, but it also identifies three contributory elements: customers, people and processes and corporate lea- rning. See **Figure 1**.

Organizations expect governments to abstain from over-regulating their markets, as these are jeopardizing their profits and interfere with their sense of freedom. Governments should create and maintain "level playing fields" and allowing companies a "license to grow". According to Orange norms, the voluntary character of corporate sustainability and responsibility particularly must never be violated.

Activities best done in Success are entrepreneurship and marketing, sales and promotion activities in order to boost the commercial capacity of the organization.

People with a lot of Orange tend to be pragmatic. This attitude gives rise to ethical issues since the end is more important than the means. With profits gained at the expense of the weaker, the Entrepreneurial system generates dropouts. Tending to elitism, Orange is inattentive to a fair distribution. With a hang to quantity and profits instead of quality and durability, Success creates "consumerism" and a huge waste stream. Moreover striving for success often becomes compulsive, leaving orangists no time to enjoy their fruits.

The spillover of the entrepreneurial successes gave rise to a new value system, shortly introduced in the next section.

3.4. Care-Driven, Based on Community (the Egalitarian Order: Green)

Introduction of the Value System

The Purple reciprocity and Orange accumulation of material wealth paved the way for Green redistribution of society's resources among all. The self is once more being sacrificed, but this time in a world where compassion and belonging are paramount, where everything is relative and "truth" is a matter of context and the group's needs. Community liberates humans from dogma and greed, promoting a sense of community and unity. Solidarity is felt with the weaker and dropouts, victims of a system exploiting resources and causing an unequal distribution of material wealth.

People and organizations with a lot of Community-sense try to explore the inner beings of themselves or others. They refresh spirituality and seek to bring New Harmony. Generally Community is anti-dogmatic, and since everyone is unique, anti-labeling and anti-hierarchy, but highly tolerant.

Organizational features associated with Community

In Community, the process of organizing has become an end in itself. Not the organization as such matter that much, but a group of people engaged in a process of organizing. It implies the involvement of all others, within and outside the organization. Community values support competences enhancing the ability to involve everyone (engagement) and listen carefully (dialogue). In Community one tend to recognize the human being "behind" the employee and the customer. As Peter Drucker already noticed in 1952 "when hiring a worker, one gets a whole man": along with the muscles and brainpower comes the emotional and spiritual dimension. These capacities allow persons to better understand one other, to create a two-way flow of information, turning conversations into dialogues. Teamwork improves, as people are better able to work together.

Persons and organizations with a lot of Green are convinced that individual achievements alone are not sufficient to adequately confront the challenges Community Organizations are facing. In Community one believes that cooperation beats competition: "together we stand strong". Fairness is a highly regarded value, both in the supply chain, especially when suppliers come from emerging economies, and in the pricing policy towards customers.

Success organizations mainly exploit their own resources and existing competences in trying to become better and better, while Community organizations learn to collaborate first internally and secondly by engaging with outside stakeholders. Examples for increasing internal coherence are quality orientations shifting from process to organization-wide, a people-driven philosophy and significantly improving workplace culture and practices. The newly acquired skills in dialogues and teamwork, support the engagement with outside stakeholders such as customers, suppliers, and neighborhood representatives. The engagement primarily commences as a consequence of corporate responsibility, expressing that the organization is accountable for its impact on others. By effectively working together with internal and external stakeholders, thus tapping into their competences and capacities, organizations find new opportunities to boost their performance. This time with respect to the triple bottom line: people, planet and profits.

The archetype leadership style in Community is "coaching"—the servant leader. The servant leader, a term coined by Robert Greenleaf, implies a state of being, not doing: the first and important choice a leader can make is the choice to serve, without which one's capacity to lead is profoundly limited [6]. Hierarchies are replaced by supportive structures. A typical expression is: "We take care of the people, the people take care of the business."

Instead of providing solutions, managers should allow the group to create the answers. With typical values such as consensus, conflict avoidance, teamwork, equality, participation, honesty, openness, being a decent person and harmony, decision making in the context of Community is an-often time consuming-group process. Once the decision is reached, the buy-in is guaranteed and implementation can be done quickly. This type of consensus-oriented decision-making implies that a new type of corporate governance structure has emerged, including a new role of management, a flat organization structure and shareholder value being balanced against the interest of other legitimate stakeholders.

In Community Organizations, the term Human Resources is no longer applicable to employees, and their satisfaction as indicator is surpassed by the level of trust which (ought to) exist between management and employees, between employees and among stakeholders such as customers, suppliers, shareholders and neighborurs. Human Talent Management is more appropriate, indicating its emphasis on the development of individual employees and the recognition of employees being assets

instead of costs.

The traditional focus on the material and commercial organizational competences are fading somewhat in favor for the socialization [7] among employees and other stakeholder groups: the ability to engage with people and uniting them in an attempt to achieve common goals. Previous organization types were resource oriented, but organizations applying engagement and collaboration as key concepts in Community strategies are stakeholder oriented. Stakeholders have become co-makers and co-creators. Strategic partnerships are common and institutional arrangements on sector level emerge.

The bulk of management tools supports Order and Success. Community related tooling is still rare. The ECSF project created an innovative measurement format: the Responsive Business Scorecard. This format includes four stakeholder groups, each with an interactive relationship with a fifth entity, the organizations itself. See **Figure 1**. The box in the middle—Corporate Performance Improvements—functions as an anchor point linking Community with Success, as much as Financiers and Owners linked the Balanced Business Scorecard with the Financial Report (Order).

The word "responsive" emphasize the Communion principle [8] and represents its willingness to interact with stakeholders and be accountable for their actions and impact to others. The Responsive Business Scorecard emphasizes the relationships with the main stakeholder groups and the extent to which these outcomes contribute to the improvement of the corporate goals.

The relationships with the stakeholders can be managed by applying the old Deming learning cycle Plan-Do-Check-Improve, or more appropriate to Community: Identify-Engage-Involve-Agree-Deliver-Learn and Improve.

Trying to be a decent person, nice and loving, is a highly regarded quality in Community. Conflict avoidance, how ever, also have negative consequences. With criticism smothered by love and judgments made relative to the

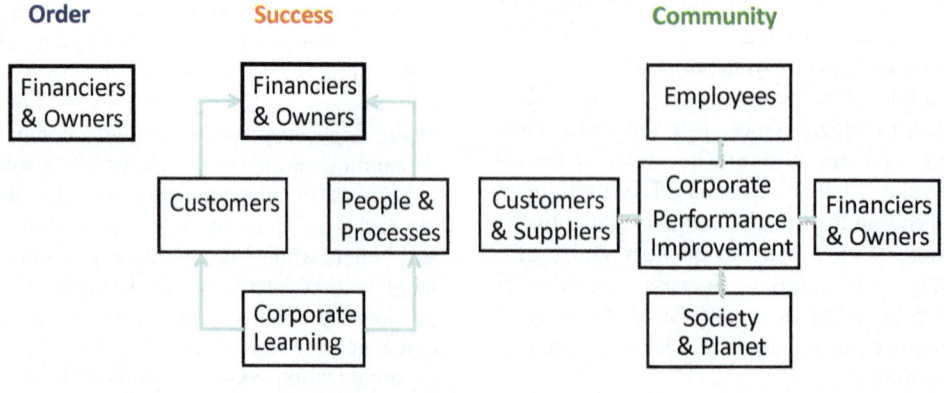

Financial Report   Balanced Business Scorecard   Responsive Scorecard

Figure 1. Three manifestations of business reporting formats aligning specific development phases.

situation at hand, decision-making risk non-functional and abstract outcomes.

Using each other's qualities for mutual growth, Community is able to create good learning conditions. However, the aura of an expert is badly regarded in Green: consensus is more important than expertise and incompetence is not a reason to be laid off. With rising complexity levels, Community does no longer provide the ultimate solutions to the problems at hand. Furthermore, equality and consensus building may lead to pooling of ignorance.

Being confronted by chaos in a world at-risk, typical Community features such as the lack of leadership and expertise and the emotional and economic cost of caring are important arguments to develop new ways to cope with more complex challenges.

3.5. Synergy (the Integrating Self: Yellow)

<u>Introduction of the Value System</u>

Comprehension, understanding and synergy are the buzzwords of Synergy. A person and organization with a lot of yellow, express itself, but never at the expense of others or the earth, so that all life may continue in the most natural, sustainable, and fitting ways. They recognize the inevitability of nature's flows. They understand that the complexity of today's world cannot be solved within the current systems, as their awareness of broad interconnections grows.

Synergy can find its way in a mix of conflicting "truths", for it is able to see more colors and uses more senses at the same time. By focusing on functionality and applying competencies to get buy—in from others, Synergy is able to create win-win options, seeking self-interest without doing harm to others and nature.

In discussing ideas, persons with a lot of yellow do not get personalized. They will not say: "These people can't cook", but "This food is not of good taste". Furthermore, in Yellow there is room for authenticy, since internal motivations matter a lot. Existentialism is strong.

<u>Organizational features associated with Synergy</u>

In order to meet its drive—to be, to learn and to discover—persons with a lot of Synergy function best in a network with a strong sense of direction: Yellow demands flexibility and open systems. Values such as insight, long-term orientation, ability to reflect and tolerance for uncertainty and paradoxes support the drive for self-development and boost people's ability to learn and apply knowledge. They are able to learn from any source. With a mind that quickly wanders, they have difficulty in maintaining focus.

Larger organizational entities transforming-or breaking up-into network structures, demonstrate the drive behind Synergy. The Hollywood movie scene is a good example of a once highly successful oligopoly, which broke up in numerous small professional clusters, who work together in a network for the duration of a project. Not far from Hollywood, in Silicon Valley, one can witnessed a network structure that emerged bottom up, independent professionals clustering into networks, creating the necessary competences to meet the challenges facing Synergy.

The archetype activity in Synergy is the "Emergence or connected Leader", who is both "visionary" and able to link the various qualities into one effective and coherent approach. The leadership style dominated by Synergy causes breakthroughs, supports transitions, directing its organisation into new innovative ways that alter business. Jim Collins' [9] "Good to Great"—concept of level five leadership fully coincides.

Real leadership is no longer confined to what people *do*, but grounded in who people *are*. An authentic choice *to serve life* increases ones capacity to lead by allowing life to unfold through you. The hierarchy between the leader and the led remains healthy: leadership is never dominating or abusing raw power. The leadership potential can be developed in everyone. It implies identifying the personal responsibility and the alignment between one's personality and ambitions with one's role within the network. Therefore, essentially, leadership is about learning how to shape the future [6].

The basic guiding principle between people and their organization is the alignment between collective and individuals needs and motives. Alignment also takes place between the various entities within the network, including the stakeholders. Corporate behavior associated with this context can be characterized as "motivational". Managers support their employees, often professionals, in order to bring them into the flow, accomplishing both their own as well as their organization's objectives and creating a feeling of self-actualization.

Employees accept career advancements only when they feel they are competent and when it is a nice job. Typical negative manifestations of synergy-driven people and organizations are the lack of commitment to organization and colleagues. They might appear aloof and uninterested or operate as loners. When they do not get enough interesting work they will abandon their position. Furthermore they are intolerant to rigidity and demands open access to information.

4. Final Remarks

4.1. Transition Matrix

The institutional structures of each ideal type can be summarized and structured according the enablers of the Global Excellence Model, one of the fundaments of the Cubrix [4]. See **Table 2**, below.

In coherent ideal type institutional structures, one can distinguish the left quadrant dimensions, introduced by

Ken Wilber [10,11], specifically the ideal type cultures and intentional values people apply while coping with the challenges the ideal type organization is facing. These two topics are summarized below (see **Table 3**).

The ideal type organizations, introduced in this paper, cannot be recognized as actual organizations. However, in studying or monitoring organization development one can distinguish various elements from these ideal types. It also supports the gap analyses between ambitions, actual behavior and policies and the structural elements of these types. When these are not coherent, one should transform towards, or adopt institutional elements from the types that align better with the intentions and challenges organizations are facing.

In practices, several challenges remain intact and groups of people often have a mix of values from various value systems, making it quite a challenge to determine which types of organization align best with the given goals. Vice versa, an actual set of institutions can jeopardize the ambitions when these ambitions cannot be met within the contemporary setting. Again, there are no simple cause relation effects in organization development.

This matrix can also be used as a framework for structuring, for instance, management literature, or all management tools, methods and theories, as these methods

Table 2. A developmental approach to corporate enablers, structured according to the GEM [4].

Development Labels	Compliance-driven Order (Blue)	Profit-driven Success (Orange)	Care-driven Community (Green)	Systemic-driven Synergy (Yellow)
1. Leadership	Manager	Entrepreneur	Servant Leader	Emergent Leader
2. Strategy	Mergers & acquisitions	Autonomous growth due to competitive qualities	Stakeholder engagement; Chain related	Industry related, seeking breakthroughs
3. People Management	Personnel & Administration	Human Resources Management	Human Talent Management	Human Capital Management
4. Communication & Decision Making	Top down, while applying the procedures from higher authorities	Top down, but valuable info from the bottom is always welcome	Bottom-up; group decides based on consensus; sociocratic	Consent principle decides who should make the decision, as understanding of the matter prevails
5. Learning & Innovation	Product innovation based on technical expertise	Process innovation, and product diversification	Social Innovations, developing supportive structures to boost learning and innovation	System innovations, based on in-depth understanding of dynamics, sustain-ability, and needs
6. Resources	Price competition	Maintenance on process indicators	Outsourcing with strong relationships, peer audits	Co-creating; together- win; Sustainable Purchasing
7. Processes	Activity Orientation	Process Orientation	(Internal) System Orientation	Chain Orientation

Table 3. A developmental approach to corporate enablers-context related (GEM).

Development Labels	Order (Blue)	Success (Orange)	Community (Green)	Systemic-driven Synergy (Yellow)
1. Culture	Bureaucratic; procedural; compliance-driven	Entrepreneurial, calculative; profit-driven	Retiree Consensus; Empathetic; care-driven	Open, flexible, transparent; network oriented; Systemic-driven
2. Values	Clarity, discipline, one truth, loyalty, duty, guilt, justice, quality, conformity, obedience, orderliness, craftmanship	Results, reward, entrepreneurial, image, career advancement, productivity, guts, creativity, control, satisfaction	Consensus, conflict avoidance, team-work, equality, participation, honesty and openness, being a decent person, harmony	Insight, integrity, learning, long-term orientation, visionary, ability to reflect, flexibility, tolerance for uncertainty and paradoxes

often align with specific contexts only. It is as if one simply opens up a specific drawer, from a wide chest of drawers, finding a full set of business institutions, management tools and concepts, whatever. Although it is a complicated framework, users only need to know the relevant aspects, the aspects related to their context only. By determining A and B, referring to an initial context and situation and a desired state, the user will get a full-management reference, indicating the various steps and sets of relevant information that will help getting them to the espoused situation. The framework can be used as an expert system, raising the right questions as well as providing the best answers.

A foundation has started—Stichting Koploperz (Leading Organizations Foundation) that will benchmark the best practices, structured according this framework.

In practice, some drawers are still empty, others are not fully filled and lacking coherence. So there is still a lot of work to do. However, we did analyze over 100 management tools, according their characteristics related to this framework, coined the Cubrix. In the near future we will create an online expert system. If you want to be involved, someway, let us know!

5. References

[1] M. van Marrewijk, "A Value Based Approach to Organisation Types: Towards a Coherent Set of Stakeholder Oriented Management Tools," *Journal of Business Ethics*, Vol. 55, No. 2, December 2004, pp. 147-158.

[2] D. Beck and C. Cowan, "Managing Values, Leadership, and Change," *Spiral Dynamics*, Blackwell Publishers, London, 1996.

[3] M. van Marrewijk and M. Werre, "Multiple Levels of Corporate Sustainability," *Journal of Business Ethics*, Vol. 44, No. 2-3, May 2003, pp. 107-119.

[4] M. van Marrewijk, "The Cubrix, an Integral Framework for Managing Performance Improvement and Organisational Development," *Journal of Technology and Investment*, Vol. 1, No. 1, 2010, pp. 1-13.

[5] J. W. Newstrom and K. Davis, "Organizational Behavior," 10th Edition, Mc. Graw-Hill, New York, 1997.

[6] J. Jaworski, "Synchronicity: The Inner Path of Leadership," Indigo, 2000.

[7] T. W. Hardjono, "Ritmiek en Organisatiedynamiek: Vierfasenmodel," Kluwer, 1995.

[8] M. van Marrewijk, "Concepts and Definitions of Corporate Sustainability," *Journal of Business Ethics*, Vol. 44, No. 2-3, May 2003, pp. 95-105.

[9] J. C. Collins, "Good to Great," Harper Collins Publishers, New York, 2001.

[10] K. Wilber, "Sex, Ecology, Spirituality: The Spirit of Evolution," 2nd Shambhala Publications, Boston, 1995.

[11] K. Wilber, "A Theory of Everything: An Integral Vision for Business," Politics, Science and Spirituality, Shambhala Publications, Boston, 2000.

Abreviations

CEO	Chief Executive Officer
CS	Corporate Sustainability
CSR	Corporate Social Responsibility
ECSF	European Corporate Sustainability Framework
ECLET	Emerging Cyclical Levels of Existence Theory
GEM	Global Excellence Model
LC	Life Conditions
MC	Mind Capacity

12

Vermiculture Technology: Reviving the Dreams of Sir Charles Darwin for Scientific Use of Earthworms in Sustainable Development Programs

Rajiv K. Sinha[1]*, Sunita Agarwal[2], Krunal Chauhan[3], Vinod Chandran[3], Brijal Kiranbhai Soni[3]

[1]**Griffith School of Engineering (Environment), Griffith University, Nathan Campus, Brisbane, Australia*
[2]*University of Rajasthan, Jaipur, India*
[3]*Vermiculture Project, Griffith University, Brisbane, Australia*

Abstract

Vermiculture technology is emerging as an "environmentally sustainable", "economically viable" and "socially acceptable" technology all over the world. 1) Vermi-composting Technology (to manage most organic wastes); 2) Vermi-filtration Technology (to treat municipal & several industrial wastewater); 3) Vermi-remediation Technology (to treat & clean up contaminated lands); 4) Vermi-agro-production Technology (to produce chemical-free organic foods by worms & vermicompost); 5) Vermi-industrial Production Technology (to produce valuable industrial raw materials from worms). The use of earthworms as "waste managers" for efficient "composting of food and farm wastes" and as "soil managers" for "fertility improvement" and enhanced "farm production" were known for ages but now it is being more scientifically and also commercially revived. The other uses of earthworms for the benefits of environment and society (wastewater treatment, land remediation & production of valuable medicines even to combat cancer and heart diseases; raw materials for rubber, lubricant, soap, detergent & cosmetic, industries and protein rich feed materials for fishery, dairy & poultry industries are some "new discoveries". We have successfully experimented with the first four technologies for management of "municipal solid wastes", treatment of "municipal & industrial wastewater", remediation of "PAHs contaminated soils" and production of "wheat & corn crops" by use of vermicompost at Griffith University, Australia, with excellent results. Wastes are degraded by over 75% faster than conventional systems and compost produced are disinfected, detoxified, richer in nutrients & beneficial soil microbes; BOD loads & TSS of wastewater is reduced by over 95%; PAHs from contaminated soils are removed by over 80% in just 12 weeks; and crops growths are promoted by 30-40% higher as compared to chemical fertilizers. Earthworms are both "protective" & "productive" for environment and society.

Keywords: Vermicomposting of Wastes, Vermifiltration of Wastewater, Vermiremediation of Contaminated Lands, Vermi-Agroproduction of Chemical-Free Organic Foods, Vermicompost—a Nutritive Biofertilizer & Soil Conditioners for Farms, Earthworms Biomass—a Valuable Resource for Pharmaceutical & Consumer Industries, Vermiculture—One Time Investment Technology with Valued By-products and End-products

1. Introduction

The global scientific community today is searching for a technology which should be "economically viable" (cheaper to be afforded by all nations), "environmentally sustainable" (friendly to the environment—flora, fauna, soil, air & water, with no adverse effect on them) and "socially acceptable" (beneficial to the society with no adverse effect on human health). Vermiculture Technology combines all these virtues and qualities together.

A revolution is unfolding in vermiculture studies (rearing of useful earthworms species) for multiple uses in environmental protection and sustainable development [1-3]. Earthworms have over 600 million years of experience as "ecosystem engineers". Vermiculture scientists all over the world knew about the role of earthworms as "waste managers", as "soil managers & fertility improvers" and "plant growth promoters" for long time. But some comparatively "new discoveries" about their role in "wastewater treatment", "contaminated soil remediation", and more recently about their potential use in modern medicine for protection of "human health" such as in lowering of blood pressure, thinning of blood and dissolving blood clots for stroke and heart patients, cure for cancer, cure for arthritis & rheumatisms, as an anti-inflammatory agent, source of antibiotics and as a rich source of "high quality protein" have brought a revolution in the vermiculture studies.

About 4,400 different species of earthworms have been identified, and quite a few of them are versatile waste eaters and bio-degraders and several of them are bio-accumulators & bio-transformers of toxic chemicals.

2. The Biology & Ecology of Earthworms

Earthworms are long, narrow, cylindrical, bilaterally symmetrical, segmented animals without bones. Usually the life span of an earthworm is about 3 to 7 years depending upon the type of species and the ecological situation. Earthworms harbor millions of "nitrogen-fixing" and "decomposer microbes" in their gut. They have "chemoreceptors" which aid in search of food. Their body contains 65% protein (70-80% high quality "lysine rich protein" on a dry weight basis), 14% fats, 14% carbohydrates and 3% ash [4-6].

Earthworms occur in diverse habitats specially those which are dark and moist. They can tolerate a temperature range between 5°C and 29°C. A temperature of 20°C to 25°C and moisture of 60-75% are optimum for good worm function. Earthworms multiply very rapidly. Studies indicate that they double their number at least every 60-70 days. Given the optimal conditions of moisture, temperature and feeding materials earthworms can multiply by 2^8 *i.e.* 256 worms every 6 months from a single individual. Each of the 256 worms multiplies in the same proportion to produce a huge biomass of worms in a short time. The total life-cycle of the worms is about 220 days. They produce 300-400 young ones within this life period [7]. Earthworms continue to grow throughout their life.

Earthworms can tolerate toxic chemicals in environment. After the Seveso chemical plant explosion in 1976 in Italy, when a vast area was contaminated with extremely toxic chemical like TCDD (2,3,7,8-tetra-chlorodibenzo-*p*-dioxin) several fauna perished except for some species of the earthworms that survived. Earthworms which ingested TCDD contaminated soils were shown to bio-accumulate dioxin in their tissues and concentrate it on average 14.5 fold [8]. Earthworms are also tolerant to moderate salt salinity in soil, but some species like the tiger worms (*Eisenia fetida*) has been found to be highly salt tolerant. In a study made by [9] at the US Department of Energy it was found that replicates with a salt concentration of 15 g/kg of soil (nearly half as salty as seawater), survival ranged from 80%-100%.

3. Technologies for Sustainable Development by Use of Earthworms

Following technologies for sustainable development with environmental protection can be envisaged by the use of useful earthworms species which promises to provide cheaper solutions to several social, economic, environmental & health problems plaguing the human society [3,10].

1) "THE VERMI-COMPOSTING TECHNOLOGY" for efficient management of municipal & industrial solid wastes (organics) by biodegradation & stabilization and converting them into useful resource (vermicompost-nutritive biofertilizer);

2) "THE VERMI-FILTRATION TECHNOLOGY" for treatment of municipal and some industrial wastewater, their purification & disinfection for reuse;

3) "THE VERMI-REMEDIATION TECHNOLOGY" for cleaning up chemically contaminated sites (lands) while also improving their physical, chemical and biological properties for reuse;

4) "THE VERMI-AGRO-PRODUCTION TECHNOLOGY" for restoring & improving soil fertility to produce safe and chemical-free food for the society by the use of vermicompost & without recourse to the destructive agro-chemicals;

5) "THE VERMI INDUSTRIAL PRODUCTION TECHNOLOGY" for use of earthworms to produce some "bioactive compounds" for pharmaceutical industries and valuable raw materials to be used in rubber, lubricant, soaps, detergent & cosmetics industries and use of rich worm proteins as feed materials to promote fishery, dairy & poultry industries to produce more nutritive foods for the society.

Vermiculture technologies based on earthworms are self-promoted, self-regulated, self-improved & self-enhanced, low or no-energy requiring zero-waste technologies, easy to construct, operate and maintain. They excel all "bio-conversion", "bio-degradation" & "bio-production" technologies by the fact that they can utilize organics that otherwise cannot be utilized by others. They excel all "bio-treatment" technologies because they achieve greater utilization than the rate of destruction achieved by other technologies. They involve about 100-1000 times higher "value addition" than other biological technologies [11,12].

Technologies based on earthworms are also "environmentally & economically sustainable" as the worms are "highly renewable resources" regenerating at a rapid rate (by 2^8 *i.e.* 256 worms every 6 months from a single individual & each of the 256 worms multiplying in the same proportion) and the products are completely "biodegradable". The best part is that application of some vermiculture technologies are based on the by-products (worm biomass & vermicompost) generated in the operation of other technologies and therefore, more sustainable. It is like "killing several birds" in one shot.

4. The Vermicomposting Technology for Efficient Management of Solid Wastes: Diverting Waste from Landfills, and Recovering Resource from Waste

Waste is a problem of the modern civilized society. We are facing the escalating socio-economic and environmental cost of dealing with current and future generation of mounting municipal solid wastes (MSW). A considerable portion of MSW consist of "Organic Wastes" that are "biodegradable" and can be vermicomposted into a highly "nutritive bio-fertilizer" 4-5 fold more powerful than conventional composts and even superior to chemical fertilizers for better crop growth and safe food production.

Another serious cause of concern today is the emission of greenhouse gases (GHG) methane (CH_4) & nitrous oxides (N_2O) resulting from the disposal of MSW either in the landfills or from their management by conventional composting systems. Molecule to molecule CH_4 is 21 times and N_2O is 310 times more powerful GHG than the CO_2. Millions of tons of MSW generated from the modern society are ending up in the landfills everyday, creating extraordinary economic and environmental problems for the local government to manage and monitor them (may be up to 30 years) for environmental safety (emission of GHG, toxic gases and leachate discharge into ground water). Construction of secured engineered landfills incurs 20-25 million U.S. dollars before the first load of waste is dumped in 2002-03. Over the past 5 years the cost of landfill disposal of waste has increased from $ 29 to $ 65 per ton of waste in Australia. During 2002-2003, waste management services within Australia cost $ 2458.2 millions.

Waste degradation & composting by earthworms is proving to be economically & environmentally preferred technology over the conventional microbial degradation & composting technology as it is rapid and nearly odorless process, reducing composting time by more than half and the end product is both "disinfected" and "detoxified" [13,14]. On an average, 2000 adult worms weigh 1 kg & one million worms approx. 1 ton. One million worms doubling every two months can become 64 million worms at the end of the year. Considering that each adult worm (particularly *Eisinia fetida*) consume waste organics equivalent to its own body weight everyday, 64 million worms (weighing 64 tons) would consume 64 tons of waste everyday and produce 30-32 tons of vermicompost per day at 40-50% conversion rate.

4.1. Community Wastes That can be Salvaged by Earthworms

Waste eater earthworms can physically handle a wide variety of organic wastes from both municipal (domestic and commercial) and industrial (livestock, food processing and paper industries) streams [2,13,15].

1) Municipal Organic Wastes

The food waste from homes (both raw & cooked kitchen wastes—fruits and vegetables, grains & beans, coffee grounds, used tea leaves & bags, crushed egg shells) and restaurants & fried food wastes from fast-food outlets The garden wastes (leaves and grass clippings) also constitute an excellent feed stock for vermi-composting. Grass clippings (high carbon waste) require proper blending with nitrogenous wastes. The "sewage sludge" (biosolids) from the municipal wastewater also provide a good feedstock for the worms. The worms digest the sludge and convert a good part of it into vermi-compost. Paunch waste materials (gut contents of slaughtered ruminants) from abattoir also make good feedstock for earthworms [14,16].

2) Agriculture and Animal Husbandry Wastes

Farm wastes such as crop residues, dry leaves & grasses. Livestock rearing waste such as cattle dung, pig and chicken excreta makes excellent feedstock for earthworms.

3) Some Industrial Organic Wastes

Solid waste including the "wastewater sludge" from paper pulp and cardboard industry, food processing industries including brewery and distillery; vegetable oil factory, potato and corn chips manufacturing industry, sugarcane industry, aromatic oil extraction industry. Sericulture industry, logging and carpentry industry also offers excellent feed material for vermi-composting by earthworms [17,18].

4.2. Some Important Studies on Vermicomposting Technology

1) Reference [6] studied vermicomposting in great details and found that most earthworms consume, at the best, half their body weight of organics in the waste in a day. *Eisenia fetida* can consume organic matter at the rate equal to their body weight every day. Earthworm participation enhances natural biodegradation and decomposition of organic waste from 60 to 80% over the

conventional aerobic & anaerobic composting. Given the optimum conditions of temperature (20-30°C) and moisture (60-70%), about 5 kg of worms (numbering approx. 10,000) can vermiprocess 1 ton of waste into vermicompost in just 30 days. Upon vermi-composting the volume of solid waste is significantly reduced from approximately 1 cum to 0.5 cum of vermi-compost indicating 50% conversion rate, the rest is converted into worm biomass.

2) References [18-22] studied the degradation and composting of "wastewater sludge" from paper pulp and cardboard industry, brewery and distillery, sericulture industry, vegetable oil factory, potato and corn chips manufacturing industry, sugarcane industry, aromatic oil extraction industry, logging and carpentry industry by earthworms. These organic wastes offer excellent feed materials for vermi-composting by earthworms. Reference [19] also studied the vermicomposting of waste from the mining industry which contains sulfur residues and creates disposal problems. They can also be fed to the worms mixed with organic matter. Optimum mixing ratio of the sulfur waste residues to the organic matter was 4%.

3) Reference [23] studied the vermicomposting of "fly-ash" from the coal power plants which is considered as a hazardous waste and poses serious disposal problem due to heavy metal contents. As it is also rich in nitrogen and microbial biomass it can be vermi-composted by earthworms. They found that 25% of fly-ash mixed with sisal green pulp, parthenium and green grass cuttings formed excellent feed for *Eisenia fetida* and the vermicompost was higher in NKP contents than other commercial manures. The earthworms ingest the heavy metals from the fly-ash while converting them into vermicompost.

4) Reference [24] successfully studied vermicomposting of "human excreta" (feces). It was completed in six months, with good physical texture, odourless and safe pathogen quality. Sawdust appeared to be the best covering material that can be used in vermicomposting toilets to produce compost with a good earthy smell, a crumbly texture and dark brown colour.

4.3. Our Studies on Vermicomposting Technology at Griffith University, Australia

1) Reference [25] studied the degradation and composting abilities of three species of earthworms on cattle dung, raw food wastes and garden wastes and found that the worm *Eudrilus euginae* was a better waste degrader followed by *Eisenia fetida*.

2) Reference [26] studied the vermicomposting of "sewage sludge" (biosolids). In 12 weeks study period there were no significant changes in the control. Most significant and rapid changes were observed in sludge which contained earthworms. Foul odor disappeared by week 2 and by week 12, the black and brittle sludge be-

came a homogenous and porous mass of brown vermicast with light texture. Upon chemical analysis, the vermicomposted sludge was over 80% free of heavy metals cadmium (Cd) and lead (Pb) and almost completely free of any pathogens.

3) Reference [27] studied the efficiency of earthworms in degradation and vermicomposting of mixed food & garden wastes and compared with conventional aerobic composting without worms. Degradation of food wastes had started within hours (5% after 24 hours) and were degraded 100% in just 15 days while garden wastes in 60 days. In wastes where the primary cellulosic materials were intact e.g. leaves and grasses, raw vegetables & fruits or where there are brittle calcium compounds e.g. egg shells, were degraded rather more slowly by the earthworms. In the conventional composting system without worms, maximum degradation of both food & garden wastes were only 35% even after 90 days.

4.4. Mechanism of Worm Action in Vermicomposting

Earthworms act as an aerator, grinder, crusher, chemical degrader and a biological stimulator and degrade waste by multiple actions.

1) Grinding action

The waste feed materials ingested is finely ground (with the aid of stones in their muscular gizzard) into small particles to a size of 2-4 microns and passed on to the intestine for enzymatic actions. The gizzard and the intestine work as a "bioreactor";

2) Enzymatic action

The gizzard and the intestine work as a "bioreactor". Worms secrete enzymes proteases, lipases, amylases, cellulases and chitinases in their gizzard and intestine which bring about rapid biochemical conversion of the cellulosic and the proteinaceous materials in the waste organics. They ingest the food materials, cull the harmful microorganisms, and deposit them mixed with minerals and beneficial microbes as "vermicasts" in the soil [28].

3) Worms Reinforce Decomposer Microbes & Act Synergistically

Worms promotes the growth of "beneficial decomposer microbes" (bacteria, actinomycetes & fungi) in waste biomass [28,29]. They hosts millions of decomposer microbes in their gut which is described as "little bacterial factory". They devour on microbes and excrete them out (many times more in number than they ingest) in soil along with nutrients nitrogen (N) and phosphorus (P) in their excreta. The nutrients N and P are further used by the microbes for multiplication and vigorous action [30]. Reference [31] showed that the number of bacteria and "actinomycetes" contained in the ingested material increased up to 1000 fold while passing through the gut. A population of worms numbering about 15,000 will in turn foster a microbial population of billions of millions. Earthworms and microbes act "symbiotically & synergistically" to accelerate and enhance the decomposition of the organic matter in the waste. It is the microorganisms that break down the cellulose in the food waste, grass clippings and the leaves from garden wastes [32].

4) Humification

The final process in vermi-processing and degradation of organic matter is the "humification" in which the large organic particles are converted into a complex amorphous colloid containing "phenolic" materials. About one-fourth of the organic matter is converted into humus. Humus is essential in soil for plant growth & survival. It takes several years in conventionally produced compost to generate "humus" through slow disintegration, whereas, earthworms excrete "humus" in its compost.

4.5 Advantages of Vermicomposting Technology

1) Salvage Human Wastes & Divert Huge MSW from Landfills

A big advantage of great economic & environmental significance is that production of vermicompost from "organic wastes" divert huge amount of MSW from ending up in the landfills thus also saving cost on waste disposal and reducing discharge of toxic leachate and gases and emission of greenhouse gases (GHG) which occurs from waste landfills.

2) Rapid and Efficient Process & Takes Half the Time than the Conventional System

Earthworms have the real potential to accelerate and enhance the natural biodegradation and decomposition of organic materials from 60 to 80% by promoting the growth of "beneficial decomposer aerobic bacteria" in the waste biomass. They hosts millions of decomposer microbes in their gut and also act as an aerator, grinder, crusher, chemical degrader and a biological stimulator [25]. As compared to the conventional composting systems, it takes nearly half the time to convert waste into vermicompost and the process becomes faster with time as the degrader worms and microbes multiply in number. Given the optimum conditions of temperature and moisture, about 1/2 kg of adult worms (approx. 1000) or 5 kg of worms (approx. 10,000) can vermicompost 10 kg of waste or 1 ton of waste respectively in just 30 days [6].

3) Earthworms Disinfect, Detoxify and Add Value to the End Products

Vermicomposting excels all conventional composting systems by the fact that it can utilize organics that otherwise cannot be utilized by others and achieves greater "utilization" than the rate of "destruction" achieved by others and also involves about 100-1000 times higher "value addition" than other technologies [33]. Another matter of considerable significance is that the earthworms stabilize the organic residues in the waste remov-

ing any "harmful pathogens" and "toxic chemicals" from the compost. They partially "detoxify" and "disinfect" the end product which is nearly "odorless" [34]. Several studies have found that earthworms effectively bio-accumulate or biodegrade several organic and inorganic chemicals including "heavy metals", "organochlorine pesticide" and "polycyclic aromatic hydrocarbons" (PAHs) residues in the medium in which it inhabits [26]. The quality of vermicompost is significantly better, rich in key minerals & beneficial soil microbes. In fact in the conventional composting technology which is thermophilic (temperature rising up to 55°C) many beneficial microbes are killed and nutrient especially nitrogen is lost (due to gassing off of nitrogen). The end product is more homogenous, richer in "plant-available nutrients & humus" and significantly low contaminants. They are "soft", "highly porous" with greater "water holding capacity" [1,11,35].

4) No or Low Energy Use in Vermi-composting Process

Normal microbial composting requires energy for aeration (constant turning of waste biomass and even for mechanical airflow) and sometimes for mechanical crushing of waste to achieve uniform particle size. Vermi-composting does not involve such use of energy. Earthworms aerate the system constantly by burrowing actions.

5) Generate No or Low Odor

Earthworms create aerobic conditions in the waste materials by their burrowing actions, inhibiting the action of anaerobic micro-organisms which release foul-smelling hydrogen sulfide and mercaptans.

6) Low Greenhouse Gas Emissions in MSW Disposal

High volumes of carbon dioxide (CO_2), methane (CH_4) and nitrous oxides (N_2O) is emitted from the conventional composting process especially in anaerobic conditions. Worms significantly increase the proportion of "aerobic to anaerobic decomposition" in the compost pile by "burrowing and aerating action" leaving very few anaerobic areas in the pile, and thus significantly reducing emission these gases and also volatile sulfur compounds. Analysis of vermicompost samples has shown generally higher levels of available nitrogen (N) as compared to the conventional compost samples made from similar feedstock. This implies that the vermicomposting process by worms is more efficient at retaining nitrogen (N) rather than releasing it as nitrous oxide (N_2O).

Our study found that on average the anaerobic composting systems emitted the highest amount of CO_2 (2950 mg/m^2/hour) and CH_4 (9.54 mg/m^2/hour), while the aerobic systems (both with and without worms) emitted the least amount of CO_2 (880 mg/m^2/hour) and CH_4 (2.17 mg/m^2/hour). Vermicomposting systems had the "lowest emission" of N_2O which is most powerful GHG [2,36].

4.6. Global Movement for Vermicomposting MSW to Divert Waste from Landfills

Large scale vermicomposting of MSW including the "sewage sludge" on commercial scale is a movement going on to divert solid waste from ending up in the landfills [37]. Municipal councils and composting companies are also participating in vermicomposting business, composting all types of organic wastes on commercial scale and selling them to the farmers. This has dual benefits. Cutting cost on landfill disposal of waste while earning revenues from sale of worms & vermicompost [1,10,38]. First serious experiments for management of municipal/industrial organic wastes were established in Holland in 1970, and subsequently in England, and Canada. Later vermiculture were followed in USA, Italy, Philippines, Thailand, China, Korea, Japan, Brazil, France, Australia, Israel & Russia.

1) USA: U.S. has some largest vermicomposting companies and plants in world and States are encouraging people for "backyard vermicomposting" to divert wastes from landfills [39]. The American Earthworm Company started a "vermi-composting farm" in 1978-79 with 500 t/month of vermicompost production [40]. A farm in LA rears 1,000,000 worms to treat 7.5 tons of garbage each month. Nearly 300 large-scale vermiculturist formed an "International Worms Growers Association" in 1997 and is having booming business. Vermicycle Organics produced 7.5 million pounds of vermicompost every year in high-tech greenhouses. Its sale of vermicompost grew by 500% in 2005. Vermitechnology Unlimited has doubled its business every year since 1991 [41,42].

US scientists are also searching for life-saving "vermimedicines" from the bioactive compounds in earthworms [43].

2) Canada: Canada is also ahead in vermicomposting business on commercial scale for both "vermicompost" and "vermimeal" production. Large-scale vermicomposting plants have been installed at several places to vermicompost municipal and farm wastes and their use in agriculture [44]. An "Organic Agriculture Centre of Canada" has been established whose objective is to replace "Chemical Agriculture" by Vermiculture [38].

3) UK: UK is also following US and Canada in promoting vermiculture mainly for waste management and to reduce the needs of "waste landfills". Large 1000 metric ton vermi-composting plants have been erected in Wales to compost diverse organic wastes [45].

4) France: France is also promoting vermiculture on commercial scale to manage all its MSW and reduce the needs of landfills. About 20 tons of mixed household wastes are being vermi-composted everyday using 1000 to 2000 million red tiger worms (*Eisenia andrei*) [6].

5) New Zealand: It is also a leading nation in vermiculture. The Envirofert Company of New Zealand is vermicomposting thousands of tons of green waste every year. They put the green waste first to a lengthy thermophilic cooking, and then to vermicomposting by worms after cooling. Cooking of green waste help destroy the weeds and pathogens which may come from the feces of pets in grasses. They claim that each worm eat the cooked green waste at least 8 times leaving an end product rich in key minerals, plant growth hormones, enzymes, and beneficial soil microbes. Envirofert is also planning to vermicompost approximately 40,000 tones of food wastes from homes, restaurants and food processing industries every year (www.envirofert.co.nz) [45,46].

6) Australia: Vermicomposting is being done on large scale in Australia as a part of the "Urban Agriculture Development Program" utilizing the urban solid wastes [1]. The Sydney Waters in New South Wales have set up a vermiculture plant of 40 million worms to degrade up to 200 ton of urban wastes a week. The Gayndah Shire Council in Queensland, Australia, is vermi-composting over 600 tons of organic waste into valuable organic fertilizer (vermi-compost) and selling to the local farmers. Vermicomposting of sludge from the sewage and water treatment plants is being increasingly practiced in Australia and as a result it is saving over 13,000 cum of landfill space every year in Australia [47]. The Hobart City Council in Tasmania, vermicompost and stabilize about 66 cum of sewage sludge every week.

7) India: India also launched vermicomposting program of MSW in the 1990s and and Bhawalkar Earthworms Research Institute (BERI) in Pune were among the pioneer institutions. Tata Energy Research Institute (TERI) in Delhi is also doing commendable works. In recent years it is growing as a part of "sustainable non-chemical agriculture" program combined with "poverty eradication" program. Farmers are using vermicompost on large scale and a revolution is going on. Vermicomposting business has enhanced the lives of poor in India and generated self-employment opportunities for the unemployed. In several Indian villages NGO's are freely distributing cement tanks and 1000 worms and encouraging men and women to collect waste from villages and farmers, vermicompost them and sell both worms and vermicompost to the farmers. People are earning from Rupees 5 to 6 lakhs (Approx. AU $ 15-20 thousands) every year from sale of both worms and their vermicompost to the farmers. Mostly they use farm waste and also MSWs collected from streets and waste dumpsites [48,49].

Bihar, Karnataka, Tamil Nadu, Gujarat and Maharashtra are leading states in vermiculture revolution. The Karnataka Compost Development Corporation established a first vermicomposting unit in the country to handle all municipal urban solid wastes and is producing 150 to 200 tons of vermicompost every day from city garbage [50]. She has listed several farmers whose life has been changed from a poor "farm labourer" to a "rich farmer" who embraced vermiculture.

8) Philippines: Vermiculture and vermicomposting were introduced in the Philippines in the 1970s. Vermicompost is being used by farmers on large scale replacing the chemical fertilizers. Recently, commercial production of "vermimeal" from earthworms biomass has been started as a substitute to "fishmeal" for promoting fishery industries [51].

9) Argentina: Vermiculture is an expanding business in Argentina especially for the development of rural and farming communities. "Worms Argentina" is a growing company which reports to be exporting "composting worms" on large scales to European, South American, Caribbean and Middle East nations. They are in high demands from Middle East countries for recycling of polluting dairy effluents [52].

10) China: Vermiculture is a fast growing industry in China for the development of rural communities. It is in fact "revival" of the traditional culture practiced by ancient medicinemen who used earthworms for treatment of several diseases. Earthworms are now being used for vermicomposting of "waste", promoting "organic farming" and for the development of "vermi-medicines" and "nutritive vermimeals". A dietary supplement in the name of PLASMIN is being marketed in China [42,53, 54].

11) Russia: Vermiculture is being promoted on large scale in Russia for management of MSW and development of life-saving "vermi-medicines" from the worms for treatment of human diseases for which conventional medicine do not have an answer. Scientists have developed a special breed of the versatile species *Eisenia fetida* which can tolerate and survive in cold climates [55].

12) Japan: Japan is also promoting vermiculture since 1970s mainly for management of MSW and production of worm biomass to isolate "bioactive compounds" for production of "vermi-medicines" [12,56].

5. The Vermifiltration Technology for Wastewater Treatment, Disinfection & Detoxification for Reuse

We are also facing the escalating socio-economic and environmental cost of dealing with current and future generation of mounting municipal and industrial wastewater. Over 80% of the potable water used by society return as wastewater. Conventional treatment results into formation of "sludge" which requires safe disposal in "secured landfills" at additional cost.

Vermifiltration of wastewater using waste eater earthworms is a newly conceived novel technology with several advantages over the conventional systems. Earthworms body work as a "biofilter" and they have been found to remove the 5 days biological oxygen demand

(BOD_5) by over 90%, chemical oxygen demand (COD) by 80-90%, total dissolved solids (TDS) by 90-92% and the total suspended solids (TSS) by 90-95% from wastewater by the general mechanism of "ingestion" and biodegradation of organic wastes and also by their "absorption" through body walls. Suspended solids are trapped on top of the vermifilter and processed by earthworms and fed to the soil microbes immobilized in the vermifilter. Worms also remove chemicals including heavy metals and pathogens from treated wastewater [57] and the treated water becomes fit for "reuse" in non-potable purposes.

5.1. Some Important Studies on Vermifiltration Technology

1) Reference [58] studied the use of earthworm for the management of effluents from intensively housed livestock which contain very heavy loads of BOD, TDSS and nutrients nitrogen (N) and phosphorus (P). The worms produced clean effluents and also nutrient rich vermicompost.

2) Reference [59] studied the treatment of domestic wastewater using vermifilter beds and concluded that worms can reduce BOD and COD loads as well as the TDSS (total dissolved and suspended solids) significantly by more than 70-80%.

3) Reference [60] studied the vermifiltration of municipal wastewater in a pilot plant for treating wastewater of 1000 inhabitants and found that the BOD load was removed by 99%, TSS by 95%, VSS (volatile suspended solids) by 96%, nitrogen (N) by 89% and phosphorus (P) by 70%. The vermifilter bed was prepared of stones at the bottom and sawdust above with 20-30 cm humus at the top in which 5000-10,000 earthworms (*Eisenia andrea*) per square meter was released. *E. coli* (M.P.N.) was removed by 1000 fold. Such systems allowed to treat 1000 L/m^2 of wastewater per day. They have commercialized and patented the technology in Chile.

4). A pilot study on vermifiltration of sewage was made by [61] at Shanghai Quyang Wastewater Treatment Facility in China. The earthworm bed which was 1 m (long) × 1 m (wide) × 1.6 m (high), was composed of granular materials and earthworms. The worm's number was kept at about 8000 worms/sqm. The average chemical oxygen demand (COD) value of raw sewage used was 408.8 mg/L that of 5 days biological oxygen demand (BOD_5) was 297 mg/L that of suspended solids (SS) was 186.5 mg/L. The hydraulic retention time varied from 6 to 9 hours and the hydraulic loading from 2.0 to 3.0 m^3/(m^2.d) of sewage. The removal efficiency of COD ranged between 81-86%, the BOD_5 between 91-98%, and the SS between 97-98%.

Vermiculture Technology: Reviving the Dreams of Sir Charles Darwin for Scientific Use of Earthworms in Sustainable Development Programs

125

5.2. Our Studies on Vermifiltration Technology at Griffith University, Australia

1) Reference [62] studied the vermifiltration of sewage obtained from the Oxley Wastewater Treatment Plant in Brisbane, Australia. Results showed that the earthworms removed BOD (BOD$_5$) loads of sewage by over 99% at hydraulic retention time (HRT) of 1-2 hours. Average COD removed from the sewage was over 50%. Although the COD removal by vermifiltration system was not significant like BOD, it was still higher than the value of COD removed by the control system without worms. This clearly signifies the role of earthworms in the degradation of "complex chemicals" in wastewater to reduce the Chemical Oxygen Demand. Earthworms also removed the total suspended solids (TSS) from the sewage by over 90%. More significant was that there was "no formation of sewage sludge".

2) Reference [63] also studied the vermifiltration of brewery and milk dairy wastewaters in Brisbane which have very high BOD$_5$ and TSS loadings e.g. 6780 mg/L & 682 mg/L respectively from brewery and 1,39,200 mg/L & 3,60,00 mg/L respectively from the dairy industry. Earthworms removed the high BOD$_5$ loads by 99% in both cases and TSS by over 98%. But the hydraulic retention times (HRTs) in case of brewery wastewater was 3-4 hours and 6-10 hours for the dairy wastewater.

An important observation was that the control system (devoid of earthworms) frequently got choked. The organic solids in the wastewater accumulated as peat in the soil layer and also attracted heavy "fungal infection". It became un-operational after sometimes. In the vermifiltration system the earthworms constantly fed upon the solids and the fungus and never allowed the system to be choked and become un-operational.

3) Currently Reference [64] are working on vermifiltration of wastewater from "fruit juice processing industry" in Brisbane. The fruit juice wastewater contain very high BOD, COD, TSS and TDS loads. The initial 5 days biological oxygen demand (BOD$_5$) was reduced from 1340 ppm to 3 ppm (99.77%), chemical oxygen demand (COD) from 2730 ppm to 112 ppm (95.89%), total suspended solids (TSS) from 190 ppm to 16 ppm (91.57%), total dissolved solids (TDS) from 440 ppm to 12 ppm (97.27%), and the turbidity from 130 NTU (naphelometric units) to 6 NTU (95.38%). The vermifiltration system (vermifilter bed) contained a 4 inches layer of vermicompost (humus) and on the top of it a 6 inches layer of soil containing 450-500 "adult healthy earthworms" (*Eisenia fetida*) @ 5000 worms per cubic meter of soil.

5.3. The Mechanism of Worm Action in Vermifiltration

The twin processes of microbial stimulation & biodeg-radation, and the enzymatic degradation of waste solids by worms simultaneously work in the vermifiltration system. Vermifilters provide a high specific area—up to 800 sq m/g and voidage up to 60%. Suspended solids are trapped on top of the vermifilter and processed by earthworms and fed to the soil microbes immobilized in the vermifilter.

Intensification of soil processes and aeration by the earthworms enable the soil stabilization and filtration system to become effective and smaller in size. Earthworms intensify the organic loadings of wastewater in the vermifilter soil bed by the fact that it granulates the clay particles thus increasing the "hydraulic conductivity" of the system. They also grind the silt and sand particles, thus giving high total specific surface area, which enhances the ability to "adsorb" the organics and inorganic from the wastewater passing through it.

Earthworms vermicompost in the vermifilter beds provides wonderful sites for "adsorption" of heavy metals and pollutants in wastewater due to presence of "lignin" contents. The vermicast in the soil bed also offers excellent hydraulic conductivity of sand (being porous like sand) and also high adsorption power of clay [48].

5.4. Advantages of Vermifiltration Technology over the Conventional Wastewater Treatment Technologies

1) Low Energy Requirement

Vermi-filtration of wastewater is low energy & efficient system and has distinct advantage over all the conventional wastewater treatment systems—the "Activated Sludge Process", "Trickling Filters" and "Rotating Biological Contactors" which are highly energy intensive, costly to install and operate and do not generate any income. In the vermifilter process there is 100% capture of organic materials, the capital and operating costs are less, and there is high value added end products e.g. vermifiltered "nutrient rich" water with potential for farm irrigation and vermicompost retrieved from the vermifiltered beds.

2) No Formation of Sewage Sludge and No Foul Odor

Since the conventional technologies are mostly the flow-processes and have finite hydraulic retention time (HRT) it always results into a "residual stream" of complex organics and heavy metals (while only the simple organics are consumed by decomposer microbes) in the form of "sludge". This plagues most municipal councils in world as the sludge is a "biohazard" and requires safe landfill disposal at high cost. The greatest advantage of vermifiltration system is that there is no formation of "sewage sludge" [65]. The worms decompose the organics in the wastewater and also devour the solids (which forms the sludge) synchronously. There is no foul odor as the earthworms arrests rotting and decay of all putrescible matters in the wastewater and the sludge. In all developed nations a "worm farm" has become a necessity in all wastewater & water treatment plants to resolve the sludge problems. Earthworms feed readily upon the sludge components, rapidly convert them into vermicompost, reduce the pathogens to safe levels and ingest the heavy metals [26].

3) Detoxified and Disinfected Treated Water for Reuse

Vermifiltered wastewater is free of pathogens and toxic chemicals (heavy metals & endocrine disrupting chemicals) and suitable for "reuse" as water for farm irrigation. & other non-potable uses. The worms devour on all the pathogens (bacteria, fungus, protozoa & nematodes) in the medium in which they inhabit. They have the capacity to bio-accumulate high concentrations of toxic chemicals in their tissues and the resulting wastewater becomes almost chemical-free. Earthworms have also been reported to bio-accumulate "endocrine disrupting chemicals" (EDCs) from sewage which otherwise is not removed by our conventional sewage treatment plants (STPs). Reference [66] have reported significantly high concentrations of EDCs (dibutylphthalate, dioctylphthalate, bisphenol-A and 17 β-estrdiol) in tissues of earthworms (*E. fetida*) living in sewage percolating filter beds and also in garden soil.

5.5. Vermifiltration Technology: Destined to Become a Global Movement

Due to its simplicity and cost-effectiveness vermifiltration of both municipal and industrial wastewater is destined to become a global movement. In Chile, over 100 sewage treatment plants of different sizes, going from individual houses to plants for 12,000 persons and bigger plants for industries are already working. It has been introduced on commercial scale in Mexico and Venezuela [60]. India and Brazil is also introducing the technology on commercial scale. Some companies in Pune (India) have already started pilot plants.

If a vermifilter bed of 0.3 cum soil is prepared with approximately 5000 worms (over 2.5 kg) to start with, it can easily treat 950-1000 L of domestic wastewater/ sewage generated by (on an average) a family of 4 people with average BOD value ranging between 300-400 mg/L, COD 100-300 mg/L, TSS, 300-350 mg/L everyday with hydraulic retention time (HRT) of the wastewater in the vermifilter bed being approximately 1-2 hours. Given that the worms multiply and double its number in at least every 60 days under ideal conditions of temperature and moisture, even starting with this number of earthworms a huge population (biomass) of worms with robust vermi-filtration system can be established quickly within few months which will be able to treat greater amount of wastewater generated in the fam-

ily. An important consideration is the peak hour wastewater generation which is usually very high and may not comply with the required HRT (1-2 hrs) which is very critical for sewage treatment by vermi-filtration system. To allow 1-2 hrs HRT in the vermifilter bed an onsite domestic wastewater storage facility will be required from where the discharge of wastewater to the vermifilter tank can be slowly regulated through flow control.

6. Vermiremediation Technology for Cleanup of Chemically Contaminated Lands & Soil for Re-Use & Re-Development

Large tract of arable land is being chemically contaminated due to mining activities, heavy use of agrochemicals in farmlands, landfill disposal of toxic wastes and other developmental activities like oil and gas drilling. Traditionally, remediation of chemically contaminated soils involves "off-site" management by excavating and subsequent disposal by burial in secured landfills. This method of remediation is very costly affair and merely shifts the contamination problem elsewhere. Additionally, this involves great risk of environmental hazard while the contaminated soils are being transported and "migration of contaminants" from landfills into adjacent lands and water bodies by leaching. Soil washing for removing inorganic contaminants from soil is another alternative to landfill burial, but this technique produce a "residue" with very high metal contents which requires further treatment or burial.

Since the late 1980s, after the chemical and mechanical treatments of lands and water bodies and thermal treatment (incineration) of hazardous wastes proved economically and environmentally unsustainable, focus shifted towards the biological methods which are cost-effective as well as environmentally sustainable and also socially acceptable.

Vermiremediation (using chemical tolerant earthworm species) is emerging as a low-cost and convenient technology for cleaning up the chemically polluted/contaminated sites/lands in world. Earthworms have been used for land recovery, reclamation and rehabilitation of suboptimal soils such as poor mineral soils, polder soils, open cast mining sites, closed landfill sites and cutover peat [67,68].

6.1. Some Important Studies on Vermiremediation Technology

1) Studies on Removal of Heavy Metals

Reference [69] studied that earthworms can bio-accumulate high concentrations of heavy metals like cadmium (Cd), mercury (Hg), lead (Pb) copper (Cu), manganese (Mn), calcium (Ca), iron (Fe) and zinc (Zn) in their tissues without affecting their physiology and this

Vermiculture Technology: Reviving the Dreams of Sir Charles Darwin for Scientific Use of Earthworms
in Sustainable Development Programs

127

particularly when the metals are mostly non-bioavailable. They can particularly ingest and accumulate extremely high amounts of zinc (Zn), lead (Pb) and cadmium (Cd). Cadmium levels up to 100 mg per kg dry weight have been found in tissues. Ireland (1983) reported that the earthworms species *Lumbricus terrestris* can bio-accumulate in their tissues 90-180 mg lead (Pb)/gm of dry weight, while *L. rubellus* and *D. rubida* it was 2600 mg /gm and 7600 mg/gm of dry weight respectively. Zinc (Zn), manganese (Mn), and iron (Fe) were shown to be excreted through the calciferous glands of earthworms. Contreras-Ramos *et al.* (2005) also confirmed that the earthworms reduced the concentrations of chromium (Cr), copper (Cu), zinc (Zn) and lead (Pb) in the vermicomposted sludge (biosolids) below the limits set by the USEPA in 60 days.

2) Studies on Removal of Polycyclic Aromatic Hydrocarbons (PAH's)

PAHs are priority pollutants and cause great concern with respect to human health and environment. They are inherently "recalcitrant hydrocarbons", and the higher molecular weight PAHs are very difficult to remediate. Reference [70] studied the influence of earthworms species *L. rubellus* on the disappearance of spiked PAHs phananthrene & fluoranthene (100 µg/kg of soil) and found that the losses of both PAHs occurred at a faster rate in soils with earthworms, than the soil without worms. After 56 days (8 weeks), 86% of the phenanthrene was removed. Reference [71] studied the uptake of three PAHs viz. phenanthrene, anthracene and benzo(a)pyrene at different concentrations by *E. fetida* and found that the concentration of anthracene decreased by 2-fold after addition of earthworms, benzo(a)pyrene decreased by 1.4-fold and phenanthrene was completely removed (100%) by earthworms

3) Studies on Removal of Petroleum and Crude Oil Hydrocarbons

References [72] & [73] studied earthworm species *E. fetida* with varying organic wastes to an oil contaminated soil and found that worms significantly degraded and decreased oil contents in comparison to the control. Reference [74] also studied the use of earthworms *E. fetida* and vermicomposting in the treatment of high molecular weight hydrocarbons "asphaltens" from the Prestige Oil Spill. Earthworms mineralized the asphaltens thus eliminating it from the system.

4) Studies on Removal of Agrochemicals

Studies indicate that the earthworms bio-accumulate or biodegrade "organochlorine pesticide" and "polycyclic aromatic hydrocarbons" (PAHs) residues in the medium in which it lives. References [75-78] found that the worm vermicasts sorbed higher amount of herbicides from the contaminated soil than the control soil due to the higher levels of organic carbon & more finer size of fractions in worm worked contaminated soils. Reference [79] found that due to earthworm burrowing actions, a

greater degree of bound pesticides residues in soil was released as compared to those without worms. Earthworms restricted the formation of bound fraction of pesticides and also enhanced the release and mineralization of bound pesticides residues.

5) Studies on Removal of Polychlorinated Biphenyls (PCBs)

PCBs are a group of oily, colorless, organic fluids belonging to the same chemical family as the pesticide DDT. PCBs are categorized as unusually toxic and "persistent organic pollutant" (POPs). Reference [80] found that PCB contaminated soil treated with earthworms resulted in significantly greater PCB losses (average 52%) when compared to the soil without earthworm treatment which was 41%.

6.2. Our Studies on Vermiremediation Technology at Griffith University, Australia

Reference [81] studied the remedial action of earthworms on PAHs contaminated soils obtained from a former gas works site in Brisbane where gas was being produced from coal. The initial concentration of total PAHs compounds in the soil at site was greater than 11, 820 mg/kg of soil. The legislative requirements for PAHs concentration in soil in Australia is only 100 mg/kg for industrial sites and 20 mg/kg for residential sites. Results showed that the earthworms could remove nearly 80% of the PAHs as compared to just 47% & 21% where it was not used and only microbial degradation occurred. This was just in 12 weeks study period. It could have removed by 100% in another few weeks. More significant was that the worm added soil became odor-free of chemicals in few days and were more soft and porous in texture.

6.3. Mechanism of Worm Action in Vermiremediation

Earthworms uptake chemicals from the soil through passive "absorption" of the dissolved fraction through the moist "body wall' in the interstitial water and also by mouth and "intestinal uptake" while the soil passes through the gut. Earthworms apparently possess a number of mechanisms for uptake, immobilization and excretion of heavy metals and other chemicals. They either "bio-transform" or "biodegrade" the chemical contaminants rendering them harmless in their bodies. Some metals are bound by a protein called "metallothioneins" found in earthworms which has very high capacity to bind metals. The chloragogen cells in earthworms appears to mainly accumulate heavy metals absorbed by the gut and their immobilization in the small spheroidal chloragosomes and debris vesicles that the cells contain [70,76] found that earthworms biodegrade organic contaminants like phthalate, phenanthrene and fluoranthene.

6.4. Advantages of Vermiremediation Technology over the Mechanical & Chemical Treatment of Contaminated Sites

The greatest advantage of the vermiremediation technology is that it is "on-site" treatment and there are no additional problems of "earth-cutting", "excavation" and "transportation" of contaminated soils to the landfills or to the treatment sites incurring additional economic and environmental cost. Vermiremediation would cost about $ 500-1000 per hectare of land as compared to $ 10,000-15,000 per hectare by mechanical excavation of contaminated soil & its landfill disposal.

Significantly, vermiremediation leads to total improvement in the quality of soil and land where the worms inhabit. Earthworms significantly contribute as soil conditioner to improve the physical, chemical as well as the biological properties of the soil and its nutritive value. They swallow large amount of soil everyday, grind them in their gizzard and digest them in their intestine with aid of enzymes. Only 5-10 percent of the digested and ingested material is absorbed into the body and the rest is excreted out in soil in the form of fine mucus coated granular aggregates called "vermicastings" which are rich in NKP (nitrates, phosphates and potash), micronutrients and beneficial soil microbes including the "nitrogen fixers" and "mycorrhizal fungus".

Of considerable economic and environmental significance is that the worm feed used in vermiremediation process is necessarily an "organic waste" product. This means that it would also lead to reuse and recycling of vast amount of organic wastes which otherwise end up in landfills for disposal at high cost. And what is of still greater economic and environmental significance is that the polluted land is not only "cleaned-up" but also "improved in quality". The soil becomes lighter and porous rich in biological activities and the productivity is increased to several times. During the vermi-remediation process of soil, the population of earthworms increases significantly benefiting the soil in several ways. A "wasteland" is transformed into "wonderland". Earthworms are in fact regarded as "biological indicator" of good fertile soil and land.

6.5. Vermiremediation Technology Destined to Become a Global Movement

Vermiremediation by commercial vermiculture in U.K. "Land Reclamation and Improvements Programs" has become an established technology for long-term soil decontamination, improvement & maintenance, without earth-cutting, soil excavation and use of chemicals". U.S., Australia and other developed nations are also following [82,83].

7. Vermi-Agroproduction Technology for Sustainable Agriculture & Production of Safe Organic Food for Society

Vermi-agroproduction technology promises to usher in the "Second Green Revolution" by completely replacing the destructive agro-chemicals which did more harm than good to both the farmers and their farmland during the "First Green Revolution" of the 1950-60's. Studies indicate that vermicompost is a wonderful growth promoter and at least 4 times more nutritive than the conventional composts and gives 30-40% higher yield of crops over chemical fertilizers [84,85]. In Argentina, farmers consider it to be seven (7) times richer than conventional composts in nutrients and growth promoting values [52]. The "humic acid" in vermicompost (excreted by worms) stimulate plant growth even in small amount [86].

Earthworms restore & improve soil fertility and boost crop productivity by the use of their excreta (vermicast). They excrete beneficial soil microbes, and secrete polysaccharides, proteins and other nitrogenous compounds into the soil [87]. They promote soil fragmentation and aeration, and bring about "soil turning" and dispersion in farmlands. Worm activity can increase air-soil volume from 8-30%. One acre of land can contain up to 3 million earthworms the activities of which can bring up to 8-10 tons of "top soil" to the surface (in the form of vermicast) every year. Presence of worms improves water penetration in compacted soils by 50%. U.S. study indicates that 10,000 worms in a farm plot provides the same benefit as three farmers working 8 hours in shift all year round with 10 tons of manure applied in the plot [42]. Indian study showed that an earthworm population of 0.2-1.0 million per hectare of farmlands can be established within a short period of three months. On an average 12 tons/hectare/year of soil or organic matter is ingested by earthworms, leading to upturning of 18 tons of soil/year, and the world over at this rate it may mean a 2 inches of fertile humus layer over the globe [48].

7.1. Some Important Studies on Vermi-Agroproduction Technology

1) Reference [85] studied the agronomic impacts of vermicompost and found that it consistently improved seed germination, enhanced seedling growth and development, and increased plant productivity much more than would be possible from the mere conversion of mineral nutrients into plant-available forms. The growth responses of plants from vermicompost appears more like "hormone-induced activity" associated with the high levels of nutrients, humic acids and humates in vermicompost rather than boosted by high levels of plant-available nutrients.

2) Studies made by [88] at CSIRO Australia found that

the earthworms can increase growth of wheat crops by 39%, grain yield by 35%, lift protein value of the grain by 12% & fight crop diseases. Reference [89] also studied that earthworms & its vermicast improve the growth and yield of wheat by more than 40%.

3) Reference [90] studied the agronomic impacts of vermicompost and inorganic (chemical) fertilizers on strawberries when applied separately and also in combination. The "yield" of marketable strawberries and the "weight" of the "largest fruit" was greater on plants in plots grown on vermicompost as compared to inorganic fertilizers. Also, farm soils applied with vermicompost had significantly greater "microbial biomass" than the one applied with inorganic fertilizers.

4) Reference [91] studied the agronomic impact of vermicompost on cherries and found that it increased yield of "cherries" for three (3) years after "single application" inferring that use of vermicompost in soil builds up fertility and restore its vitality for long time and its further use can be reduced to a minimum after some years of application in farms.

5) Reference [92] reported two-fold yield of grapes by vermicompost as compared to chemical fertilizers.

7.2. Our Studies on Vermi-Agroproduction Technology at Griffith University, Australia

1) Reference [93] studied the growth impacts of earthworms and their vermicompost on potted corn crops and compared with chemical fertilizers. Vermicompost with earthworms in soil achieved excellent growth over chemical fertilizers. While the plants on chemicals grew only 5 cm in 7 weeks, those on vermicompost with worms grew 15 cm within the same period. Corn plants with worms & vermicompost also attained maturity (appearance of male & female reproductive organs) very fast. Another significant finding was that plants on vermicompost demanded "less water" for irrigation.

2) Reference [93] also studied the growth impacts of earthworms with vermicompost on potted wheat plants and compared with chemical fertilizers & conventional compost (cow manure). Wheat crops on vermicompost with worms maintained very good growth from the very beginning & achieved maturity very fast. The striking rates of seed germination were very high, nearly 48 hours (2 days) ahead of others and the numbers of seed germinated were also high by nearly 20%. Plants were greener and healthier over others, with large numbers of tillers & long seed ears at maturity. Seeds were healthy and nearly 35-40% more as compared to plants on chemical fertilizers. What they achieved in just 5 weeks was achieved by others in 10 weeks. More significant was that the pot soil with vermicompost was very soft & porous and retained more moisture. Pot soil with chemical fertilizers was hard and demanded more water frequently.

3) Reference [93] also studied the growth impacts of vermicompost on farmed wheat crops and compared it with conventional cattle dung compost and chemical fertilizers. Exclusive application of vermicompost@25 quintal/ha boosted yield 18% higher over the chemical fertilizers (NPK: 120:40:60). On conventional compost applied @ 100 Q/ha (4 times more than vermicompost) the yield was 17% less than that on vermicompost. The requirement of irrigation was also reduced in vermicompost applied farm plots by 30-40%. Test results indicated better availability of essential micronutrients and useful microbes in vermicompost applied soils. Most remarkable was the significantly reduced (nearly 75%) incidences of "pest & disease attack" on vermicompost grown crops.

7.3. Vermiculture Technology can Reduce Soil Salinity & Improve Fertility of Sodic Soils

Studies indicate that *Esinea fetida* can tolerate soils nearly half as salty as seawater *i.e.* 15 gm/kg of soil and also improve its biology and chemistry. (Average seawater salinity is around 35 g/L). Farmers at Phaltan in Satara district of Maharashtra, India, applied live earthworms to their sugarcane crop grown on saline soils irrigated by saline ground water. The yield was 125 tones/hectare of sugarcane and there was marked improvement in soil chemistry. Within a year there was 37% more nitrogen, 66% more phosphates and 10% more potash. The chloride content was less by 46% [93].

Reference [94] studied the production of potato (*Solanum tuberosum*) by application of vermicompost in a reclaimed sodic soil in India. With good potato growth the sodicity (ESP) of the soil was also reduced from initial 96.74 to 73.68 in just about 12 weeks. The average available nitrogen (N) content of the soil increased from initial 336.00 kg/ha to 829.33 kg/ha.

7.4. Advantages of Vermi-Agroproduction Technology

1) Can Replace Destructive & Costly Chemical Fertilizers from Farm Production

Vermicompost has potential to replace the destructive chemical fertilizers from farm production. It can alone produce food over 30-40% higher than those produced by chemical fertilizers. It is at least 75% cheaper than the chemical fertilizers which are produced in factories from vanishing petroleum products generating huge waste & pollution.

2) Produce Nutritive, Chemical-free Farm Products with Greater Storage Value

The biggest advantage of great social significance is that the food produced is completely organic "safe & chemical-free". Use of vermicompost enhances size, color, smell, taste, flavour and keeping quality (storage value) of flowers, fruits, vegetables and food grains.

3) Restore Natural Fertility of Farmland Soil

Upon successive years of application, vermicompost build-up the soils "natural fertility" improving its total physical (porous), chemical (rich in nutrients) and biological (beneficial soil microbes) properties. It also regenerates a rich population of worms in the farm soil from the cocoons which further help improve soil fertility and subsequently lesser amount of vermicompost is required to maintain a good yield and productivity. On the contrary, with the continued application of chemical fertilizers over the years the "natural fertility of soil is destroyed" and it becomes "addict". Subsequently greater amount of chemicals are required to maintain the same yield & productivity of previous years.

4) Reduces Water for Farm Irrigation

Vermicompost has very "high porosity", "aeration", "drainage" and "water holding capacity" and thus its application in soil reduces the requirement of water for irrigation by 30-40%.

5) Kills Pests without Pesticides

Another big advantage of great social & environmental significance is that vermicompost "suppress plant disease" in crops and inhibit the soil-born fungal diseases. In field trials with pepper, tomatoes, strawberries and grapes significant suppression of plant-parasitic nematodes has been found. There is also significant decrease in arthropods (aphids, buds, mealy bug, spider mite) populations with 20% and 40% vermicompost additions [95]. Humus in vermicast extracts "toxins", "harmful fungi & bacteria" from soil & protects plants. Actinomycetes in vermicast induces "biological resistance" in plants against pests & diseases. As such use of vermicompost significantly reduces the need for "chemical pesticides". Our studies indicated over 75%.

7.5. The Global Movement for VAPT to Replace the Destructive Chemical Fertilizer

Worldwide farmers are desperate to get rid of the vicious circle of the use of chemical fertilizers as their cost have been constantly rising and also the amount of chemicals used per hectare has been steadily increasing over the years to maintain the yield & productivity of previous years. Nearly 3-4 times of agro-chemicals are now being used per hectare what was used in the 1960s. In Australia, the cost of MAP fertilizer has risen from AU $ 530.00 to AU $ 1500.00 per ton since 2006. So is the story everywhere in world because the chemical fertilizers are produced from "vanishing resources" of earth. Farmers urgently need a sustainable alternative which is both economical and also productive while also maintaining soil health & fertility. The new concept is "Ecological Agriculture" which is by definition different from "Organic Farming" that was focused mainly on production of chemical-free foods. Ecological agriculture emphasize

on total protection of food, farm & human ecosystems while improving soil fertility & development of secondary source of income for the farmers. UN has also endorsed it. Vermiculture technology provides the best answer for ecological agriculture which is synonymous with "sustainable agriculture".

8. The Vermi-Industrial Production Technology for Producing Raw Materials for Pharmaceutical & Consumer Industries

1) Raw Materials for Rubber, Lubricant, Detergent, Soaps and Cosmetic Industries

Some biological compounds from earthworms are also finding industrial applications. Being "biodegradable" they are environmentally friendly and sustainable. Stearic acid found in earthworms is a long chain saturated fatty acid and is widely used as "lubricant" and as an "additive" in industrial preparations. It is used in the manufacture of metallic stearates, pharmaceuticals soaps, cosmetics and food packaging. It is also used as a "softner", "accelerator activator" and "dispersing agents" in rubbers. Industrial applications of lauric acid and its derivatives are as "alkyd resins", "wetting agents", a "rubber accelerator" and "softner" and in the manufacture of "detergents" and "insecticides" [54,96]. Worms are also finding new uses as a source of "collagen" for pharmaceutical industries.

2) Nutritive Feed Materials for Poultry, Dairy and Fishery Industries

Earthworms are rich in high quality protein (65%) and are "complete protein" with all essential amino acids. There is 70-80% high quality "lysine" and "methionine". Glumatic acid, leucine, lysine & arginine are higher than in fish meals. Tryptophan is 4 times higher than in blood powder and 7 times higher than in cow liver. Worms are also rich in Vitamins A & B. There is 0.25 mg of Vitamin B_1 and 2.3 mg of Vitamin B_2 in each 100 gm of earthworms. Vitamin D accounts for 0.04-0.073% of earthworms wet weight. Thus worms are wonderful probiotic feed for fish, cattle and poultry industry. They are being used as "additives" to produce "pellet feeds" in the USA, Canada and Japan [42].

As earthworm protein is complete with 8-9 essential amino acids especially with the tasty "glutamic acid" it can be used for human beings as well. Worm protein is higher than in any meat products with about 2% lower fats than in meats and ideal for human consumption [51].

3) Bioactive Compounds for Pharmaceutical Industries to Produce Life Saving Medicines

A great news for the world vermitech scientists appeared in Philippines "News Today" on November 25, 2005 telling "Earthworms can help dissolve blood clots for stroke patients" [97]. In the last 10 years, a number

Vermiculture Technology: Reviving the Dreams of Sir Charles Darwin for Scientific Use of Earthworms
in Sustainable Development Programs

131

of earthworm's "clot-dissolving", "lytic" and "immune boosting" compounds have been isolated and tested clinically [98,99]. Current researches made in Canada, China, Japan and other countries on the identification, isolation and synthesis of some "bioactive compounds" from earthworms (*Lumbricus rubellus* & *Eisenia fetida*) with potential medicinal values for treatment of heart diseases have brought revolution in the vermiculture studies [12,100,101]. Some of these compounds have been found to be enzymes exhibiting "anti-blood clotting" effects. Oral administration of earthworms powder & enzymes were found to be effective in treating "thrombotic diseases", "arthritis", "diabetes mellitus", "pulmonary heart disease", "lowering blood pressure", "epilepsy", "schizophrenia", "mumps", "exzema", "chronic lumbago", "anemia", "vertigo" and "digestive ulcer" [44,102,103]. Scientist have also isolated "bronchial dilating" substance from earthworms.

Researchers at Quinghua University, China has extracted 4 valuable medicinal compounds from earthworms —a large molecular compound which has "anti-carcinogenic" effects [104]; medium molecular compound which has "anti-thrombosis" & "thrombus dissolution" effects [105]; a small molecular compounds which contain 17 kinds of amino acids, polymers, trace elements and vitamins; and a 4th product which can cure burns and scalds [42]. Reference [102] also extracted enzymes lumbritin, lumbrofebrin, terrestrolumbrolysin and "lumbrokinase" enzymes from *Lumbricus rubellus* useful in thrombolytic therapy.

The coelomic fluid of earthworms have been reported to have anti-pathogenic activities and are good biological compound for the production of "antibiotics" [34]. Several fatty acids have been isolated from earthworms. Important among them are "lauric acid" which are known for its "anti-microbial" properties. It is a precursor to "monolaurin" which is a more powerful "anti-microbial" agent that has potential to fight lipid-coated RNA and DNA viruses, several pathogenic Gram-positive bacteria, yeasts and various pathogenic protozoa [54]. Peptide "lumbricin I" isolated from *L. lumbricus* also exhibits antimicrobial activity against both Gram positive and Gram negative bacteria as well as fungi.

9. Conclusions & Remarks

Vermiculture technologies for waste and land management and for improving soil fertility to promote crop productivity and production of valuable bioactive compounds of great medicinal values has grown considerably in recent years all over the world and has been scientifically improved [106]. It is like getting "gold from garbage" (highly nutritive biofertilizer) by vermi-composting technology; "silver from sewage" (disinfected & detoxified water for reuse in agriculture & industries) by

vermi-filtration technology; "converting a wasteland (chemically contaminated lands) into wonderland" (fertile land) by vermi-remediation technology; harvesting "green gold" (food crops) by using "black gold" (vermicompost) by agro-production technology; creating a "worm factory" to produce medicines & materials for societal use. The three versatile species *E. fetida, E. euginae* and *P. excavatus* performing wide social, economic & environmental functions occur almost everywhere.

The vermi-composting & vermi-agro-production technologies can together maintain the "global human sustainability cycle" & "circular economy"—using food wastes (negative economic & environmental value) of the society to produce food (positive socio-economic value) for the society again" while also protecting farm soil and improving its fertility (positive economic & environmental value). And if vermicompost can "replace" the "chemical fertilizers" for production of "safe organic foods" which has now been proved worldwide, it will be a giant step towards achieving global social, economic & environmental sustainability. With the growing global popularity of "organic foods" which became a US $ 6.5 billion business every year by 2000, there will be great demand for vermicompost in future. US Department of Agriculture estimates 25% of Americans purchase organically grown foods at least once a week [42].

In all developed nations a "worm farm" has become a necessity in all wastewater & water treatment plants to resolve the problems of "sludge" which is a biohazard and needs safe disposal in secured landfills at high cost. Earthworms readily feed on them and convert into vermicompost.

In any vermiculture practice, "worm biomass" comes as a valuable by-product. It is finding uses and applications in modern medicine and in several industries for sustainable production of essential goods for societal use and consumption [107]. On commercial scale tons of worm biomass can result every year as under favorable conditions worms "double" their number at least every 60-70 days.

All infrastructure based on vermiculture technologies (vermicomposting, vermifiltration, vermiremediation & vermi-agroproduction) using earthworms are easy to construct, install and operate with minimum engineering considerations. They are highly economical and cost-effective with highly valued by-products and end-products. It is basically a "one-time investment" technology as the earthworms multiply at a fast rate under favorable conditions of temperature and moisture and increase the pace and rapidity of the technological process.

Earthworms are truly justifying the beliefs and fulfilling the dreams of Sir Charles Darwin who called them as *"unheralded soldiers' of mankind"* and *"friends of farmers"* and said that *"there may not be any other creature in world that has played so important a role in the his-*

tory of life on earth". It is also justifying the beliefs of great Russian scientist Dr. Anatoly Igonin who said "*Nobody and nothing can be compared with earthworms and their positive influence on the whole living Nature. They create soil & improve soil's fertility and provides critical biosphere's functions: disinfecting, neutralizing, protective and productive*". Future of mankind on earth beholds with the earthworms and our relationship must be maintained.

10. Acknowledgements

The authors thank Mr. Scott Byrnes and Ms. Jane Gifkins—the in-charge of various laboratories and Mr. Ehsram Werner—the in-charge of glasshouses in the Faculty of Environmental Sciences of Griffith University, Nathan Campus for providing all laboratory and glasshouse facilities availed during the various research projects on vermiculture studies.

11. References

[1] M. Lotzof, "Vermiculture: An Australian Technology Success Story," *Waste Management Magazine*, Australia, February 2000.

[2] R. K. Sinha, J. Nair, G. Bharambe, S. Patil and P. S. Bapat, "Vermiculture Revolution: A Low-Cost & Sustainable Technology for Management of Municipal & Industrial Organic Wastes (Solid & Liquid) by Earthworms with Significantly Low Greenhouse Gas Emissions," In: J. I. Daven and R. N. Klein, Eds., *Progress in Waste Management Research*, NOVA Science Publishers, Hauppauge, 2008, pp. 159-227.

[3] R. K. Sinha, S. Herat, G. Bharambe, S. Patil, P. S. Bapat, K. Chauhan and D. Valani, "Vermiculture Biotechnology: The Emerging Cost-Effective and Sustainable Technology of the 21st Century for Multiple Uses from Waste & Land Management to Safe & Sustained Food Production," *Environmental Research Journal*, NOVA Science Publishers, Hauppauge, Vol. 3, No. 1, 2009, pp. 41-110.

[4] C. A. Edwards and J. R. Lofty, "Biology of Earthworms," Chapman & Hall, London, 1972, p. 283.

[5] C. A. Edwards and P. J. Bohlen, "Biology and Ecology of Earthworms," 3rd Edition, Chapman and Hall, London, 1996.

[6] C. Visvanathan, J. Trankler, K. Jospeh and R. Nagendran, (Eds.) "Vermicomposting as an Eco-Tool in Sustainable Solid Waste Management," Asian Institute of Technology, Annamalai University, Chidambaram, 2005.

[7] P. Hand, "Earthworm Biotechnology," In: R. Greenshields, Ed., *Resources and Application of Biotechnology: The New Wave*, Macmillan Press Ltd, US, 1988.

[8] J. E. Satchell, "Earthworm Ecology from Darwin to Vermiculture," Chapman and Hall Ltd., London, 1983, pp. 1-5.

[9] M. Kerr and A. J. Stewart, "Tolerance Test of *Eisinia fetida* for Sodium Chloride," *Journal of Undergraduate Research*, U.S Department of Energy, 2002. http:www.scied.science.doe.gov

[10] R. K. Sinha, "Earthworms: The Miracle of Nature (Charles Darwin's 'Unheralded Soldiers of Mankind and Farmer's Friends')," *The Environmentalist*, Vol. 29, No. 4, August 2009, pp. 339-340.

[11] M. Appelhof, "Worms Eat My Garbage," 2nd Edition, Flower Press, Kalamazoo, Michigan, 1997. http://www.wormwoman.com

[12] Z. W. Wang, "Research Advances in Earthworms Bioengineering Technology," *Medica*, Vol. 31, No. 5, 2000, pp. 386-389.

[13] R. C. Loehr, J. H. Martin, E. F. Neuhauser and M. R. Malecki, "Waste Management Using Earthworms—Engineering and Scientific Relationships," Project Report ISP-8016764, National Science Foundation, Washington, D.C., 1984.

[14] C. A. Edwards, "The Use of Earthworms in the Breakdown and Management of Organic Wastes," In: C. A. Edwards, Ed., *Earthworm Ecology*, CRC Press, Boca Raton, 1998, pp. 327-354.

[15] M. T. Datar, M. N. Rao and S. Reddy, "Vermicomposting: A Technological Option for Solid Waste Management," *Solid Waste Technology and Management*, Vol. 24, No. 2, 1997, pp. 89-93.

[16] G. Fraser-Quick, "Vermiculture—A Sustainable Total Waste Management Solution," *What's New in Waste Management?* Vol. 4, No. 6, 2002, pp. 13-16.

[17] C. A. Edwards, "Breakdown of Animal, Vegetable and Industrial Organic Wastes by Earthworms," In: C. A. Edward and E. F. Neuhauser, Ed., *Earthworms in Waste and Environmental Management*, SPB Academic Publishing, The Hague, 1988, pp. 21-32.

[18] R. D. Kale, "Earthworms: Nature's Gift for Utilization of Organic Wastes," In: C. A. Edward, Ed., *Earthworm Ecology*, St. Lucie Press, NY, 1998.

[19] R. D. Kale and N. S. Sunitha, "Efficiency of Earthworms (*E. Eugeniae*) in Converting the Solid Waste from Aromatic Oil Extraction Industry into Vermicompost," *Journal of IAEM*, Vol. 22, No. 1, 1995, pp. 267-269.

[20] S. N. Seenappa, J. Rao and R. Kale, "Conversion of Distillery Wastes into Organic Manure by Earthworm *Eudrillus euginae*," *Journal of IAEM*, Vol. 22, No. 1, 1995, pp.244-246.

[21] K. Gunathilagraj and T. Ravignanam, "Vermicomposting of Sericultural Wastes," *Madras Agricultural Journal*, Coimbatore, 1996, pp. 455-457.

[22] B. L. Lakshmi and G. S. Vizaylakshmi, "Vermicomposting of Sugar Factory Filter Pressmud Using African Earthworms Species (*Eudrillus eugeniae*)," *Pollution Research*, Vol. 19, No. 3, 2000, pp. 481-483.

[23] M. Saxena, A. Chauhan and P. Asokan, "Flyash Vermicompost from Non-Friendly Organic Wastes," *Pollution Research*, Vol. 17, No. 1, 1998, pp. 5-11.

[24] O. Bajsa, J. Nair, K. Mathew and G. E. Ho, "Pathogen Die-Off in Vermicomposting Process," Paper Presented at the International Conference on *Small Water and Wastewater Treatment Systems*, Perth, 2004.

[25] R. K. Sinha, A. S. Herat, R. Asadi and E. Carretero, "Vermiculture Technology for Environmental Management: Study of Action of Earthworms *Eisenia fetida, Eudrilus euginae* and *Perionyx excavatus* on Biodegradation of Some Community Wastes in India and Australia," *The Environmentalist*, Vol. 22, No. 2, 2002, pp. 261-268.

[26] R. K. Sinha, S. Herat, G. Bharambe and A. Brahambhatt, "Vermistabilization of Sewage Sludge (Biosolids) by Earthworms: Converting a Potential Biohazard Destined for Landfill Disposal into a Pathogen Free, Nutritive & Safe Bio-Fertilizer for Farms," *Journal of Waste Management & Research*, 2009. http://www.sagepub.com

[27] R. K. Sinha, S. Herat, D. Valani, K. Singh and K. Chauhan, "Vermitechnology for Sustainable Solid Waste Management: A Comparative Study of Vermicomposting of Food & Green Wastes with Conventional Composting Systems to Evaluate the Efficiency of Earthworms in Sustainable Waste Management with Reduction in Greenhouse Gas Emissions," NOVA Science Publications, Hauppauge, 2010.

[28] M. C. Dash, "Role of Earthworms in the Decomposer System," In: J. S. Singh and B. Gopal, Eds., *Glimpses of Ecology*, India International Scientific Publication, New Delhi, 1978, pp. 399-406.

[29] F. Binet, L. Fayolle and M. Pussard, "Significance of Earthworms in Stimulating Soilmicrobial Activity," *Biology and Fertility of Soils*, Vol. 27, No. 1, 1998, pp. 79-84.

[30] D. R. Singleton, B. F. Hendrix, D. C. Coleman and W. B. Whitemann, "Identification of Uncultured Bacteria Tightly Associated with the Intestine of the Earthworms *Lumricus rubellus*," *Soil Biology and Biochemistry*, Vol. 35, 2003, pp. 1547-1555.

[31] C. A. Edwards and K. E. Fletcher, "Interaction between Earthworms and Micro-Organisms in Organic Matter Breakdown," *Agriculture Ecosystems and Environment*, Vol. 24, No. 1-3, 1988, pp. 235-247.

[32] M. Morgan and I. Burrows, "Earthworms/Microorganisms Interactions," Rothamsted Experimental Station, USA, 1982.

[33] M. Appelhof, "Notable Bits," In: *WormEzine*, Vol. 2, No. 5, May 2003. http://www.wormwoman.com

[34] V. Pierre, R. Phillip, L. Margnerite and C. Pierrette, "Anti-Bacterial Activity of the Haemolytic System from the Earthworms *Eisenia fetida andrei*," *Invertebrate Pathology*, Vol. 40, No. 1, 1982, pp. 21-27.

[35] R. Hartenstein and F. Hartenstein, "Physico-Chemical Changes Affected in Activated Sludge by the Earthworms *Eisenia fetida*," *Journal of Environmental Quality*, Vol. 10, No. 3, 1981, pp. 377-382.

[36] R. K. Sinha, and A. Chan, "Study of Emission of Greenhouse Gases by Brisbane Households Practicing Different Methods of Composting of Food & Garden Wastes: Aerobic, Anaerobic and Vermicomposting," NRMA—Griffith University Project Report, 2009.

[37] R. Sherman, "Commercial Systems Latest Development in Mid-to-Large Scale Vermicomposting," *Biocycle*, November 2000, p. 51.

[38] G. Munroe, "Manual of on-Farm Vermicomposting and Vermiculture," Organic Agriculture Centre of Canada, 2007, p. 39.

[39] P. Bogdanov, "Commercial Vermiculture: How to Build a Thriving Business in Redworms," VermiCo Press, Oregon, 1996, p. 83.

[40] C. A. Edward, "Potential of Vermicomposting for Processing and Upgrading Organic Waste," Ohio State University, Ohio, 2000.

[41] NCSU, "Large Scale Vermi-Composting Operations— Data from Vermi-Cycle Organics, Inc.," North Carolina State University, 1997.

[42] K. M. Li and P. Z. Li, "Earthworms Helping Economy, Improving Ecology and Protecting Health," In: R. K. Sinha, *et al.*, Eds., *International Journal of Environmental Engineering* (Special Issue on 'Vermiculture Technology'), 2010.

[43] H. Mihara, M. Sumi, H. Mizumoto, T. Yoneta, R. Ikeda and M. Maruyama, "Oral Administration of Earthworm Powder as Possible Thrombolytic Therapy," *Recent Advances in Thrombosis and Fibrinolysis*, Academic Press, New York, 1990, pp. 287-298.

[44] GEORG, "Feasibility of Developing the Organic and Transitional Farm Market for Processing Municipal and Farm Organic Wastes Using Large-Scale Vermicomposting," Good Earth Organic Resources Group, Halifax, Nova Scotia, 2004. http://www.alternativeor- ganic.com

[45] J. Frederickson, "The Worm's Turn," *Waste Management Magazine*, UK, August 2000.

[46] M. Gary, "Personal Communication from Envirofert (on Commercial Vermicomposting of Green Waste in New Zealand," 2009. http:www.envirofert.co.nz

[47] S. Komarowski, "Vermiculture for Sewage and Water Treatment Sludge," *WATER*, July 2001.

[48] U. S. Bhawalkar, "Vermiculture Eco-Technology," Publication of Bhawalkar Earthworm Research Institute (BERI), Pune, 1995.

[49] P. K. Singh, "Production and Use of Vermicompost in India," College of Horticulture, Rajendra Agriculture University, Bihar, 2010.

[50] R. D. Kale, "The Role of Earthworms and Research on Vermiculture in India," In: R. Guerrero and M. Guerrero, Eds., *Vermitechnologies for Developing Countries*, *Proceedings of the International Symposium on Vermi Technologies for Developing Countries*, Philippines, 2005, pp. 66-88.

[51] R. Guerrero, "Commercial Vermimeal Production," In: R. Guerrero and M. Guerrero, Eds., *Vermitechnologies for Developing Countries*, *Proceedings of the International Symposium on Vermi Technologies for Developing Countries*, Philippines, 2005, p. 175.

[52] S. Pajon, "The Worms Turn – Argentina," Intermediate Technology Development Group, Case Study Series 4, Munroe, 2007.

[53] Z.-J. Sun, "Vermiculture and Vermi Protein," China Agricultural University Press, Beijing, 2003, p. 366.

[54] A. Lopez and R. Alis, "Indigenous Use of Native Earthworms and its Fatty Acids Profile," Paper Presented at the *Inernational Symposium on Vermitechnologies for Developing Countries*, Laguna, Philippines, Also in *Utilization of Earthworms for Health Remedies*, 2005. http://www.wormsphilippines.com/docs/IKs%20on%20Earthworms.htm

[55] I. N. Titov and B. M. Anokhin, "The Ten-Year Results of Treatment with the Extract of Earthworm Tissues," Innovation Centre, Moscow, Russia, In: R. Guerrero and M. Guerrero, Eds., *Vermitechnologies for Developing Countries; Proceedings of the International Symposium on Vermi Technologies for Developing Countries*, Philippines, 2005, pp. 148-149.

[56] B. Tanaka and S. Nakata, "Studies of 'Antipyretic Components' from the Japanese Earthworm," *Tokyo Igaku Zasshi*, Vol. 29, 1974, pp. 67-97.

[57] O. Bajsa, J. Nair, K. Mathew and G. E. Ho, "Vermiculture as a Tool for Domestic Wastewater Management," *Water Science and Technology*, IWA Publishing, Vol. 48, No. 11-12, 2003, pp. 125-132.

[58] R. Hartenstein and M. S. Bisesi, "Use of Earthworm Biotechnology for the Management of Effluents from Intensively Housed Livestock," *Outlook Agriculture*, Vol. 18, No. 2, 1989, pp. 72-76.

[59] M. Taylor, W. P. Clarke and P. F. Greenfield, "The Treatment of Domestic Wastewater Using Small-Scale Vermicompost Filter Beds," *Ecological Engineering*, Vol. 21, No. 2-3, 2003, pp. 197-203.

[60] M. A. Soto and J. Toha, "Ecological Wastewater Treatment," *Advanced Wastewater Treatment, Recycling and Reuse*, AWT 98, Milano, 14-16 September 2008.

[61] M. Xing, J. Yang and Z. Lu, "Microorganism-Earthworm Integrated Biological Treatment Process—A Sewage Treatment Option for Rural Settlements," ICID 21st European Regional Conference, Frankfurt, 15-19 May 2005.

[62] R. K. Sinha, G. Bharambe and U. Chowdhary, "Sewage Treatment by Vermi-Filtration with Synchronous Treatment of Sludge by Earthworms: A Low-Cost Sustainable Technology over Conventional Systems with Potential for Decentralization," *The Environmentalist*, Springer, Vol. 28, No. 4, 8 April 2008, pp. 409-420.

[63] R. K. Sinha, G. Bharambe and P. D. Bapat, "Removal of High BOD & COD Loadings of Primary Liquid Waste Products from Dairy Industry by Vermi-Filtration Technology Using Earthworms," *Indian Journal of Environmental Protection*, Vol. 27, No. 6, 2007, pp. 486-501.

[64] V. Chandran and B. Soni, "Vermifiltration of Fruit Juice Processing Wastewater from in Brisbane," 40 CP Vermiculture Project, School of Engineering (Environment), Griffith University, Nathan Campus, Brisbane, Australia, (Supervisors Dr. Rajiv K. Sinha & Dr. Sunil Herat), 2010.

[65] R. J. Hughes, J. Nair and K. Mathew, "The Implications of Wastewater Vermicomposting Technologies: On-Site Treatment Systems for Sustainable Sanitation," WAMDEC Conference, Zimbabwe, 27-30 July 2005.

[66] S. I. Markman, A. Guschina, S. Barnsleya, L. Katherine,

B. David and C.T. Muller, "Endocrine Disrupting Chemicals Accumulate in Earthworms Exposed to Sewage Effluents," *Chemosphere*, Vol. 70, No. 1, 2007, pp. 119-125.

[67] C. N. Lowe and K. R. Butt, "Inoculation of Earthworms into Reclaimed Soils: Experiences from Britain," *Proceedings of 9th International Waste Management and Landfill Symposium*, Sardinia, 2003.

[68] K. R. Butt, C. N. Lowe, J. Frederickson and A. J. Moffat, "The Development of Sustainable Earthworm Populations at Calvert Landfill Site, UK," *Land Degradation & Development*, Vol. 15, No. 1, 2004, pp. 27-36.

[69] R. Hartenstein, E. F. Neuhauser and J. Collier, "Accumulation of Heavy Metals in the Earthworm *E. foetida*," *Environmental Quality*, Vol. 9, No. 1, 1980, pp. 23-26.

[70] W. C. Ma, J. Imerzeel and J. Bodt, "Earthworm and Food Interactions on Bioaccumulation and Disappearance of Pahs: Studies on Phenanthrene and Flouranthene," *Ecotoxicology and Environmental Safety*, Vol. 32, No. 3, 1995, pp. 226-232.

[71] S. M. Contreras-Ramos, D. Alvarez-Bernal and L. Dendooven, "*Eisenia fetida* Increased Removal of Polycyclic Aromatic Hydrocarbons (PAHs) from Soil," *Environmental Pollution*, Vol. 141, No. 3, 2006, pp. 396-401.

[72] Y. Tomoko, K. Toyota and S. Hiroaki, "Enhanced Bioremediation of Oil-Contaminated Soil by a Combination of the Earthworm (*Eisenia Fetida*) and Tea Extraction Residue," *Edaphologia*, Vol. 77, 2005, pp. 1-9.

[73] M. Schaefer, "Earthworms in Crude Oil Contaminated Soils: Toxicity Tests and Effects on Crude Oil Degradation," *Contaminated Soil Sediment & Water*, Vol. 35, 2005, pp. 7-8.

[74] J. Martin-Gil, L. M. Navas-Gracia, E. Gomez-Sobrino, A. Correa-Guimaraes, S. Hernandez-Navarro and M. Sanchez-Bascones, "Composting and Vermicomposting Experiences in the Treatments and Bioconversion of Asphaltens from the *Prestige* Oil Spill," *Journal of Bioresource Technology*, Vol. 99, No. 6, 2007, pp. 1821-1829.

[75] B. Davis, "Laboratory Studies on the Uptake of Dieldrin and DDT by Earthworms," *Soil Biology and Biochemistry*, Vol. 3, 1971, pp. 221-223.

[76] M. P. Ireland, "Heavy Metals Uptake in Earthworms," *Earthworm Ecology*, Chapman & Hall, London, 1983.

[77] J. Haimi, J. Salminen, V. Huhta, J. Knuutinen and H. Palm, "Bioaccumulation of Organochlorine Compounds in Earthworms," *Soil Biology & Biochemistry*, Vol. 24, No. 12, 1992, pp. 1699-1703.

[78] N. S. Bolan and S. Baskaran, "Characteristics of Earthworm Casts Affecting Herbicide Sorption and Movement," *Biological Fertility of Soils*, Vol. 22, No. 4, 1996, pp. 367-372.

[79] B. Gevao, C. Mordaunt, K. T. Semple, T. G. Piearce and K. C. Jones, "Bioavailability of Nonextractable (Bound) Pesticide Residues to Earthworms," *Environmental Science & Technology*, Vol. 35, No. 3, 2001, pp. 501-507.

[80] A. C. Singer, W. Jury, E. Leupromchai, C.-S. Yahng and D. E. Crowley, "Contribution of Earthworms to PCB

Vermiculture Technology: Reviving the Dreams of Sir Charles Darwin for Scientific Use of Earthworms in Sustainable Development Programs

135

Bioremediation," *Journal of Soil Biology & Biochemistry*, Vol. 33, No. 6, 2001, pp. 765-775.

[81] R. K. Sinha, G. Bharambe and D. Ryan, "Converting Wasteland into Wonderland by Earthworms: A Low-Cost Nature's Technology for Soil Remediation: A Case Study of Vermiremediation of PAH Contaminated Soil," *The Environmentalist*, Vol. 28, No. 4, 14 May 2008, pp. 466-475.

[82] K. R. Butt, "Inoculation of Earthworms into Reclaimed Soils: The UK Experience," *Land Degradation and Development*, Vol. 10, No. 6, 1999, pp. 565-575.

[83] G. B. Brown and B. M. Doube, "On Earthworms Assisted Bioremediation," In: C. A. Edward, Ed., *Earthworm Ecology*, 2nd Edition, CRC Press, Boca Raton, 2004, pp. 213-239.

[84] R. D. Kale and K. Bano, "Field Trials with Vermicompost: An Organic Fertilizer," *Proceedings of National Seminar on Organic Waste Utilization by Vermicomposting*, GKVK Agricultural University, Bangalore, 1986.

[85] C. A. Edwards and I. Burrows, "The Potential of Earthworms Composts as Plant Growth Media," In: C. A. Edward and E. F. Neuhauser, Eds., *Earthworms in Waste and Environmental Management*, SPB Academic Publishing, The Hague, The Netherlands, 1988, pp. 21-32.

[86] L. P. Canellas, F. L. Olivares, A. L. Okorokova and R. A. Facanha, "Humic Acids Isolated from Earthworm Compost Enhance Root Elongation, Lateral Root Emergence, and Plasma Membrane H^+-Atpase Activity in Maize Roots," *Plant Physiology*, Vol. 130, No. 4, 2002, pp. 1951-1957.

[87] H. I. Chaoui, L. M. Zibilske and T. Ohno, "Effects of Earthworms Casts and Compost on Soil Microbial Activity and Plant Nutrient Availability," *Soil Biology and Biochemistry*, Vol. 35, No. 2, 2003, pp. 295-302.

[88] G. H. Baker, P. M. Williams, P. J. Carter and N. R. Long, "Influence of Lumbricid Earthworms on Yield and Quality of Wheat and Clover in Glasshouse Trials," *Journal of Soil Biology and Biochemistry*, Vol. 29, No. 3-4, 1997, pp. 599-602.

[89] S. Palaniswamy, "Earthworm and Plant Interactions," Paper Presented in ICAR Training Program, Tamil Nadu Agricultural University, Coimbatore, 1996.

[90] N. Q. Arancon, C. A. Edwards, P. Bierman, C. Welch and J. D. Metzger, "Influences of Vermicomposts on Field Strawberries-1: Effects on Growth and Yields," *Bioresource Technology*, Vol. 93, No. 2, 2004, pp. 145-153.

[91] K. A. Webster, "Vermicompost Increases Yield of Cherries for Three Years after a Single Application," *EcoResearch*, South Australia, 2005. http:www.ecoresearch.com.au

[92] J. C. Buckerfield and K. A. Webster, "Worm-Worked Waste Boost Grape Yield: Prospects for Vermicompost Use in Vineyards," *The Australian and New Zealand Wine Industry Journal*, Vol. 13, No. 1, 1998, pp. 73-76.

[93] R. K. Sinha, S. Herat, D. Valani and K. Chauhan, "Vermiculture and Sustainable Agriculture," *American-Eurasian Journal of Agricultural and Environmental Sciences*, IDOSI Publication (Special Issue), 2009, pp. 1-55. http: www.idosi.org

[94] A. A. Ansari, "Effect of Vermicompost on the Productivity of Potato (*Solanum tuberosum)* Spinach (*Spinacia oleracea*) and Turnip (*Brassica campestris*)," *World Journal of Agricultural Sciences*, Vol. 4, No. 3, 2008, pp. 333-336.

[95] C. A. Edwards and N. Arancon, "Vermicompost Suppress Plant Pests and Disease Attacks," *REDNOVA NEWS*, 2004. http://www.rednova.com/ display/?id = 55938

[96] G. F. de Boer and O. Sova, "Vermicomposting as a Resource for Biodegradable Detergents," 4th ZERI World Congress, Windhoek, Namibia, 1998.

[97] C. H. Cordero, "Earthworms Can Help Dissolve Blood Clots for Stroke Patients," 2005. http://www.thenewstoday.info/20051125/earthworms.can.help.dissolve.blood.cl-ots.for.strokepatients.html

[98] W. L. Cheng and Z. J. Sun, "Pharmaceutical Value and Uses of Earthworms," Vermillenium Abstracts, Flowerfield Enterprizes, Kalamazoo, 2000.

[99] E. Cooper, "New Enzymes Isolated from Earthworms is Potent Fibrinolytic," ACAM Integrative Medicine Blog, *Oxford University Press Journal*, 2009. http://acam.typepad.com/blog/2009/04/ index.html

[100] C. M. Hwang, D. Kim and S. H. Huh, "In-vivo Evaluation of Lumbrokinase Extracted from Earthworms *Lumbricus rubellus* in a Prosthetic Vascular Graft," *Cardiovascular Surgery*, Vol. 43, No. 6, 2002, pp. 891-894.

[101] C. Qingsui, "A New Medicine for Heart Diseases Containing Enzyme Activator Extracted from Earthworms," In: Lopez & Alis, *The Utilization of Earthworms for Health Remedies*, 2003.

[102] H. Mihara, M. Maruyama and H. Sumi, "Novel Thrombolytic Therapy Discovered in Oriental Medicine Using the Earthworms," *SE Asian Journal of Tropical Medicine & Health*, Vol. 23, Suppl 2, 1992, pp. 131-140.

[103] S. L. Li, "Research on *di long's* (Earthworms) Effect in Lowering Blood Pressure," *Journal of Information*, Vol. 12, No. 3, 1995, pp. 22-24.

[104] R. Moss, "Of Enzymes, Worms & Cancer: The War on Cancer (Lumbrokinsae enzyme from Earthworms)," *Worm Digest*, 2004. http://www.wormdigest.org/content view/161/2/

[105] L. Jin, H. Jin, G. Zhang and G. Xu, "Changes in Coagulation and Tissue Plasminogen Activator after the Treatment of Cerebral Infarction with Lumbrokinsae (from Earthworms)," *Clinical Hemorheology and Microcirculation*, Vol. 23, 2000, pp. 213-218.

[106] UNSW, ROU, "Best Practice Guidelines to Managing On-Site Vermiculture Technologies," University of New South Wales Recycling Organics Unit, Sydney, 2002. http:www.resource.nsw.gov.au/data/Vermiculture%20BPG.pdf

[107] R. A. Dynes, "Earthworms: Technology Information to Enable the Development of Earthworm Production," Rural Industries Research and Development Corporation, Government of Australia, Canberra, 2003.

13

Discrete Time Markov Reward Processes a Motor Car Insurance Example[*]

Guglielmo D'Amico[1], Jacques Janssen[2], Raimondo Manca[3]

[1]*Università "G. D'Annunzio" di Chieti, Dip. di Scienze del Farmaco, via dei Vestini, Chieti, Italy*
[2]*Jacan &, EURIA, Université de Bretagne Occidentale, 6 avenue le Gorgeu, Brest, France*
[3]*Università "La Sapienza", Dip. di Matematica per le Decisioni Economiche, Finanziarie ed Assicurative, via del Castro Laurenziano, Roma, Italy*

Abstract

In this paper, a full treatment of homogeneous discrete time Markov reward processes is presented. The higher order moments of the homogeneous reward process are determined. In the last part of the paper, an application to the bonus-malus car insurance is presented. The application was constructed using real data.

Keywords: Markov Rewards Processes, Higher Order Moments, Bonus-Malus Systems

1. Introduction

In the sixties and seventies, Markov reward processes were developed, mainly in the engineering fields in discrete and continuous time [1]. In [2] an application of Continuous Time Markov Reward Processes in life insurance was presented.

In this paper, we present the Discrete Time Markov Reward Processes (DTMRWP) as given in [3]. The evolution equation of the expected value of the DTMRWP is presented with different reward structures. Furthermore, the relations useful for the computation of the higher order moments of the Markov reward process are presented and they are given in matrix form too. To the authors' knowledge, it is the first time that higher moments of a discrete time Markov reward process and the matrix approach for the first n moments are given. The matrix approach facilitates the algorithm construction as for example it is explained in [4] for semi-Markov reward processes.

We believe that DTMRWP can describe any kind of premiums or benefits involved in a generic insurance contract then they represent tool to approach in a general way actuarial problems.

In the last section an example on the application of DTMRWP in the motor car insurance is given using real data applied to the bonus-malus Italian rules.

2. Reward Structure, Classifications and Notation

The association of a sum of money to a state of the system and to a state transition assumes great relevance in the study of financial phenomena. This can be done by linking a reward structure to a stochastic process. This structure can be thought of as a function associated with the state occupancies and transitions [1].

In this paper the rewards are considered as amounts of money. These amounts can be positive, if they are benefits for the system and negative if they are costs.

A classification scheme of different kinds of DTM RWP is reported in [5] page 150.

2.1. Discounting Factors

The following notations will be used:
$r(1), r(2), \ldots, r(t), \ldots$, for the discrete time homogeneous interest rates and

$$\dot{v}(t) = \begin{cases} 1 & \text{if } t = 0, \\ \prod_{h=1}^{t}\left(1+r(h)\right)^{-1} & \text{if } t > 0, \end{cases}$$

for the discrete time discount factors.

See [6] or [7] for further details on this topic.

2.2. Reward Notation

ψ_i, $\psi_i(t)$, denote the reward that is given for the per-

---

[*]Work supported by a MURST grant.

manence in the i-th state; it is also called rate reward, see [8]; the first is paid in the cases in which the period amount in state i is constant in time, the second when the payment is a function of the state and the time of payment. ψ represents the vector of these rewards.

γ_{ij}, $\gamma_{ij}(t)$, denote the reward that is given for the transition from the ith state to the jth one (impulse reward). Γ is the matrix of the transition rewards.

The different kinds of ψ rewards represent an annuity that is paid because of remaining in a state. This flow is to be discounted at starting time. In the *immediate case,* the reward will be paid at the end of the period before the transition; in the *due case* the reward will be paid at the beginning of the period. On the other hand, γ represents lump sums that are paid at the instant of transition. As far as the impulse reward γ is concerned, it is only necessary to compute the present value of the lump sum paid at the moment of the related transition.

Reward structure can be considered a very general structure linked to the problem being studied. The reward process evolves together with the evolution of the Markov process which it is linked. When the studied stochastic system is in a state then a reward of type ψ is paid; once there is a transition an impulse reward of γ type is paid.

This behaviour is particularly efficient at constructing models which are useful to follow, for example, the dynamic evolution of insurance problems e.g. [9] and [10].

2.3. Matrix Operations

We give some matrix operation notation useful to describe the equations of the moments of the Markov reward processes in matrix form.

Given the two matrices $\mathbf{A}$, $\mathbf{B}$ with the notations

$$\mathbf{A} * \mathbf{B} \quad \text{and} \quad \mathbf{A} \cdot \mathbf{B}$$

are denoted, respectively, the usual row column product and the element by element product.

Definition 2.1 Given two matrices $\mathbf{A}, \mathbf{B}$ that have row order equal to m and column order equal to n, the following operation is defined:

$$\mathbf{c} = \mathbf{A} \circ \mathbf{B}$$

where $\mathbf{c}$ is the m elements vector in which the i-th component is obtained in the following way:

$$c(i) = \sum_{j=1}^{n} a_{ij} b_{ij} = \mathbf{a}_{i*} * \mathbf{b}_{i*}$$

3. Homogeneous DTMRWP

Markov reward processes are a class of stochastic proc-

esses each of them with different evolution equations. The differences from the analytic point of view can be considered irrelevant but from the algorithmic point of view they are very significant and must be taken into account in the construction of the algorithms.

Let consider a discrete time homogeneous Markov chain with state space $I = \{1, 2, ..., m\}$ and transition probability matrix $\mathbf{P} = \left[p_{ij} \right]_{i,j \in I}$. As it is well known the n-step transition probability matrix is given by $\mathbf{P}(n) = (\mathbf{P})^n$.

Definition 1: Let denote by $\xi_i(n)$ the discounted rewards accumulated in n periods given that at time 0 the system was in the state i and the reward are paid in the immediate case. It is defined recursively as follows:

$$\xi_i(n) = \xi_i(n-1) + v(n) \sum_{i,j=1}^{m} 1_{\{X(n-1)=i, X(n)=j\}} \left(\psi_j(n) + \gamma_{ij}(n) \right)$$

(1)

where $\xi_i(0) = 0$

Similar relations can be easily written for discounted homogeneous due cases. We denote by:

$$V_i(n) = E\left(\xi_i(n) \right); \quad \mathbf{V}(n) = \left[V_1(n), V_2(n), ..., V_m(n) \right]$$

With $\ddot{V}_i(n) = E\left(\xi_i(n) \right)$; the mean present value of the rewards paid in the investigated horizon time in the due cases is represented. In this case, in the definition of the $\xi_i(n)$ process we put $\xi_i(0) = \psi_i$.

For the sake of understanding, first we present the simplest case in immediate and due hypotheses after only the general relations in the discrete time environment will be given.

The immediate homogeneous Markov formula in the case of fixed permanence and without transition rewards is the first relation presented. The DTMRWP present value after one payment is:

$$V_i(1) = (1+r)^{-1} \psi_i = (1+r)^{-1} \psi_i$$

after two payments,

$$V_i(2) = (1+r)^{-1} \psi_i + v^2 \sum_{k=1}^{m} p_{ik}^{(1)} \psi_k = V_i(n) + v^2 \sum_{k=1}^{m} p_{ik}^{(1)} \psi_k$$

and in general, taking into account the recursive nature of relations, at n-th period it is:

$$V_i(n) = V_i(n-1) + v^n \sum_{k=1}^{m} p_{ik}^{(n-1)} \psi_k$$

that in matrix form becomes:

$$\mathbf{V}(n) = \mathbf{V}(n-1) + \left(v^n \mathbf{P}^{(n-1)} \right) * \psi = v\psi + \cdots + \left(v^n \mathbf{P}^{(n-1)} \right) * \psi$$

The general case with variable permanence, transition rewards and interest rates is presented. The present value after one period is:

$$V_i(1) = v(1)\left(\psi_i(1) + \sum_{j=1}^{m} p_{ij}\gamma_{ij}(1)\right),$$

after two payments,

$$V_i(2) = v(1)\left(\psi_i(1) + \sum_{j=1}^{m} p_{ij}\gamma_{ij}(1)\right) +$$

$$v(2)\sum_{k=1}^{m} p_{ik}\left(\psi_k(2) + \sum_{j=1}^{m} p_{kj}\gamma_{kj}(2)\right)$$

$$= V_i(1) + v(2)\sum_{k=1}^{m} p_{ik}\left(\psi_k(2) + \sum_{j=1}^{m} p_{kj}\gamma_{kj}(2)\right),$$

and in general, taking into account the recursive nature of relation, at n-th period it is:

$$V_i(n) = V_i(n-1) +$$

$$v(n)\sum_{k=1}^{m} p_{ik}^{(n-1)}\left(\psi_k(n) + \sum_{j=1}^{m} p_{kj}\gamma_{kj}(n)\right). \quad (2)$$

This relation can be written in matrix notation in the following way:

$$\mathbf{V}(n) = v(1)\boldsymbol{\psi}(1) + \cdots + \left(v(n)\mathbf{P}^{(n-1)}\right)*\boldsymbol{\psi}(n) +$$

$$v(1)\left(\mathbf{P}\circ\boldsymbol{\Gamma}(1)\right) + \cdots + \left(v(n)\mathbf{P}^{(n-1)}\right)*\left(\mathbf{P}\circ\boldsymbol{\Gamma}(n)\right).$$

In the case of payment due the permanence reward is paid at beginning of the period and the transition reward at the end. It results:

$$\ddot{V}_i(1) = \psi_i(1) + v(1)\sum_{j=1}^{m} p_{ij}\gamma_{ij}(1),$$

$$\ddot{V}_i(2) = \psi_i(1) + v(1)\sum_{k=1}^{m} p_{ik}\gamma_{ik}(1) + v(1)\sum_{j=1}^{m} p_{ij}\psi_j(2) +$$

$$v(2)\sum_{k=1}^{m} p_{ik}\sum_{j=1}^{m} p_{kj}\gamma_{kj}(2)$$

$$= \ddot{V}_i(1) + v(1)\sum_{k=1}^{m} p_{ik}\psi_k(1) + v(2)\sum_{k=1}^{m} p_{ik}\sum_{j=1}^{m} p_{kj}\gamma_{kj}(2).$$

$$\ddot{V}_i(n) = \ddot{V}_i(n-1) + v(n)\sum_{k=1}^{m} p_{ik}^{(n-1)}\sum_{j=1}^{m} p_{kj}\gamma_{kj}(n) +$$

$$v(n-1)\sum_{k=1}^{m} p_{ik}^{(n-1)}\psi_k(n). \quad (3)$$

That in matrix notation is:

$$\ddot{\mathbf{V}}(n) = \mathbf{I}*\boldsymbol{\psi}(1) + \left(v(1)\mathbf{P}\right)*\boldsymbol{\psi}(2) + \cdots +$$

$$\left(v(n-1)\mathbf{P}^{(n-1)}\right)*\boldsymbol{\psi}(n) + \left(v(1)\mathbf{P}\right)\circ\boldsymbol{\Gamma}(1) + \cdots +$$

$$\left(v(n)\mathbf{P}^{(n-1)}\right)*\left(\mathbf{P}\circ\boldsymbol{\Gamma}(n)\right).$$

Remark 3.1 In this section, general formulas were presented. In the construction of the algorithms the dif-

ferences between the possible cases should be taken into account. For example in the non-discounting case the following can be stated $v(k) = 1$, $k = 1,...,n$.

4. The higher Order Moments of Markov Reward Processes

In [11] relations for higher order moments of the integral of a generic function that evolves following a semi-Markov process were given. In more recent works (see [4] and [12]), the relations for higher moments of rewards associated to a semi-Markov backward system were presented.

In this section, following the methodology used in the last two quoted papers, the recursive relations useful for computing the higher moments in a Markov reward environment are provided.

It should be stated that the equations of this paper are different from that of [4] and [12] because we consider the conditioning on the starting state but also on the arriving state.

We will give only the discounted case.

According to Section 3 let us define the following stochastic process:

Definition 2: Let denote by $\xi_{ij}(n)$ the accumulated discounted rewards in n periods given that at time 0 the system was in the state i and at time n it will be in state j:

$$\xi_{ij}(n) = 1_{\{X(n)=j\}}\cdot\xi_i(n-1) +$$

$$1_{\{X(n)=j\}}\cdot v(n)\sum_{a,b=1}^{m} 1_{\{X(n-1)=a,X(n)=b\}}\left(\psi_b(n) + \gamma_{ab}(n)\right)$$

$$= 1_{\{X(n)=j\}}\cdot\xi_i(n-1) +$$

$$v(n)\sum_{a=1}^{m} 1_{\{X(n-1)=a,X(n)=j\}}\left(\psi_a(n) + \gamma_{aj}(n)\right).$$

$$(4)$$

Moreover we denote

$$V_i(n) = E\left[\xi_i(n)\mid X(0) = i\right] = E_{(i,0)}\left[\xi_i(n)\right];$$

$$\mathbf{V}(n) = \left[V_1(n), V_2(n),..., V_m(n)\right]$$

$$V_{ij}(n) = E[\xi_{ij}(n)\mid X(0) = i, X(n) = j] = E_{((i,0);(j,n))}[\xi_{ij}(n)];$$

$$\mathbf{W}(n) = \left[V_{ij}(n)\right]_{i,j\in\{1,2,...,m\}}$$

and the higher order moments are defined as

$$V_i^{(r)}(n) = E_{(i,0)}\left[\left(\xi_i(n)\right)^r\right];$$

$$\mathbf{V}^{(r)}(n) = \left[V_1^{(r)}(n), V_2^{(r)}(n),..., V_m^{(r)}(n)\right]'$$

$$V_{ij}^{(r)}(n) = E\left[\left(\xi_{ij}(n)\right)^r\mid X(0) = i, X(n) = j\right] = E_{((i,0);(j,n))}\left[\left(\xi_{ij}(n)\right)^r\right];$$

$$\mathbf{W}^{(r)}(n) = \left[V_{ij}^{(r)}(n) \right]_{i,j \in \{1,2,\dots,m\}}$$

and it results for all r that $V_i^{(r)}(n) = \sum_{j=1}^{m} p_{ij}^{(n)} V_{ij}^{(r)}(n)$.

Similar relations can be easily written for non discounted cases

Theorem 4.1 The moments of $\xi_{ij}(n)$ in the discounted immediate case, in matrix form, are given by:

$$\mathbf{W}^{(r)}(n) = \left(\left(\mathbf{P}^{(n-1)} \cdot \mathbf{W}^{(r)}(n-1) \right) * \mathbf{P}(n) \right) \cdot \tilde{\mathbf{P}}^{(n)} + $$
$$\sum_{l=1}^{r-1} \frac{r!}{l!(r-l)!} \left[\dot{v}(n) \right]^{r-l} \cdot \tag{5}$$
$$\left(\left(\mathbf{P}^{(n-1)} \cdot \mathbf{W}^{(l)}(n-1) \right) * \left(\mathbf{P} \cdot \mathbf{C}^{(r-l)}(n) \right) \right) \cdot \tilde{\mathbf{P}}^{(n)} + $$
$$\left[\dot{v}(n) \right]^r \cdot \left(\mathbf{P}^{(n-1)} * \left(\mathbf{P} \cdot \mathbf{C}^{(r)}(n) \right) \right) \cdot \tilde{\mathbf{P}}^{(n)}$$

where:

$$\tilde{\mathbf{P}}^{(n)} = \left(\frac{1}{p_{ij}^{(n)}} \right)_{i,j \in E} ,$$

$$\mathbf{C}^{(l)}(n) = \left(c_{ij}^{(l)}(n) \doteq \left(\psi_i(n) + \gamma_{ij}(n) \right)^l \right)$$

Proof From (4.1) it results:

$$V_{ij}^{(r)}(n) = E_{((i,0);(j,n))} \left[\left(\xi_i(n) \right)^r \right]$$
$$= E_{((i,0);(j,n))} \left[\left(1_{\{X(n)=j\}} \xi_i(n-1) + \right. \right.$$
$$\left. \left. \dot{v}(n) \sum_{a=1}^{m} 1_{\{X(n-1)=a, X(n)=j\}} \left(\psi_a(n) + \gamma_{aj}(n) \right) \right)^r \right].$$

$$= E_{((i,0);(j,n))} \left[\sum_{l=0}^{r} \frac{r!}{l!(r-l)!} \left(1_{\{X(n)=j\}} \xi_i(n-1) \right)^l \cdot \right.$$
$$\left. \left(\dot{v}(n) \sum_{a=1}^{m} 1_{\{X(n-1)=a, X(n)=j\}} \left(\psi_a(n) + \gamma_{aj}(n) \right) \right)^{r-l} \right]$$

$$= \sum_{l=0}^{r} \frac{r!}{l!(r-l)!} E_{((i,0);(j,n))} [E_{((i,0);(j,n))} [\left(1_{\{X(n)=j\}} \xi_i(n-1) \right)^l \cdot$$
$$\left(\dot{v}(n) \sum_{a=1}^{m} 1_{\{X(n-1)=a, X(n)=j\}} \left(\psi_a(n) + \gamma_{aj}(n) \right) \right)^{r-l}$$
$$| X(n-1)]]$$

The random variables $\xi_i(n-1)$ and $\xi_{ij}(n-1) - \xi_i(n-1)$ are independent given $X(n-1)$ then we get in:

$$= \sum_{l=0}^{r} \frac{r!}{l!(r-l)!} E_{((i,0);(j,n))} [E_{((i,0);(j,n))}$$

$$[\left(1_{\{X(n)=j\}} \xi_i(n-1) \right)^l | X(n-1)] \cdot$$

$$E_{((i,0);(j,n))} [\left(\dot{v}(n) \sum_{a=1}^{m} 1_{\{X(n-1)=a, X(n)=j\}} \left(\psi_a(n) + \gamma_{aj}(n) \right) \right)^{r-l} $$
$$X(n-1)]]$$

by independence between $1_{\{X(n)\}}$ and $\xi_i(n-1)$ given $X(n-1)$ and by measurability of $1_{\{X(n)\}}$ with respect to the information set $\{ X(0) = i, X(n-1) = k, X(n) = j \}$ it results:

$$= \sum_{l=0}^{r} \frac{r!}{l!(r-l)!} E_{((i,0);(j,n))} \left[E_{((i,0);(j,n))} [1_{\{X(n)=j\}} | X(n-1)] \right.$$
$$\cdot E_{((i,0);(j,n))} [\xi_i(n-1) | X(n-1)]$$
$$\cdot E_{((i,0);(j,n))} [\left(\dot{v}(n) \sum_{a=1}^{m} 1_{\{X(n-1)=a, X(n)=j\}} \left(\psi_a(n) + \gamma_{aj}(n) \right) \right)^{r-l}$$
$$\left. \cdot X(n-1)] \right]$$

$$\sum_{l=0}^{r} \frac{r!}{l!(r-l)!} E_{((i,0);(j,n))} \left[V_{i,X(n-1)}^{(l)}(n-1) \right.$$
$$\left. \cdot \left(\dot{v}(n) \left(\psi_{X(n-1)}(n) + \gamma_{X(n-1)j}(n) \right) \right)^{r-l} \right]$$

$$= \sum_{l=0}^{r} \frac{r!}{l!(r-l)!} \sum_{k=1}^{m} P_i \left[X(n-1) = k | X(n) = j \right]$$
$$\cdot V_{i,k}^{(l)}(n-1) \left(\dot{v}(n) \left(\psi_k(n) + \gamma_{kj}(n) \right) \right)^{r-l}$$

$$= \sum_{l=0}^{r} \frac{r!}{l!(r-l)!} \sum_{k=1}^{m} \frac{P \left[X(n) = j | X(n-1) = k \right] P_i \left[X(n-1) = k \right]}{P_i \left[X(n) = j \right]}$$
$$\cdot V_{i,k}^{(l)}(n-1) \cdot \left(\dot{v}(n) \left(\psi_k(n) + \gamma_{kj}(n) \right) \right)^{r-l}$$

$$= \sum_{l=0}^{r} \frac{r!}{l!(r-l)!} \sum_{k=1}^{m} \frac{p_{ik}^{(n-1)} p_{kj}}{p_{ij}^{(n)}} V_{i,k}^{(l)}(n-1)$$
$$\cdot \left(\dot{v}(n) \left(\psi_k(n) + \gamma_{kj}(n) \right) \right)^{r-l}$$

Consequently we obtain:

$$V_{ij}^{(r)}(n) = \sum_{k=1}^{m} \frac{p_{ik}^{(n-1)} p_{kj}}{p_{ij}^{(n)}} V_{ik}^{(r)}(n-1) + $$
$$\sum_{l=1}^{r-1} \frac{r!}{l!(r-l)!} \sum_{k=1}^{m} \frac{p_{ik}^{(n-1)} p_{kj}}{p_{ij}^{(n)}} V_{ik}^{(l)}(n-1)$$
$$\cdot \left\{ \left(\psi_k(n) + \gamma_{kj}(n) \right) \dot{v}(n) \right\}^{r-l} + $$
$$\sum_{k=1}^{m} \frac{p_{ik}^{(n-1)} p_{kj}}{p_{ij}^{(n)}} \left\{ \left(\psi_k(n) + \gamma_{kj}(n) \right) \dot{v}(n) \right\}^r$$

that in matrix form gives (5)

Now since $V_i^{(r)}(n) = \sum_{j=1}^{m} p_{ij}^{(n)} V_{ij}^{(r)}(n)$, by direct computation we get $V_i^{(r)}(n)$.

Corollary 4.1 The evolution equation of the higher order moment of the $\xi_i(n)$ process in the discounted immediate case, in matrix form is:

$$\mathbf{V}^{(r)}(n) = \mathbf{V}^{(r)}(n-1) + \left[\dot{v}(n)\right]^r \cdot$$

$$\left(\mathbf{P}^{(n-1)} * \left(\mathbf{P} \circ \mathbf{C}^{(r)}(n)\right)\right) +$$

$$\sum_{l=1}^{r-1} \frac{r!}{l!(r-l)!} \left[\dot{v}(n)\right]^{r-l} \cdot \left(\mathbf{P}^{(n-1)} \cdot \mathbf{W}^{(l)}(n-1)\right) * \qquad (6)$$

$$\left(\mathbf{P} \circ \mathbf{C}^{(r-l)}(n)\right).$$

By means of similar procedures, the following corollaries can be obtained.

Corollary 4.2 The higher moments of $\xi_{ij}(n)$ in the discounted due case, in matrix form, are given by the following relation:

$$\ddot{\mathbf{W}}^{(r)}(n) = \left(\left(\mathbf{P}^{(n-1)} \cdot \ddot{\mathbf{W}}^{(r)}(n-1)\right) * \mathbf{P}\right) \cdot$$

$$\tilde{\mathbf{P}}^{(n)} + \sum_{l=1}^{r-1} \frac{r!}{l!(r-l)!} \left[\dot{v}(n-1)\right]^{r-l} \cdot$$

$$\left(\left(\mathbf{P}^{(n-1)} \cdot \ddot{\mathbf{W}}^{(l)}(n-1)\right) * \left(\mathbf{P} \cdot \ddot{\mathbf{C}}^{(r-l)}(n)\right)\right) \cdot \tilde{\mathbf{P}}^{(n)} +$$

$$\left[\dot{v}(n-1)\right]^r \cdot \left(\mathbf{P}^{(n-1)} * \left(\mathbf{P} \cdot \ddot{\mathbf{C}}^{(r)}(n)\right)\right) \cdot \tilde{\mathbf{P}}^{(n)}$$

$$(7)$$

where: $\ddot{\mathbf{C}}^{(l)}(n) = \left(\ddot{c}_{ij}^{(l)}(n) \doteq \left(\psi_i(n-1) + \gamma_{ij}(n)\right)^l\right).$

Remark 4.2 The possibility of computing the second order moments permits the obtaining of the variance and the sigma square, having in this way the opportunity to have a risk measure.

5. Motorcar Insurance Application

As it is well known, the bonus-malus motor car insurance model can be studied by means of Markov chains, see [13] for a complete description of bonus-malus systems. As far as the authors know, the premiums received and the benefits paid by the insurance company have never been studied simultaneously inside the evolution equation of the model as we propose here. In this way it is possible to have information on the future evolution of cash flows of the insurer and the possibility of computing higher order moments permits the obtaining of risk measures.

In order to apply DTMRWP we will construct a bonus-malus Markov reward model.

It should be noted that, as explained in [14], motor car insurance premiums could be a function of many factors such as type of car, mileage, age of the driver, region, sex and so on.

In Italy the only official distinctions are the province in which the car is insured and the power of its engine.

This example will use a transition matrix related to the motor car bonus-malus insurance rules that apply in Italy. In this case, the Markov model fits quite well because:

1) the position of each insured person is given at the beginning of each year,

2) there are precise rules that give the change of states in function of the behaviour of the policyholder person during the year,

3) the future state depends only on the present one.

The Italian bonus-malus rules are expressed by the function $T : I \times \mathbb{N} \to I$ that to each rating class $i \in I$ and number of accidents $k \in \mathbb{N}$ associates a new rating class $j \in I$ by means of the following law:

$$T(i,k) = 1_{\{k=0\}} \max\left(1, i-1\right) +$$

$$1_{\{0<k<4\}} \min\left(18, (i-1)+3k\right) + \qquad (8)$$

$$1_{\{k\geq4\}} \min\left(18, (i-1)+4k\right)$$

The range of values of T is $\{1,2,....,18\}$ expressing the classes of risk in which all drivers are classified. The stochastic process $X(t)$ describing the rating risk class evolution of the policyholder is assumed to be a Markov chain with state space $I = \{1,2,...,18\}$. This choice is determined by the fact that the next risk class is determined through rule (5.1) as a function of the current risk class i and the number of accidents k the policyholder carried out in the current year.

The authors are in possession of the history of 105627 insured persons over a period of three years. This means that it was possible consider 316881 real or virtual transitions. The data are related to the years 1998, 1999 and 2000. The estimated Markov transition matrix obtained from the available data taking into account the bonus-malus Italian rules is given in the **Table 1**. In this table we report only the transition probability that are possible to be observed, the remaining are impossible due to the Italian BMS rules. Then for example, in one step, from state 1 it is possible to migrate only towards state 1 (0 accident), to state 3 (1 accident), to state 6 (2 accident), to state 9 (3 accident) and to state 12 (4 or more accident). The other transitions are not allowable and then their probabilities are zero and then not reported in the table.

The payment of a claim by the insurance company can be seen as a lump sum (impulse or transition reward) paid by the insurer to the insured person.

In **Figure 1** the premiums (they can be seen as permanence rewards) that are paid in Naples for a car of 2300 c.c. and in Oristano (a small Sardinian province) for a small car (about 1000 c.c.) are reported.

Table 1. One step transition probability matrix.

Starting state	Next state and related probability				
1	**1** 0.941655	**3** 0.056264	**6** 0.001973	**9** 0.000081	**12** 0.000027
2	**1** 0.935097	**4** 0.062379	**7** 0.002427	**10** 0.000097	**13** 0
3	**2** 0.941646	**5** 0.056611	**8** 0.001574	**11** 0.000169	**14** 0
4	**3** 0.948892	**6** 0.049364	**9** 0.001744	**12** 0	**15** 0
5	**4** 0.945231	**7** 0.052354	**10** 0.002314	**13** 0.000067	**16** 0.000034
6	**5** 0.949204	**8** 0.04908	**11** 0.00157	**14** 0.000146	**17** 0
7	**6** 0.934685	**9** 0.061856	**12** 0.00339	**15** 0.000069	**18** 0
8	**7** 0.92227	**10** 0.073137	**13** 0.004246	**16** 0.00026	**18** 0.000087
9	**8** 0.914103	**11** 0.082621	**14** 0.003185	**17** 0	**18** 0.000091
10	**9** 0.923854	**12** 0.071989	**15** 0.003827	**18** 0.00033	
11	**10** 0.92933	**13** 0.066723	**16** 0.003696	**18** 0.000251	
12	**11** 0.930156	**14** 0.066697	**17** 0.002994	**18** 0.000153	
13	**12** 0.937854	**15** 0.059651	**18** 0.002495		
14	**13** 0.920681	**16** 0.074704	**18** 0.004615		
15	**14** 0.885204	**17** 0.107143	**18** 0.007653		
16	**15** 0.777568	**18** 0.222432			
17	**16** 0.876733	**18** 0.123267			
18	**17** 0.888614	**18** 0.111386			

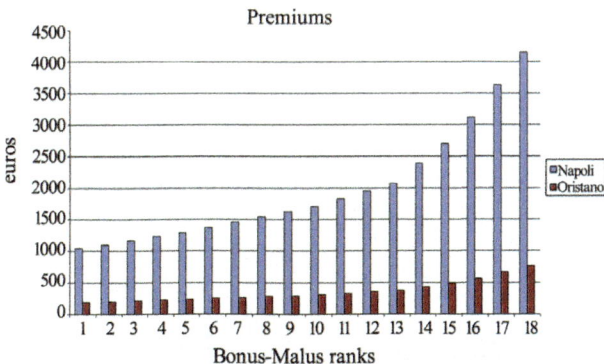

Figure 1. Naples and Oristano premiums.

The example is constructed from the point of view of the insurance company and premiums are an entrance for the company. It is to precise that these values correspond to the real premiums (that is loaded premiums covering costs and risk) paid by an insured in the year 2001 and officially given in the internet site of Assicurazioni Generali for that year.

In the example we suppose that the rewards are fixed in the time. Furthermore we suppose to have a yearly fixed discount factor of 1/1.03.

Table 2 gives the mean values of the expenses that the insurance company should pay for the claims made by the insured person.

More clearly stated, the element –7772.51 represents the expenses that, on average, the company has to pay for the two accidents that an insured person that was in the state 1 (lowest bonus-malus class) had and which then took him to state 6.

This table was constructed starting from the observed data in the authors' possession.

From the point of view of the model, the elements of this table are transition rewards. More precisely, as already mentioned, they can be seen as lump sums (impulse rewards) paid by the company at the time of the accident. In this case, being expenses for the company, they result negative.

Table 2. Mean insurance payments.

State	Expenses mean values in function of next state			
1	**3** –2185.57	**6** –7772.51	**9** –3240.77	**12** –7728.78
2	**4** –1956.4	**7** –3196.16	**10** –9004.43	**13** 0
3	**5** –2188.25	**8** –2846.52	**11** –4498.34	**14** 0
4	**6** –2853.19	**9** –2920.39	**12** 0	**15** 0
5	**7** –2245.02	**10** –3945.44	**13** –3240.77	**16** –6274.95
6	**8** –2676.12	**11** –3076.05	**14** –6703.61	**17** 0
7	**9** –2086.66	**12** –3391.18	**15** –1572.09	**18** 0
8	**10** –2198.02	**13** –4027.26	**16** –3286.39	**18** –3629.14
9	**11** –2017.77	**14** –6397.63	**17** 0	**18** –3687.5
10	**12** –2103.01	**15** –4931.93	**18** –5165.44	
11	**13** –3110.63	**16** –4710.94	**18** –5993.19	
12	**14** –3048.69	**17** –3893.94	**18** –11602.3	
13	**15** –2613.27	**18** –8271.51		
14	**16** –3564.01	**18** –4145.45		
15	**17** –2468.23	**18** –7356.78		
16	**18** –2883.68			
17	**18** –3764.32			
18	**18** –2578.55			

In **Figure 2** are resumed in the first part the reward mean present values and in the second the related sigma square.

The permanence reward (insurance premium) increases in function of the state and, therefore, the money earned by the company increases in function of the starting state too. It is to observe that the Insurance company always earns. Only in one case in Oristano (the first year of the 16th rank) it looses some small sum.

The illustrated case is very particular. In Naples the premiums are higher than in the other part of Italy, the car is big and also for this reason the premiums are very high. In Oristano the premiums are among the lowest in Italy and we consider a small car.

6. Conclusions

The description of homogeneous Markov reward processes was presented. For the first time, at author knowl-

edge, the relations useful to compute the higher moments for homogeneous Markov reward processes conditioned on the starting and arriving states are given. By means of the higher order moments it is possible to obtain variability indices.

The model was applied to motor car insurance regulations in Italy. The mean present values of rewards were computed. The results related to Naples and Oristano provinces were shown.

The authors hope to get a wider data set to construct a more reliable example and to understand if these first results that were obtained by the available data could be confirmed.

7. Acknowledgements

The authors are grateful to colleagues and friends Patrizia Gigante, Liviana Piceh and Luciano Sigalotti that

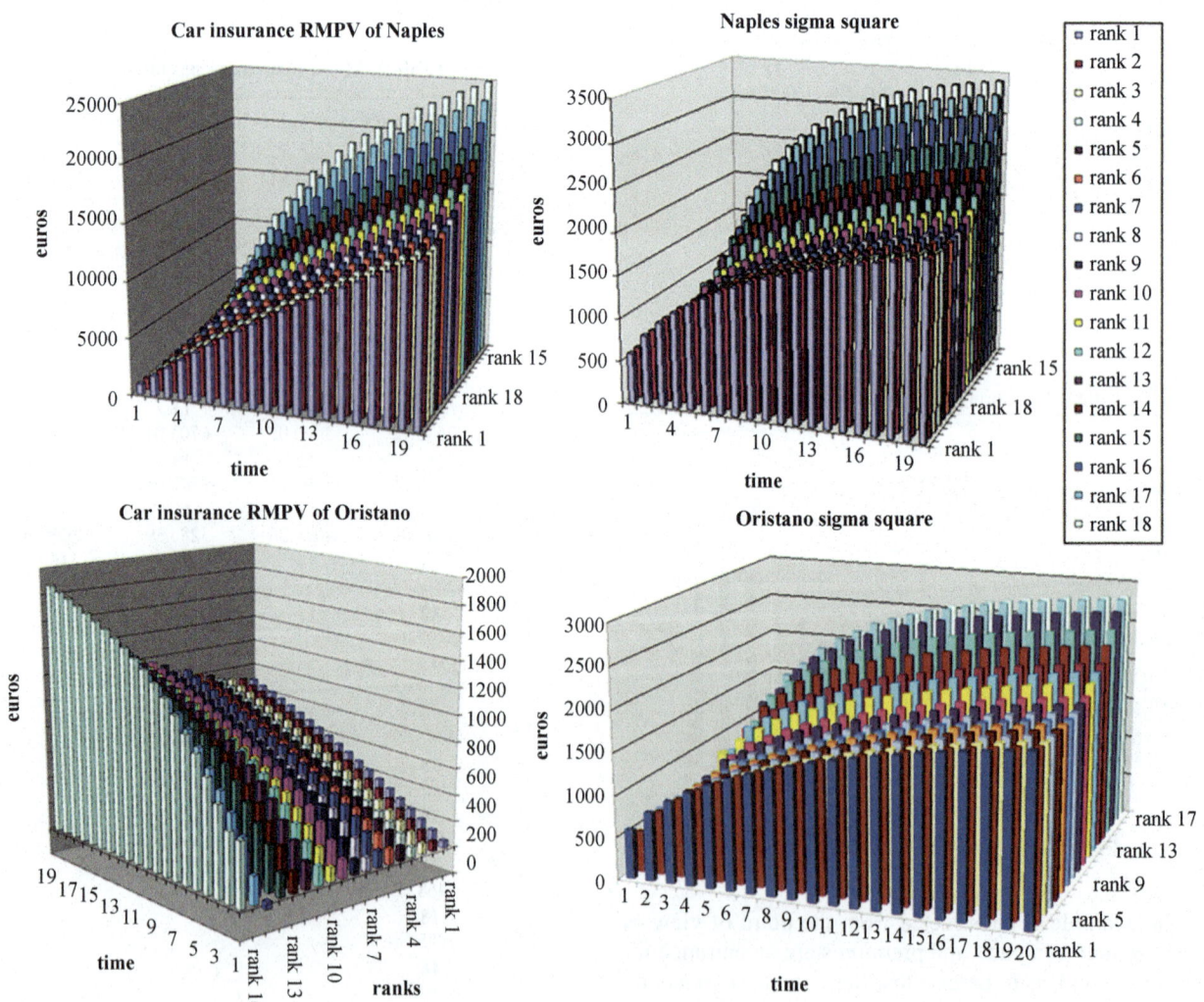

Figure 2. Mean present values and variances of Naples and Oristano rewards.

gave the data for the applications. The work was supported by a PRIN-MIUR and a Università di Roma "La Sapienza" grants.

8. References

[1] Howard R, "Dynamic Probabilistic Systems," Vol. 1-2, Wiley, New York, 1971.

[2] R. Norberg, "Differential Equations for Moments of Present Values in Life Insurance," *Insurance*: *Mathematics and Economics*, Vol. 17, No. 2, 1995, pp.171-180.

[3] J. Janssen and R. Manca, "Applied Semi-Markov Processes," Springer, New York, 2006.

[4] F. Stenberg, R. Manca and D. Silvestrov, "An Algorithmic Approach to Discrete Time Non-Homogeneous Backward Semi-Markov Reward Processes with an Application to Disability Insurance," *Methodology and Computing in Applied Probability*, Vol. 9, No. 4, 2007, pp. 497-519.

[5] J. Janssen and R. Manca, "Semi-Markov Risk Models for Finance, Insurance and Reliability," Springer, New York. 2007.

[6] J. Janssen, R. Manca and di P. E. Volpe, "Mathematical Finance: Deterministic and Stochastic Models," STE and Wiley, London, 2008.

[7] S. G. Kellison, "The Theory of Interest," 2nd Edition, Homewood, Irwin, 1991.

[8] M. A. Qureshi and H. W. Sanders, "Reward Model Solution Methods with Impulse and Rate Rewards: An Algorithmic and Numerical Results," *Performance Evaluation*, Vol. 20, No. 4, 1994, pp. 413-436.

[9] J. M. Hoem, "The Versatility of the Markov Chain as a Tool in the Mathematics of Life Insurance," *Transactions of the 23rd International Congress of Actuaries*, Vol. 3, 1988, pp. 171-202.

[10] H. Wolthuis, "Life Insurance Mathematics (the Markovian Model)," 2nd Edition, Peeters Publishers, Herent. 14, 2003.

[11] E. Çinlar, "Markov Renewal Theory," *Advances in Applied Probability*, Vol. 1, 1969, pp. 123-187.

[12] F. Stenberg, R. Manca and D. Silvestrov, "Semi-Markov Reward Models for Disability Insurance," *Theory of Stochastic Processes*, Vol. 12, No. 28, 2006, pp. 239-254.

[13] J. Lemaire, "Bonus-Malus Systems in Automobile Insurance," Kluwer Academic Publisher, Boston, 1995.

[14] B. Sundt, "An Introduction to Non Life Insurance Mathematics," Veroffentlichungen des Istitute fur Versich-erun gswissenschaft der Universitat Mannheim, 3rd Edition, 1993.

14

The Feasibility of Using an Automated Net Asset Value Validation Tool in an International Investment Bank

Sammer Markos, Nhien-An Le-Khac, M-Tahar Kechadi
School of Computer Science & Informatics, University College Dublin, Belfield, Dublin, Ireland

Abstract

Fund administration is a relatively new service that some banks and back office offer Investment Company's. This service was regarded as "boutique" in some countries as it was not a necessity hence not enforced by law to have independent calculation and verification of a fund price. However, this sector of business was and has been a major factor in the economic boom for many countries worldwide. In general most companies have many human resources tagged to this service. This is mainly due to the high volume of manual work that needs to be carried out to validate a Net Asset Value. If the Net Asset Value is calculated incorrectly and hence not validated correctly then there is huge repercussions for the company that calculated the Net Asset Value (monetary, reputation, losing a client). With the turn in the current climate the operational requirements that was once affordable has snowballed out of control, this is why invest company's are finding ways to reduce costs and hence use less labour intensive methods or relocate these specific jobs to lower cost countries such as Eastern Europe and India. However, this is not without its own set of problems, some being that most companies and in our case, the company always employs a distributed service requirement. Within the scope of a collaboration project which focuses on a Net Asset Value automated validation solution to replace a labour intensive manual approach. In this paper, we research the feasibility of using such a tool in a funds business of an international investment bank where parts of this process are based in Asia and Europe. Our approach is based on surveying people that are currently working in the Net Asset Value validation process, and in turn analyse the results attained. Throughout this process, we must not only focus on the efficient method of applying a Net Asset Value validation automated solution but we must also provide an overview of the important factors in building a solutions to be used in a fund administration environment.

Keywords: Data Mining, Funds, Investment Banking, Alternative Investment, NAV, Hedge Funds

1. Introduction

Funds administration is a subsection of the investments industry, *i.e.* trading on the stock exchange [1]. When it comes to trading on the stock exchange there are three tiers in administration, at the front line is front office- these are the traders, they execute the trades on behalf of a client. The second tier is middle office, here is where all the actual trade information and others are tabulated and sent in an agreed format to the final tier; back office [2]. Back office is were the accountancy work is carried out for all trades as per front office's instructions hence the price or Net Asset Value (NAV) of a fund is calculated. A NAV is the price at which an investor can buy/sell shares of a fund, a fund is a collective investment entity hence a pool of different instruments.

There are many steps in the pricing or valuation of a fund. This depends on what type of fund it is, however, all funds consist of six core pieces: 1) Stock reconciliation, 2) reflection of corporate actions, 3) pricing of instruments, 4) Booking, calculating and reconciling fees and interest accruals, 5) cash reconciliation and finally, 6) NAV/price validation.

The NAV validation piece is so vital as this is were the verification for accuracy and correctness occurs, hence is the stock reflected correctly and in line with the prospectus or legal contract between client and administrator, are then prices correct and so on. In short the verification of points 1-5 of the NAV preparation. If a NAV price is released to a client is incorrect then the fund administrator is liable according to the fund administration agreement, this in cases can be hundreds of thousands of monetary compensation to investors and the client. This is why it is imperative that if the administrator is verifying the NAV manually that there should be a way to automate the NAV validation piece to not only reduce cost but also to reduce if not eliminate human error. One major factor as previously discussed is to cut costs, must reduce expenditure in the current climate, working on the Toyota LEAN methodology *"Increase efficiency and decrease waste—more value less work"* [1]. Hence reducing human resources and maintaining service we can theoretically run the business with a reduction in cost. A second reason is that most fund administration companies are located in the financial district IFSC (International Financial Services Centre-Dublin); therefore are regulated by the financial regulator (FR). and are audited yearly, so according to the Irish and EU directives there are many checks and standard reports that must be available, these reports are always checked for manual intervention, hence using a large amount of human interaction in a process increases the possibility of errors occurring. As this is an international fund administration company, their operation is spread throughout the world *i.e.* Europe, Asia, North America etc. There needs to be an improved approach to maintain and track all operations across this distributed environment.

The funds administration industry is trying to reduce the cost of the operational cost by implementing a NAV validation tool. Net asset Value (NAV) or the price at which a fund or pool of investments is priced in the market. Even though this process involves some human interaction hence solving an exception.

There are four companies that are regarded as the leaders in the market when it comes to a NAV validation tool, Comit (NAV Audit), Linedata (NavQuest), Moneymate (MoneyMate Control Platform) and Milestone (pControl), all these applications have an acceptable standard for compliance reasons and are therefore accepted as an automated tool by the FR.

However, they all have one weakness; the tools are generic for all companies, hence not tailor made to the organisations needs. For example, company A has a certain set of rules that are used for fund X and therefore only need certain rules to be applied; also, this company uses ± 20% tolerances as its parameters. Therefore, they have no dynamic rule selection; hence, if field A is populated then Rule Y should apply. As an extension to this study, we will explore the potential of automatic rule selection.

This study was a natural extension to that, we would like to investigate what are the obstacles in implementing such a radical solution, choosing the correct validation software, data integration, rule sets used, dynamic rule selection and not forgetting the infamous obstacle of the cultural issues associated.

However, in an economy that is currently very volatile and fragile, this reflects on the workers that implement this automated service. At this time, culture and human reactions take precedence. These obstacles are placed at the forefront of the discussion, as people feel threatened.

This paper is organised as follows: Section 2 is a brief review of the background in NAV validation and preparation in banking and finance. Section 3 shows the current operating model of an international investment bank. We present our approach in Section 4. We analyse some of the results achieved in Section 5. Finally, we conclude in Section 6

2. Background in NAV Validation and Preparation in Banking and Finance

2.1. What is a NAV?

A NAV is a price for an entity that is published on the stock exchange, which then allows investors to buy shares/invest in to this entity.

Fund administration is the name given to the set of activities that are carried out in support of the actual process of running a collective investment scheme, whether the scheme is a traditional mutual fund, a hedge fund, pension fund, unit trust or something in between. (**Figure 1**)

These administrative activities in the scope of this document would include the calculation of the Net Asset Value (NAV) of a fund (investment scheme or pool of money). Some investment management companies calculate their own NAV. However if it is an Irish regulated fund then the NAV must be calculated and verified independently (EU UCITS Regulations 1989) hence back office fund administrators. **Figure 1** illustrates the components of a fund. A NAV can be calculated daily, weekly, bimonthly, quarterly, semi annually. Therefore, the NAV frequency is dependent on the characteristics of the fund.

2.2. What is Involved in the Calculation and Preparation of a NAV?

The core pieces for calculating a NAV on a specific day are: stock or portfolio reconciliation; executing any potential corporate actions on some of the securities held on the portfolio, pricing the securities/instruments on the portfolio, booking, calculating and reconciling fees and interest accruals; these could be legal fees, audit fees and some NAV based fees (calculated on the size of the NAV) such as administration fees, management fees and performance fees (the latter two are more common in hedge funds rather than mutual funds), reconciling the cash accounts of the fund and finally validating the NAV, once all aspects are completed (**Figure 2**).

2.2.1. Stock or Portfolio Reconciliation

This is the first step in NAV preparation; this is where the fund accountant will collate and reflect the below all shares bought and sold by the investment/portfolio manager on to the fund accounting system generally this step is either completely manual or has a considerable amount of manual intervention.

2.2.2. Executing any Potential Corporate Actions on Some of the Securities Held on the Portfolio

Once all trades/shares are reflected, corporate actions such as acquisitions, mergers, ISIN changes, dividends etc must be also reflected on the fund. These can impact the funds cash *i.e.* dividends payable/receivable, and also the number of holdings/name/entity *i.e.* ISIN change, merger etc. This is also a completely manual process no automation at all hence prone to human error.

2.2.3. Pricing the Securities/Instruments on the Portfolio

Once all stock positions and corporate actions are reflected on the fund accounting system, the next step is to price the stock/securities held on the funds portfolio. Pricing is a very important issue to many back office fund administered because they must be independent with the prices. They must reflect the price according to the legal contract or prospectus, this legal document outlines the strategy of the fund and that includes pricing sources and price types for example: The pricing hierarchy of equity in fund X is bid price source Extel, Telekurs then Bloomberg. That means the fund administrator must use first try to source the price from Extel if there is no price available from this source then they move to Telekurs and so on. This is a semi automatic process.

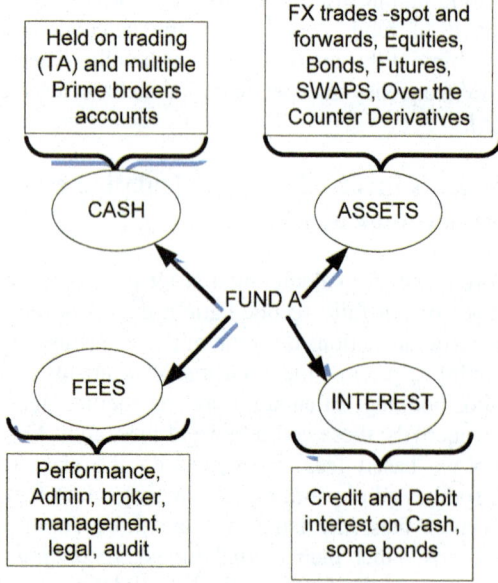

Figure 1. Components of a fund.

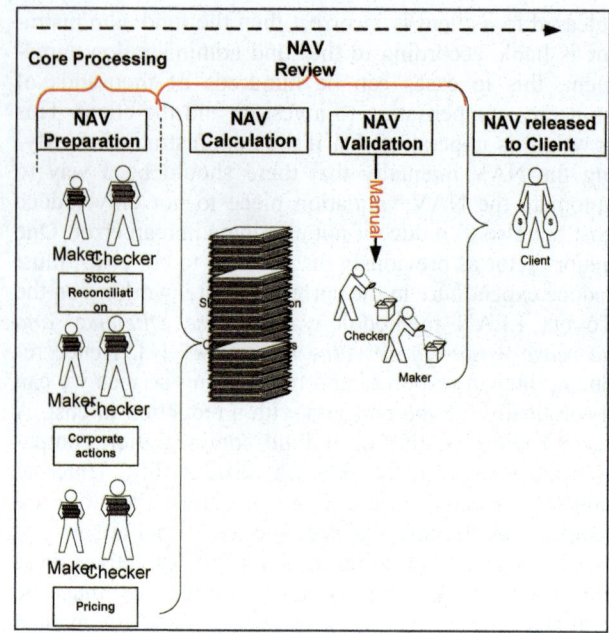

Figure 2. Flow chart of a NAV preparation/validation process.

2.2.4. Booking, Calculating and Reconciling Fees

Some of the fees/income are legal fees, audit fees and some NAV based fees (calculated on the size of the NAV) such as administration fees, management fees and performance fees (the latter two are more common in hedge funds rather than mutual funds), on the income side, it is more like credit interest accruals.

There are e parts when it comes to fees. First, the calculation of the correct amount of the fund charged as at particular NAV date. For example the NAV is monthly, the audit fees are € 12,000 annually, so the amount that should be reflected as an accrual on the NAV is € 1,000, however if these fees are prepaid then the amount that would be reflected is a prepaid expense that is reduced every month. Another scenario is that the fund paid the investment manager 1,000 of the 12,000, and then this amount must be reflected as leaving the fund cash account (more about this in cash reconciliation section below) and a reduction in the accrual. This process is semi automatic, the accrual is calculated by the accounting system, however any payments are reflected manually.

2.2.5. Reconciling the Cash Accounts of the Fund

At this stage of the NAV preparation has one final stage and it is reconciling all the cash accounts that the fund holds, these accounts can be multicurrency and be held in multiple locations. For Example: there is a EURO account held with JPMorgan, a USD margin account held at Goldman Sacs. Before the recession that hit the economy the funds used one broker, now the common investment manager strategy is to spread their liquid cash across many brokers to reduce the exposure to the market.

This step is reconciling all cash statements with what is reflected on the fund accounting system. This is a manual process no automation.

2.2.6. Validating and Publishing the NAV

Once all the core pieces of the NAV are executed. The validation process of the NAV must then occur. This is the most time consuming and at present exclusively manual process. In this step, all points carried out in producing a NAV are checked. The figures that are reflected on the fund accounting system are checked against broker statements, pricing vendor reports, cash statements etc. This step is normally completed by eye balling the reports and making sure that the external reports match what is reflected on the NAV (in the fund accounting system). If the figures do not match or are not within the allowable tolerance dictated by the prospectus then valid evidence must be attained to answer why not, this evidence is attached as a hard copy within the file for audit purposes. This where it was decided that there is too much emphases on manual process and that there is a need for human resources as it is labour intensive and also implementing a automated solution reduces the risk of errors.

3. Current Operating Model in BIP[1] Bank

In Section 2, the process of NAV preparation and validation was outlined in brief, NAV process can be completed by the same individual, however BIP bank employs a scatted model:

- Stock or portfolio reconciliation is carried out in Eastern Europe and Asia
- Corporate actions is carried out in Ireland, UK
- Pricing the securities/instruments on the portfolio: Luxembourg, India
- Booking, calculating and reconciling fees, audit fees is calculated in Ireland, UK
- Reconciling the cash accounts of the fund occurs in India and Eastern Europe
- Validating the NAV, once all aspects above are completed in the UK and Ireland

Currently the means by which funds are administered in BIP bank is using a scattered approach. This is the same model employed by many other fund administration companies globally. Model currently deployed by BIP multinational bank to fund administration only (not including TA)

Figure 3 shows an example for Fund XYZ administered using a scattered approach. Poland will complete the trade/stock reconciliation part of the NAV. Poland

will then inform Ireland as the NAV validation piece occurs in Ireland. Ireland valuation team will then ask the corporate actions team in the UK to execute all appropriate corporate actions on the fund. Once that is complete the Irish NAV validation team send a an email to Luxembourg to ask the team to price the securities on the fund Luxembourg once again inform the valuation team in Ireland to inform them that the task is complete. Ireland once again informs the cash team in Poland to complete the process of cash reconciliation. At this time, the valuation team in Ireland calculates the accruals on the fund. Upon completion of the cash reconciliation, the NAV should be ready for validation, and this as discussed above occurs in Ireland.

Using this approach is not cost effective, can have security and hence audit issues as all communication between the teams is via email and not one core system. This is why we recommend an automated solution, which is currently being researched for the current business; this is an automated solution where all actions will be centralised using one core validation application. All systems will feed into this tool hence points 1 to 5 as outlined in section 2.0. All resources in the multiple locations will have full visibility in to the process and hence no need for emails/other communication. First step in this analysis is to see:

1) Can an automated solution be applied to the hedge business technically?
2) What will the challenges be in adopting this model?
3) Is the business ready for this solution?
4) Is their a cost saving using this approach?
5) and anything else that the data showed?

Figure 4 illustrates the new automated solution and how it will affect the overall process.

In order to answer these questions, we carried out some research on the feasibility of this approach by making use of a survey on the daily activities of the NAV validation team and in turn analysing these results.

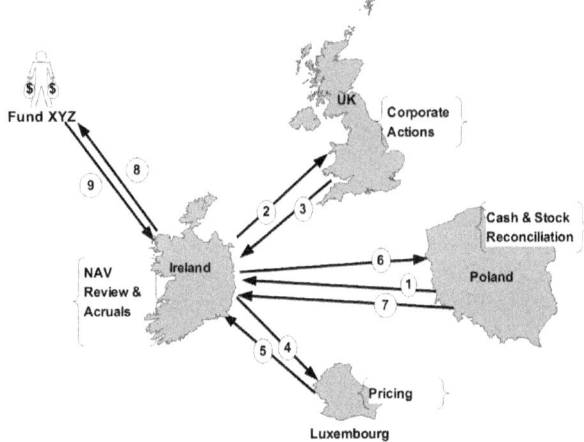

Figure 3. Current manual operating model of BIP bank.

---

[1]Real name of fund cannot be disclosed due to confidentiality agreement of the project

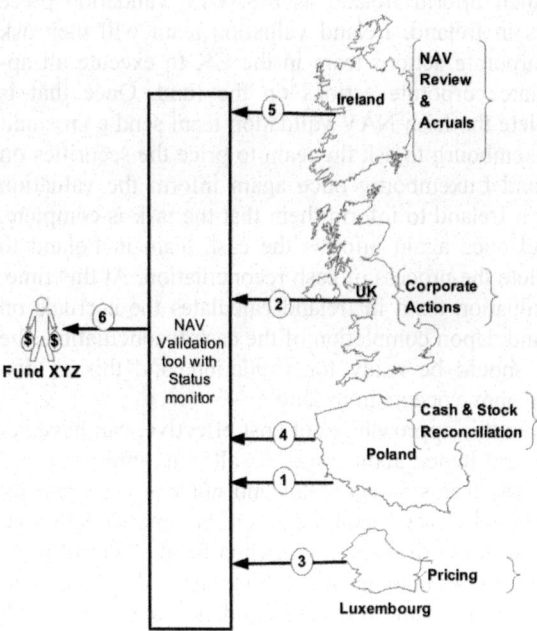

Figure 4. Automated solution.

4. Methodology

The evaluation of the NAV validation tool is a complicate task [3-5] in terms of resource capacities and to the best of our knowledge there is no related works on this axe. Therefore, our approach is composed of two main steps: preparing data and analysing of data collected to extract useful knowledge. This second step will be presented in Section 5.

As the purpose of this research is to efficiently apply a new NAV validation tool that has not been deployed yet and there is no experience of using same tools in the company profile, the data should be collected from the real activities of NAV validation teams. As a consequence, pre-processing step is also needed to make datasets ready and meaningful enough to analyse.

4.1. Data Collection

The raw data was collected through a survey carried out by interviewing experts in the fund accounting world [6]. The Survey was designed using knowledge of the funds business. It was agreed that the data will be collected using interviews and responses. These responses were categorical in nature and hence will assist in the analysis. Data collection segment involved interviewing 162 people across 2 sites. The data collection lasted approximately 15 business days, this process involved holding separate interviews which spanned between 5 and 20 min. Using this technique we were able to collect other important information which was more in line with cultural

issues and procedures, this will be discussed further in the result section. Data collected included the following attributes:

- Number of people tagged to each fund and subsequently each client. This is important to collate exactly who does what and hence assist in collating information about cost savings with resource capacity in mind.

- Client Name: this was an informative field that acted as a marker—a descriptive field for purposes of reporting.

- Fund Legal Name and Fund Type e.g. Stand alone, master feeder fund of funds. This field was used for analytics and fund characterisation; hence when thinking about a validation tool can the validation tool take a hold of a specific type of fund hence is it "able" to mimic a manual approach or is the fund type too complex.

- Base CCY and Asset Value of a fund, this field was used also as a marker to convert non euro NAV balances to EUR so as to standardise the total that each fund holds-used in resource capacity for instance. If the NAV of fund A is 5 million and there are 4 people tagged to this fund and the cost to me is 4 million per year, will I have a cost saving if we automated the validation instead of manual validation; hence reduce cost and human resource.

- Prime Broker, this field was vital as a precursor to NAV validation tool because if we know what prime brokers are used by the clients then all the reports in question must be streamed into the software. This step needs iteration with prime brokers.

- NAV Frequency, monthly, weekly etc, this field was used to see how out time was spent on each client and subsequently fund and in future will dictate the checks that will need to be put in place for the validation of a NAV—for example if the NAV is monthly then there should be a rule that states that checking monthly price tolerance is irrelevant as stock prices will dramatically fluctuate however this rule needs to be in place for a daily NAV as you will not expect a large movement in price in one day.

- Type of instruments held on portfolio e.g. bonds, futures, options etc. This was used to dictate what is needed to value and validate a NAV, there are certain rules for each type of instrument hence this should give us an actual idea of the complexity of a fund, i.e. does it need more resources? Does the resource need extra time to validate the NAV?

- Number of open positions on the portfolio, volumes of trading per NAV period and Portfolio Size., these important in calculating man hours and resources, hence to check a portfolio of 10 instruments should - using logic be less time and resource draining than a portfolio with 1000 open positions. If a fund trades

100 times a month then this must also be less resource draining as 2500 trades per month. The asset size is important to evaluate the cost of providing a service compared to fees charged to the company.

- Perceived complexity of the fund: this was a vital indicator in the assessment of what the user thought was a complex fund. We used this as a comparison to actual complexity keeping mind variables outlined above.
- Processing time of checking the fund locally, processing time of checking the fund abroad, processing time of preparing the fund in Ireland and finally processing time of preparing the fund abroad. These attributes were used to evaluate the cost effectiveness of moving certain services to Asia and Eastern Europe, and also to ensure resource capacity of the NAV validation teams in Western Europe.

The information collected above was deemed necessary to evaluate the resource capacity according to certain attributes such a: how many people are needed to complete a NAV for a specific client, the level of the person was used as a marker. The characteristics of a fund were also defined by instrument that are held and others. We used the size of the portfolio as a bench mark for income and expenditure. Once this data was collected the data was normalised [7] hence upon data input, the interviewer could use difference abbreviations for the same question. This is discusses in the section following.

5. Analysis of Results

Most of the techniques used to analyse the results are standard descriptive statistics with an evaluation of correlated variables [8] e.g. are the complexity of the funds correlated to the type of fund? Is it negatively/positively correlated? The results are outlined and discussed in the following paragraphs.

There were 162 people surveyed across 2 sites, over 286 funds analysed (**Table 1**), we chose to analyse some funds that are going to liquidate therefore the figures can be somewhat skewed, we chose to do this as they are still part of the persons duties, the number of 286 include all run off classes - which in other words are feeders. The breakdown of fund types include: 113 master feeders, 72 standalone *i.e.* no feeders and 101 feeders/run-offs. The majority of the funds are administered monthly 91% of the total are monthly and only 1% are daily funds (**Table 2**).

We can therefore deduce that there are 450 (where funds liquidated are a total of 164) funds administered every month by 162 people which is 2.8 funds per person including feeder, if you were to remove the feeder count then the figure would be 337 funds for 162 = 2 funds per person/month.

Table 1. Abstract results.

Description	Total number
Persons in total	162
Total Clients	49
No. population to each client	3
No. of population to standalone fund and master feeder only	1
Total no. of funds	286
Total Standalone funds	72
Total Master feeders	113
Total Feeder funds	101
No of prime brokers	33
List of Prime brokers	See **Table 4**
No. of Instruments	
List of Instruments	See **Table 6**
No of funds administered in India not inc feeders	124
% of funds administered in India not inc feeders	67%
% similar to Mutual funds	83%

Table 2. NAV frequency of all funds.

NAV Frequency	Total	%
DAILY	2	1%
MONTHLY	261	91%
QUARTERTLY	6	2%
SEMI ANNUAL	1	0.3%
WEEKLY	16	6%
Grand Total	**286**	

All fund types were then analysed and certain information deemed necessary was collected, such as instruments held on the portfolio, list of prime brokers (**Table 4**), time that it takes to prepare the NAV, time to check the NAV, perceived complexity etc. Using this data we were able to ascertain whether the funds in question can be automated by using the validation software.

The next step in the analysis was the Ratio of people to standalone and master feeders was found to be 1 fund to 1 person. The total number of clients is 49 and that shows a ratio of 3 people per client. Classifying this proportion down into "level" of person *i.e.* Vice President, Assistant Vice President, Account Manager and Maker then the ratios are as per **Table 3**, for Funds not including feeders: there are approx 31 funds per VP, 11 funds per AVP almost 5 funds per account manager/checker and approx 2 funds per maker Even though there are over 67% of these funds (not feeders/run off classes) are partially administered in India (up to the GAV, therefore all that is needed to completed in Ireland is accrual calculation and reflection on the trial balance and P&L).

Automating the NAV validation step of the NAV preparation will logically reduce head count *i.e.* human resource as all manual checks done by humans can be automated. For example price checking, instead of eye balling 2 reports and ticking the reports using a red pen, the software can be fed the 2 figures from the 2 reports and it will complete the task automatically without manual tampering/error.

Upon further inspection into the variables that were attained from the analyses, people that administered the fund were asked to rate the complexity in terms of the difficulty, bearing in mind the duration of completion and the instruments on the portfolio etc. as they perceive it from 1 to 10, 1 being not complex to 10 which is equivalent to highly complex as per characterisation explained in the methodology, we cross referenced this to the size of the portfolio.

An important question when trying to improve a process by applying a validation tool is to show how to cut costs and hence become more efficient without diluting the service/the controls put in place, hence can we statistically justify the ratios seen above involving resources. Does the size of the portfolio dictate the complexity of the fund? (**Table 5**).

Figure 5 clearly shows that this is not the case as both high and medium levels fit a standard normal distribution hence bell shape yet the low complexity is high for all sizes of the portfolio this is shown as the trend line is skewed proving the size of the portfolio has no influence on the perceived complexity of the fund.

Another Hypothesis that was deemed necessary to be analysed when analysing the applicability of a validation tool is: does the volume of trading have a direct influence on the complexity of the fund (**Figure 6** and **Table 6**).

Table 3. Breakdown of population into "Level" in organisation.

	Human Resource Per Fund – (Not inc Feeders)	Human Resource Per Client
Funds (Master and stand-alone only)	185	49
Vice President	6 30.83	8.17
Assistant Vice President	17 10.88	2.88
Account Manager	39 4.74	1.26
NAV Preparation	100 1.85	0.49
Total	162	

Table 4. List of prime brokers according to most commonly used.

JPMN	136	BOP	1
DB2	61	CARGRILL	1
CSI	59	CARNEGIEP	1
MSI	58	CIEP	1
UBA	40	IMAREXA	1
CITIP	31	Marcuma	1
GSM	24	PITETO	1
MLP	13	RBSI	1
HTBC	10	SATANDER	1
BNO	3	SEBA	1
CITCOP	3	SWISSE	1
Benkollman	2	Syzo	1
Bircluys	2	NEWEGE	2
SCOTIBANK	2	SUISSEP	2
Macquary	2	UBI	2

Table 5. Perceived complexity of fund V's the size of the fund.

	% Complexity of fund				
% Portfolio Size V's Complexity of fund	High	Medium	Low	Total	% of total
LARGE	22%	31%	7%	49	17%
MEDIUM	15%	26%	12%	49	17%
SMALL	63%	44%	81%	188	66%
Total	41	98	147	286	
	14%	34%	51%		

Table 6. Perceived complexity of fund V's the volume of trading.

	Complexity				
Volume	High Complexity	Medium Complexity	Low Complexity	Total	Total %
HIGH	1%	10%	3%	42	15%
MEDIUM	2%	3%	4%	27	9%
LOW	11%	21%	44%	217	76%
Total	41	98	147	286	

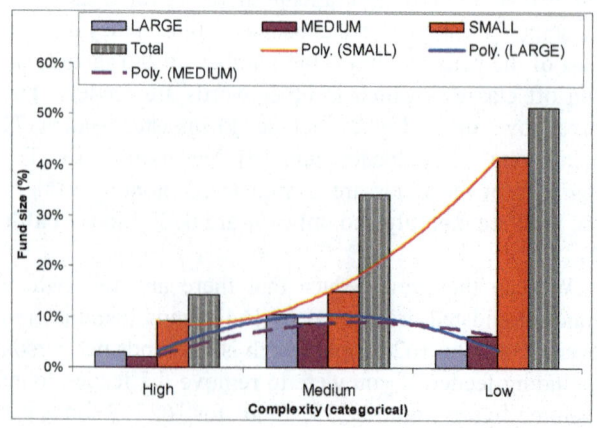

Figure 5. Size of the portfolio V's the complexity of the fund.

From the figures it shows that 76% of the funds that are administered have a low volume of trades per month, so can this statistic account for the high ratio?

Figure 6 shows this is not the case as high and volumes fit a standard normal distribution and the medium volumes seems to be linear yet the low complexity is high for all volumes of the portfolio this is shown as the trend line is skewed proving the volumes of trading has no influence on the perceived complexity of the fund.

The final relevant statistic was to see how long it takes to prepare and check an official NAV on a monthly basis and how does this compare to our operations overseas (Asia and Eastern Europe) (**Table 7** and **Figure 7**).

We used SPSS V.16.0 [9] to run a simple one way ANOVA test, to see if there was any significant difference between Asia/E. Europe and Ireland preparation time. The Results showed that there was no significant at the 95% level of confidence meaning that Ireland is still taking just as long collating and checking overseas work then we are preparing the NAV fully in Ireland. Keeping in mind that organisations are trying to keep costs down by being efficient at a minimum cost, hence minimal number of resources to carry out the tasks at hand yet still optimising their service.

Throughout the data collection and the hypothesis testing it seems there does not seem to be statistical reason why there is such a high resource drain *i.e.* too many human resources in place and apparently this is not to due to any technical factor but merely due to the process being manually intensive. Other factors that seemed to shine through during the interview process were cultural —people will complicate their daily task so as to secure their job, hence put obstacles in the path of an automated less labour intensive process. All that remains to discuss and show is how there could be another reason, not quantifiable explanation. Keeping in mind the bias of our sample size. When conducting this study some by-products of the study were discovered. Some of which are listed below.

1) All the process is Excel based.

2) It is based heavily on manual work from the teams; this is a huge hindrance when it comes to using a validation instrument.

3) Migration on to a new platform.

4) Difficult to price securities.

5) Market value manual reconciliation (main check-eyeballing over 1000 securities and making sure they match the broker, last months NAV figures and the investment manager).

6) All reports sent to client are via email in excel format (11 spreadsheets linked into one another huge compliance risk).

7) The NAV is prepared and checked section by section using a 15 page check sheet not all at once.

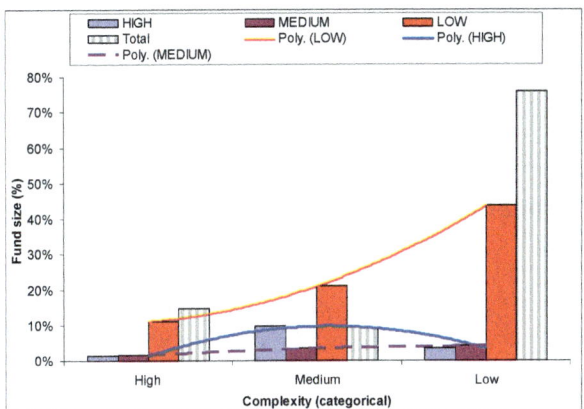

Figure 6. Volume of trading V's perceived complexity of fund.

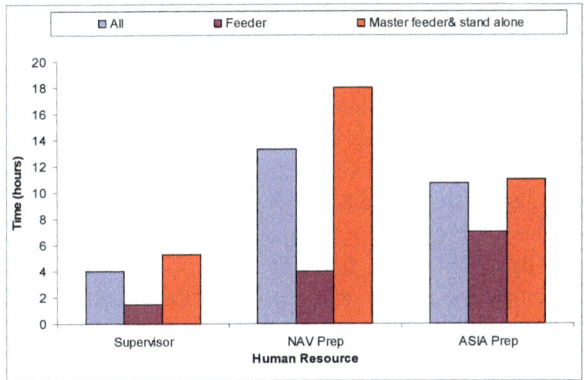

Figure 7. Preparation time classified into human resource.

Table 7. Perceived hours per fund preparation.

Fund Type	Checker	Maker	COE
All	4	13.3	10.7
Feeder	1.5	4	7
Master feeder& stand alone	5.3	18	11

There are 2 level checks for all funds (even funds partially administered in Asia hence this makes over a 4 level checks), this is waste of resources and hence profit.

We now discuss how to improve performance by using an automated NAV validation tool and improving the process flow of the NAV Preparation. Using the basis that there is no valid reason why an automated NAV validation tool cannot be used, there is nothing too complex that logical/SQL rules cannot handle. This tool should eliminate the above manual based approach and hence should reduce the number of checks that need to be carried out by multiple people, also manual spreadsheets need to be eliminated due to the fact that this manually intensive process hinders the ability for companies to pass audits [10,11] and also makes it difficult for companies to keep in line with the flaws laid down by financial regulators. And finally using a manual approach blinds management as there is no way of measuring performance of their staff, what is used is not system based it is once again manually based excel spreadsheets with manual statistics not system generated statistics.

6. Conclusions and Further Discussion

We found through this study using the strategy employed *i.e.* our statistical approach using the correct interview technique (friendly approach) and the selection of the correct data elements used in the interviews was essential to the success of the research. These was an underlying hypothesis that this study was designed for and that was can an automated NAV validation tool be fitted to the funds administration business for BIP bank replacing the current operating model.

The study was successful and all staff co-operated and seemed very eager to learn and be involved. We proved that a validation tool can be applied to this book of business, the only hindrance is cultural. The *"this it's the way it's always been done"* scenario. We found that there is no logical/statistical reason for a high human resource account, once again it's the manually driven process and the reliance on excel. It seems some of the checks that are being done are "over the top" the one that stands out the most is checking the monthly price of a security against the previous months price—this does not seem logical as you would more than likely expect a movement unless it's a fund of funds that has a NAV calculated quarterly.

One of the most astonishing findings was that even when funds are migrated to the new applications, the Excel spreadsheet will still be used and this once again falls in to culture rather than necessity. Upon further inspection into the checks that are being made almost 39% are manual and excel related and for this reason we can theoretically apply validation software.

From this study we recommend that processes are reviewed and recommendations are made to eliminate unnecessary manual checks hence rule validation can we according to the study results use an automated validation tool integrated in data/knowledge analysing framework [12-14].

7. References

[1]   http://www.investopedia.com/

[2]   L. L. Gremillion, "Mutual Fund Industry Handbook: A Comprehensive Guide for Investment," John Wiley & Sons, New York, 2005.

[3]   H. Levy and M. Sarnat, "Principles of Financial Management", Prentice Hall, Upper Saddle River, 1988.

[4]   "Mutual Fund Fact Book," Investment Company Institute (U.S.). http://www.icifactbook.org/

[5]   G. N. Gregoriou and J. Zhu, "Evaluating Hedge Fund and CTA Performance: Data Envelopment Analysis Approach," John Wiley & Sons, New York, 2005.

[6]   P. Giudici, "Applied Data Mining Statistical Methods for Business and Industry," American Statistical Association Publisher, Alexandria, 2006.

[7]   J. Han and M. Kamber, "Data Mining: Concept and Techniques," 2nd Edition, Morgan Kaufmann Publishers, San Francisco, 2006, pp. 67-73.

[8]   P-N. Tan, M. Steinbach and V. Kumar, "Introduction to Data Mining Errata," Addison-Wesley Publisher, Boston, 2006, pp. 66-83.

[9]   http://spss.com

[10] W. A. Rini, "Mathematics of the Securities Industry," McGraw-Hill, New York, 2003.

[11] L. Jaeger, "The New Generation of Risk Management for Hedge Funds and Private Equity," Institutional Investor Book, 2004.

[12] N.-A. Le-Khac, M.-T. Kechadi and J. Carthy, "ADMIRE Framework: Distributed Data Mining on Data Grid platforms," *Proceedings of International Conference on Software and Data Technologies*, Setubal, 11-14 September 2006.

[13] N.-A. Le-Khac, L. M. Aouad and M.-T. Kechadi, "Knowledge Map: Toward a New Approach Supporting the Knowledge Management in Distributed Data Mining," *Proceedings of 3rd IEEE International Conference on Autonomic and Autonomous Systems*, Computer Society Press, Athens, 19-25 June 2007.

[14] N.-A. Le Khac, S. Markos, M. O'Neill, A. Brabazon and M.-T. Kechadi, "An Efficient Search Tool for an Anti-Money Laundering Application of an Multi-National Bank's Dataset," *Proceedings of International Conference on Information and Knowledge Engineering*, Las Vegas, 13-16 July 2009.

15

Environmental Policy and Firm Investment Behaviour when Energy Saving Technologies are Available

Emanuela Giusi Gaeta*
University of Rome "Tor Vergata", Rome, Italy

Abstract

This paper investigates upon the effects of taxation on firm investment behaviour in presence of alternative energy (oil) saving technologies and scarce resources in competitive markets. Socially optimal policies are compared to a decentralized regulatory framework: the paper shows that taxation affects the adoption of different energy saving technologies hence the aggregate amount of energy saving. To our knowledge, there are few works that underline the relationship between environmental policies and firms' incentives to adopt oil saving technologies. For this reason, we follow the theoretical literature focusing on the effects of environmental policy applied to pollution and climate change by adapting it to the energy saving perspective. We perform a static comparison of environmental policies to show that different levels of the same instrument lead to different results in terms of the number of firms adopting energy saving technologies; multiple equilibrium are possible but there is only one which is socially optimal.

Keywords: Environmental Policies, Fiscal Policies, Technological Change, Energy Saving, Welfare Analysis

1. Introduction

In the last decade, debates around environmental economics and policy have become increasingly permeated by issues related to technological change. One aspect of this issue relates to the effects that environmental policies have on firms' behaviour. In particular the literature has focussed on the comparison of alternative policy instruments targeted to reduce social costs, paying specially attention to pollution and climate change, rather than to energy saving. There are few works underlining the relationship between environmental policy and firms' incentives to adopt oil saving technologies and this paper follows such research line. In general, a large number of papers aim at establishing a ranking between alternative environmental policy instruments regarding the extent to which they enhance the adoption and diffusion of pollution control technology both at industry level [1-3] and firm level [4]. The goal in evaluating the different instruments is to compare the cost before and after adoption of the abatement technology, where the latter differs from a conventional "dirty" technology in terms of a lower marginal abatement cost [5]. However the literature is rather scattered: some authors focus on the ranking of market-based instruments by taking into account the time inconsistency of the environmental policy related to the delay between announcement and actual implementation [6,7]. Other authors investigate upon the effect that uncertainty—on the arrival time of the advanced technology—plays on firms' choice, distinguishing by the case where the regulator anticipates or not the arrival of new technology.

Unlike the cited literature, this paper investigates upon the effects of taxation on firm investment behaviour in presence of alternative energy (oil) saving technologies and scarce resources in competitive markets. Socially optimal policies are compared to a decentralized regulatory framework: the paper shows that taxation affects the adoption of different energy saving technologies hence the aggregate amount of energy saving and decentralized policies are succesfull in achieving first best outcome [8,9]. The paper is strongly inspired by the theoretical analysis of Requate and Unold [4], but their research is focused on the comparison of policy instruments (taxes, auctions permits and standards) to reduce pollution in competitive markets rather than investigate upon the adoption of oil-saving technologies. They show that different policy instruments lead to quite different results in terms of emissions, if the number of firms which adopt

*I am indebted to the IAD—University of Rome Tor Vergata (http: www. scuolaiad.it) that provides funds for my research.

the new technology is determined endogenously through equilibrium consideration.

Following their research, we try to define the optimal policy by comparing "market-based instruments", to a "command-and-control" policy. Unlike the recent literature, we do not assume that all firms, belonging to the same industry, will adopt the new technology. Following Requate and Unold [4], we endogenize the number of adopting firms by analysing two scenarios that differ with respect to the order of first mover in a two-stage game: regulator—by setting the level of his policy instruments (e.g. tax rate)—or the firm by investing.

In the first one, called ex-ante optimal policy, we assume that the regulator makes a commitment both to the choice and level of his policy instrument. In this case the regulator moves at first, while the firms invest in the second stage, after observing the new tax rate and decide for the possible adoption of the new technology. In the second strategy, named ex post optimal policy, we are going to assume that, before the game starts, the regulator makes a commitment to the choice of his policy instrument only, although we are focusing on taxation only. Then she observes how many firms invest in the first stage and finally she chooses the level of the instrument. In the first case, for each implementation cost F, a particular number of firms should invest for an optimal outcome. This would require coordination among firms. Since firms, however, are indifferent between investing and not when the tax rate equals the socially optimal marginal damage—which is a necessary condition for optimality—inefficient outcomes are likely to occur in this case. So, for the first scenario, we confirm the result found by Requate, Unold [4]: there are multiple equilibria, a lot of these are inefficient and the runic solution that can be pursued is the second best.

In the second situation, the planner moves after observing firms choice. In such a way the first best policy is a sub-game perfect equilibrium. Nevertheless, the implementation of such an equilibrium depends on the way the game is played between firms and planner. In such a case, Requate and Unold [4] find that there exists a unique subgame perfect equilibrium where the optimal number of firms invests and the regulator chooses the optimal tax rate. But firms move simultaneously and in an uncoordinated way, so nothing assures that the optimal number of firms investing in the advanced technology (first best) will be, in fact, implemented. Unlike Requate and Unold, [4], we are going to show that, if players act in a different way, the solution of first best will be implemented in a decentralized economy. This is possible in a "multi-stage game with observed actions and perfect information" [10] where the planner moves at the last stage and backward induction is a viable solution. This result can be considered as the original aspect of our paper (a previous investigation is found in Gaeta [11]), which makes a little but substantial difference with the research made by Requate and Unold [4].

This paper is organized as follows: In the next section, we discuss the characteristics of the model. Section 3 describes firms' behaviour. In Section 4 we present the social optimum and derive the socially optimal allocation. In Section 5 we study two scenarios, in the first the regulator announces the instrument and fixes the relative level, while in the second she announces the instrument, but fixes the instrument in a second stage, after observing the firm's behaviour. In Section 6 we present a numerical example which summarises the model. Conclusions follow in Section 7. Technical proofs are found in Appendix.

2. The Model

There are n small firms operating in a competitive market. Every firm produces by means of a production function characterized by DRS, where the argument is oil (O). Under a laisser-faire policy, the firms choose the first best quantity $O_{\max}$. Taxation on oil makes it expensive and firm are induced to substitute oil with an alternative input: e.

The firms can choose between two technologies: the first one, that we call conventional technology, is oil intensive, while the second one, called advanced technology, is "oil saving". This means that, for the same output level, the advanced technology uses a lower level for O. However, the implementation of the second technology is costly, according to a sunk cost F. We are going to assume that each firm starts with the conventional technology.

We assume that oil price is given. This is so because the domestic oil demand is not able to affect the international oil price.

$O_{\max}$ is the oil usage in the first best equilibrium, *i.e.* when the firms operate without taxation. With oil taxation, the level O chosen by the firm can be reduced throughout an alternative input e. The e usage depends on O, $e(O)$, with $e'(O) < 0$, $e \in [0, e_{\max}]$. $C_e(e)$ is the usage cost for e with $C_e(e_{\max}) = \infty$, $C_e(0) = 0$. It is helpful using O as the unit of reference for the model and expressing $C_e(e)$ in terms of O; so we call $C(O)$ the substitution cost, between e and O, in terms of O. Given the relationship $e(O)$, we conclude that $C(O_{\max}) = 0$, $-C'(O) > 0$, $C(0) = \infty$

Figure 1 highlights the relationship between $C_e(e)$ and $C(O)$.

The picture must be read clockwise: starting from a given $O \in [0, O_{max}]$ in the first diagram (e.g. C in the picture), we can obtain the implied level of e in the second one (the D point); the latter shows the assumed linear inverse relationship between e and O. The 45 degree line in the third diagram brings the point D in the fourth diagram. The latter shows the $C_e(e)$ cost function. By linking the O quantity with $C_e(e)$ we obtain a point in $C(O)$; by iterating the proces we obtain the cost function in the O space depicted in the first diagram.

Without taxation, the firm chooses the first best level of $O = O_{Max}$ by using the conventional technology; this involves $e = 0$ (point A).

When two technologies are available the situation is the one shown in figure two. The first technology, that we call "conventional", labeled 0, is immediately available to firms free of additional implementation costs. The second one, that we call "advanced" and labelled 1, is more efficient and allows firms to save e for each level of O with respect the conventional technology; however firms adopting such a technology incur in a sunk cost F. **Figure 2** shows that $O_{Max}^1 < O_{Max}^0$ and that $\forall O < O_{Max}^1 \rightarrow C^1(O) < C^0(O)$. As an example, for a given O' oil usage we have $C^0(O) > C^1(O)$.

Given the assumptions on the cost functions, the marginal oil saving costs $MC = C'(O)$ have the following characteristics: $-C_i'(O) > 0 \ \forall O < O_{Max}^i, \quad i \in \{0,1\}$ and strictly increasing in oil saving, $C_i''(O) > 0 \quad \forall O < O_{Max}^i, i \in \{0,1\}$. In other words, everytime the firm reduces the quantity O, the MC increases. It is worth stressing that, for the same MC, i.e. $MC_O = MC_1$, we have $O_1 < O_0$.

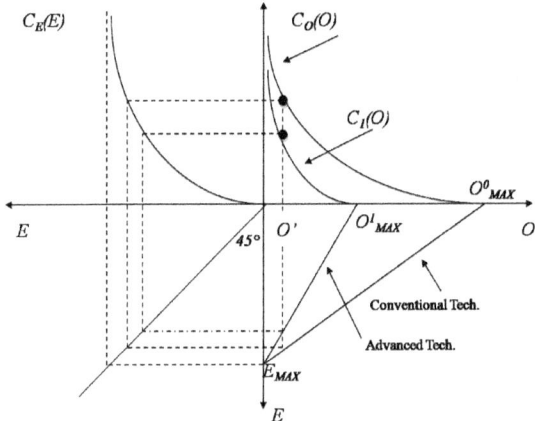

Figure 2. Energy saving costs with two technologies.

3. Equilibrium in Competitive Markets

We know that the solution of first best under competitive market conditions is to produce with the quantity O_{Max}.

The profit function is:

$$V(O) = PQ(O_{max}) - P_o O_{max}$$

where P is the output price, normalized to one and $Q(O_{max})$ is the quantity in the first best situation. $P_o O_{max}$ is the cost of using O_{max} at the international price P_o.

When oil taxation is at work, profits are as follows:

$$V(O) = PQ(O, e(O)) - P_o O - C(e(O)) - \tau O$$

where $Q(O, e(O))$ is the output quantity which depends on O throught e, while $C(e(O))$ is the cost for oil saving and τO is the fiscal burden.

Let us rewrite the previous equation for the two technologies in this way:

$$V(O_0) = \pi(O_0) - C(e(O_0)) - \tau O_0$$

$$V(O_1) = \pi(O_1) - C(e(O_1)) - \tau O_1 - F$$

where F is the sunk cost of adopting the advanced technology. $\pi(O_i)$ is the profit gross of tax and adjumest cost. By deriving with respect to $O_i, i \in \{0,1\}$ we obtain the following F.O.C.:

$$\frac{\partial \pi_0(O_0)}{\partial O_0} - \frac{\partial C_0(O_0)}{\partial O_0} = \tau \qquad (1)$$

$$\frac{\partial \pi_1(O_1)}{\partial O_1} - \frac{\partial C_1(O_1)}{\partial O_1} = \tau \qquad (2)$$

By taxing oil usage, the government induces firms to adopt or not the advanced technology. Now we are going to show that does exist only one tax rate that leaves firms indifferent in adopting or not.

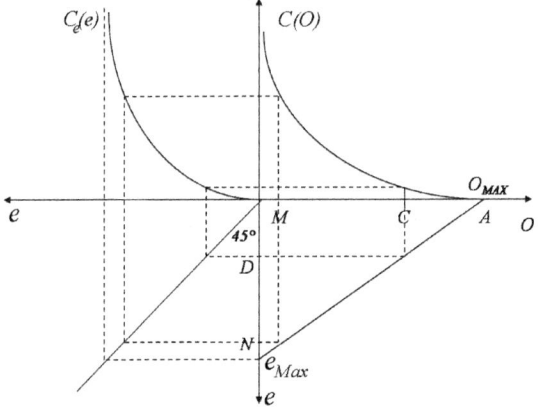

Figure 1. Energy saving costs with one technology.

By assuming technology satisfies $\pi(O_0) = \pi(O_1)$, for a fixed τ, firms are indifferent to the adoption of new technology if:

$$C_0(O_0(\tau)) + \tau O_0 = C_1(O_1(\tau) + \tau O_1 + F \qquad (3)$$

where $O_i, i \in \{0,1\}$ is the optimal oil usage under technology 0 and 1 respectively. The indifference condition is quite simple: it claims that firms are indifferent when the costs of oil saving, inclusive of taxation, are equal under both technologies.

Lemma 1 shows that does exist τ satisfating equation indifference:

Lemma *There exists at most one tax rate, $\tilde{\tau}$, such that firms are indifferent between adopting and not adopting the new technology. For this $\tilde{\tau}$, there exists a unique oil quantity $\tilde{O}_1$ and $\tilde{O}_0$ chosen by the firms with and without advanced technology, respectively. If $\tau > \tilde{\tau}$ ($\tau < \tilde{\tau}$) all firms (no firm) want to adopt the new technology. Moreover, $\tilde{\tau}$ is increasing in F.*

The proof is given in Appendix. Rationale is straightforwad. If $\tau < \tilde{\tau}$, the taxation is too low to induce firms to afford the sunk cost F in order to adopt the advanced technology; no firm chooses to do that. The result is the maximum oil wasting in the economy, as all firms remain on the inefficient technology: it amounts to $\overline{O} = n\tilde{O}_0$, where n is the number of firms in the economy. Conversely, when taxation is sufficiently high, $\tau > \tilde{\tau}$, it is too costly remaining with the conventional technology and all firms are induced to adopt the advanced one. In such a case the oil usage in the economy is lower than the previous case $\underline{O} = n\tilde{O}_1$. Lemma 1 shows that between these two opposite case there exists an equilibrium of partial adoption, where firms are indifferent to adopt or not $\tau = \tilde{\tau}$. The number of adopting firms is undetermined and the total oil usage in the economy lies in the closed set $O \in [\underline{O}, \overline{O}]$.

4. Social Optimum

The previous lemma shows that the government is able to affect firms choice about the adoption of the technology. The amount of oil wasting in the economy is under the indirect control of central authority. If the government goal were to reduce the oil wasting in the economy it should fix a higher tax rate; as lemma 1 shows, in such a case, all firms invest in the new technology. Nevertheless this involves a private cost F for each firm that reduces the social welfare. There is a trade-off between the private cost of increasing tax and the social benefit of oil saving induced by a high taxation. Hence, the social planner's problem is to minimize the social costs by balancing in-

dustry's total saving costs against the damage caused by the oil wasting. To do so, it chooses the optimal taxation filling the goal; this involves an optimal aggregate oil usage in the economy and a corresponding optimal number of adopting firms n_1^*. The social equilibrium is given by the triple $\{O_o^*, O_1^*, n_1^*\}$.

The social cost can be represented by a loss function $D(W)$, with $W = n_1 O_1 + (n - n_1)O_0$, which evaluates the aggregate oil wasting in monetary terms. This implies that only aggregate oil wasting matters [4]. We assume that the damage function is increasing and convex in W, i.e. $D'(W) > 0$ and $D''(W) > 0$. If the regulator wants to minimize the social cost, she has to resolve this equation:

$$\min_{\{O_o^*, O_1^*, n_1^*\}} V = \left\{ \begin{array}{l} -n_1[\pi_1(O_1) - C_1(O_1) - F] - n_0[\pi_0(O_0) \\ -C_0(O_0)] + D(n_1 O_1 + n_0 O_0) \end{array} \right\}$$

$$(4)$$

The socially optimal allocation can be characterized as follows:

Proposition *There is an interval of fixed costs $[\underline{F}, \overline{F}]$ such that:*

1) No firm should adopt the new technology for $F > \overline{F}$;

2) All the firms should adopt the new technology for $F < \underline{F}$;

3) For $F \in [\underline{F}, \overline{F}]$ partial adoption is optimal.

The optimal number of firms n_1^* adopting the new technology is decreasing in F. The optimal marginal damage $MD^*(F)$ is decreasing in F.

The proof is given in Appendix. The intuition is that if the fixed cost F of installing the advanced technology is extremely high, firms do not adopt this technique. Conversely, if F is sufficiently low, all the firms should adopt the new technology. In both cases, the optimal aggregate oil wasting $\underline{O}$ and $\overline{O}$ are independent of F.

5. Optimal Policy: Two Possible Scenarios

In this last section we are going to analyze how social planner can implement the socially optimal equilibrium. We are doing so by following two possible strategies. In the first one, called ex-ante optimal policy, we assume that the regulator makes a commitment both to the choice and level of his policy instrument. In this case the regulator moves at first, while firms invest in the second stage, after observing the tax rate, and decide for the possible adoption of the new technology. This is summarized in the following proposition:

Proposition (*Ex ante optimal policy*). *If the welfare-maximizing regulator moves first, then: for* $F < \underline{F}$ *and* $F > \overline{F}$ *, there exits a unique subgame perfect equilibrium leading to a first best outcome. For* $F \in \left[\underline{F}, \overline{F}\right]$ *there are multiple equilibria. One of these equilibria is efficient but there are also many inefficient equilibria with too little and too much investment.*

(See Appendix)

In the second strategy, ex post optimal policy, we are going to assume that, before the game starts, the regulator makes a commitment to the choice of his policy instrument only, so she observes firms investing in the first stage, then she chooses the level of the instrument in the second stage. Unlike the previous case, with such a strategy the socially optimal equilibrium can be implemented in the economy.

Proposition (*ex post optimal policy*). *If the regulator sets his optimal policy after observing the number of investing firms, then under taxes there is a unique subgame perfect equilibrium where the optimal number of firms invests, and the regulator sets the first best tax rate.*

The first part of the proposition follows Requate and Unold [4]. In a two stage game with informed and rational players, we can use the backward induction for proving the statement. In fact, firms know that, in the second stage of the game, the governement is going to set the optimal tax rate coherently with the optimal number of adopting firms n_1^* (first best). If n_1^* is chosen by firms in the first stage of the game, then this is a sub game perfect equilibrium as neither firms nor planner has an incentive to modify their choice. If firms choose $n_1 > n_1^*$, then the best strategy of the planner is to set the tax rate conditional on n_1, i.e. $\tau(n_1) < \tau^*(n_1^*)$ in the second stage, as the social damage reduce with respect to n_1 and tax must be reduced consequently. But this means that some firms that was adopting in stage 1 would be better off from not adopting, as the tax rate is lower than expected. So we conclude that n_1 is not an equilibrium. Same result holds when $n_1 < n_1^*$. Nevertheless, the game analyzed by Requate and Unold [4] shows only that an equilibrium exists under subgame perfection, but this does not imply that such equilibrium will be effectively implemented. Unlike Requate and Unold [4], we are going to show that, if players act in a different way, n_1^* will be implemented in a decentralized economy. This is possible in a "multi-stage game with observed actions and perfect information" [10]. In such a game, the choice set of each player is enlarged by the move "do nothing". As an example, any single firm strategy set, per each game stage, is composed by {*adopting, not adopting, "do*

nothing"}. Moreover, any player knows the history of the game, as everyone observes past actions.

We say that a multi-stage game has perfect information if, for every stage k and history h^k, exactly one player has a nontrivial choice set—a choice set with more than one element—and all the others have the one-element choice set "do nothing" [10].

The planner moves at the last stage, so backward induction is still a viabile solution. Everyone knows the optimal taxation level chosen by the planner at the last stage of the game as consequence of n_1^*. The game is composed by $n+1$ stages. At each stage one firm chooses whether adopting or not, knowing what happened up to now; the other one choose "do nothing". Once the single firm has played either "adoption" or "not adoption" it will choose "do nothing" in the rest of the game. In such a way, when n_1^* has been achieved in the economy it becomes common knowledge, as everyone knows the past history of the game. From now and on, rational firms do choose "not adopting" as they know that if $n_1 > n_1^*$ the taxation rate chosen by the planner at the last stage is not choerent with their choice, following the reasoning of the sub-game perfection used for the first part of the proposition..

6. A Numerical Example

In this section we discuss a numerical example to show in detail the mechanism of the model.

We know that the firm can choose between two techniques that are characterized by different costs.

For each technology, the firm supports an energy saving cost: $C_0(O), C_1(O)$. We suppose that this kind of cost functions has the following explicit form, choerently with the assumptions described in Section 1:

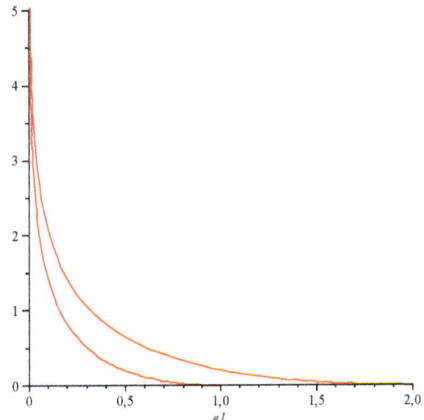

Figure 3. Oil saving costs.

$C_0(O) = 0.5(O_0) - \ln(O_0) - 0.3$ *"oil intensive"*

$C_1(O) = O_1 - \ln(O_1) - 1$ *"advanced technology"*

These functions are depicted in **Figure 3**, which corresponds to the graph of the first diagram reported in **Figure 2**.

As shown by the graph, for each technique, we obtain a monotonic decreasing function on its closed domain, that describes the negative relationship between the energy saving costs: $C_o(O)$, $C_1(O)$ and the oil quantity.

The marginal energy saving costs: $C_o'(O)$ and $C_1'(O)$ are described by the two functions presented in **Figure 4**, where, $C_1'(O) = 1 - \frac{1}{O}$ and $C_o'(O) = 0,5 - \frac{1}{O}$ and they respect the assumptions made in Section 2.

Now, we give a numerical explanation of Lemma 1.

The **Figure 5** shows that for a fixed F, there exists at most one tax rate, such that firms are indifferent between adopting and not adopting the new technology. In fact, for $F = 1.4142$ there is only intersection point that individuates: $\widehat{\tau} = 0,66$ that satisfies the indifference condition.

If we vary F, we can observe the positive relation between F and $\widetilde{\tau}$, as shown by **Table 1**.

By proposition 2, we know that if the new technology is available, the social planner seeks to minimize total social costs expressed by the equation lagra which is a numerical example of the equation lagrth.

By assuming $Q(O_i) = 2(O_i)^{0.7} + 2$ the Lagrangian that solves this problem is reported in the following equation:

$$L = -n_1[(3 - 3O_1 + 2(O_1)^{0.7} + \ln(O_1) - F] - (1 - n_1)$$
$$[1.3 - 2.5(O_0) + 2(O_0)^{0.7} + \ln(O_0)] + [n_1 e_1 + (1 - n_1)e_0]^2$$

This numerical example shows the existence of the values of first best: O_o^*, O_1^*, n_1^*.

The **Table 2** shows the content of proposition 2.

If we vary F, we can observe that there is an interval of fixed costs $[\underline{F}, \overline{F}]$ such that for:

$1,445 < F < 1,458$ we obtain $n_0, n_1 > 0$, so there is partial adoption, while for $F \leq 1,445$ or $F \geq 1,458$ we observe corner solutions.

7. Conclusions

The paper shows the existence of an optimal policy that reduces the social cost represented by oil usage. The regulator can implement this policy throughout two alternative strategies: the ex ante optimal policy or the ex post optimal policy. The choice depends on the sunk cost of

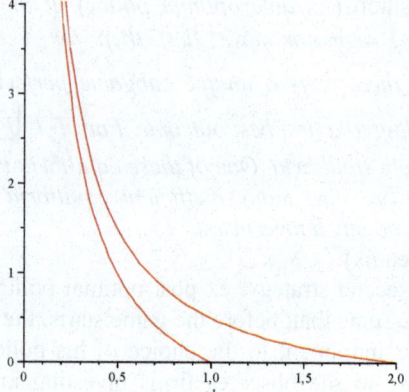

Figure 4. Marginal energy saving costs.

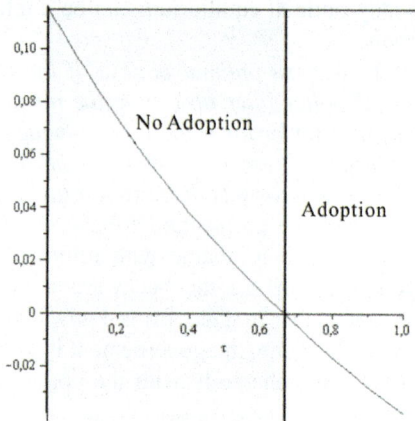

Figure 5. Lemma 1.

Table 1. Relationship between F and $\widetilde{\tau}$.

F	1,3	1,33	1,36	1,39	1,42	1,45
$\widetilde{\tau}$	0,008	0,14	0,30	0,49	0,71	0,98

Table 2. Proposition 2.

O_0	O_1	F	n_1	$\widetilde{\tau}$
0,000	0,463	1,445	1	0.832
0,563	0,460	1,446	0,9	0.842
0,559	0,458	1,447	0,8	0.851
0,559	0,458	1,448	0,8	0,861
0,555	0,455	1,449	0,7	0,871
0,552	0,453	1,450	0,6	0,881
0,552	0,453	1,451	0,6	0,891
0,549	0,450	1,452	0,5	0,900
0,545	0,448	1,453	0,4	0,912
0,542	0,446	1,454	0,3	0,922
0,542	0,446	1,455	0,3	0,932
0,539	0,444	1,456	0,2	0,943
0,536	0,442	1,457	0,1	0,953
0,533	0,000	1,458	0	0,964

adopting the oil saving technology. If the implementation cost is outside the range $[\underline{F}, \overline{F}]$ the regulator is indifferent between the two strategies: both strategies lead to the first best. If the implementation cost is within the range, the regulator can implement the optimal policy only by choosing the ex post optimal policy, where firms move according to a multi-stage game with informed and rational players. So the paper confirms that policies ruled by the market are viable instruments for environmental control. We also show that, unlike the current literature, first best solution is actually implemented when firms and the regulator play a sequential game.

The sunk cost F plays a leading role for results; in a following paper we are going to investigate how results change when such a cost is made endogenous by assuming an R&D sector in the economy.

8. References

[1]   P. B. Downing and L. J. White, "Innovation in Pollution Control," *Journal of Environmental Economics and Management*, Vol. 13, No. 1, 1986, pp. 18-29.

[2]   S. R. Milliman and R. Prince, "Firms Incentives to Promote Technological Change in Pollution Control," *Journal of Environmental Economics and Management*, Vol. 17, No. 3, 1989, pp. 247-265.

[3]   Ch. Jung, K. Krutilla and R. Boyd, "Incentives for Advanced Pollution Abatement Technology at the Industry Level: An Evaluation of Policy Alternatives," *Journal of Environmental Economics and Management*, Vol. 30, No. 1, 1996, pp. 95-111.

[4]   T. Requate and W. Unold, "Environmental Policy Incentives to Adopt Advanced Abatement Technology: Will the True Ranking Please Stand up?" *European Economic Review*, Vol. 47, No. 1, 2003, pp. 123-146.

[5]   T. Requate, "Dynamics and Incentives by Environmental Policy Instruments—A Survey," *Ecological Economics*, Vol. 54, No. 2-3, 2005, pp. 175-195.

[6]   D. P. van Soest, "The Impact of Environmental Policy Instruments on the Timing of Adoption of Energy-Saving Technologies," *Resource and Energy Economics*, Vol. 27, No. 3, 2005, pp. 235-247.

[7]   A. von Döllen and T. Requate, "Environmental Policy and Incentives to Invest in Advanced Abatement Technology if Arrival of Future Technology is Uncertain," Economics Working Paper No 2007-04, 2007.

[8]   J. Montero, "Permits, Standards, and Technology Innovation," *Journal of Environmental Economics and Management*, Vol. 44, No. 1, 2002, pp. 23-44.

[9]   C. Carraro and D. Siniscalco, "Environmental Policy Reconsidered: The Role of Technological Innovation," *European Economic Review*, Vol. 38, No. 3-4, 1994, pp. 545-554.

[10]   D. Fudenberg and J. Tirole, "Game Theory," MIT Press, Cambridge, 1991.

[11]   E. G. Gaeta, "Environmental Policy, Innovation and Adoption of Energy Saving Technologies," Phd Dissertation, University of Rome, "La Sapienza", 2009.

Appendix

Proof of Lemma 1

Now we focus on the total difference of the net value of the i-th firm:

$$\Delta V(O) = V_0(O_0) - V_1(O_1) \qquad \text{A.1}$$

So we can write A.1 as follows:

$$\Delta V(O) = [\pi_0(O_0(\tau)) - C_0(O_0(\tau)) - \tau O_0(\tau)]$$
$$-[\pi_1(O_1(\tau)) - C_1(O_1(\tau)) - \tau O_1(\tau) - F] \qquad \text{A.2}$$

We differentiate A.2 respect to τ to demonstrate that there exists at most one tax rate such that firms are indiferent to adption or not adoption.

$$\frac{\partial \Delta V(O)}{\partial \tau} = \left[\frac{\partial \pi_0}{\partial O_0} \frac{\partial O_0}{\partial \tau} - \frac{\partial C_0}{\partial O_0} \frac{\partial O_0}{\partial \tau} \right] - O_0(\tau) - \tau \frac{\partial O_0}{\partial \tau}$$
$$- \left\{ \left[\frac{\partial \pi_1}{\partial O_1} \frac{\partial O_1}{\partial \tau} - \frac{\partial C_1}{\partial O_1} \frac{\partial O_1}{\partial \tau} \right] - O_1(\tau) - \tau \frac{\partial O_1}{\partial \tau} \right\}$$

A.3

substituting Equations (1), (2) into A.3 we obtain:

$$\frac{\partial \Delta V(O)}{\partial \tau} = O_1(\tau) - O_0(\tau) < 0 \qquad \text{A.4}$$

which is always negative, because as previously stressed, the same MC involves $O_1 < O_0$.

When $\tau = 0 \rightarrow \Delta V(O) = F > 0$, since $\pi_0(O_0) = \pi_1(O_1)$ by the competitive market assumtion. We know that $\Delta V(O)$ is a monotonic function and it decreases if τ increases, as A.4 shows; this means that there is a unique τ called "$\hat{\tau}$" which ensures that firms are indifferent between the two technologies, i.e. when $\Delta V(O) = 0$.

Now we demonstrate that $\tilde{\tau}$ is increasing in F.

Differentiating the net value A.2 with respect to F and remembering the F.O.C., we obtain:

$$\frac{\partial \tau}{\partial F} [O_1(\tau(F)) - O_0(\tau(F))] = -1$$

$$\frac{\partial \tau}{\partial F} = -\frac{1}{[O_1(\tau(F)) - O_0(\tau(F))]} > 0$$

which is always positive because, as previously stressed, $O_1 < O_0$. This result demonstrates that $\tilde{\tau}$ is increasing in F.

Proof of Proposition 2:

The Lagrangian of the minimization problem is given by:

$$L = -n_1[\pi_1(O_1) - C_1(o_1) - F] - n_0[\pi_0(O_0) - C_0(o_0)]$$
$$+ D(n_1 O_1 + n_0 O_0) - \lambda_0 n_0 - \lambda_1 n_1 - \mu(n_0 + n_1 - n)$$

A.5

where λ_i are the Kuhn_Tucker multipliers of the non negative constraints for n_1 and $n_0 = n - n_1$. We denote $W = n_1 O_1 + n_0 O_0$ as the total use of oil choosen by firms under taxation. Differentiating the A.5 respect to O_i, n_i we obtain the first order conditions:

$$\frac{\partial L}{\partial O_0} = -\frac{\partial \pi_0}{\partial O_0} + \frac{\partial C_0}{\partial O_0} + \frac{\partial D(W)}{\partial O_0} = 0$$
$$\frac{\partial L}{\partial O_1} = -\frac{\partial \pi_1}{\partial O_1} + \frac{\partial C_1}{\partial O_1} + \frac{\partial D(W)}{\partial O_1} = 0$$

A.6

$$\frac{\partial L}{\partial n_0} = -\pi_0(O_0) + C_0(O_0) + \frac{\partial D(W)}{\partial W} O_0 - \lambda_0 - \mu = 0$$

$$\frac{\partial L}{\partial n_1} = -\pi_1(O_1) + C_1(O_1) + F + \frac{\partial D(W)}{\partial W} O_1 - \lambda_1 - \mu = 0$$

eliminating μ yields:

$$-\pi_1(O_1) + \pi_0(O_0) + C_1(O_1) - C_0(O_o) + (O_1 - o_0) \frac{\partial D(W)}{\partial W}$$
$$+ F - \lambda_1 + \lambda_0 = 0$$

A.7

First, suppose that there exists an interior solution, i.e. $\lambda_0 = \lambda_1 = 0$.

Differentiating system A.6 and A.7 w.r.t. F and using the chain rule in A.7 we have the following equations:

$$-\frac{\partial^2 \pi_0(O_0)}{\partial O_0^2} \frac{\partial O_0}{\partial F} + \frac{\partial^2 C_0}{\partial O_0^2} \frac{\partial O_0}{\partial F} + \frac{\partial^2 D(W)}{\partial W^2} \frac{\partial W}{\partial F} = 0$$

$$-\frac{\partial^2 \pi_1(O_1)}{\partial O_1^2} \frac{\partial O_1}{\partial F} + \frac{\partial^2 C_1}{\partial O_1^2} \frac{\partial O1}{\partial F} + \frac{\partial^2 D(W)}{\partial W^2} \frac{\partial W}{\partial F} = 0$$

A.8

$$\frac{\partial^2 D(W)}{\partial W^2} (O_1 - O_0) \frac{\partial W}{\partial F} + 1 = 0$$

Given that $O_0 > O_1 \forall \tau$ we can write

$$\frac{\partial^2 D(W)}{\partial W^2} (O_0 - O_1) \frac{\partial W}{\partial F} - 1 = 0$$

This yields

$$\frac{\partial W}{\partial F} = \frac{1}{\frac{\partial^2 D(W)}{\partial W^2}(O_0 - O_1)} > 0 \qquad \text{A.9}$$

i.e. optimal aggregate use of oil is increasing in F. Substituting A.9 into A.8 yields:

$$\frac{\partial O_1}{\partial F} = -\frac{1}{(O_0 - O_1)} \frac{1}{[\frac{\partial^2 C_1}{\partial O_1^2} - \frac{\partial \pi_1(O_1)}{\partial O_1}]} \qquad \text{A.10}$$

Unlike Requate and Unold [4] the Equation A.10 is

negative only if: $\dfrac{\partial^2 C_1}{\partial O_1^2} > \dfrac{\partial^2 \pi_1(O_1)}{\partial O_1^2}$. and we assume this condition holds. So we have: $\dfrac{\partial O_i}{\partial F} < 0 \ \ \forall i = 0,1$. Hence, optimal use of oil by each firm is *decreasing* in F.

Now total energy wasting can be written as

$$W(F) = n_1(F)O_1(F) + n_0(F)O_0(F) \qquad \text{A.11}$$

Differentiating A.11 w.r.t. F and solving for $\dfrac{\partial n_1(F)}{\partial F}$ yields:

$$\frac{\partial n_1}{\partial F} = \frac{+\frac{\partial W(F)}{\partial F} - \frac{\partial O_1(F)}{\partial F} n_1(F) - \frac{\partial O_0(F)}{\partial F} n_0(F)}{(O_1 - O_0)} < 0$$

From Equation A.7 we know that

$$C_1(O_1) - C_0(O_o) + (O_1 - O_0)\frac{\partial D}{\partial W} - (\pi_1 - \pi_0) + F =$$
$$+ \lambda_1 - \lambda_0$$
$$\qquad \text{A.12}$$

If F is large, the LHS of the A.12 is positive since that $O \in [0, O_{\max}]$ so we have $\lambda_0 = 0$ and $\lambda_1 > 0$ $\rightarrow n_1 = 0$. So, when F is large, there exists an $\overline{F}$ such that if $F \geq \overline{F}$ no firm should adopt the advanced technology.

Let us rewrite Equation A.12 in the following way:

$$[\pi_1 - C_1(O_1) - F] - [\pi_0 - C_0(O_0)] -$$
$$(O_1 - O_0)\frac{\partial D}{\partial W} = \lambda_0 - \lambda_1$$
$$\qquad \text{A.13}$$

if F is very small we have $[\pi_1 - C_1(O_1) - F] > [\pi_0 - C_0(O_0)]$ and the LHS of Equation A.13 is positive. This involves $\lambda_0 > 0$ that means $n_0 = 0$. So when $F \approx 0$, there exists an $\underline{F}$ such that if $F \leq \underline{F}$ all firms adopt the advanced technology.

So far we have demonstrated that n_0 (and consequently n_1) is one for F large and zero for F small. However, being the functions of Equation A.13 continuos is F, there exist values for F such that both n_1 and n_0 are outside the corner solutions: $[n_1 = 0, n_0 = 1]$ and $[n_1 = 1, n_0 = 0]$. So we conclude that for $F \in [\underline{F}, \overline{F}]$ we have $n_1, n_0 > 0$. In this case there is partial adoption.

Proof of Proposition 3:

When the regulator chooses the instrument (taxation) and fixes the instrument's level in the same time, there are three possible cases:

1) $F \leq \underline{F}$

We have shown that in such a case $n_1 = 1$ and $n_o = 0$ this means that F.O.C for the Equation A.5 involves :

$$-\frac{\partial C(O_1)}{\partial O_1} + \frac{\partial \pi_1}{\partial O_1} = \frac{\partial D(W)}{\partial O_1}$$

but for the firm F.O.C. we know that $-\dfrac{\partial C(O_1)}{\partial O_1} + \dfrac{\partial \pi_1}{\partial O_1} = \tau$.

So finally, the government sets $\tau = \dfrac{\partial D(W)}{\partial O_1}$. By so doing, the optimal taxation is coherent with firm profit maximization and there is a subgame perfection.

2) $F \geq \overline{F}$

Similar analysis holds. In such a case $n_1 = 0$ and $n_o = 1$ this means that F.O.C for the Equation A.5 involves :

$$-\frac{\partial C(O_0)}{\partial O_0} + \frac{\partial \pi_0}{\partial O_0} = \frac{\partial D(W)}{\partial O_0}$$

but for the firm F.O.C. we know that $-\dfrac{\partial C(O_{0\_})}{\partial O_0} + \dfrac{\partial \pi_0}{\partial O_0} = \tau$.

So finally, the government sets $\tau = \dfrac{\partial D(W)}{\partial O_0}$. and the strategy is subgame perfect .

3) $\underline{F} < F < \overline{F}$

In this case the regulator sets τ by minimizing Equation A.5. This involves a particular value for n_1 and n_o. Nevertheless as firms play in the second stage in an uncoordinated way, there is no certainty that n_1 and n_o will be effectively implemented. For the same reason, is possible that, for pure chance, firms choose n_1 and n_o coherently with the optimal value chosen by the government. Hence multiple equilibria are possible, but only one is the efficient one.

16

Do Leveraged ETFs Increase Volatility

William J. Trainor Jr.
East Tennessee State University, Johnson City, USA

Abstract

The 2008 financial crisis has produced volatility levels not seen since the 1987 stock market crash more than 20 years ago. During that time, the culprit was thought to be index futures and program trading. This time, leveraged ETFs and their rebalancing trades have been singled out by some to explain both the spike in volatility and the appearance of large price swings at the end of the trading day. This study examines the merit of these accusations and whether the increase in volatility and end of the day price momentum is indeed linked to leveraged ETFs and their rebalancing trades. For the S&P 500, the relationship appears to be a spurious coincidence.

Keywords: Leveraged ETFs, Volatility, Momentum

1. Introduction

"Whenever high market volatility occurs, the tendency seems to be to blame it on whatever new is going on at the time," [1]. This is the first line of Franklin Edward's piece, "Does Futures Trading Increase Stock Market Volatility" in the *Financial Analyst Journal* over 20 years ago. As the old French proverb goes, "The more things change, the more they stay the same." Then, much as now, the market was in a turbulent period. The stock market crash on Oct. 20, 1987 is still the biggest one day percentage loss in U.S. history and many were looking for a scapegoat to place the blame. Index futures seemed to fit the bill as they had become increasingly popular among sophisticated investors, while at the same time were not completely understandable to many. They were further demonized by their use in program trading and were thought to be the sole province of greedy "speculators".

However, the overriding conclusion from most of the research suggests that index futures had little or nothing to do with the increased volatility being experienced at that time [1-3]. The accuracy of this conclusion has been further evidenced by the historically low volatility the market experienced in the 1990's and through most of this 21st century despite the tremendous growth in the use of index futures.

Jumping forward, the volatility associated with the 2008 financial crisis has not been seen since the 1987 stock market crash, and some of the blame is being placed on the latest investment vehicle that has become popular with the more sophisticated investors, leveraged ETFs.

Much like index futures in the late 80's, leveraged ETFs have also been somewhat demonized by their critics since they are supposedly used primarily by those greedy day traders and speculators. This study takes a more rigorous examination of leveraged ETF's impact in the market place and whether critic's assertions that leveraged ETFs cause increased volatility and big moves in prices at the end of the day actually hold up to scrutiny [4,5]. The answer to this question is becoming increasingly relevant as there are now more than 150 levered and inverse ETFs with total assets of $ 30 billion [6].

2. Research Past and Present

2.1. The Past

A great deal of research was done on volatility after index futures were initially espoused as the cause of the last great leap in volatility in the late 80's. Not surprisingly, even without "something" to blame for the market volatility during the financial crisis of 2008-09, past research would predict that high volatility should be expected. Schwert [7] found that stock market volatility increases during recessions and after a large drop in stock prices. Even more enlightening is that Schwert found the higher the financial leverage of the market, the greater the volatility. This is clearly seen today in the financial sector where many firms use unprecedented levels of financial leverage, some to their own demise, e.g. Lehman Brothers. Thus, the increased volatility at the height of the financial crisis should be expected while firms continue to unwind some of their financial leverage exposure. The market environment during the financial crisis has all the critical factors identified more than 20 years ago as working towards increased volatility: a recession, a significant drop in stock prices, and high levels of firm leverage.

Additional research more directly related to leveraged ETFs deals with changing margin requirements. The expectation is that reducing margin requirements allows investors to create greater leverage which in turn causes increasing levels of volatility. Hardouvelis [8] concluded that increasing margin requirements would indeed stifle volatility. However, Hsieh and Miller [9], Kupiec [10,11], and Salinger [12] found a weak relationship at best while Schwert [7] found only a spurious relationship in that the Fed reacts after the fact, *i.e.* volatility changes, then the Fed changes margin requirements. Thus, results suggest that the use of leveraged funds by investors which in effect is similar to buying on margin, likely has little or no effect on market volatility.

2.2. The Present

Moving forward, some efforts have been made to quantify what role, if any, leveraged ETFs have on the increased volatility being experienced since the financial market meltdown. Deshpande, Devapriya, and Bhatia [13] suggest the impact is likely very small based on volume analysis, especially on the S&P 500 where the percentage of market capital traded daily by leveraged ETFs is only 0.0079% of the total volume. For smaller indexes, there may be more of an effect such as on the DJ US Real Estate Index. However, even the percentage traded by leveraged ETFs on this index is only 0.254% of the total.

A report from Credit Suisse [14] has similar conclusions finding that leveraged ETFs account for only 2% of end-of-day trading and thus, are unlikely to have any significant effect. Finally, a report by Direxion [15] also found similar results and suggests that leveraged ETFs do not exacerbate market volatility or compound directional moves from 3:00 p.m. to market close. In fact, they found creation unit activity is actually negatively correlated with market movements. This means that if the market is falling, more units are being created/purchased which goes against the flow, not with.

However, Cheng and Madhavan [16] find that leveraged ETFs may indeed have a large impact based on market-on-close (MOC) volume. MOC volume is the amount of trades that are specified to be filled at the market close price. In fact, orders for this to occur can begin with 20 minutes until close. Based on a theoretical model developed in their paper, they find that if stock indexes have moved 1% in a particular direction during the day, leveraged ETF trading could account for 16.8% of the MOC volume. If the market moves 5%, 50% of the MOC volume could be accounted for by leveraged ETF

trading. Thus, broad moves could be exacerbated by the rebalancing that leveraged ETFs undertake towards the end of the day.

3. The Rebalancing Argument

One of the theoretical arguments that suggests leveraged ETFs can exacerbate market moves and increase volatility is due to the fact that current leveraged ETFs are set up to only provide a daily multiple of the underlying index. For example, a 3x fund is set up to provide three times the daily index return while a −3x fund is set up to provide three times the opposite return of the index. Because of this, daily rebalancing is required for any market move to maintain a constant leverage ratio. The rebalancing, for both long and short leveraged ETFs will create additional demand or selling pressure in the same direction as the market move.

The example depicted in **Table 1** will best illustrate the point above. Assume the underlying index and levered fund's NAVs start at 100. For the 3x fund, $ 300 in market exposure is needed. This exposure is usually created by holding some of the underlying index securities, and some combination of swaps and futures with swaps usually being primary. For the −3x fund, −$ 300 in market exposure is required. In period 1, assume the underlying index increases to 105 for a 5% gain. The 3x fund will gain 15% while the −3x fund will lose 15%. For the 3x fund to maintain its exposure at 3, it will need $ 345 in exposure since its underlying asset value increased to $ 315. Thus, at the end of the day, $ 45 in additional exposure will be needed.

For the −3x fund, the NAV falls to $ 85 so it will need −$ 255 (−3*85) in exposure. Thus, at the end of the day, it will also be a net buyer, in this case $ 45 of swaps or some combination of instruments to attain less negative exposure to the market. This creates an interesting market dynamic. When the market increases, both levered long and short funds will be net buyers and add to any existing buying pressure already being felt in the market.

Conversely, when the market decreases, both long and short funds will be net sellers in the market. For example, **Table 1** shows that as the index falls from 105 back to 100 in period 2, the 3x fund will need to reduce its exposure by −$ 49.3 while the −3x fund will also need to change exposure by −$ 36.4. Depending on the magnitudes of these values relative to all trading in the last hour, the rebalancing issue can theoretically increase pressure on the market to continue whatever direction it may be moving during the last hour of trading.

As a point of exercise, assume this is the case. That is, leveraged ETFs cause the market to overshoot at the end of each day. If this is indeed the case, two types of investors could step in. Both types would know that leveraged ETFs would be net buyers or sellers at the end of

Table 1. Rebalancing to maintain daily leverage ratio for a 3x and –3x fund

Pe-riod	Index Value	Index Return	3x Index Return	–3x Index Return	3x Fund NAV	3x Fund Needed Exposure	3x Change in Exposure	–3x Fund NAV	–3x Fund Needed Exposure	–3x Change in Exposure
0	100				100	300		100	–300	
1	105	5%	15%	–15%	115	345	45	85	–255	+45
2	100	–4.76%	–14.28%	14.28%	98.58	295.7	–49.3	97.14	–291.4	–36.4

each day based on what the market had done up until that point of time. The first type of investor would take the same actions as the leveraged ETFs knowing that the additional buying or selling pressure from the ETFs would continue to move the market in the same direction. They would of course be forced to sell right at the close or after hours to reverse their positions and profit from the likely market move.

However, a second type of investor would likely be more successful. This investor would take the opposite direction knowing that the market would reverse itself the next morning, assuming of course even moderate market efficiency in which market prices do indeed revert to their fundamental values, or at least what investors perceive them to be. This investor would reduce and most likely eliminate any arbitrage profits from front running, and eliminate any preponderance for the market to trend. Thus, any short-term abnormal price pressure causing the market to overshoot at the end of the day should theoretically be arbitraged away. This should occur as more and more investors take opposite positions of the leveraged ETFs on the expectation that the market open price the next day would be in the opposite direction that the market closed the previous day. Only if the leveraged ETF trading was so large that it could not be arbitraged away in this fashion, would extended volatility and price effects remain. Fortunately, this hypothesis is easily testable.

4. Volatility and Price Effects

4.1. Volatility Effects from Rebalancing

To attain a historical perspective on volatility, **Figure 1** shows the moving 60 day annualized standard deviation of the daily S&P 500 returns. As one can see, volatility in the early 80's was fairly subdued. With the stock market crash of 1987, volatility sky rocketed and stock index futures were blamed by some even though they were actually introduced on February 24, 1982 with no discernable increased in volatility. However, as volatility quickly fell back to "normal" levels, even the casual observer must admit that blaming stock index futures for the increased volatility in 1987 appears to be a stretch as volatility was very low with them in existence before 1987, and very low with them after 1987.

Volatility didn't increase to any substantial level until the 2001 tech crash and 9/11. However, by 2003, volatil-

ity again fell to very low levels, sometimes below 10%. Only with the financial meltdown has volatility spiked, but as the financial crisis has mitigated, volatility levels have again returned to more reasonable levels. Thus, the critics who blame leveraged ETFs for the increased market volatility during the financial crisis, similarly to the critics of index futures in 1987/88, may be hard pressed to explain why volatility levels have since fallen, and so far continue to remain at more "normal" levels. In fact, the evidence appears to be almost identical to the 1980s since leveraged funds have actually been around since 1993. ETFs have made them more popular and recognized, but their initial introduction and growth did not lead to any perceptible increase in volatility.

Figure 2 shows why there has been a minor furor of increased volatility at the end of the day. The 60 day moving average of 30 minute volatility measured by the standard deviation of beginning and ending values of the S&P 500 between 9:30 a.m. and 10 a.m. and 3:30 p.m. and 4:00 p.m. EST is depicted. The first thing to note is that the opening 30 minutes is more volatile than the closing 30 minutes. This holds for the entire 12 year sample and on average, the opening 30 minutes has a standard deviation of 0.52% while the final 30 minutes has a standard deviation of 0.33%. It is also quite clear that both morning and afternoon volatility increased dramatically with the financial market crises.

However, afternoon volatility only exceeds morning volatility for approximately 3 months, November 2008 through January 2009. Since then, the afternoon volatility fell dramatically and is again, significantly less than morning volatility. Thus, at least to casual observation, it

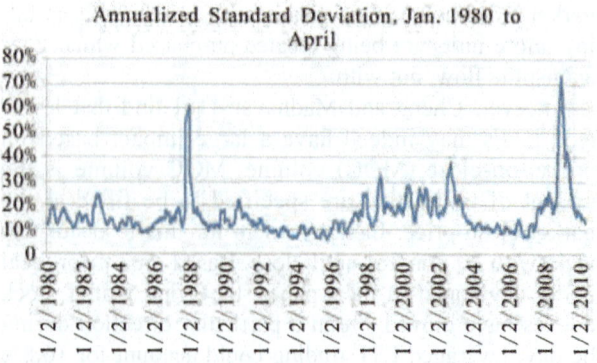

Figure 1. S&P 500 annualized standard deviation, *60 day annualized daily standard deviation.

does not appear leveraged ETF's rebalancing trades are creating increased volatility in the last 30 minutes of trading in the S&P 500. Despite continual flows to these funds, afternoon volatility has fallen dramatically, even relative to morning volatility.

To further investigate whether the increase in afternoon volatility from December 2008 to January 2009 may have been caused by rebalancing efforts of leveraged ETFs, the 10:00 a.m. to 10:30 a.m. period was compared to the 3:00 p.m. to 3:30 p.m. time period. This is done to see if the spike in afternoon volatility occurs during a time period when rebalancing should not be a significant force.

Figure 3 shows the results. On average, the two 30 minute time period's standard deviations are virtually the same, 0.33% and 0.30% respectively. However, much like **Figure 2**, the November 2008 to January 2009 time period dealing with the 10:00-10:30 a.m. and 3:00-3:30 p.m. show the same relationship. By March, the volatility for both time periods returns to being virtually equal. Thus, even though leveraged ETF's rebalancing doesn't begin in earnest until the last 30 minutes of the trading day, the same relationship appears from 3:00 to 3:30 p.m. giving at least some initial evidence that rebalancing is not the major issue. Although not shown, the 2:30 to 3:00 p.m. time period also had the same spike in volatility (from an average of 0.26% to 0.90%) and virtually no rebalancing occurs this early.

4.2. Price Effects from Rebalancing

Although it appears rebalancing is not the root cause of the increase in volatility, at least in the S&P 500, rebalancing still may cause price effects. To address this issue, a rolling 60 day average of price changes is calculated. **Figure 4** shows the probability of a positive move in the market from the opening to 3:30 p.m. being followed by a positive move from 3:30 p.m. to close. Evidence suggests that positive momentum did increase substantially during the financial market crisis. Starting in August of 2008, the probability of a continuation of a positive market move increased to over 70% and remained there until November 2008.

However, it soon fell quite dramatically. For the entire 1998 to 2010 time period, this probability has actually averaged 58% although with quite a bit of volatility. A statistical test does find the August through November 2008 positive price momentum to be statistically significant relative to the average of the previous 10 years. Examining the average from August 2008 through April 2010, there is no discernable difference as the average momentum before August 2008 is 58% and after is 61%.

Figure 5 shows the results for a negative market move throughout the day being reinforced by a negative move the last 30 minutes. For the entire time period, a negative move has reinforced the daily move 52% of the time. Similar to **Figure 4**, the probability a negative move

would continue through the last 30 minutes of the day also increased to above 70% from August to November 2008. Thus, **Figures 4** and **5** do suggest there is some momentum in stock returns and leveraged ETFs are theorized to cause or exacerbate this exact price momentum.

However, these extreme values have been seen before and neither the positive or negative price momentum has remained a systematic phenomena. In fact, before 2006, every year saw positive momentum greater than 70% at least once during the year. In addition, the probability of a move continuing has also seen probabilities at the opposite spectrum. For example, in early 2001, the probability of positive momentum fell to less than 20% and in 2009, the probability of negative momentum fell to less than 30%. With the extreme moves in these values and the fact that this price momentum has not remained even as levered ETFs have continued to grow in size suggests the relationship between leveraged ETFs and price momentum to be a spurious coincidence.

On the other hand, if rebalancing does cause the price to overshoot as suggested earlier in this paper, then the increased price momentum should be associated with a next day opening that is negatively related to the previous day's close. **Figure 6** shows the probability of the opening being greater than the previous day's close if the market

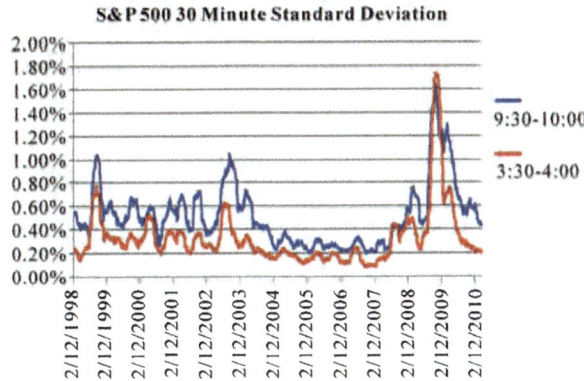

Figure 2. S&P 500 30 minute volatility from January 1998 to April 2010.

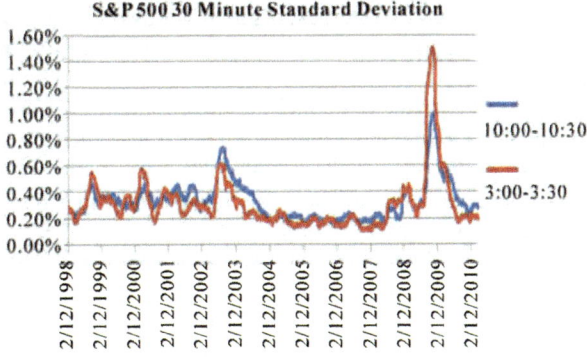

Figure 3. S&P 500 30 minute volatility from January 1998 to April 2010.

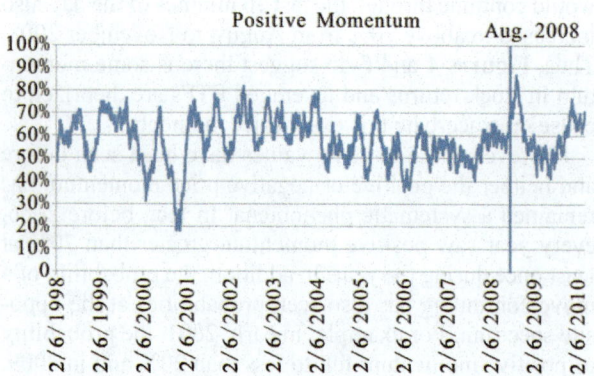

Figure 4. Probability a positive market move will be reinforced in the last 30 minutes of trading.

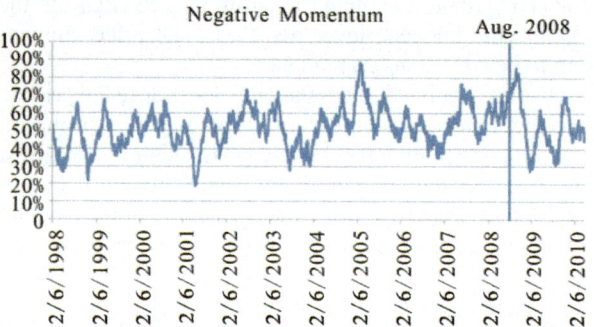

Figure 5. Probability a positive market move will be reinforced in the last 30 minutes of trading.

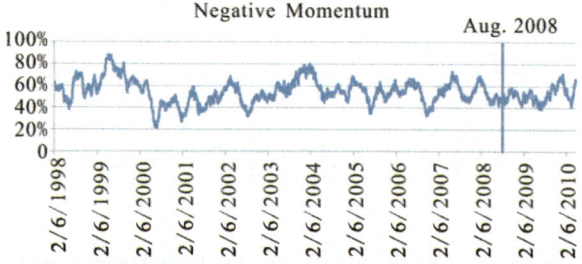

Figure 6. Probability market will increase the next day if market falls last 30 minutes the day before.

fell over the last 30 minutes of the previous day. For the entire time period studied, there was a 54% chance that this would occur.

During the financial market meltdown, the probability the next day's opening would be higher if the market fell the last 30 minutes of the previous day did not deviate from historical norms as can easily be discerned in **Figure 6** which a statistical test confirms.

To test whether the magnitude of the previous day's final 30 minute decline is related to a positive reversal, the previous day's percentage decline is regressed on the next day's opening reversal percentage return. Specifically,

$$\text{Reversal} = \alpha + \beta(\text{ret30}) + \varepsilon \qquad (1)$$

where:
reversal = percentage return of day t; and
ret30 = percentage return of last 30 minutes of previous day if last 30 minute return is negative.

The results are shown below for the August to November 2008 time period:

Reversal =	−0.027	−0.023(ret30)	+ ε
t-stat =	(−0.32)	(−0.71)	

This indicates that for each one percent additional decline during the previous day's final 30 minutes, the opening is expected to be 0.023% higher the next day relative to the previous day's close. Economically, this is not overly significant and based on the t-stat, certainly not statistically significant. Thus, there is no confirming evidence that leverage fund rebalancing is causing additional price momentum that leads to overshooting.

To be complete, **Figure 7** shows the probability that the market will decrease the next day if the market increases the last 30 minutes the day before. For the entire time period, the average probability that this would occur is 49%. The August through November 2008 time period did see this increase to 61% which is statistically significant. However, this value has fallen to the 40% level twice since then. Regardless, there is some minor evidence here that suggests a negative reversal is more likely after an increase over the last 30 minutes from the day before.

Similarly to above, the magnitude of the reversal is also tested using Equation (1) with the only difference being that ret30 = percentage return of last 30 minutes of previous day if last 30 minute return is positive instead of negative. The results are shown below:

Reversal =	−0.082	− 0.007(ret30)	+ ε
t-stat =	(−0.96)	(−0.23)	

In this case, the economic reversal is a trivial 0.007% and statistically insignificant based on the 0.23 t-stat. Although the probability of reversal appears to be greater, the magnitude is even smaller relative to the positive reversal case.

To further test the robustness of this negative reversal, the reversal probability is also calculated based on the previous day's move, not just the last 30 minutes. Interestingly, the same basic result found above is also attained based on whether the market is up or down for the entire day the day before, not just the last 30 minutes. In fact, the negative reversal based on the previous day's move was 67% during August to November 2008 as opposed to only 61% based on the last 30 minutes. Thus, the supposed market overreaction as evidence by higher than a 50% probability of reversal is not based just on the 30 minute price change of the index from the day before, but more on a general buy into the declines and sell into the increases irrespective of what leveraged ETFs are doing.

Figure 7. Probability market will decrease the next day if market increases last 30 minutes the previous day.

5. Conclusions

Leveraged ETFs are a growing market segment and have received a great deal of scrutiny. It has been suggested by some that they have played a role in increasing market volatility. The fact they were becoming increasingly popular when the financial market crisis hit made them an obvious scapegoat for explaining the tremendous increase in volatility at the time. Two major points refute this idea: 1) the abnormally high market volatility has now mostly subsided despite the continued growth in levered ETFs, and 2) historical evidence suggests the volatility that accompanied the financial crisis should have been expected irrespective of levered ETFs existence based on the economic recession, the tremendous leverage held by financial firms, and the large drop in stock prices.

This study has not found evidence that volatility has systematically increased due to the rebalancing issue associated with leveraged ETFs. Intra-daily volatility in time periods not associated with rebalancing saw the same spikes in volatility as the last 30 minutes did. Furthermore, price momentum and reversal during the height of the financial crisis also does not appear to be related to leveraged ETF rebalancing for the following four reasons: 1) these effects have not continued even though leveraged ETFs continue to grow, 2) the magnitudes during the financial crisis have been seen before, 3) the magnitude of the previous day's 30 minute move is not related to higher percentage reversal returns the next day, and 4) the significant next day reversal associated only when the market was up during the financial crisis is more related to a move during the previous day, not just to the last 30 minutes.

Thus, the trading associated with leveraged ETFs does not appear to have any substantial effect on the market. However, the S&P 500 is a large market. If leveraged ETFs make up a greater percentage of the trading in some smaller markets, it is possible they could have an effect, although it seems likely any systematic pricing bias would be quickly arbitraged away.

6. References

[1] F. Edwards, "Does Futures Trading Increase Stock Market Volatility?" *Financial Analysts Journal*, Vol. 44, No. 2, 1988, pp. 63-69.

[2] G. W. Schwert, "Why does Stock Market Volatility Change over Time?" *Journal of Finance*, Vol. 19, No. 5, December 1987, pp. 3-29.

[3] G. W. Schwert, "Stock Market Volatility," *Financial Analysts Journal*, Vol. 46, No. 3, May/June 1990, pp. 23-34.

[4] T. Lauricella, S. Pulliam and D. Gullapalli, "Are ETFs Driving Late-Day Turns? Leveraged Vehicles Seen Magnifying Other Bets; Last-Hour Volume Surge," *Wall Street Journal*, 15 December 2008.

[5] J. Zweig, "How Managing Risk with ETFs can Backfire," *Wall Street Journal*, 27 February 2009.

[6] J. Spence, "Leveraged ETFs are under SEC Scrutiny," *Wall Street Journal*, 13 April 2010.

[7] G. W. Schwert, "Stock Volatility and the Crash of 87," *The Review of Financial Studies*, Vol. 3, No. 1, 1990, pp. 77-102.

[8] G. Hardouvelis, "Margin Requirements and Stock Market Volatility," Federal Reserve Bank of New York Quarterly Review, 1988, pp. 80-89.

[9] D. Hsieh and M. Miller, "Margin Regulation and Stock Market Volatility," *Journal of Finance*, Vol. 45, No. 1, 1990, pp. 3-29.

[10] P. Kupiec, "Initial Margin Requirements and Stock Returns Volatility: Another Look," *Journal of Financial Services Research*, Vol. 3, No. 2-3, December 1989, pp. 287-301.

[11] P. Kupiec, "Margin Requirements, Volatility, and Market Integrity: What have We Learned Since the Crash?" *Journal of Financial Services Research*, Vol. 13, No. 3, 1998, pp. 231-255.

[12] M. Salinger, "Stock Market Margin Requirements and Volatility: Implications for Regulation of Stock Index Futures," *Journal of Financial Services Research*, Vol. 3, No. 2-3, December 1989, pp. 121-138.

[13] M. Deshpande, D. Mallick and R. Bhatia, "Understanding Ultrashort ETFs," Barclays Capital Special Report, 5 January 2009.

[14] "What is the Real Impact of Leveraged ETFs?" Credit Suisse Portfolio Strategy, 2009.

[15] Direxion Report, Meeting with SEC Staff, 16 April 2009.

[16] M. Cheng and A. Madhavan, "The Dynamics of Leveraged and Inverse Exchange-Traded Funds," *Journal of Investment Management*, Vol. 7, No. 4, 2009, pp. 43-62.

17

Coordination of a Supply Chain with Advertising Investment and Allowing the Second Ordering

Tiaojun Xiao*, Xinxin Yan, Jiabao Zhao
School of Management Science and Engineering, Nanjing University, Nanjing, China

Abstract

This paper develops a game theoretic model of a one-manufacturer and one-retailer supply chain allowing the second ordering to investigate how to coordinate the order quantity and advertising investment via a markdown money-cooperative advertising contract. We focus on the effects of allowing the second ordering on equilibrium outcome and coordination mechanism. We find: the relationship between the unit wholesale prices and the chargeback rate depends on whether allowing the second ordering; the coordination mechanism is robust to demand uncertainty; the unit wholesale price in period 2 increases with the unit production cost in period 2, the unit delayed delivery cost and unit salvage value if and only if the chargeback rate is sufficiently small while that in period 1 is independent of them. In addition, we study the Pareto condition of coordination mechanism under which both manufacturer and retailer are better off using the coordination mechanism and find that the unit production costs in different periods may have contrary effects on the bounds of Pareto range.

Keywords: Advertising Investment, Supply Chain Management, Markdown Money-Cooperative Advertising Contract, Reorder, Game Theory

1. Introduction

In business world, advertising is an important tool of sales promotion for retailer/seller, which raises the supply chain's profitability. However, retailer only reaps a part of the benefit of advertising, which implies that the retailer may invest less in advertising than that of the centralized supply chain. For seasonal products, market demand is highly uncertain, which discourages the purchase behavior of the retailer. To stimulate the retailer's order, the manufacturer may share the risk of demand uncertainty with the retailer, say, offering returns policy and markdown money policy. This paper focuses on how to coordinate the supply chain via a markdown money-cooperative advertising contract.

The members of supply chain usually cannot accurately make decisions under demand uncertainty, especially, order quantity and investment decisions. Hence, the retailer often orders a lower quantity to reduce operation risk. In order to satisfy the market demand, the manufacturer may allow the second ordering. Specifically, at the end of selling season, the retailer is allowed to make the second ordering for unsatisfied demand. They use this policy to reduce the loss incurred by demand

uncertainty. The reorder policy becomes very important in business operation management. Lots of companies allow the retailers to reorder. For example, according to [1], Sport Obemeyer LTD is a company that sells fashion skiwear. If there were unsatisfied demand, Obemeyer would allow retailers to make the second ordering to replenish for popular items during the selling season. In fashion industry, the second ordering is often adopted, say Zara, Lilanz. This also happened in electronics industry, say, Irico group electronics company limited.

In this paper, we develop a game theoretic model of a supply chain consisting of one manufacturer and one retailer under demand uncertainty to investigate how to coordinate the order quantity and advertising investment decisions, and explore the effects of allowing the second ordering on the coordination mechanism. The manufacturer offers a markdown money-cooperative advertising contract to coordinate the supply chain. We assume that the manufacturer allows the retailer to make the second ordering at the end of selling season. The manufacturer uses a fast production mode to satisfy the second ordering, which incurs a higher unit production cost. We focus on the effect of some factors related to the second ordering on the coordination mechanism. We find that the relationship between the unit wholesale price and chargeback rate differs from that without the second ordering. In addition, we study Pareto condition of the coordination mechanism.

The remainder of this paper is organized as follows. Section 2 reviews related literature. Section 3 introduces the basic model. Section 4 investigates the coordination mechanism of the supply chain with general distribution function. Section 5 analyzes Pareto conditions of the coordination mechanism under uniform distribution. Finally, we summarize this paper and point out some directions for future research in Section 6.

2. Literature Review

This paper is closely related to cooperative advertising, coordination management and reorder policy.

It is well known that advertising can stimulate the market demand while also incurs an advertising cost. Thus, the seller must make a trade-off between the benefit and the cost when it determines advertising investment. Jørgensen et al. [2] pointed out that cooperative advertising is a popular incentive mechanism for advertising investment. Huang and Li [3] introduced a cooperative advertising model of a supply chain consisting of one manufacturer and one retailer, where the manufacturer invests in national advertising and pays the retailer a subsidy to stimulate the local advertising investment of the retailer. Nagler [4] offered an exploratory empirical investigation of the determinants of cooperative advertising participation rates and examined the relationship between participation rates and national advertising expenditures by brand. In this paper, we consider a cooperative advertising contract between one manufacturer and one retailer and investigate how to coordinate advertising investment.

About supply chain coordination contract, it has been widely studied in the literature, such as returns/buyback policy [5], markdown money [6,7], revenue-sharing contract [8], and option contract [9]. Donohue [10] investigated how to coordinate supply chain with forecast updating and two production modes. Zhang et al. [11] examined coordination of an assemble-to-order system involving a short-life-cycle product. Hsieh et al. [12] examined coordinated decisions in a decentralized supply chain faces random demand of a short-life-cycle product. Returns policy/buyback contract is a good coordination mechanism for the retailer to order more, where the retailer can return some or all unsold items at the end of selling season to the manufacturer and receives a full or partial refund. Kandel [13] investigated the allocation of responsibility for unsold items and concluded that monopolistic manufacturer prefers a buyback contract, while monopolistic retailer prefers a no-buyback policy. He et al. [14] developed a model to

determine the optimal returns policy for single-period products in the presence of risk preferences and considered a markdown money contract stimulating order quantity. In a sense, markdown money contract is similar to buyback contract. Their difference lies in who disposes the leftovers to obtain the salvage value. Nair and Closs [15] evaluated the implications of coordinating price markdown policy with supply chain policies of inventory replenishment, and transportation expediting on retail performance of a short lifecycle product. Wang and Webster [7] pointed out that markdown money is frequently used between manufacturers and retailers selling perishable goods. In this paper, we combine markdown money contract with cooperative advertising contract to coordinate the supply chain.

There are many publications has discussed demand uncertainty [16-18]. Under demand uncertainty, there may be unsatisfied demand at the end of selling season. Some publications assumed that the unsatisfied demand is lost [18,19]. However, a few publications assumed that the seller reorders to satisfy the unsatisfied demand, say [20]. We consider the case where the retailer reorders to satisfy the unsatisfied demand at the end of selling season. Because of the delayed delivery, there is penalty cost for all unsatisfied demand. The reorder policy research mainly focused on two issues: reorder time and the second ordering. Most of the literature about reorder focused on reorder time. For example, Chen [21] compared the installation stock policy with the echelon stock policy to analyze the optimal reorder points. Seo et al. [22] defined the order risk policy to decide reorder time to develop the optimal reorder policy for a distribution system with one-warehouse and multiple retailers. Dogru et al. [23] used echelon stock newsvendor equations to optimize the reorder policy in an N-echelon stochastic serial inventory system with a given fixed batch size and linear penalty costs. Leng and Parlar [24] developed a simple profit-sharing contract to achieve supply chain coordination where the retailer manages the inventory system using reorder policy. A few publications only allowed the second ordering at the end of selling season and investigated the effect of allowing the second ordering. For example, Donohue [10] examined the problem of developing supply contracts and production decisions of high fashion, seasonal products operating in a two-mode production environment, and the second ordering was expensive but offered quick turnaround. Weng [20] developed a generalized newsvendor model to analyze the coordinated quantity decisions between the manufacturer and the buyer where allows the second ordering at the end of the period if the demand exceeds stock on hand. Seo [25] extended the order risk policy to general multi-echelon systems, and assumed that excessive customer demands at retailers are fully backordered and incur a linear penalty cost. We assume that the retailer makes the second ordering at the end of selling season and the second order quantity is equal to the quantity of unsatisfied demands, and focus on the effect of allowing the second ordering on the coordination mechanism. The unit production cost in the first setup often is lower than that in the second setup because the former has a longer delivery time. We incorporate this characteristic into model and investigate its effect on the coordination mechanism.

This paper is closely related to [26] that considered how to coordinate the order quantity and advertising investment decisions in a single period model with single production mode. However, we assume that the manufacturer has two production modes and explore how allowing the second ordering influences the equilibrium outcome and coordination mechanism. In addition, we consider how some factors influence the Pareto condition of coordination mechanism. We try to find the new results and managerial insights relative to [26]. In fact, we find some contrary results, for example, the relationship between the unit wholesale prices and chargeback rate depends on whether allowing the second ordering or not. We will point the main difference between them.

This paper complements the literature by investigating coordination of a two-stage supply chain allowing the second ordering to satisfy the unsatisfied demand at the end of selling season via a markdown money-cooperative advertising mechanism. Especially, we focus on the effects of allowing the second ordering on the coordination mechanism. In addition, we study Pareto condition of coordination mechanism when the random demand is uniformly distributed.

3. The Basic Model

We consider a supply chain consisting of one manufacturer and one retailer. The manufacturer produces a seasonal product and sells it through the retailer who carries out (local) advertising investment to stimulate market demand, where the second ordering is allowed. Owing to the market demand's uncertainty, there may be some unsatisfied demands at the end of selling season. Thus, at the end of selling season, to set up a good reputation and obtain a higher profit, the retailer must reorder to satisfy all of unsatisfied demands, i.e., this paper allows backorder but shortage will incur a loss of goodwill. The unsatisfied customer demands incur a delayed delivery cost. We assume that the manufacturer has enough capacity to satisfy the retailer's ordering within a given lead-time and only the second ordering is allowed at the end of selling season due to a long lead-time. The two players independently maximize their own expected profits.

Similar to [19], we assume that the retail price is exogenously given. Owing to the fact that there exists a long delivery lead-time and a short selling season, the manufacturer only allows the retailer to order two times, one occurring before the selling season, the other occurring at the end of selling season. In response to the retailer's orders, the manufacturer should produce items over two periods. In the first period, the production mode is relatively cheap but needs a long lead-time. And in the second period, the manufacturer uses a faster but typically more expensive production mode. Similar to [10], we use two different production costs to express two different production modes.

The event sequence of this game is as follows:

1) the manufacturer determines the unit wholesale prices, cooperative advertising subsidy rate and charge-back rate;

2) the retailer decides the advertising investment level and the first order quantity;

3) if there are unsatisfied demands at the end of selling season, the retailer makes the second ordering to satisfy the market demand.

We have following notation:

c_i the unit production cost of the manufacturer in period i ($i = 1,2$), $c_1 < c_2$;

w_i the unit wholesale price of the manufacturer in period i ($i = 1,2$), $w_1 < w_2$;

p the unit retail price, $p > b + s$;

s the salvage value per unit unsold item for the retailer, $0 \le s < c_1$;

Q the first order quantity of the retailer;

c_d the delayed delivery cost rate for per unit unsatisfied product, $c_d > 0$;

b the chargeback rate per unit unsold product, $b > 0$;

I the advertising investment per unit expected demand for the retailer, referring to as *advertising level*, $I < p - c_2$;

t the fraction of advertising expenditure shared by the manufacturer, $0 \le t \le 1$;

k scaling constant for deterministic demand part, $k > 0$;

β the advertising elasticity of the demand, $0 < \beta < 1$;

x the stochastic demand for the retailer.

Similar to [26,27], we assume that the retailer faces a random demand $x = D(I) + \varepsilon = kI^{\beta} + \varepsilon$, where ε is distributed over $[\underline{B}, \bar{B}]$ with a density function of $f(\varepsilon)$, a cumulative distribution function of $F(\varepsilon)$ and a mean of μ, $kI^{\beta} + \underline{B} \ge 0$. Furthermore, the total advertising investment is $I \cdot \mathrm{E}(x) = I(D(I) + \mu)$.

Since the market demand is uncertain, it is necessary to divide the profit function of the retailer into two cases,

$x \leq Q$ and $x > Q$. At the end of selling season, if $x \leq Q$, the unsold items are disposed in the secondary market by the retailer for a unit salvage value. Further, the retailer's profit function is

$$\Pi_R(x \mid x \leq Q) = px + (b+s)(Q-x) - w_1 Q - (1-t)I(D+\mu)$$
$$= px - (b+s)x + (b+s-w_1)Q - (1-t)I(D+\mu)$$

In the first line, the first term represents the selling revenue; the second term represents the total revenue of the leftovers from salvage value and chargeback money; the third term is the purchase cost; and the fourth term represents the advertising investment cost bear by the retailer.

If $x > Q$, the retailer makes the second ordering to satisfy all the unsatisfied demand. Similar to [22], unsatisfied demand incurs a shortage cost. In this paper, the retailer makes the second ordering to satisfy those unsatisfied demands. The customers at last receive those items a few days later, which incurs a unit delayed delivery cost c_d. And the retailer's profit function is

$$\Pi_R(x \mid x > Q) = px - w_1 Q - (w_2 + c_d)(x-Q)$$
$$- (1-t)I(D+\mu)$$
$$= px - (w_2 + c_d)x + (w_2 + c_d - w_1)Q - (1-t)I(D+\mu)$$

In the first line, the third term represents the sum of the reordering purchase cost and the delayed delivery cost.

Furthermore, the expected profit of the retailer is

$$\pi_R = \int_{\underline{B}}^{Q-D} \Pi_R(x \mid x \leq Q) f(\varepsilon) d\varepsilon + \int_{Q-D}^{\overline{B}} \Pi_R(x \mid x > Q) f(\varepsilon) d\varepsilon$$
$$= p(D+\mu) - (1-t)I(D+\mu)$$
$$+ \int_{\underline{B}}^{Q-D} [(b+s-w_1)Q - (b+s)(D+\varepsilon)] f(\varepsilon) d\varepsilon$$
$$+ \int_{Q-D}^{\overline{B}} [(w_2+c_d-w_1)Q - (w_2+c_d)(D+\varepsilon)] f(\varepsilon) d\varepsilon$$
$$= [p - (1-t)I - b - s](D+\mu) + (b+s-w_1)Q$$
$$+ (b+s-w_2-c_d) \int_{Q-D}^{\overline{B}} (D+\varepsilon-Q) f(\varepsilon) d\varepsilon \quad (1)$$

In (1), the term $\int_{Q-D}^{\overline{B}} (D+\varepsilon-Q) f(\varepsilon) d\varepsilon$ represents the expected shortage quantity.

If $x \leq Q$, the profit function of the manufacturer is

$$\Pi_M(x \mid x \leq Q) = (w_1 - c_1)Q - tI(D+\mu) - b(Q-x)$$

The first term represents the gross profit; the second term represents the advertising cost bear by the manufacturer; and the last term represents the chargeback cost for the leftovers. If $x > Q$, the manufacturer setups the second production to satisfy the second ordering, and the manufacturer's profit function is

$$\Pi_M(x \mid x > Q) = (w_1 - c_1)Q + (w_2 - c_2)(x-Q) - tI(D+\mu).$$

The second term represents the gross profit for the reorder quantity of the retailer. Furthermore, the expected profit of the manufacturer is

$$\pi_M = \int_{\underline{B}}^{Q-D} \Pi_M(x \mid x \leq Q) f(\varepsilon) d\varepsilon + \int_{Q-D}^{\overline{B}} \Pi_M(x \mid x > Q) f(\varepsilon) d\varepsilon$$
$$= \int_{\underline{B}}^{Q-D} b(D+\varepsilon-Q) f(\varepsilon) d\varepsilon + \int_{Q-D}^{\overline{B}} (w_2-c_2)(D+\varepsilon-Q) f(\varepsilon) d\varepsilon$$
$$+ (w_1-c_1)Q - tI(D+\mu)$$
$$= (w_1 - c_1 - b)Q + (b-tI)(D+\mu)$$
$$+ (w_2 - c_2 - b) \int_{Q-D}^{\overline{B}} (D+\varepsilon-Q) f(\varepsilon) d\varepsilon \quad (2)$$

The total expected profit of supply chain is the sum of the expected profit functions of the retailer and the manufacturer. Thus, the total expected profit of supply chain is

$$\pi_C = \pi_R + \pi_M = (p - I - s)(D+\mu) + (s - c_1)Q$$
$$+ (s - c_2 - c_d) \int_{Q-D}^{\overline{B}} (D+\varepsilon-Q) f(\varepsilon) d\varepsilon \quad (3)$$

4. Coordination Mechanism

It is well known that the decentralized supply chain has a lower profitability than the centralized supply chain at the absence of supply chain competition. That is, coordinating the behavior of the member firms can improve the performance of supply chain. In order to coordinate the supply chain, the manufacturer offers a markdown money-cooperative advertising (MMCA) mechanism (w_1, w_2, b, t) to induce the retailer to replicate the optimal advertising level and order quantity of the centralized supply chain. When the supply chain is coordinated, the supply chain achieves the profit of the centralized system.

4.1. Optimal Decisions in the Centralized Setting

To provide a benchmark, we first consider a centralized system where the central decision maker determines all decisions (advertising level and quantity) to maximize the channel profit π_C.

From (3), we derive the following.

Proposition 1. *In the centralized setting, the optimal solution of the channel profit satisfies the first-order conditions*

$$G(Q,I) = c_2 + c_d - c_1 - (c_2 + c_d - s)F(Q - kI^\beta) = 0 \ (for \ Q)$$

$$H(I) = (p - I - c_1)k\beta I^{\beta-1} - kI^\beta - \mu = 0 \quad (for \ I).$$

Proposition 1 implies that the optimal advertising level is independent of the unit salvage value s and the unit production cost c_2 while the quantity depends on them. That is, when they change, the central decision-maker would like to adjust quantity to react to their effects. Let the optimal quantity and advertising level of the supply chain be Q_C^* and I_C^*. The effects of c_1, μ and k on Q_C^* and I_C^* are similar to those in [26], omitting them. From Proposition 1, we find that Q_C^* is an increasing function of c_2, c_d and s. Specifically, when the unit production cost c_2 or the unit delayed delivery cost c_d increases, the central decision maker should raise the production quantity in period 1 to reduce the cost for the shortage product. When the unit salvage value s increases, the central decision maker raises the production quantity in period 1 due to a lower loss for the leftovers.

4.2. Coordination Mechanism

Now, we investigate how to coordinate the decentralized supply chain in which the manufacturer and the retailer maximize their own profits independently.

Similar to Proposition 1, we derive the following.

Proposition 2. *The optimal decisions of the retailer satisfy the first-order conditions*

$$w_2 - w_1 + c_d - (w_2 + c_d - b - s)F(Q - kI^\beta) = 0 \quad (for\ Q) \quad (4)$$

$$-kI^\beta(1+\beta)(1-t) + k\beta I^{\beta-1}(p - w_1) - (1-t)\mu = 0 \quad (for\ I) \quad (5)$$

Proposition 2 implies that, a higher fraction (t) of advertising expenditure shared by the manufacturer induces a higher advertising level, which in turn induces a higher order quantity in period 1.

When the supply chain is coordinated, the MMCA mechanism should induce the retailer to order quantity Q_C^* and invest I_C^*. Proposition 3 summarizes the MMCA mechanism.

Proposition 3. *The MMCA mechanism* (w_1, w_2, b, t) *with* $w_1^* = tp + c_1(1-t)$ *and*

$$w_2^* = \frac{\begin{cases} -b(c_2 + c_d - c_1) - c_2 s + c_1(s - c_d) \\ + (c_2 + c_d - s)[tp + c_1(1-t)] \end{cases}}{c_1 - s}$$

can coordinate the supply chain.

Proposition 3 implies that the MMCA coordination mechanism is robust to demand uncertainty, *i.e.*, independent of the distribution of demand uncertainty, which differs from that in [26]. When the fraction t increases, the manufacturer will raise the unit wholesale prices in two periods to offset a part of the increased advertising cost. It is worthy to note that a higher chargeback rate is along with a lower unit wholesale price in period 2 and the unit wholesale price in period 1 is independent of the chargeback rate, which differs from that without the second ordering, see [19,26]. That is, if the manufacturer decreases the chargeback rate to reduce the excessive ordering, it should raise the unit

wholesale price in period 2 to stimulate the order quantity in period 1. The unit wholesale price in period 1 is independent of the unit production cost c_2, the unit delayed delivery cost c_d and the unit salvage value s because they are not related to period 1. The unit wholesale price w_2^* increases with the unit production cost c_2 if and only if the chargeback rate is sufficiently low ($b < c_1(1-t) - s + pt$); and increases with the unit delayed delivery cost c_d and the unit salvage value s if and only if the chargeback rate is sufficiently low ($b < (p - c_1)t$). In addition, although a higher unit production cost in period 1 raises the unit wholesale price in period 1, it decreases the unit wholesale price in period 2 if the chargeback rate is sufficiently low ($b < (p - s)t$), which results in a lower order quantity in period 1.

5. Pareto Analysis of Coordination Mechanism under Uniform Distribution

In Section 4, we discuss the MMCA coordination mechanism without giving the optimal quantity and advertising level decisions in the setting with general distribution function. Now, we use a specific form of distribution function to obtain the optimal decisions and discuss the Pareto condition of the coordination mechanism. For analytical tractability, we use the uniform distribution function for ε, defined over a finite range $[-A, A]$, $A > 0$, which implies that the mean is $\mu = 0$. Here, the density function is $f(\varepsilon) = 1/(2A)$, the cumulative distribution function is $F(\varepsilon) = (\varepsilon + A)/(2A)$ and A reflects the degree of demand uncertainty.

5.1. Equilibrium Outcome in the Centralized Setting

From Proposition 1, we derive the following.

Corollary 1. *Under uniform distribution, the optimal decisions of the centralized system are*

$$I_C^* = \frac{(p - c_1)\beta}{(1+\beta)} \quad and \quad Q_C^* = k(I_C^*)^\beta - A + 2A\frac{c_2 - c_1 + c_d}{c_2 + c_d - s}.$$

The equilibrium channel profit is

$$\pi_C^* = \frac{\begin{bmatrix} k(p - c_1)(c_2 + c_d - s)(\dfrac{(p - c_1)\beta}{1+\beta})^\beta \\ - A(c_2 + c_d - c_1)(c_1 - s)(1+\beta) \end{bmatrix}}{(c_2 + c_d - s)(1+\beta)}$$

In the centralized setting, from Corollary 1 and [26], we know that the optimal advertising level is independent of whether allowing the second ordering while the optimal quantity depends on it. Corollary 1 implies that the channel profit is positive if and only if

$$A < \hat{A} = \frac{k(p-c_1)(c_2+c_d-s)(\frac{(p-c_1)\beta}{1+\beta})^\beta}{(c_2+c_d-c_1)(c_1-s)(1+\beta)}$$

That is, the channel can make a positive profit if and only if the demand uncertainty is not too large ($A < \hat{A}$). In the following, we assume that the condition $A < \hat{A}$ is satisfied. It follows from $p > c_1$ that both I_C^* and Q_C^* increase with β. It is surprising that the channel profit is decreasing with the advertising elasticity β if $(p-c_1-1)\beta < 1$. One expects that the advertising elasticity always have a positive effect on the channel profit because this raises the market demand. However, higher advertising elasticity also incurs a higher advertising cost (negative effect). As a consequence, if the unit net profit is sufficiently small ($p-c_1 < 1$) or the advertising elasticity β is sufficiently small, the channel profit decreases with the advertising elasticity because the negative effect is larger than the positive effect; otherwise, it increases. Corollary 1 implies that, when the retail price increases, the central decision maker increases the optimal advertising level to stimulate the market demand due to a higher unit profit.

5.2. Equilibrium Outcome in the Decentralized Setting

Now, we discuss the decentralized system without coordination contract. Here, the manufacturer and the retailer maximize their profits independently. The manufacturer first jointly determines the unit wholesale price in two periods and then the retailer determines the order quantity and advertising level.

Similar to Section 3, when allowing the second ordering, we get the expected profit of the retailer is

$$\bar{\pi}_R = (p-I-s)D + (s-w_1)Q$$
$$+ (s-w_2-c_d)\int_{Q-D}^A (D+\varepsilon-Q)/(2A)d\varepsilon$$
$$= (p-I-s)D + (s-w_1)Q + (A+D-Q)^2(s-w_2-c_d)/(4A)$$
$$(6)$$

and the expected profit of the manufacturer is

$$\bar{\pi}_M = (w_1-c_1)Q + (w_2-c_2)\int_{Q-D}^A (D+\varepsilon-Q)/(2A)d\varepsilon$$
$$= (w_1-c_1)Q + (w_2-c_2)(A+D-Q)^2/(4A)$$
$$(7)$$

Similar to Corollary 1, from (6), it follows that, given the unit wholesale prices (w_1,w_2), the optimal reactions

of the retailer are $\bar{I}(w_1) = \frac{\beta(p-w_1)}{(1+\beta)}$ and

$$\bar{Q}(w_1,w_2) = k(\bar{I}(w_1))^\beta + \frac{A(c_d+s+w_2-2w_1)}{c_d+w_2-s}$$

Inserting $\bar{I}(w_1)$ and $\bar{Q}(w_1,w_2)$ into (7), we can obtain the expected profit of the manufacturer $\bar{\pi}_M(w_1,w_2)$. By search the maximum value of $\bar{\pi}_M(w_1,w_2)$ under the constraint $-A \le Q-D \le A$, we can obtain the optimal unit wholesale prices $(\bar{w}_1^*,\bar{w}_2^*)$. Furthermore, we can obtain the equilibrium decisions of the retailer and the profits of the players. Let the optimal profit of the retailer be $\bar{\pi}_R^*$ and that of the manufacturer $\bar{\pi}_M^*$ in the decentralized setting.

5.3. Pareto Analysis

When the supply chain is coordinated, the supply chain achieves the profit of the centralized system that is higher than that of the decentralized supply chain. However, the profit allocation of the coordinated supply chain depends on the specific MMCA contract. It is possible that a member of the coordinated supply chain gains a lower profit than that in the decentralized setting. Thus, it is necessary to study when both firms are better off using MMCA coordination mechanism, *i.e.*, Pareto dominant.

Proposition 4 summarizes the Pareto condition of coordination mechanism.

Proposition 4. *The MMCA mechanism is Pareto dominant over the decentralized setting if $b \in (\hat{b}_L, \hat{b}_H)$, where*

$$\hat{b}_L = c_1(1-t)+pt-s+\frac{(c_2+c_d-s)[\bar{\pi}_R^* - kI_C^{*\beta}(1-t)(p-c_1-I_C^*)]}{A(c_2+c_d-c_1)}$$

and $\hat{b}_H = c_1(1-t)+pt-s$

$$+\frac{(c_2+c_d-s)[\pi_C^* - \bar{\pi}_M^* - kI_C^{*\beta}(1-t)(p-c_1-I_C^*)]}{A(c_2+c_d-c_1)}.$$

Proposition 4 implies that, the retailer is better off accepting the MMCA coordination mechanism only if the chargeback rate is not too low and the manufacturer is better off offering the MMCA mechanism only if the chargeback rate is not too high because a higher chargeback rate decreases the unit wholesale price in period 2 (see Proposition 3), which differs from that in [26]. That is, only when the chargeback rate is appropriate ($b \in (\hat{b}_L, \hat{b}_H)$), the two players are better off using the MMCA coordination mechanism.

Since it is difficult to find the analytic results on the

bounds of chargeback rate, we investigate how some factors influence the results using a numerical example, where the default values of parameters are used as: $A = 25$, $c_1 = 8$, $c_2 = 18$, $c_d = 4$, $k = 20$, $p = 35$, $s = 6$, $t = 0.7$ and $\beta = 0.5$.

Figure 1 describes the effect of the chargeback rate on the profits of the players when the supply chain is coordinated. **Figures 2-5** describe how the unit delayed cost, the unit production cost in period 2, the advertising elasticity and the fraction of advertising expenditure influences the bounds of chargeback rate. Since the effects of the unit production cost in period 1 and salvage value on the bounds are similar to those of the unit delayed delivery cost, we omit them. We also omit the effect of scaling constant because it is similar to that of advertising elasticity.

From **Figure 1** and Proposition 3, we know that a higher chargeback rate is more beneficial to the retailer because the manufacturer charges the retailer a lower unit wholesale price in period 2 and the retailer obtains a higher chargeback for the unsold quantity in period 1, which is different from that in [26]. From **Figure 2**, we know that when the unit delayed delivery cost increases, the retailer has a higher incentive to use the MMCA mechanism while the manufacturer has a lower incentive to choose it because the manufacturer bears a part of the

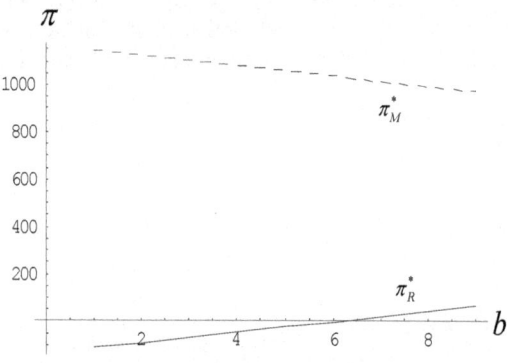

Figure 1. Profits versus chargeback rate.

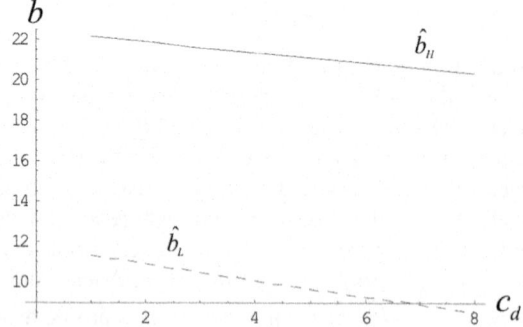

Figure 2. Bounds of chargeback rate versus delayed delivery cost.

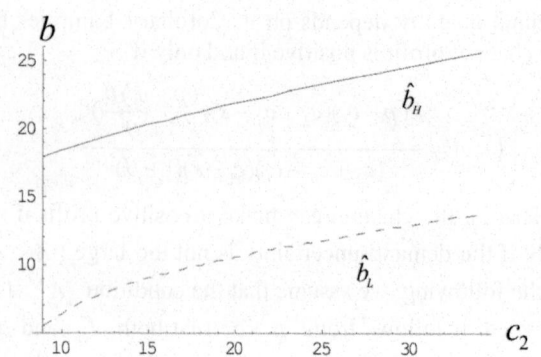

Figure 3. Bounds of chargeback rate versus unit production cost.

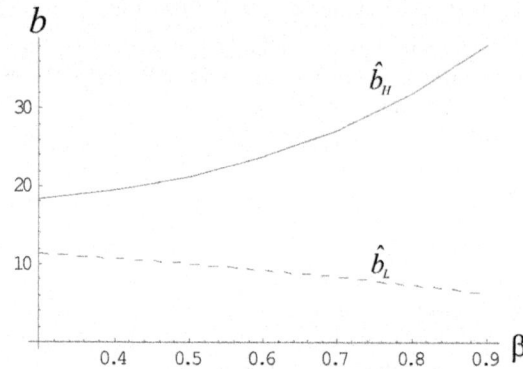

Figure 4. Bounds of chargeback rate versus advertising elasticity.

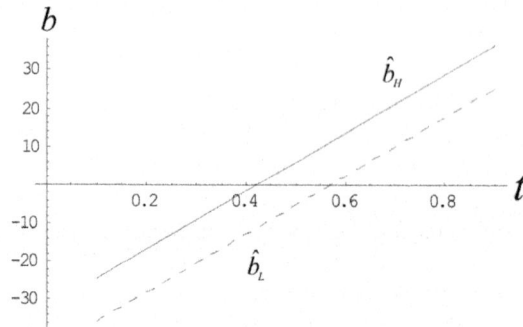

Figure 5. Bounds of chargeback rate versus the fraction.

delayed delivery cost in the coordinated setting. **Figure 3** implies that, when the unit production cost in period 2 increases, the retailer has a lower incentive to use the coordination mechanism while the manufacturer has a higher incentive because the manufacturer can better transfer the production cost in period 2 to the retailer via the MMCA mechanism than the decentralized setting. Furthermore, the unit production cost difference between the two periods plays an important role in the motivation of the players to choose the MMCA mechanism. From **Figure 4**, we know that, when the advertising elasticity is not too small, higher advertising elasticity implies a larger range of chargeback rate in which both the manufacturer and the retailer are better off using coordination mechanism because the cooperative advertising can stimulate a higher advertising level and demand rate. From **Figure 5**, we know that, when the fraction t is sufficiently small, coordination is always beneficial to the retailer but harmful to the manufacturer. Thus, the manufacturer would like to offer a high fraction to stimulate the advertising investment. In fact, from Proposition 3, we know that the manufacturer offers a higher unit wholesale price to access a higher unit profit, which offsets a part cost of the advertising subsidy as the fraction increases. A higher fraction often is along with a higher chargeback rate because it needs a higher chargeback rate to induce the retailer to use coordination mechanism.

6. Conclusions

Seasonal products own high demand uncertainty such that there are often leftovers or shortage at the end of selling season. Local advertising plays an important role in promoting the marketing of seasonal products. This paper investigates how to coordinate the order quantity and advertising investment decisions via a MMCA mechanism when the second ordering is allowed.

We allow the retailer to make the second ordering to satisfy the market demand when there exists shortage at the end of selling season and focus on the effects of allowing the second ordering on equilibrium outcome and coordination mechanism. We find that whether allowing the second ordering influences the coordination mechanism to a large degree and even fully changes the results. For example, it inverts the relationship between the unit wholesale prices and chargeback rate and the motivation of the players to use the MMCA mechanism. In addition, we focus on the effects of the new factors related to allowing the second ordering (the unit production cost c_2 and the unit delayed delivery cost c_d) on the results and the characteristics of the unit wholesale price (w_2) in period 2. We also illustrate the effects of the changing of economic environment on the Pareto range of coordination mechanism and find that the unit production cost difference between the two production modes remarkably influences the Pareto range, *i.e.*, the unit production costs in different periods may have contrary effects on the bounds of Pareto range.

This paper assumes that there is a monopoly retailer in the retail market. One may extend it to the case with multiple retailers to consider the effects of competition on equilibrium outcome and coordination mechanism. We assume that the manufacturer does not carry out (national) advertising investment. Incorporating the national advertising investment into our model may be interesting.

7. Acknowledgements

This research was supported in part by the National Natural Science Foundation of China under Grant 70971060, 70671055, 70971063 and 70731002.

8. References

[1] D. Simchi-Levi, P. Kaminsky and E. Simchi-Levi, "De-signing & Managing Supply Chain: Concepts, Strategy & Case Studies," McGraw-Hill, Irwin, 2003, pp. 76-90.

[2] S. Jørgensen, S. P. Sigué and G. Zaccour, "Dynamic Cooperative Advertising in a Channel," *Journal of Retailing*, New York, Vol. 76, No. 1, 2000, pp. 71-92.

[3] Z. Huang and S. X. Li, "Co-op Advertising Models in Manufacturer-Retailer Supply Chains: A Game Theory Approach," *European Journal of Operational Research*, Elsevier, Vol. 135, No. 3, December 2001, pp. 527-544.

[4] M. G. Nagler, "An Exploratory Analysis of the Deter-minants of Cooperative Advertising Participation Rates," *Marketing Letters*, Springer Netherlands, Vol. 17, No. 2, April 2006, pp. 91-102.

[5] H. S. Lau and A. H. L. Lau, "Manufacturer's Pricing Strategy and Return Policy for a Single-Period Com-modity," *European Journal of Operation Research*, Elsevier, Vol. 116, No. 2, July 1999, pp. 291-304.

[6] T. A. Taylor, "Supply Chain Coordination under Channel Rebates with Sales Effort Effects," *Management Science*, INFORMS, Vol. 48, No. 8, August 2002, pp. 992-1007.

[7] C. X. Wang and S. Webster, "Markdown Money Con-tracts for Perishable Goods with Clearance Pricing," *European Journal of Operational Research*, Elsevier, Vol. 196, No. 3, August 2009, pp. 1113-1122.

[8] Z. Yao, S. C. H. Leung and K. K. Lai, "Manufacturer's Revenue-Sharing Contract and Retail Competition," *European Journal of Operational Research*, Elsevier, Vol. 186, No. 2, April 2008, pp. 637-651.

[9] N. X. Xu and L. Nozick, "Modeling Supplier Selection and the Use of Option Contracts for Global Supply Chain Design," *Computers & Operations Research*, Elsevier, Vol. 36, No. 10, October 2009, pp. 2786-2800.

[10] K. L. Donohue, "Efficient Supply Contracts for Fashion Goods with Forecast Updating and Two Production Modes," *Management Science*, INFORMS, Vol. 46, No. 11, November 2000, pp. 1397-1411.

[11] X. H. Zhang, J. H. Ou and S. M. Gilbert, "Coordination of Stocking Decisions in an Assemble-to-Order Environ-ment," *European Journal of Operational Research*, Elsevier, Vol. 189, No. 2, September 2008, pp. 540-558.

[12] C. C. Hsieh, C. H. Wu and Y. J. Huang, "Ordering and Pricing Decisions in a Two-Echelon Supply Chain with Asymmetric Demand Information," *European Journal of Operational Research*, Elsevier, Vol. 190, No. 2, October 2008, pp. 509-525.

[13] E. Kandel, "The Right to Return," *Journal of Law and*

Economics, University of Chicago, Vol. 39, April 1996, pp. 329-356.

[14] J. He, K. S. Chin, J. B. Yang and D. L. Zhu, "Return Policy Model of Supply Chain Management for Single-Period Products," *Journal of Optimization Theory and Applications*, Springer Netherlands, Vol. 129, No. 2, May 2006, pp. 293-308.

[15] A. Nair and D. J. Closs, "An Examination of the Impact of Coordinating Supply Chain Policies and Price Markdowns on Short Lifecycle Product Retail Performance," *International Journal of Production Economics*, Elsevier, Vol. 102, No. 2, August 2006, pp. 379-392.

[16] H. P. Marvel and H. Wang, "Inventories, Return Policy, and Equilibrium Price Dispersion under Demand Uncertainty," China Center for Economic Research, Beijing University, Working Paper, 2002.

[17] K. Kogan and A. Herbon, "A Supply Chain under Limited-Time Promotion: The Effect of Customer Sensitivity," *European Journal of Operational Research*, Elsevier, Vol. 188, No. 1, July 2008, pp. 273-292.

[18] Y. J. He and J. Zhang, "Random Yield Risk Sharing in a Two-Level Supply Chain," *International Journal of Production Economics*, Elsevier, Vol. 112, No. 2, April 2008, pp. 769-781.

[19] C. H. Lee and B. D. Rhee, "Channel Coordination Using Product Returns for a Supply Chain with Stochastic Salvage Capacity," *European Journal of Operational Research*, Elsevier, Vol. 177, No. 1, February 2007, pp. 214-238.

[20] Z. K. Weng, "Coordinating Order Quantities between the Manufacturer and the Buyer: A Generalized Newsvendor Model," *European Journal of Operational Research*, Elsevier, Vol. 156, No. 1, July 2004, pp. 148-161.

[21] F. Chen, "Echelon Reorder Points, Installation Reorder Points, and the Value of Centralized Demand Information," *Management Science*, INFORMS, Vol. 44, No. 12, December 1998, pp. S221-S234.

[22] Y. Seo, S. Jung and J. Hahm, "Optimal Reorder Decision Utilizing Centralized Stock Information in a Two-Echelon Distribution System," *Computers & Operations Research*, Elsevier, Vol. 29, No. 2, February 2002, pp. 171-193.

[23] M. K. Dogru, G. J. Houtum and A. G. Kok, "Newsvendor Equations for Optimal Reorder Levels of Serial Inventory Systems with Fixed Batch Sizes," *Operations Research Letters*, Elsevier, Vol. 36, No. 5, September 2008, pp. 551-556.

[24] M. Leng and M. Parlar, "Lead-Time Reduction in a Two-Level Supply Chain: Non-Cooperative Equilibria vs. Coordination with a Profit-sharing Contract," *International Journal of Production Economics*, Elsevier, Vol. 118, No. 2, April 2009, pp. 521-544.

[25] Y. Seo, "Controlling General Multi-Echelon Distribution Supply Chain with Improved Reorder Decision Policy Utilizing Real-Time Shared Stock Information," *Computers & Industrial Engineering*, Elsevier, Vol. 51, No. 2, October 2006, pp. 229-246.

[26] T. J. Xiao and X. X. Yan, "Coordinating a Two-Stage Supply Chain via a Markdown Money and Advertising Subsidy Contract," *International Journal of Information and Decision Sciences*, Inderscience, 2010, in press.

[27] F. J. Arcelus, S. Kumar and G. Srinivasan, "Evaluating Manufacturer's Buyback Policies in a Single-Period Two-Echelon Framework under Price-Dependent Stochastic Demand," *Omega*, Elsevier, Vol. 36, No. 5, October 2008, pp. 808-824.

Appendix

Proof of Proposition 1. Differentiating π_C with respect to Q, we can obtain the first-order condition

$$\frac{\partial \pi_C}{\partial Q} = s - c_1 - (s - c_2 - c_d)(1 - F(Q - kI^\beta))$$

$$= c_2 - c_1 + c_d - (c_2 + c_d - s)F(Q - kI^\beta) = 0 \quad (A.1)$$

Note that D is a function of I. Differentiating π_C with respect to I, we obtain the first-order condition

$$\frac{\partial \pi_C}{\partial I} = -kI^\beta - \mu + k\beta I^{\beta-1}(p - I - s) + k\beta I^{\beta-1}(s - c_2 - c_d)(1 - F(Q - kI^\beta))$$

$$= -kI^\beta - \mu + k\beta I^{\beta-1}[(p - I - c_2 - c_d) + (c_2 + c_d - s)F(Q - kI^\beta)]$$

$$= 0 \quad (A.2)$$

From (A.1), it follows that the first-order condition (A.2) is equivalent to

$$(p - I - c_1)k\beta I^{\beta-1} - kI^\beta - \mu = 0 \quad (A.3)$$

From (1), $p > c_2 > c_1 > s$ and $I < p - c_2$, it follows that, the second-order derivatives are

$$\frac{\partial^2 \pi_C}{\partial Q^2} = -(c_2 + c_d - s)f(Q - kI^\beta) < 0$$

$$\frac{\partial^2 \pi_C}{\partial Q \partial I} = k\beta I^{\beta-1}(c_2 + c_d - s)f(Q - kI^\beta) > 0$$

$$\frac{\partial^2 \pi_C}{\partial I^2} = -k\beta I^{\beta-2}[2I + (1 - \beta)(p - I - c_1) + k\beta I^\beta(c_2 + c_d - s)f(Q - kI^\beta)] < 0$$

$$\frac{\partial^2 \pi_C}{\partial Q^2} \cdot \frac{\partial^2 \pi_C}{\partial I^2} - (\frac{\partial^2 \pi_C}{\partial Q \partial I})^2$$

$$= k\beta I^{\beta-2}(c_2 + c_d - s)f(Q - kI^\beta)[2I + (1 - \beta)(p - I - c_1)] > 0 .$$

Thus, π_C is a jointly concave function of (Q, I), i.e., the second-order condition is satisfied. Thus, the solution of the first-order conditions is optimal.

Proof of Proposition 2. Given the MMCA mechanism of the manufacturer, the retailer determines Q and I to maximize π_R given by (1). Differentiating π_R with respect to Q and I, we can obtain the first-order conditions

$$\frac{\partial \pi_R}{\partial Q} = b + s - w_1 - (b + s - w_2 - c_d)(1 - F(Q - kI^\beta))$$

$$= w_2 - w_1 + c_d - (w_2 + c_d - b - s)F(Q - kI^\beta) = 0 \quad (A.4)$$

$$\frac{\partial \pi_R}{\partial I} = -(1 - t)(kI^\beta + \mu) + k\beta I^{\beta-1}[p - (1 - t)I - b - s]$$

$$+ k\beta I^{\beta-1}(b + s - w_2 - c_d)(1 - F(Q - kI^\beta))$$

$$= -(1 - t)(kI^\beta + \mu) + k\beta I^{\beta-1}[p - (1 - t)I - w_2$$

$$- c_d - (b + s - w_2 - c_d)F(Q - kI^\beta)] = 0 \quad (A.5)$$

From (A.4), it follows that the first-order condition

(A.5) is equivalent to

$$-kI^\beta(1 + \beta)(1 - t) + k\beta I^{\beta-1}(p - w_1) - (1 - t)\mu = 0 \quad (A.6)$$

Similar to Proposition 1, we can show that π_R is a concave function of (Q, I), i.e., the second-order condition is satisfied.

Proof of Proposition 3. By comparing (A.1) with (A.4), we know that, if the manufacturer wants to induce the retailer to replicate the outcome of the centralized system, the optimal unit wholesale price for two periods should satisfy

$$w_2(w_1) = \frac{b(c_1 - c_2 - c_d) - c_2 s + c_1(s - c_d) + (c_2 + c_d - s)w_1}{c_1 - s}$$

Rewriting (A.3) and (A.6), we have

$$kI^\beta(1 + \beta) + \mu = (p - c_1)k\beta I^{\beta-1} \quad (A.7)$$

$$kI^\beta(1 + \beta) + \mu = k\beta I^{\beta-1}(p - w_1)/(1 - t) \quad (A.8)$$

From (A.7) and (A.8), we know that

$$(p - c_1)k\beta I^{\beta-1} = k\beta I^{\beta-1}(p - w_1)/(1 - t) \quad (A.9)$$

Solving (A.9) for w_1, we have

$$w_1^* = p - (p - c_1)(1 - t) = tp + c_1(1 - t)$$

Proof of Corollary 1. From Proposition 1 and $F(\varepsilon) = (\varepsilon + A)/(2A)$, it follows that the first-order conditions (A.1) and (A.3) are equivalent to

$$2A(c_2 + c_d - c_1) - (A + Q - kI^\beta)(c_2 + c_d - s) = 0 \quad (A.10)$$

$$(p - c_1)k\beta I^{\beta-1} - kI^\beta(1 + \beta) = 0 \quad (A.11)$$

Solving (A.10) and (A.11) for Q and I, we obtain Q_C^* and I_C^*, given in Corollary 1.

Proof of Proposition 4. Inserting w_1^*, w_2^* and Q_C^* into (1), we have

$$\pi_R^*(b) = kI_C^{*\beta}(1 - t)(p - c_1 - I_C^*)$$

$$+ \frac{A(c_2 + c_d - c_1)[b + s - c_1(1 - t) - pt]}{c_2 + c_d - s}$$

which is an increasing function of b following from $c_2 > c_1 > s$.

Solving $\pi_R^*(b) = \overline{\pi}_R^*$ for b, we get

$$\hat{b}_L = c_1(1 - t) + pt - s$$

$$+ \frac{(c_2 + c_d - s)[\overline{\pi}_R^* - kI_C^{*\beta}(1 - t)(p - c_1 - I_C^*)]}{A(c_2 + c_d - c_1)}$$

Thus, the retailer is better off using coordination mechanism if $b > \hat{b}_L$.

The equilibrium profit of the coordinated manufacturer is $\pi_M^*(b) = \pi_C^* - \pi_R^*(b)$, which is a decreasing function of b. By solving $\pi_M^*(b) = \overline{\pi}_M^*$ for b, we obtain $\hat{b}_H$, given in Proposition 4. Furthermore, the manufacturer is better off using coordination mechanism if $b < \hat{b}_H$.

18

Cost Benchmarking of Generation Utilities Using DEA: A Case Study of India

Shafali Jain, Tripta Thakur, Arun Shandilya
Department of Electrical Engineering, National Institute of Technology, MANIT-Bhopal, India

Abstract

Technical efficiency of electric utility is the critical element for its competitiveness in the electricity market and very relevant in the Indian electricity sector presently. This paper is aimed to measure the efficiencies of 30 state owned electric generation utilities/companies for the year 2007-08 by applying DEA models with single input and two outputs. The input used is total cost and outputs are units of energy generated and total energy sold or consumed. Cost benchmarking has been carried out so that cost controls can be implemented. In addition, the target evaluation for input cost has also been done. The result of this model shows that GENCOs are generally inefficient in cost frontier and there is an urgent need for intro inspection. This will help for GENCOs. The result shows that the total average of overall, technical and scale efficiencies are 46%, 75.1% and 60% respectively. This efficiency measurement assists the utilities by identifying their shortcomings, setting targets and trying to reach the set targets.

Keywords: Data Envelopment Analysis (DEA), Generation Company (GENCO), Cost Benchmarking, Target Evaluation

1. Introduction

Recent electricity sector reforms in the form of liberalization, privatization, and implementation of a new regulatory design around the world have been radically transformed the power sector. Enhancing efficiency, productivity and quality are the goals behind these reforms. A similar had been followed by India which experienced electric power reforms in early 1991. Today's competitive electricity market has heightened the need for methods to evaluate the technical efficiency of the electric utility [1]. Among many possible efficiency measurement methods, Data Envelopment Analysis (DEA) is one method that has been used especially for the complicated systems with lots of inputs and outputs for benchmarking since its introduction by Charnes, Cooper and Rhodes in 1978 based on previous work by Farrell on production efficiency [2]. DEA methodology has been most commonly used for calculating the efficiency of utilities and benchmarking their performances to establish the best practices [3].

The deficiency in power availability in India is a significant obstacle to the smooth development of the economy [4-5]. The deficits experienced in India during the last two decades can be attributed to two main reasons. One reason is the huge growth in demand for electricity, mostly from industries and agriculture. The other reason is the unbelievable level of inefficiencies at all stages between electricity generation and its end use. India exhibits one of the lowest levels of efficiency in the overall management of electricity. The peak power deficit is 13.9% and base energy deficit has gone up to 9.3%. To bridge its future demand–supply gap, India would need capacity addition of nearly 100,000 MW in the coming 10-12 years [6]. The Ministry of Power (MoP) estimates that the additional capacity requirement to meet these shortages is about 10,000 MW every year. This translates into an asset of about US$10 billion per annum. To fulfill the objective of Indian Government to provide power to all by 2012, and to bridge the demand-supply gap country needs huge investment requirements [7]. Country has already done vast investment in reform programs with the aid of internal/external investors. Before going for further investment it is necessary to have empirical analysis of the extent to which the structural change of Indian electric power industry is working. Improving the efficiency levels would be able to remove the deficits completely but there have not been serious efforts to improve the efficiency levels to the international best practice levels [8-9]. Bridging the gap in demand and supply has become significant and accordingly this strongly necessitates assessment of performance of generation utilities [10].

This paper presents the cost benchmarking of Indian electric generation companies by analyzing their efficiency using DEA methodology for the year 2007-2008.

2. Indian Generation Sector

India is world's fifth largest consumer of energy. It is sixth largest generating company in the world and third largest in Asia. The Indian power sector is divided into five Regions: Northern, Western, Southern, Eastern, and the North-Eastern Region; and each state in India has its own state owned electric utility (SOEU). The Central Electricity Authority (CEA) is responsible for power planning at the national level. CEA advises the Ministry of power (MOP) on matters concerning the national power policy, and national power planning. Regulatory matters in the center are taken care by the Central Electricity Commission (CERC) and the State Electricity Regulatory Commission (SERC) take care corresponding regulatory issue at the state level.

The electricity sector in India is predominantly controlled by the Government of India's public sector undertakings (PSUs). Major PSUs involved in the generation of electricity include National Thermal Power Corporation (NTPC), National Hydroelectric Power Corporation (NHPC) and Nuclear Power Corporation of India (NPCI). In electricity generation, the contribution of state, central and private sectors are 52.5, 34 and 13.5% respectively. As on 31st march, 2008, there were eight State Electricity Boards and thirteen Electricity Departments in the States and Union Territories and total fifteen utilities have been unbundled.

3. Methodology

DEA occasionally called frontier analysis was first place ahead by Charnes, Cooper and Rhodes in 1978 [4]. It is a performance measurement technique which, can be used for evaluating the relative efficiency of decision-making units (DMU's)[1] in organizations. The most basic DEA model is CCR based on Charnes, Cooper & Rhodes (1978) which have constant returns to scale; however there is also DEA models which address varying returns

---

[1]DMU is a distinct unit within an organization that has flexibility with respect to some of the decisions it makes, but not necessarily completes freedom with respect to these decisions. Banks, police stations, hospitals, tax offices, prisons, defense bases (army, navy, and air force) schools and university departments, are examples of such units to which DEA has been applied.

to scale known as BCC based on Banker, Charnes and Cooper (1984) [11].

DEA has been applied for both production and cost data [12]. By using the selected input and output variables, DEA software finds for the points with the lowest input value for any given output, connecting those points to form the efficiency frontier. The utility which is not on the frontier is considered to be inefficient. A numerical coefficient is given to each firm, defining its relative efficiency. This method can easily accommodate a multiplicity of inputs and outputs. This method is also useful because returns to scale is taken into consideration in calculating efficiency, thus allowing for the concept of increasing or decreasing efficiency based on size and output levels.

The most important job in this efficiency analysis is the right selection of inputs and outputs. No universally applicable rational template is available for selection of variables [13]. An inherent assumption in DEA is that there is some relationship between the input and the output. Correlation is a statistical test which enables us to investigate for a statistical relationship between two variables. Input variables chosen for DEA model are: total cost in Rs. Crores and the outputs are units generated (GWh) and energy sold (GWh), their correlation is shown in **Table 1**.

3.1. DEA Models

There can be two DEA models: CCR and BCC model and both of these models are applied in this analysis.

1) CCR Model

The CCR model was suggested by Charnes et al. (1978), and hence is named as CCR model and assumes constant returns to scale (CRS) assumption. If assuming data on K inputs and M outputs for each of N firms, then for the i-th firm these are represented by the column vectors x_i and y_i respectively. The $K \times N$ input matrix, X, and the $M \times N$ output matrix, Y, represent the data for all N firms. A measure of the ratio of all outputs over all inputs would be obtained for each firm, such as uy_i / vx_i, where u is an $M \times 1$ vector of output weights and v is a $K \times 1$ vector of input weights [14]. The optimal weights are obtained by solving the mathematical programming problem:

$$\max_{u,v} (uy_i / vx_i),$$
$$\text{st} \quad uy_j / vx_j \leq 1, \quad j = 1,2,....N,$$
$$u,v \geq 0. \quad (1)$$

It is required to calculate values of u and v, such that the efficiency measure for the i-th firm is maximized, subject to the constraints that all efficiency measures must be less than or equal to one. The difficulty in this ratio formulation is that it has an infinite number of solutions. This can be avoided by imposing the constraint $vx_i = 1$, which provides:

$$\max_{\mu,v} (\mu y_i),$$
$$st \quad vx_i = 1,$$
$$\mu y_j - vx_j \leq 0, \quad j = 1,2,....N,$$
$$\mu,v \geq 0, \quad (2)$$

where the notation is changed from u and v to μ and v, to stress that this is a different linear programming problem. Equation (2) is known as the multiplier form of the DEA linear programming problem. By the duality in linear programming, equivalent envelopment form of this problem can be derived as:

$$\min_{\theta,\lambda} \theta,$$
$$st \quad -y_i + Y\lambda \geq 0,$$
$$\theta x_i - X\lambda \geq 0,$$
$$\lambda \geq 0, \quad (3)$$

where θ is a scalar and λ is a $N \times 1$ vector of constants. The efficiency score for the i-th firm will be the value of θ According to the Farell (1957) definition, it will satisfy: $\theta \leq 1$, with a value of 1 indicating a point on the frontier and hence the firm is technically efficient firm.

2) BCC Model

BCC model was suggested by Banker, Charnes and Cooper (1984) investigates whether the performance of each DMU was conducted in region of increasing, constant or decreasing returns to scale in multiple outputs and multiple inputs situations. The CCR efficiency can be decomposed into the pure technical and scale efficiency components by this BCC model, thus investigating the scale effects [15]. According to this model an inefficient firm is only "benchmarked" against firms of a similar size.

The CRS linear programming problem can be easily modified to account for VRS by adding the convexity constraint: $N1\lambda = 1$ to (3) to provide:

$$\min_{\theta,\lambda} \theta,$$
$$st \quad -y_i + Y\lambda \geq 0,$$
$$\theta x_i - X\lambda \geq 0,$$
$$N1\lambda = 1$$
$$\lambda \geq 0, \quad (4)$$

where N1 is an $N \times 1$ vector of ones. This approach forms a convex hull of interesting planes which envelope the data points more tightly than the CRS conical hull and thus provides technical efficiency scores which are greater than or equal to those obtained using the CRS model. The VRS specification has been the most commonly used specification in the 1990s.

3.2. DEA Variables

The most important job in this efficiency analysis is the right selection of inputs and outputs. No universally applicable rational template is available for selection of variables [16-17]. An inherent assumption in DEA is that there is some relationship between the input and the outpu t. Correlation is a statistical test which enables us to investigate for a statistical relationship between two variables. Input variables chosen for DEA model are: total cost in Rs. Crores and the outputs are units generated (GWh) and energy sold (GWh) and input output correlation has been shown in **Table 1**. Total cost (Totex), which represents the cost incurred by the utility to supply electricity to the ultimate consumers. The components considered for calculating the total cost are: cost of the fuel, operating and maintenance cost (O & M), administrative and general cost (A & G), interest payment liability, depreciation and the cost of power purchase.

3.3. Orientation

Efficiency can be evaluated either on an input-oriented or output-oriented basis. For this paper, an input- oriented or input-minimizing approach has been selected since the purpose of the analysis was to suggest benchmarks for efficiency and reduction of cost input chosen in order to produce a given output.

3.4. Data Collection

Data was collected for 30 SOEUs in which 8 entities were the State Electricity Boards (SEBs), 7 entities comprised various electricity or power departments (PDs), and 15 entities comprised the unbundled SOEUs. The physical data for various states were obtained for the different years from "General Review 2009" published by CEA [18]. The cost data were taken from the "Power Finance Corporation" report 2005-2006 to 2007-2008 [19]. Descriptive statistics of the data for year 2007-2008 is presented in **Table 2** in the form of mean, median, standard deviation, minimum and maximum values.

4. Result & Analysis

4.1. Overall Efficiency Scores

The overall efficiency is measured by CCR model with

Table 1. Input/output correlations.

Variable	Totex	Units Generated	Total Energy Sold
1. Totex	1		
2. Units Generated	0.88561	1	
3. Energy Sold	0.88623	0.974358	1

Table 2. Descriptive statistics.

Variables	Mean	Median	Standard Deviation	Min	Max
Totex	1960.03	458	2465.15	20	7770
Units Generated	14477.57	5427.61	18407.74	21.08	72770.46
Energy Sold	16547.84	10956.17	18604.46	169.51	67930.96

CRS assumption. The results are presented in **Table 4**. It is evident from **Table 4** that the utilities display significant variations in efficiency levels. The total efficiency had a mean score of 46 % for all the utilities and nearly two- third of utilities lie below this average value. Only three generation companies (Himachal Pradesh- HPSEB, Jammu & Kashmir- J & K SEB and Puducherry-PCL) turned out to be the best practices and the remaining 27 utilities exhibited varying degree of inefficiencies. With the exception of the best practices and eight utilities -Sikkim, Assam- APGCL, Manipur, Meghalaya, Nagaland, Tripura, Arunachal Pradesh and Mizoram, exhibited decreasing returns to scale suggesting that these

utilities exceeded their most productive scale size. This outcome supports the unbundling policy of the GoI, as envisaged in the Electricity Act. Five Utilities –Sikkim PD, APGCL, Manipur PD, Arunachal Pradesh (PD) and Mizoram (PD), exhibited increasing returns to scale, which indicates that these utilities are smaller than the most productive scale size.

4.2. Calculation of Scale Efficiency

The scale efficiency is calculated by the BCC formulation that assumes a VRS by taking into consideration the sizes of utilities. This formulation ensures that similar sized utilities are benchmarked and compared with each other [20-21]. In this model the total efficiency is decomposed into pure technical and scale efficiency. The scale efficiency is given by the ratio of CRS efficiency (overall efficiency) to VRS efficiency (pure technical efficiency). The results are presented in **Table 3**. In BCC model, the number of utilities that appear as efficient increased to 11, while remaining 19 utilities showed inefficiencies. The average technical efficiency is 75.1%. The results indicate the possibility of restructuring of several utilities that display low scale efficiencies.

Table 3. Results of CCR and BCC Model.

S.No.	Genco	Total efficiency	Technical efficiency	Scale efficiency	Returns to scale	Benchmarks		
1	HPGCL	0.092	0.175	0.524	drs	16	17	20
2	HPSEB	1	1	1	-	2		
3	J & K PDC	1	1	1	-	3		
4	PSEB	0.242	0.545	0.445	drs	16	14	12
5	RRVUNL & RVPNL	0.239	0.485	0.493	drs	21	12	
6	UPRVUNL &UPJUVNL	0.294	0.872	0.337	drs	17	20	
7	UJVNL	0.95	1	0.95	drs	7		
8	IPGCL & PPCL	0.376	0.856	0.44	drs	17	20	
9	GSECL	0.345	0.789	0.437	drs	12	21	
10	MPPGCL	0.377	0.813	0.464	drs	16	14	17
11	CSEB	0.373	0.508	0.733	drs	21	12	
12	MAHAGENCO	0.419	1	0.419	drs	12		
13	Goa PD	0.383	0.394	0.973	drs	3	18	
14	APPGCL	0.4	1	0.4	drs	14		
15	KPCL	0.431	0.97	0.444	drs	16	12	14
16	KSEB	0.826	1	0.826	drs	16		
17	TNEB	0.37	1	0.37	drs	17		
18	PCL	1	1	1	-	18		
19	BSEB	0.689	0.812	0.848	drs	20	3	
20	JSEB	0.779	1	0.779	drs	20		
21	OPGCL & OHPCL	0.767	1	0.767	drs	21		
22	WBPDCL	0.47	0.971	0.484	drs	21	12	
23	Sikkim PD	0.387	1	0.387	irs	23		
24	APGCL	0.317	0.339	0.937	irs	2	18	23
25	Manipur PD	0.087	0.364	0.238	irs	23		
26	MeSEB	0.307	0.429	0.716	irs	23	2	
27	Nagaland PD	0.141	0.513	0.275	irs	23		
28	Tripura PD	0.433	0.6	0.721	irs	2	23	
29	Arunachal Pradesh PD	0.154	0.439	0.351	irs	2	23	
30	Mizoram PD	0.156	0.645	0.242	irs	23		
	Mean	0.46	0.751	0.6				

Table 4. Input cost target values.

S.No.	GENCO	Original value	Target value
1	HPGCL	7104	1244.01
2	HPSEB	166	166
3	J & K PDC	110	110
4	PSEB	4863	2648.36
5	RRVUNL & RVPNL	4810	2331.24
6	UPRVUNL &UPJUVNL	3948	3442.99
7	UJVNL	261	261
8	IPGCL & PPCL	1153	987.14
9	GSECL	6266	4943.1
10	MPPGCL	2296	1865.83
11	CSEB	1399	711.11
12	MAHAGENCO	7770	7770
13	Goa PD	164	64.58
14	APPGCL	4851	4851
15	KPCL	3401	3298.09
16	KSEB	501	501
17	TNEB	5229	5229
18	PCL	50	50
19	BSEB	154	125.04
20	JSEB	415	415
21	OPGCL & OHPCL	647	647
22	WBPDCL	2631	2555.29
23	Sikkim PD	20	20
24	APGCL	253	85.73
25	Manipur PD	55	20
26	MeSEB	96	41.21
27	Nagaland PD	39	20
28	Tripura PD	70	42
29	Arunachal Pradesh PD	48	21.08
30	Mizoram PD	31	20

4.3. Benchmarking

Benchmarking is the process of creating a standard/best practice against which the performance of utility can be measured [22]. For every inefficient DMU, DEA identifies a set of corresponding efficient units that can be utilized as benchmarks for improvement. The benchmarks for inefficient utilities are shown in **Table 3**. For example the benchmarks for Haryana (HPGCL) are Kerala SEB, Tamil Nadu (TNSEB) and Jharkhand (JSEB). This inefficient utility will be benchmarked or compared against these three efficient utilities.

4.4. Input Cost Target Values

For each inefficient utility target value for input variable is calculated so as to make them efficient and shown in the **Table 4**. The input cost target values for most of the utilities is lower than their actual values. In the case of HPGCL, the input cost should be reduced by 82% to make it technically efficient. The mean technical efficiency of all the utilities is 75.1% which means utilities could reduce their inputs by 24.9% without reducing their outputs.

4.5. Cost Savings

The mean technical efficiency of all the utilities is 75.1% which means utilities could reduce their inputs by 24.9% without reducing their outputs. That means by cost benchmarking the utilities we can have the cost reduction by nearly 25% with the same output. For the case of generation company of Haryana (HPGCL), the input cost is 7104 Rs crores, so on an average we can reduce its cost by 25% which is a huge money saving which can be utilize by this utility for further generation.

5. Conclusions

The cost benchmarking has been carried out so that cost controls can be implemented. This analysis would be useful for the regulators in decreasing the electricity price and offer valuable lessons to ensure that the new structure being adopted is better than the regulatory and legislative framework designed a few decades back. The results show that the total generation cost reduction can be 25% with the same output of energy generated, as the mean technical efficiency is nearly 75%. The mean overall efficiency is 46%. The numbers of GENCOs that appear as efficient entities are 3 in case of CRS while under VRS condition, it increased to 11. In addition to this, for each inefficient GENCO target value for input cost is calculated so as to make them efficient. Himachal Pradesh (HPSEB), Jammu & Kashmir (J & K SEB) and Puducherry (PCL) display the best performance. This efficiency measurement assists the companies by identifying their shortcomings, setting targets and trying to achieve the set targets.

6. References

[1] K. Sarica and I. Or, "Efficiency Assessment of Turkish Power Plants Using Data Envelopment Analysis," *Energy policy*, Vol. 32, 2007, pp. 1484-1499.

[2] A. Charnes, W. W. Cooper and E. Rhodes, "Measuring the Efficiency of Decision Making Units," *European journal of operational research*, Vol. 2, No. 6, 1978, pp 429-444.

[3] B. Golany, Y. Roll and D. Rybak, "Measuring efficiency of power Plants in Israel by data envelopment analysis," *IEEE transactions on engineering management*, Vol. 41, No. 3, 1994, pp. 291-301.

[4] K. P. Kannan and N. V. Pillai, "Plight of the power sector in India: SEBs and their saga of inefficiency", Centre for development studies, Thiruvananthapuram, working paper, No. 308, 2000.

[5] V. K. Yadav, N. P. Padhy and H. O. Gupta, "Assessing the performance of electric utilities of developing countries: An inter country comparison using DEA," *Power and energy general meeting*, No. 308, November 2000, pp. 1-87.

[6] Ministry of power website. www.powermin nic in

[7] T. Thakur, "Benchmarking Study for the Indian Electric utilities Data Envelopment Analysis," *IEEE Transactions on Power Systems*, 2005, pp. 545-549.

[8] D. K. Jha and R. Shrestha, "Measuring Efficiency of Hydropower Plants in Nepal Using Data Envelopment Analysis," *IEEE Transactions on Power Systems*, Vol. 21, No. 4, November 2006, pp. 1502-1511.

[9] M. Saleem, "Technical efficiency in electricity sector of Pakistan-The impact of private and public ownership," 2007. www.pide.org.pk

[10] T. Thakur, S. G. Deshmukh, S. C. Kaushik and M. Kulshrestha, "Impact Assessment of the Electricity Act 2003 on the Indian Power Sector," *Energy Policy*, Vol.

33, No. 9, 2005, pp. 1187-1198.

[11] T. Coelli, D. S. P. Rao and G. E. Battese, "An introduction to efficiency and productivity analysis,"

[12] R. F. Lovado, "Benchmarking the efficiency of Philippines electric cooperatives using stochastic frontier analysis and data envelopment analysis," *Third east west center international graduate student conference*, Hawaii, 2004.

[13] T. Thakur, S. G. Deshmukh, S. C. Kaushik and M. Kulshrestha, "Impact Assessment of the Electricity Act 2003 on the Indian Power Sector," *Energy Policy*, Vol. 33, No. 9, 2005, pp. 1187-1198.

[14] W. W. Cooper and K. Tone, "Measures of Inefficiency in Data Envelopment Analysis and Stochastic Frontier Estimation," *European Journal of Operational Research*, Vol. 99, 1997, pp. 72-88.

[15] D. K. Jha, N. Yorino and Y. Zoka, "A Modified DEA Model for Benchmarking of Hydropower Plants," *Power Technology*, July 2007, pp. 1374-1379.

[16] A. Vaninsky, "Efficiency of electric power generation in the United States: Analysis and Forecast Based on Data Envelopment Analysis," *Energy Economics*, Vol. 28, 2006, pp. 326-338.

[17] R. Meenakumari and N. Kamraj, "Measurement of Relative Efficiency of State Owned Electric Utilities in India Using Data Envelopment analysis," *Modern Applied Science*, Vol. 2, No. 5, September 2008, pp 61-71.

[18] CEA, "All India Electricity Statistics, General Review 2009," *Central Electricity Authority*, New Delhi, India, 2009, pp. 1-235.

[19] "Report on the Performance of the State Power Utilities for the years 2005-06 to 2007-08," Power Finance Corporation Ltd, New Delhi.

[20] M. Abbott, "The Productivity and Efficiency of the Australian Electricity Supply Industry," *Energy Economics*, Vol. 28, 2006, pp. 444-338.

[21] A. Pahwa, X. Feng and D. Lubkeman, "Performance Evaluation of Electric Distribution Utilities Based on Data Envelopment Analysis," *IEEE Transactions on Power Systems*, Vol. 18, No. 1, February 2003, pp. 400-405.

[22] P. Chitkara, "A Data Envelopment analysis Approach to Evaluation of Operational Inefficiencies in Power Generating Units: A Case Study of Indian Power Plants," *IEEE Transactions on Power Systems*, Vol. 14, No. 2, May 1999, pp. 419-425.

19

Do Regional Investment Grants Improve Firm Performance? Evidence from Sweden

Mattias Ankarhem[1], Sven-Olov Daunfeldt[2,4], Shahiduzzaman Quoreshi[3], Niklas Rudholm[4,5]

[1]*Ministry of Finance, Stockholm, Sweden*
[2]*The Ratio Institute, Stockholm, Sweden*
[3]*University of Bergen, Bergen, Norway*
[4]*Dalarna University, Borlänge, Sweden*
[5]*The Swedish Retail Institute, Stockholm, Sweden*

Abstract

The effect of Swedish regional investment grants during 1990-1999 on firm performance, in terms of returns on equity and number of employees, were studied using a propensity-score matching-method to control for sample selection. Firms that received grants did not perform better in terms of returns on equity when compared to matched firms in the control group. In most years, recipient firms also did not hire more employees. The results thus cast doubt on the use of regional investment grants as a general policy instrument to improve firm performance.

Keywords: Economic Efficiency, Propensity Score Matching, Sample Selection, Logit Regression, Panel Data

1. Introduction

Regional investment grants (RIG) distributed directly to firms are common in most industrialized countries around the world. Their goals are different, sometimes being focused on promoting economic growth in the region, other times more oriented towards alleviating the impact of structural changes in the economy. In either case, their existence is based on the assumption that they improve performance of the firms to which they are directed.

A few empirical studies have investigated whether RIG actually influence firm performance. Wren [1] found that Regional Selective Assistance (RSA) in the UK had been successful in promoting new jobs, and thus supporting its expansion. Harris [2] found that Selective Financial Assistance (SFA) in Northern Ireland contributed to more jobs and investments in the region, while Harris and Trainor [3] found that total factor productivity would have been 7-10% lower if the Northern Ireland firms had not received SFA. Harris and Trainor [4] also found that SFA reduced the probability of plant closure by 15-24%. More supportive evidence was presented by [5], who found that Greek capital subsidies targeted at food and beverage manufacturing firms contributed to higher total factor productivity.

On the other hand, Harris and Robinson [6] found that RSA in the UK had no effect on productivity when targeted plants where compared to other plants within the assisted area. Similarly, Bergström [7] found no effect of capital subsidies on total factor productivity in Sweden, while Lee [8] found that industrial targeting in Korea actually lowered total factor productivity of the targeted firms. Thus, the evidence on whether RIG improve firm performance is mixed and inconclusive.

The purpose of this paper is to study whether regional investment grants to firms in Sweden during 1990-1999 had a positive impact on firm performance, indicated by more employees and higher returns on equity. If RIG were successful, we expect that firms receiving grants will have raised employment and returns more than has a control group of firms with similar characteristics.

The analysis is based on comprehensive panel-data set covering all limited firms in Sweden during the study period. From this dataset a sub-sample of firms from the two support areas were selected, thus guaranteeing that firms receiving the grant were not compared to firms from other parts of Sweden. There were considerable differences, on average, between firms that received RIG and the other firms, differences that were controlled for in the analysis using a propensity-score matching-method developed by [9]. Propensity-score matching makes it possible to compare firms that had or had not received RIG but are similar in all other relevant aspects. To our knowledge this method has not been previously applied to RIG.

We find that firms receiving RIG did not have better development of returns on equity than others that did not receive grants. In addition, in most cases, RIG did not influence employment either. The exceptions were in 1994 and 1995, during the last years of the 1990 recession. Thus, our results cast doubt on the general efficiency of RIG in promoting firm performance.

The next section describes the RIG in Sweden, while Section 3 presents the data and the method of propensity-score matching as well as discussing the difference-in-difference estimation procedure. Results are then presented and discussed in Section 4, while Section 5 details our conclusions.

2. Regional Grants in Sweden

In Sweden, regional investment grants directly to firms go back to the 1960s, when firms were given grants if they made new investments in outlying regions with free capacity. RIG became even more common during the 1970s and more oriented towards reducing distributional differences across regions. However, from 1990 onwards, grants have been targeted more towards promoting economic growth. Grants are limited to firms that have a market outside their own county or that face competition from outside the county. Firms are not given grants that it is believed might undermine local competition.

In order to receive RIG, the firm must apply in writing to the County Administration Board (Länsstyrelsen) or the Swedish Agency for Economic and Regional Growth (NUTEK), including a business plan and a description of the expected results. A processing officer decides whether the application is entitled of receiving support, taking into account the economic situation of the firm. For example, firms with lower probability of receiving financial support from commercial banks are more likely to receive grants so that high-risk projects are overrepresented. It is also evaluated whether the firm can expand and survive in the future, and any complaints to the Swedish Enforcement Authority (Kronofogden) are taken into account. Small firms and investments expected to increase integration and equality in society are also given priority.

Grants can be given for investment in machinery, buildings, inventory, patents, and licenses. In exceptional cases, grants can also be given for investment in education, consulting, participating in conferences, and research and development. Depending on the region, grants can cover at most 20-30% of the total investment cost.

RIG constitute the largest regional policy-instrument directed towards promoting firm performance in Sweden. Thus, this paper focuses on them, and excludes other grants from the empirical analysis. However, during the study period there were a number of other regional grants in Sweden, e.g., countryside-support grants, employment grants, transportation grants, and small-firm investment grants, which will also be described briefly.

Countryside-support grants, also issued by the County Administrative Board (Länsstyrelserna), aimed to contribute to sustainable rural growth in rural areas in Sweden by ensuring a minimum of commercial services. Municipalities, retail stores, and gas stations were typical recipients.

To promote growth and create new rural employment opportunities, there were two types of employment grants given to firms when they recruited new employees, or when they entered new local markets—again issued by the County Administrative Board (Länsstyrelserna), or the Swedish Agency for Economic and Regional Growth (NUTEK), or the Swedish national government itself.

Transportation grants were also available to manufacturing firms in the four most northern municipalities in Sweden to compensate them for higher transportation costs. Finally, small-firm investment grants (SFG) were available to firms with less than 50 employees but yearly revenues of more than seven million Euro.

3. Empirical Method

3.1. Data

In order to study whether regional investment grants for firms have any impact on firm performance, we need both firm-specific and region-specific data at municipality level. Firm-specific data was obtained from MM-Partner, a Swedish firm that collects economic information on firms in Sweden. The data used here is from a dataset covering the annual reports of all limited firms that were tax-based in a specific municipality and active in the market during 1990-2000[1]. The annual reports were originally submitted, as required by the law, to the Swedish patent and registration office (PRV). The dataset includes, among other items, measures of profit, number of employees, salaries, fixed costs, and liquidity. In order to include only active firms in the empirical analysis, the sample was restricted to firms with documented sales during the study period.

Municipality-specific data, including demographic measures, average income, political preferences, educational level, and unemployment, were provided by Statistics Sweden (SCB). Due to the division of some munici-

---

[1]This means that different types of limited companies are included in the dataset, e.g., both private and public companies. It is, however, unlikely that private companies will be matched with public companies when propensity score matching is used.

palities into smaller units during the study period, as well as the merger of three counties, 56 municipalities were omitted from the study, leaving 233.

Data concerning which firms received RIG during the study period was supplied by the Swedish Agency for Economic and Regional Growth (NUTEK). All data used, irrespective of original source, was collected and provided to the authors by the Swedish Institute for Growth Policy Studies (ITPS). The results have also been presented (in Swedish) previously in [10].

3.2. Propensity Score Matching

To test the effects of RIG on firm performance, we estimated the average effect on: 1) the number of employees, and 2) the return on equity[2]. The "treatment group" consists of firms that received RIG during the study period. Propensity-score matching was used to match "untreated" observations with "treated observations" if they had a similar probability, based on firm characteristics, of being treated (*i.e.*, receiving a grant).

To take account of time-invariant unobservable heterogeneity, a difference-in-difference propensity score matching-method was used. Thus, instead of studying numbers of employees and returns on equity directly, we focused on changes in those variables. If RIG were effective in promoting firm performance, we expect that firms receiving grants will have developed better after receiving grants than similar firms that did not receive grants. This method makes it possible to get an unbiased estimate of the treatment effect even if there were unobservable differences between firms that received RIG and other firms, as long as the differences were time-invariant.

Matching methods differ by how much weight is placed on the control observations. Nearest-neighbor matching was used here, putting all weight on the control (non-treated) observation with the most similar propensity score. This reduces bias, since only the best matches are used, but could lead to increased variance, compared to matching methods which use more control observations. We imposed a common support condition of-maximum 0.00001 allowed distance between the propensity-score of the treated and the control. Treated observations for which no matches could be found within this distance were excluded.

The final dataset contains 362,258 observations, of which 3,015 are from firms that received RIG. **Table 1** reports means and standard deviations for the variables included in the analysis for the treatment groups, control group, and all firms. On average, firms that received RIG differed substantially from other firms, with more employees and higher returns on equity. As mentioned, this

sample selection was controlled for by using propensity-score matching.

The first step in estimating the effects of RIG was thus to estimate propensity scores relating to the probability of belonging to the treatment group. Among a general set of models, the final specification was chosen using the Akaike consistent information criterion. As such, propensity scores were calculated using logit estimation of the equation

$$RIG_{ikt} = \alpha_j + \alpha_t + \beta_1 * Return_{ikt-1} + \beta_2 * GDPContr_{ikt-1} + \beta_3 * Employed_{ikt-1} + \beta_4 * Investments_{ikt-1} + \beta_5 * More_{ikt-1} + \beta_6 * Other_{ikt-1} + \beta_7 * Non\text{-}conservative_{kt-1} + \beta_8 * Political\ strength_{kt-1} + \beta_9 * Same_{kt-1} + \beta_{10} * University_{kt-1} + \beta_{11} * Unemployment_{kt-1} + \beta_{12} * Income_{kt-1} + \beta_{13} * Migration_{kt-1} + \beta_{14} * (Unemployment_{kt-1} * Income_{kt-1}) + \beta_{15} * (Migration_{kt-1} * Income_{kt-1}) + \beta_{16} * (dRegion_{ikt} * Income_{kt-1}) + \beta_{17} * (dRegion_{ikt} * Unemployment_{kt-1}) + \varepsilon_{ikt}, \qquad (1)$$

where α_j and α_t are region-specific and time-specific fixed effects; $Return_{ikt-1}$ is the return on equity of firm i in municipality k in the previous year; $GDPContr_{ikt-1}$ is the direct contribution of the firm to GDP; $Employed_{ikt-1}$ is the number of employees of the firm; and $Investments_{ikt-1}$ is the size of the firm's investments. $More_{ikt}$ is then an indicator variable equal to one if the firm had more than one regional investment grant, and $Other_{ikt}$ is an indicator variable equal to one if the firm also received other types of regional grants (such as employment grants or transportation grants etc., described in Section 2).

Municipality-specific information was next included in the model: $Non\text{-}conservative_{kt}$ is an indicator variable equal to one if the municipality had a left-wing majority; $Political\ strength_{kt}$ is a Herfindahl-index relating to the number of seats each party had in the local county council; and $Same_{kt}$ is an indicator variable equal to one if the political majority was the same in the municipality as at the national level. $University_{kt}$ is an indicator variable equal to one if the municipality had a university or university college; $Unemployment_{kt}$ is the share of the municipal population unemployed; $Income_{kt}$ measures average income in the municipality; and $Migration_{kt}$ measures the in- or outflow of people as a share of the municipal population.

Finally, since it is likely that there are interactions among some of the variables, the model also contains interaction-terms for $Unemployment_{kt} * Income_{kt}$, $Migration_{kt} * Income_{kt}$, $dRegion_{ikt} * Income_{kt}$, and $dRegion_{ikt} * Unemployment_{kt}$.

The results from logit estimation of (1) are presented in **Table 2**, where the region- and time-specific fixed effects, and the interactions including the region-specific fixed effects, have been excluded to save space.

---

[2]Note that the choice of output variable (e.g., employment and returns on equity) can be challenged since they are subjective indicators.

Table 1. Descriptive statistics.

	Treatment		Control		All firms	
Variable	Mean	Std. dev.	Mean	Std. dev.	Mean	Std. dev.
$Return_{ikt-1}$	0.02	0.46	0.01	13.01	0.01	13.00
$GDPCont_{ikt-1}$	10876209.00	79843067.00	3504655.80	388876425.77	3516557.30	388575726.87
$Employed_{ikt-1}$	44.63	341.91	9.96	130.19	10.01	130.81
$Investments_{ikt-1}$	1687410.00	66121978.00	869392.30	366237368.10	870630.70	365969084.53
$More_{ikt-1}$	0.10	0.31	0.00	0.00	0.00	0.01
$Other_{ikt-1}$	0.53	0.50	0.00	0.00	0.00	0.03
$Socialist_{kt-1}$	0.77	0.40	0.56	0.47	0.56	0.47
$Political\ strength_{kt-1}$	0.30	0.05	0.27	0.05	0.27	0.05
$Same_{kt-1}$	0.53	0.49	0.49	0.48	0.49	0.48
$University_{kt-1}$	0.24	0.40	0.54	0.47	0.54	0.47
$Unemployment_{kt-1}$	4.17	1.76	3.96	4.28	3.96	4.28
$Income_{kt-1}$	133476.00	16724.33	151650.50	23580.75	151621.20	23582.58
$Migration_{kt-1}$	0.62	0.47	0.29	0.43	0.29	0.43
$Unemployment_{kt-1} * Income_{kt-1}$	226435.70	93554.72	234527.50	237196.36	234514.00	237034.83
$Migration_{kt-1} * Income_{kt-1}$	34250.70	25612.36	17079.80	25606.13	17107.50	25615.41

Table 2. Estimation results, probability of receiving regional investment grants, 1990-2000.

Variable	Est.	St.err
$Return_{ikt-1}$	1.84E-04	6.27E-04
$GDPCont_{ikt-1}$	9.01E-09	2.23E-09***
$Employed_{ikt-1}$	2.29E-04	2.70E-05***
$Investments_{ikt-1}$	−1.90E-08	9.86E-09*
$More_{ikt-1}$	6.79	0.91***
$Other_{ikt-1}$	8.93	0.15***
$Socialist_{kt-1}$	0.22	0.15
$Political\ strength_{kt-1}$	3.83	0.87***
$Same_{kt-1}$	−0.54	0.18***
$University_{kt-1}$	−0.82	0.09***
$Unemployment_{kt-1}$	0.07	0.28
$Income_{kt-1}$	−0.04	0.02***
$Migration_{kt-1}$	−0.82	0.59
$Unemployment_{kt-1} * Income_{kt-1}$	2.30E-03	4.31E-03
$Migration_{kt-1} * Income_{kt-1}$	0.03	0.01**
Pseudo R^2	0.58	

* Statistically significant at the 10% level; ** Statistically significant at the 5% level; *** Statistically significant at the 1% level.

Firms with higher direct contribution to GDP and more employees had a higher probability of receiving a grant, as did those that had previously received either a regional investment grant or some other form of government grant. In addition, low investment in period t-1 increased the probability of receiving a grant. RIG were also more common in municipalities with strong political leadership (as measured by the Herfindahl index), no university or university college, and low average income.

The next step involved finding the best possible match

in the control group for each "treated" firm, and comparing outcomes. It seems reasonable to believe, however, that RIG effects are not constant over time. We therefore divided the data into yearly sub-periods to test this possibility. Thus the logit equation used to find matches was also estimated for each year (results left out in order to save space).

3.3. Difference-in-Difference Estimates

There is also a question of the timing of grant effects, since some investments might take some time to complete, and effects on employment or returns on equity might not show up for even longer. Difference-in-difference estimates were thus calculated over one, three, and five years after the grant year.

Finally, there could also be a so-called threshold effect, if grants need to reach a certain size before having any measurable effect on employment or returns. Thus the analysis was also performed using only grants exceeding one hundred thousand SEK or exceeding one million SEK.

4. Regional Investment Grants and Firm Performance

Yearly and overall difference-in-difference estimates of the effects of RIG on employment are presented (**Table 3**) for one-, three-, and five-year periods and for grants exceeding SEK 100,000 or SEK 1,000,000.

In most of the estimated models, no statistically significant effect on employment was found, indicating that, in general, recipient firms did not increase their number of employees more than similar firms that did not receive

Table 3. Difference-in-difference estimates, number of employees.

Effect in	1 year		3 years		5 years	
Year	Est.	St. err.	Est.	St. err.	Est.	St. err.
RIG						
1990-1999	1.86	2.63	5.4	8.81	9.27	13.06
1990	0.79	11.61	−23.77	25.06	−26.52	49.25
1991	6.46	4.46	0.11	5.95	14.45	10.69
1992	−2.15	1.80	−1.60	4.87	−10.16	10.72
1993	100.76	108.12	18.39	10.71*	98.79	64.17
1994	2.07	2.83	14.73	8.22*	20.50	11.13*
1995	3.14	1.60*	8.22	7.04	10.22	8.47
1996	0.18	22.92	3.56	14.77		
1997	14.98	10.74	103.25	107.59		
1998	−26.41	30.16				
1999	3.38	6.50				
Exceeding 100,000						
1990-1999	2.65	2.26	5.76	8.58	10.70	16.39
1990	2.96	15.57	−18.67	22.99	−24.68	23.86
1991	3.26	3.67	2.97	6.09	15.78	12.53
1992	0.20	0.90	2.93	1.92	2.11	11.88
1993	4.43	4.07	21.65	26.79	106.47	69.76
1994	5.18	2.73*	20.98	10.80*	30.07	13.50*
1995	2.17	1.81	2.51	5.80	2.67	9.54
1996	0.81	2.72	4.86	15.48		
1997	0.05	9.03	68.44	107.94		
1998	−29.44	29.99				
1999	1.65	4.27				
Exceeding 1,000,000						
1990-1999	7.33	6.94	19.31	33.78	26.65	41.78
1990	−1.41	26.48	−42.99	54.16	−47.86	73.71
1991	6.76	11.56	12.17	27.36	57.61	45.71
1992	2.14	3.66	9.38	4.80*	6.63	6.19
1993	13.42	6.15*	48.41	27.94*	403.76	335.81
1994	−2.30	18.07	78.94	73.73	107.15	101.23
1995	−2.05	5.95	13.00	19.74	-0.94	27.00
1996	1.85	5.13	6.48	9.84		
1997	24.41	27.80	228.96	273.05		
1998	−53.46	58.27				
1999	−0.14	6.13				

* Statistically significant at the 10 percent significance level. Standard errors are calculated by bootstrapping.

a grant. Hence, RIG do not seem to have been very successful in increasing employment during the study period.

However, there are a few exceptions. For grant of any size, there are positive and statistically significant effects after three years for 1993 and 1994 recipients; after 5 years for 1994 recipients; and after one year for 1995 recipients. Recipients in 1993, on average, employed 18 persons more during 1993-1996 than did firms not receiving a grant, and 15 persons more during 1994-1997. Recipients in 1994, on average, employed 20 more during 1994-1999 than did firms not receiving a grant. Recipients in 1995 also employed slightly more than others during that year. All these statistically significant results were in 1993 to 1995, i.e. during the end of the Swedish recession of the early 1990s, and this pattern holds for larger grants as well.

Recipients of over one hundred thousand SEK in 1994, on average, employed 5 more during that year, 21 more during 1994-1997, and 30 more during 1994-1999. Recipients of more than one million SEK in 1992 employed 9 more during 1992-1995, while recipients in 1993 employed 13 more during that year and 48 more during 1993-1996.

Similar estimates of effects on returns are presented in **Table 4**.

No statistically significant effects were found. Thus, recipient firms did not seem to perform better in terms of returns on equity than similar firms that did not receive a grant.

Table 4. Difference-in-difference estimates, the return on equity.

Effect in	1 year		3 years		5 years	
Year	Est.	St. err.	Est.	St. err.	Est.	St. err.
RIG						
1990-1999	−0.06	0.19	0.09	0.25	0.00	0.16
1990	−0.84	0.89	−0.02	0.11	0.01	0.02
1991	0.01	0.02	−1.49	1.19	−0.10	0.32
1992	0.00	0.04	−0.28	0.18	−0.23	0.25
1993	0.37	0.73	0.03	0.56	0.01	0.44
1994	0.14	0.45	−0.47	0.36	−0.02	0.08
1995	−0.10	0.13	0.05	0.07	0.05	0.08
1996	0.00	0.02	−0.02	0.04		
1997	−13.75	12.39	0.05	0.08		
1998	−0.01	0.10				
1999	−0.07	0.04				
Exceeding 100,000						
1990-1999	−0.12	0.18	−0.17	0.17	−0.04	0.05
1990	−0.44	0.88	−0.01	0.09	−0.02	0.02
1991	0.05	0.10	−1.41	1.45	0.05	0.30
1992	−0.03	0.10	0.04	0.06	−0.01	0.05
1993	1.46	1.81	0.14	0.40	0.02	0.06
1994	−0.06	0.19	−0.11	0.64	0.02	0.03
1995	−0.04	0.81	0.01	0.06	0.02	0.08
1996	0.00	0.39	−0.07	0.05		
1997	0.03	1.06	0.00	0.03		
1998	−0.12	0.11				
1999	1.33	2.04				
Exceeding 100,000						
1990-1999	−0.63	0.49	−0.47	0.42	0.09	0.12
1990	−2.67	1.60	0.00	0.27	−0.02	0.03
1991	0.05	0.07	0.07	0.08	0.02	0.07
1992	−0.01	0.04	0.03	0.25	0.02	0.16
1993	−0.03	0.06	0.05	0.15	0.06	0.09
1994	−0.55	0.33	−0.38	0.40	0.02	0.08
1995	−0.64	0.74	0.08	0.08	0.10	0.13
1996	0.02	0.03	0.00	0.05		
1997	0.15	1.92	−0.07	0.10		
1998	−0.07	0.14				
1999	−0.05	0.07				

* Statistically significant at the 10 percent significance level. Standard errors are calculated using bootstrapping.

5. Conclusions

The aim of this paper has been to study whether regional investment grants targeted towards firms affect employment or owners' returns on equity. To control for sample selection, we used propensity-score matching, whereby firms that received grants were compared to otherwise similar firms that received no grants during the study period.

Regional investment grants did not seem to have any impact on firm performance. Firms that received grants did not perform better in terms of returns on equity when compared to matched firms in the control group. In most years, recipient firms also did not hire more employees, and we thus conclude that, in general, RIG do not affect employment. The few exceptions during 1993-1995, were during the recovery from the early 1990s recession.

The results thus cast doubt on the use of regional investment grants as a general policy instrument to improve firm performance. An issue for future research is whether other types of regional grants may have been more successful, and whether the results are applicable to other outcome variables such as revenue growth, innovation, market capitalization, and the survival rate.

6. Acknowledgements

We would like to thank the Swedish Institute for Growth Policy Studies (ITPS) for supplying the data used in this study. We also thank participants at a seminar at the Ratio Institute for valuable comments and suggestions.

7. References

[1] C. Wren, "Regional Grants. Are They Worth it?" *Fiscal Studies*, Vol. 26, No. 2, 2005, pp. 245-275.

[2] R. Harris, "Regional Economic Policy in Northern Ireland 1945-1988," Avebury, Aldershot, 1991.

[3] R. Harris and M. Trainor, "Capital Subsidies and their Impact on Total Factor Productivity: Firm-Level Evidence from Northern Ireland," *Journal of Regional Science*, Vol. 45, No. 1, 2005, pp. 49-74.

[4] R. Harris and M. Trainor, "Impact of Government Intervention on Employment Change and Plant Closure in Northern Ireland, 1983-97," *Regional Studies*, Vol. 41, No. 1, 2007, pp. 51-63.

[5] D. Skuras, K. Tsekouras, E. Dimara and D. Tzelepis, "The Effects of Regional Capital Subsidies on Productivity Growth: A Case Study of the Greek Food and Beverage Manufacturing Industry," *Journal of Regional Science*, Vol. 46, No. 2, 2006, pp. 355-381.

[6] R. Harris and C. Robinson, "Industrial Policy in Great Britain and its Effect on Total Factor Productivity in Manufacturing Plants, 1990-1998," *Scottish Journal of Political Economy*, Vol. 51, No. 4, 2004, pp. 528-543.

[7] F. Bergström, "Capital Subsidies and the Performance of Firms," *Small Business Economics*, Vol. 14, No. 3, 2000, pp. 183-193.

[8] J.-W. Lee, "Government Interventions and Productivity Growth," *Journal of Economic Growth*, Vol. 1, No. 3, 1996, pp. 391-414.

[9] P. Rosenbaum and D. Rubin, "The Central Role of the Propensity Score in Observational Studies for Causal Effects," *Biometrica*, Vol. 70, No. 1, 1991, pp. 41-55.

[10] M. Ankarhem, N. Rudholm and S. Quoreshi, "Effektutvärdering av det regional utvecklingsbidraget: En studie av effekter på svenska aktiebolag," Rapport A2007:26, Institutet för Tillväxtpolitiska Studier (ITPS), Sweden, 2007.

20

An Application of Fuzzy Set Theory to the Weighted Average Cost of Capital and Capital Structure Decision

Shin-Yun Wang[1], Chih-Chiang Hwang[1,2]
[1]*Department of Finance, National Dong Hwa University, Taiwan, China*
[2]*Department of Health Business Administration, Tajen University, Taiwan, China*

Abstract

The purpose of this paper is to present the use of fuzzy logic to improve the calculation of weighted average cost of capital (WACC). The fuzzy WACC approach not only allows the pre-tax cost of debt, the effective tax rate, the tax benefit, and cost of equity to be treated as fuzzy numbers, it also offers ranking means to find the optimal debt ratio. This paper contributes to the literature by offering alternative methods to calculate the WACC and the optimal debt ratio for firms under uncertainty. Compared with the traditional WACC, the fuzzy WACC model can overcome the problems pertinent to uncertainty, complexity and imprecision. This paper thus sheds light on capital structure decision making.

Keywords: WACC, Capital Structure, Fuzzy Numbers, Capital Structure, Fuzzy Logic

1. Introduction

Sharpe [1] and Lintner [2] brought the theory of the capital asset pricing model (CAPM), which offers a very intuitive and straightforward method to gauge the cost of equity. Four decades later, the CAPM still remains the predominant model to estimate the cost of equity as shown in numerous surveys of corporate practice (Bruner et al. [3]; Bierman [4]; Gitman and Vandenberg [5]; Graham and Harvey [6]; Arnold and Hatzopoulos [7]; McLaney, Pointon, Thomas and Tucker [8]; and Brounen, De Jong and Koedijk [9]); however, a series of influential papers, based on the failure of the CAPM in empirical tests, have doubted the performance of CAPM (Chopra, Lakonishok and Ritter [10]; Fama and French [11]; Davis [12]; Barber and Lyon [13]; and Roll [14]), and argued that beta is not favorable in explaining the cross-section of stock returns. In response, several studies (Black [15]; Kothari et al. [16]; and Sharpe [17]) persisted that the CAPM is still the best model for estimating the cost of equity and all the empirical results conflicting with the CAPM are due to selection bias or the mis-measurement of beta. As the ongoing debate among researchers continues, the WACC remains a hot topic in the finance literature. Generally, multifactor models are regarded as alternatives to the CAPM for estimating the cost of equity.

The aforementioned studies have stimulated the development of asset pricing models, but both CAPM and multifactor models offer practitioners only a single rate cost of equity, which is always uncertain because the cost of equity varies over time or with market conditions in the real world, and its considerable ambiguity may mislead us to one set of optimal debt ratio calculations. So Lister [18] advocates management should cease their expensive search for the cost of equity. Furthermore, much of the evidence also implies that the cost of debt is uncertain. For example, Lund [19] has pointed out that much of the literature on the relationship between the cost of debt and taxation neglects uncertainty. Mayer [20] uses a dynamic programming model to examine the cost of debt, indicating that the current taxable earnings of the firm are highly volatile and uncertain, Graham and Harvey [6] demonstrates that the effective tax rate varies with non-debt tax shields, such as depreciation, investment tax, carry-forwards of past operating losses, and the like.

Owing to uncertainty with respect to the cost of capital, we argue that a reasonable range of the cost of capital estimates is indispensable, and then we use it in the optimal debt ratio calculations. Bruner et al. [3] conclude that best-practice companies may not give a precise number about WACC but can estimate them with an accuracy of no more than plus or minus 100 to 150 basis points. In other words, the ranges of estimated WACC are consistent with a real world, and it embeds fuzzy characteristics. In such scenario, fuzzy set theory may help mitigate uncertainty, and to our best knowledge, there is no literature applying a fuzzy set theory to the WACC and capital structure.

In addition, traditional WACC employs the marginal tax rate and assumes a constant operating income as the debt ratio increases. In our model, we modify the tax rate to reflect the potential loss of the tax benefits of debt at higher debt ratios, where the interest expenses exceed the EBIT. The effective corporate tax rate can differ from the statutory corporate tax rate because taxable income can differ from economic income due to features of the tax system, such as accelerated depreciation, industry-specific concessions or non-compliance. As a result, the effective corporate tax rate can reflect the uncertainty of future cash flows and produce meaningful estimates of tax shield and cost of debt. For this reason, we adopt the effective tax rate rather than the marginal or statutory tax rate.

In this paper we present the use of fuzzy logic as a post-processing method to improve the calculation of the WACC. The purpose of this paper is to develop fuzzy weighted average cost of capital and fuzzy capital structure with firm value maximization in mind. The fuzzy WACC approach not only allows the pre-tax cost of debt, the effective tax rate, the tax benefit, and the cost of equity to be expressed as fuzzy numbers, but also offers ranking means to find the optimal debt ratio. These fuzzy numbers can better capture the uncertainty in the computation of the WACC. Finally, In order to rank the WACC at each level of debt for seeking a precise optimal capital structure, this paper adopts the latest method for ranking generalized trapezoidal fuzzy numbers by Chen *et al.* [21], which we will discuss in more details later in Subsection 2.4. Our results are consistent with the trade-off theory. Compared with the traditional WACC, the fuzzy WACC model overcomes issues regarding uncertainty, complexity, and imprecision. The rest of this paper is organized as follows: Section 2 introduces the fuzzy WACC model and the latest method for ranking generalized trapezoidal fuzzy numbers. Section 3 gives a numerical example to calculate the cost of capital using fuzzy WACC model and the optimal debt ratio. Conclusions are presented in Section 4.

2. The Fuzzy Weighted Average Cost of Capital Approach

2.1. Fuzzy Numbers

Cheng and Mon [22] describe fuzzy number A as a fuzzy

subset in support R (real number), which is both normal and convex, where $\text{supp}(\tilde{A}) = \{x \in R \mid \mu_{\tilde{A}} > 0\}$. Normality implies that the maximum value of the fuzzy set $\tilde{A}$ in R is 1. By contrast, the maximum value of non-normal fuzzy set in R is less than 1. The concept of generalized trapezoidal fuzzy numbers attempts to deal with real problems by possibility. For a trapezoidal fuzzy number $\tilde{A} = (a_1, a_2, a_3, a_4; 1)$ with the membership function, its membership function $f_{\tilde{A}}(x)$ is given by

$$f_{\tilde{A}} = \begin{cases} \dfrac{x - a_1}{a_2 - a_1}, & a_1 \leq x \leq a_2 \\ 1, & a_2 \leq x \leq a_3 \\ \dfrac{x - a_4}{a_3 - a_4}, & a_3 \leq x \leq a_4 \\ 0, & otherwise \end{cases}$$

2.2. Generalized Trapezoidal Fuzzy Numbers

According to the characteristics of generalized trapezoidal fuzzy numbers and their operations, **Figure 1** shows two different generalized trapezoidal fuzzy numbers $\tilde{A} = (a_1, a_2, a_3, a_4; w_{\tilde{A}})$ and $\tilde{B} = (b_1, b_2, b_3, b_4; w_{\tilde{B}})$, where $0 < w_{\tilde{A}} \leq 1$ and $0 < w_{\tilde{B}} \leq 1$; $w_{\tilde{A}}$ and $w_{\tilde{B}}$ denote the degree of confidence with respect to the decision-maker's opinions A and B, respectively. We present generalized trapezoidal fuzzy numbers arithmetical operations based on the extension principle. Let $\tilde{A}$ and $\tilde{B}$ be two generalized trapezoidal fuzzy numbers, where $\tilde{A} = (a_1, a_2, a_3, a_4; w_{\tilde{A}})$ and $\tilde{B} = (b_1, b_2, b_3, b_4; w_{\tilde{B}})$. The generalized trapezoidal fuzzy numbers arithmetic operations are as follows:

1) Generalized trapezoidal fuzzy numbers addition $\oplus$:

$$\tilde{A} \oplus \tilde{B} = (a_1, a_2, a_3, a_4; w_{\tilde{A}}) \oplus (b_1, b_2, b_3, b_4; w_{\tilde{B}})$$
$$= [a_1 + b_1, a_2 + b_2, a_3 + b_3, a_4 + b_4; \min(w_{\tilde{A}}, w_{\tilde{B}})]'$$

2) Generalized trapezoidal fuzzy numbers subtraction $\ominus$:

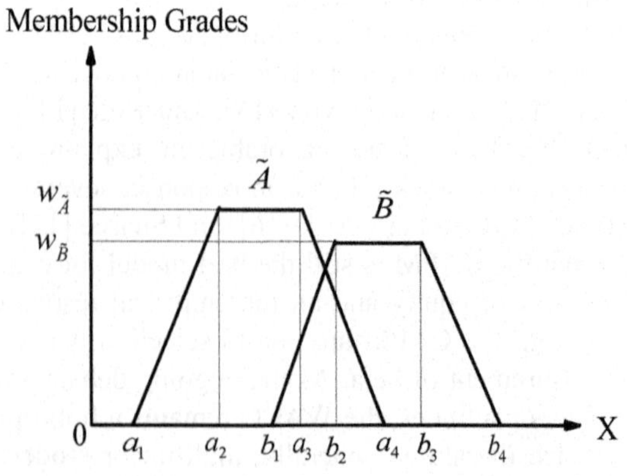

Figure 1. Generalized trapezoidal fuzzy number numbers $\tilde{A}$ and $\tilde{B}$.

$$\tilde{A} \ominus \tilde{B} = (a_1, a_2, a_3, a_4; w_{\tilde{A}}) \ominus (b_1, b_2, b_3, b_4; w_{\tilde{B}})$$

$$= \left[a_1 - b_4, a_2 - b_3, a_3 - b_2, a_4 - b_1; \min(w_{\tilde{A}}, w_{\tilde{B}}) \right],$$

3) Generalized trapezoidal fuzzy numbers multiplication $\otimes$:

$$\tilde{A} \otimes \tilde{B} = (a_1, a_2, a_3, a_4; w_{\tilde{A}}) \otimes (b_1, b_2, b_3, b_4; w_{\tilde{B}})$$

$$= \left[a_1 \times b_1, a_2 \times b_2, a_3 \times b_3, a_4 \times b_4; \min(w_{\tilde{A}}, w_{\tilde{B}}) \right],$$

4) Generalized trapezoidal fuzzy numbers division $\oslash$:

$$\tilde{A} \oslash \tilde{B} = (a_1, a_2, a_3, a_4; w_{\tilde{A}}) \oslash (b_1, b_2, b_3, b_4; w_{\tilde{B}})$$

$$= \left[a_1 / b_4, a_2 / b_3, a_3 / b_2, a_4 / b_1; \min(w_{\tilde{A}}, w_{\tilde{B}}) \right].$$

where $a_1, a_2, a_3, a_4,$ b_1, b_2, b_3 and b_4 are any real numbers.

2.3. A Fuzzy WACC Model

In this section, we use the theory of fuzzy logic to explain the WACC and capital structure decisions. When a company raises one additional dollar capital during a given time period, the costs of debt, preferred stock, and common equity begin to rise. As this happens, the marginal cost of capital (MCC) will vary according to the type of capital used. Thus, corporations cannot raise unlimited amounts of capital at a fixed cost. At some break point, the cost of each new dollar will become greater. **Figure 2** graphs the marginal cost of capital (MCC) schedule as well as the retained earnings break point. Each dollar has a weighted average cost of 9 percent until the company has raised a total of $256 million. However, if firm raises more than $256 million, the WACC jumps from 9 percent to 9.5 percent. This nu-

merical example illustrates only the concept of the increasing step function of the WACC given alternative sources of capital. The value used in each step of the WACC is by no means deterministic. In fact, WACC embeds fuzzy characteristics. This is because the decision of choosing capital structure and employing various sources of capital is fuzzy in nature. Therefore, we relate the WACC to the fuzzy logic theory and transform WACC to the fuzzy cost of capital. This can be explained in **Figure 3**, where fuzzy spaces exist in the triangle between b1 and a4, and between c1 and b4. These fuzzy spaces can be influenced by factors such as interest rates, exchange rates, the firm's bargaining ability, collateral, etc.

In general, these inputs cannot be characterized by a single number. But practitioners are able to estimate the WACC by using trapezoidal possibility distribution of the form

$$\text{FWACC} = \left[\text{fwacc}_1, \text{fwacc}_2, \text{fwacc}_3, \text{fwacc}_4 \right]$$

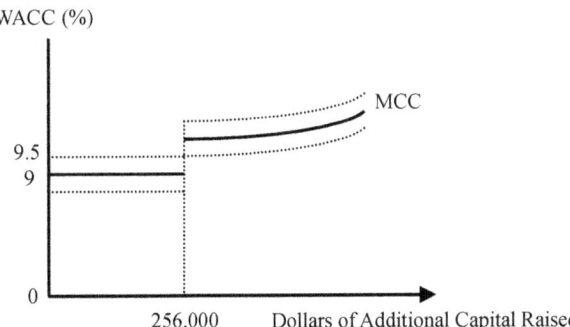

Figure 2. Marginal cost of capital schedule with the retained earnings break point.

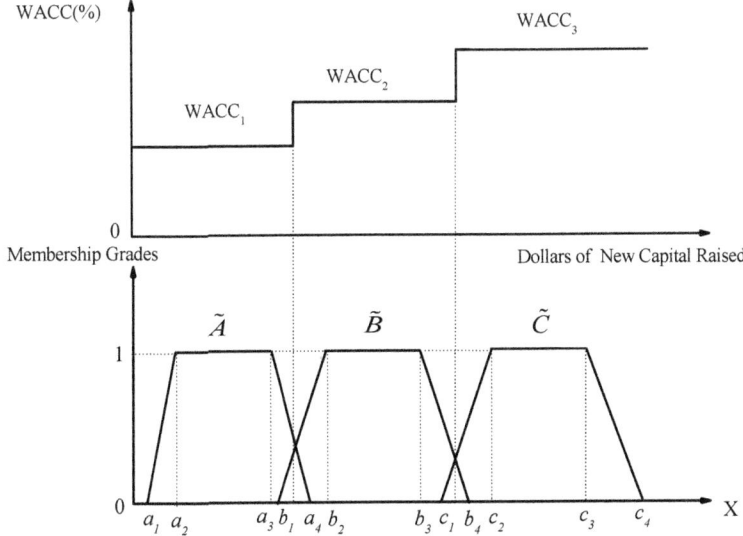

Figure 3. Combining the WACC with generalized trapezoidal fuzzy numbers.

That is, the most likely values of the WACC lie in the interval between $fwacc_2$ and $fwacc_3$ which are the core of the trapezoidal fuzzy number $FWACC$; while $fwacc_4$ is the greatest value and $fwacc_1$ is the smallest value for the WACC.

Accordingly, one can estimate the pre-tax cost of debt by using a trapezoidal possibility distribution of the form: $\tilde{K}_d = [K_{d1}, K_{d2}, K_{d3}, K_{d4}]$, i.e., the most possible values of the pre-tax cost of debt lie in the interval between K_{d2} and K_{d3} which are the core of the trapezoidal fuzzy number K_d; K_{d4} is the greatest value and K_{d1} is the smallest value for the pre-tax cost of debt .

As we have discussed earlier, we examine the approach for estimating the costs of debt, equity, and the appropriate weights to use in computing the cost of capital. To summarize, the cost of equity should reflect the risk of an equity investment and the cost of debt should reflect the default risk of the firm. The cost of debt should also reflect the effective tax rate, and the tax benefit associated with debt. Hence, we estimate these inputs by a trapezoidal possibility distribution of the form:

$$\tilde{K}_e = [K_{e1}, K_{e2}, K_{e3}, K_{e4}];$$
$$\tilde{t} = [t_1, t_2, t_3, t_4];$$
$$\tilde{K}_d * t = [K_{d1} \otimes t_1, K_{d2} \otimes t_2, K_{d3} \otimes t_3, K_{d4} \otimes t_4],$$

i.e., the most likely values of the cost of equity, the effective tax rate, and the tax benefit lie in the interval between K_{e2} and K_{e3}, t_2 and t_3, $K_{d2} \otimes t_2$ and $K_{d3} \otimes t_3$, respectively (which are the core of the trapezoidal fuzzy number $\tilde{K}_e$, $\tilde{t}$, and $\tilde{K}_d \otimes \tilde{t}$). K_{e4} is the greatest value and K_{e1} is the smallest value for the cost of equity; t_4 is the greatest value and t_1 is the smallest value for the effective tax rate; $K_{d4} \otimes t_4$ is the greatest value and $K_{d1} \otimes t_1$ is the smallest value for the tax benefit.

The information needed for the WACC is generally not known with certainty. The sources of uncertainty may be the pre-tax cost of debt, the cost of equity, the effective tax rate, the tax benefit, and the discount rate, etc. Under these circumstances we suggest the use of the following formula for computing the fuzzy WACC.

2.4. The Latest Ranking Method for Generalized Trapezoidal Fuzzy Numbers

From Cheng [23] and Chu [24], we can see that some methods have been proposed for ranking fuzzy numbers. Drawbacks exist in the existing ranking methods, i.e., they cannot correctly rank fuzzy numbers in some situations. Thus, in this paper, we adopt the latest method for ranking generalized trapezoidal fuzzy numbers. The latest method by Chen et al. [21] not only considers the centroid points, but also the standard deviations of generalized trapezoidal fuzzy numbers to deal with the fuzzy-number ranking problems.

Furthermore, the latest method also can rank more than two fuzzy numbers simultaneously. This method contains five steps described as follows:

Step 1.Standardized generalized trapezoidal fuzzy numbers

Assume that there are n generalized trapezoidal fuzzy number $\tilde{A}_1, \tilde{A}_2, ..., \tilde{A}_n$, where $\tilde{A}_j = (a_{1j}, a_{2j}, a_{3j}, a_{4j}; w_{\tilde{A}_j})$, $1 \le j \le n$, $0 < w_{\tilde{A}_j} \le 1$, $0 \le a_{1j} \le a_{2j} \le a_{3j} \le a_{4j} \le k$, and k is any real value; the value $w_{\tilde{A}_j}$ denotes the maximum membership value of the generalized trapezoidal fuzzy number $\tilde{A}_j$, where $1 \le j \le n$. For each generalized trapezoidal fuzzy number $\tilde{A}_j$, where $1 \le j \le n$, if the generalized trapezoidal fuzzy number $\tilde{A}_j$ is not a standardized generalized trapezoidal fuzzy number, where the universe of discourse of the generalized trapezoidal fuzzy number $\tilde{A}_j$ is $[0, k]$, then the generalized trapezoidal fuzzy number $\tilde{A}_j = (a_{1j}, a_{2j}, a_{3j}, a_{4j}; w_{\tilde{A}_j})$ can be translated into a standardized generalized trapezoidal fuzzy number $\tilde{A}_j$ shown as follows:

$$\tilde{A}_j^* = (\frac{a_{1j}}{k}, \frac{a_{2j}}{k}, \frac{a_{3j}}{k}, \frac{a_{4j}}{k}; w_{\tilde{A}_j^*})$$
$$= (a_{1j}^*, a_{2j}^*, a_{3j}^*, a_{4j}^*; w_{\tilde{A}_j^*}) \tag{2}$$

where $w_{\tilde{A}_j^*} = w_{\tilde{A}_j}$, $0 \le w_{\tilde{A}_j^*} \le 1$, $0 \le a_{1j}^* \le a_{2j}^* \le a_{3j}^* \le a_{4j}^* \le 1$, or $-1 \le a_{1j}^* \le a_{2j}^* \le a_{3j}^* \le a_{4j}^* \le 1$, and $1 \le j \le n$.

Step 2: Calculating the centroid point $(\hat{x}_{\tilde{A}_j^*}, \hat{y}_{\tilde{A}_j^*})$ of each standardized generalized trapezoidal fuzzy number

$$\hat{x}_{\tilde{A}} = \frac{\hat{y}_{\tilde{A}}(a_3 + a_2) + (a_4 + a_1)(w_{\tilde{A}} - \hat{y}_{\tilde{A}})}{2w_{\tilde{A}}} \tag{3}$$

$$\hat{y}_{\tilde{A}} = \begin{cases} \dfrac{w_{\tilde{A}} \times \left(\dfrac{a_3 - a_2}{a_4 - a_1} + 2 \right)}{6}, & if \quad a_1 \ne a_4 \ and \ 0 \le w_{\tilde{A}} \le 1 \\[4mm] \dfrac{w_{\tilde{A}}}{2}, & if \quad a_1 = a_4 \ and \ 0 \le w_{\tilde{A}} \le 1, \end{cases}$$

$$\tag{4}$$

$$FWACC(\tilde{K}_d, \tilde{K}_e, \tilde{t}, \tilde{K}_d \times \tilde{t}) = \frac{E}{E+D} \tilde{K}_e \oplus \frac{D}{E+D} \tilde{K}_d \otimes (1 \ominus \tilde{t}) = \frac{E}{E+D} \tilde{K}_e \oplus \frac{D}{E+D} \tilde{K}_d \ominus \frac{D}{E+D} (\tilde{K}_d \otimes \tilde{t})$$
$$= \frac{E}{E+D} (K_{e1}, K_{e2}, K_{e3}, K_{e4}) \oplus \frac{D}{E+D} (K_{d1}, K_{d2}, K_{d3}, K_{d4}) \ominus \frac{D}{E+D} (\tilde{K}_{d1} \otimes \tilde{t}_1, \tilde{K}_{d2} \otimes \tilde{t}_2, \tilde{K}_{d3} \otimes \tilde{t}_3, \tilde{K}_{d4} \otimes \tilde{t}_4)$$
$$= \frac{E}{E+D} (K_{e1}, K_{e2}, K_{e3}, K_{e4}) \oplus \frac{D}{E+D} [\tilde{K}_{d1} \ominus (\tilde{K}_{d4} \otimes \tilde{t}_4), \tilde{K}_{d2} \ominus (\tilde{K}_{d3} \otimes \tilde{t}_3), \tilde{K}_{d3} \ominus (\tilde{K}_{d2} \otimes \tilde{t}_2), \tilde{K}_{d4} \ominus (\tilde{K}_{d1} \otimes \tilde{t}_1)] \tag{1}$$

Step 3: Calculating the standard deviation, $s_{\tilde{A}_j^*}$ of each standardized generalized trapezoidal fuzzy number $\tilde{A}_j^*$ as follows:

$$s_{\tilde{A}_j^*} = \sqrt{\frac{\sum_{i=1}^{4}(a_{ij}^* - \overline{a}_j^*)^2}{3}} \qquad (5)$$

Step 4: Using the standard deviation $s_{\tilde{A}_j^*}$ and the value of the centroid point $(\hat{x}_{\tilde{A}_j^*}, \hat{y}_{\tilde{A}_j^*})$, $\hat{y}_{\tilde{A}_j^*}$, to derive a new value $\hat{y}_{\tilde{A}_j^*}^s$ shown as follows:

$$\hat{y}_{\tilde{A}_j^*}^s = \frac{w_{\tilde{A}_j^*}}{2} - \hat{y}_{\tilde{A}_j^*} \times s_{\tilde{A}_j^*} \qquad (6)$$

Step 5: Using the new point $(\hat{x}_{\tilde{A}_j^*}, \hat{y}_{\tilde{A}_j^*})$ to calculate the ranking value score of the standardized generalized trapezoidal fuzzy numbers $\tilde{A}_j^*$, where $1 \le j \le n$ as follows:

$$Score(\tilde{A}_j^*) = \sqrt{(\hat{x}_{\tilde{A}_j^*} - \min_{j=1,2,\dots,n}\left[\hat{x}_{\tilde{A}_j^*}\right])^2 + (\hat{y}_{\tilde{A}_j^*}^s)^2} \qquad (7)$$

3. Example

3.1. Fuzzy WACC

In this section, we present an example to calculate the cost of capital for Boeing using fuzzy weighted average cost of capital model, where the cost of equity, the cost of debt, the tax benefit, the effective tax rate, and the weighted average cost of capital are estimated by trapezoidal fuzzy numbers.

The inputs needed to estimate the WACC can be obtained from the annual report or other sources such as the COMPUSTAT database. We analyze the optimal capital structure for Boeing in 1999 using data from Damodaran [25]. **Table 1** is drawn from Damodaran, who calculated the cost of capital at each level of debt for Boeing. **Table 1** provides three basic inputs to compute the cost of capital —the cost of equity, the cost of debt, and the weights on debt and equity. In addition, it estimates Boeing's dollar amount of debt and interest expenses at each debt ratio, computes the interest coverage ratio that measures default risk to estimate a rating for Boeing, and then finds the rating that corresponds to that level of debt. According to Damodaran's approach, the interest expense is measured by circular reasoning. This process is reiterated for each level of debt from 10% to 90%, and the pre-tax costs of debt are achieved at each level of debt.

Now let's examine this computation in more details in **Table 1**. First, it presumes the EBIT at Boeing to be unaffected by the firm's financing decision. Second, it reflects the possible losses of the tax shields of debt at higher debt ratios by modifying the effective tax rate. To explain this point, it is important to note that the EBIT at Boeing is $1,751 million. Under the condition that inter-

est expenses are less than $1,751 million, interest expenses are fully tax deductible and earn the 35% tax benefit. For example, at a 30% debt ratio, the interest expenses are $857 million, and the tax shield is therefore 35% of this amount, and the effective tax rate is 35%. At a 60% debt ratio, however, the interest expenses rise to $2,692 million, which is greater than the EBIT of $1,751 million. At most the tax benefit on the interest expenses is $612.85 million ($1,751 million × 0.35). As the proportion of the tax benefit on the interest expenses to the total interest expenses is $612.85 million/$2,692 million, the effective tax rate is 27.76% instead of 35% on taxable income. As a matter of fact, the effective tax rate is typically a more accurate reflection of a company's tax liability than its marginal tax rate.

Based on the above-mentioned statements, the effective tax rates are unchanged and certain at the level of debt from 10% to 40%. That is, interest expenses remain fully tax deductible and earn the 35% tax benefit. But the effective tax rates are uncertain at the level of debt from 50% to 90%. Hence, only the effective tax rates at the level of debt from 50% to 90% are estimated by trapezoidal fuzzy numbers shown in **Table 2**.

Lund [19] has pointed out that much of the literature on the relationship between the cost of debt and taxation neglects uncertainty because the tax system is fiendishly complicated. Given its uncertainty and complexity, in **Table 2** we begin the illustration by computing fuzzy pre-tax cost of debt, fuzzy effective tax rate, and fuzzy tax benefit at each debt level using trapezoidal fuzzy numbers. As firms borrow more, their default risk will increase and so will the pre-tax cost of debt (Columns 1 and 2). On the other hand, the tax benefits from debt increase as the effective tax rate goes up (Columns 3 and 4).

According to a fuzzy WACC model in Subsection 2.3, we may compute fuzzy after-tax cost of debt, fuzzy cost of equity, and fuzzy WACC at each level of debt in **Table 3** using fuzzy pre-tax cost of debt, fuzzy effective tax rate, and fuzzy tax benefits obtained from **Table 2** and Equation (1).

For instance, at a 50% debt ratio in **Table 3**, fuzzy WACC (Column 4) is equal to 50% [11.18, 12.49, 13.81, 15.12] + 50% [8.5 − (11.5 × 0.35), 9.5 − (10.5 × 0.32), 10.5 − (9.5 × 0.29), 11.5 − (8.5 × 0.26)] = [7.85, 9.34, 10.80, 12.23].

3.2. Ranking Fuzzy WACC Numbers

For the purpose of calculating Boeing's optimal debt ratio, we adopt the latest method by Chen et al. [21] for ranking generalized trapezoidal fuzzy WACC numbers in **Table 4**.

Table 1. Cost of debt, debt ratios, and cost of equity for Boeing.

Debt Ratio	Debt	Interest Expense	Interest Coverage Ratio	Bond Rating	Pre-tax Cost of Debt (%)	Effective Tax Rate (%)	Cost of Equity (%)
0%	$0	$0	∞	AAA	5.2	35	9.79
10%	4,079	224	7.8	AA	5.5	35	10.14
20%	8,158	510	3.43	A-	6.25	35	10.57
30%	12,237	857	2.04	BB	7	35	11.13
40%	16,316	1,632	1.07	CCC	10	35	11.87
50%	20,394	2,039	0.86	CCC	10	30.05	13.15
60%	24,473	2,692	0.65	CC	11	22.76	15.35
70%	28,552	3,569	0.49	C	12.5	17.17	19.06
80%	32,631	4,079	0.43	C	12.5	15.02	26.09
90%	36,710	4,589	0.38	C	12.5	13.36	47.18

Table 2. Illustration of fuzzy pre-tax cost of debt, fuzzy effective tax rate, and fuzzy tax benefits.

Debt Ratio	Fuzzy Pre-tax Cost of Debt (%)	Fuzzy Effective Tax Rate	Fuzzy Tax Benefits (%)
0%	[4.42,4.94,5.46,5.98]	[0.35,0.35,0.35,0.35]	[0,0,0,0]
10%	[4.68,5.23,5.78,6.33]	[0.35,0.35,0.35,0.35]	[1.64,1.83,2.02,2.21]
20%	[5.31,5.94,6.56,7.19]	[0.35,0.35,0.35,0.35]	[1.86,2.08,2.30,2.52]
30%	[5.95,6.65,7.35,8.05]	[0.35,0.35,0.35,0.35]	[2.08,2.33,2.57,2.82]
40%	[8.50,9.50,10.50,11.50]	[0.35,0.35,0.35,0.35]	[2.98,3.33,3.68,4.03]
50%	[8.50,9.50,10.50,11.50]	[0.26,0.29,0.32,0.35]	[2.17,2.71,3.31,3.97]
60%	[9.35,10.45,11.55,12.65]	[0.19,0.22,0.24,0.26]	[1.81,2.26,2.76,3.31]
70%	[10.63,11.88,13.13,14.38]	[0.15,0.16,0.18,0.20]	[1.55,1.94,2.37,2.84]
80%	[10.63,11.88,13.13,14.38]	[0.13,0.14,0.16,0.17]	[1.36,1.69,2.07,2.48]
90%	[10.63,11.88,13.13,14.38]	[0.11,0.13,0.14,0.15]	[1.21,1.51,1.84,2.21]

Table 3. Fuzzy after-tax cost of debt, fuzzy cost of equity and fuzzy weighted average cost of capital.

Debt Ratio	Fuzzy After-tax Cost of Debt (%)	Fuzzy Cost of Equity (%)	Fuzzy WACC (%)
0%	[0,0,0,0]	[8.32,9.30,10.28,11.26]	[8.32,9.30,10.28,11.26]
10%	[2.46,3.20,3.95,4.69]	[8.62,9.63,10.65,11.66]	[8.00,8.99,9.98,10.96]
20%	[2.80,3.64,4.48,5.33]	[8.99,10.04,11.10,12.16]	[7.75,8.76,9.78,10.79]
30%	[3.13,4.08,5.02,5.97]	[9.46,10.57,11.69,12.80]	[7.56,8.63,9.69,10.75]
40%	[4.48,5.83,7.18,8.53]	[10.09,11.28,12.46,13.65]	[7.84,9.10,10.35,11.60]
50%	[4.53,6.19,7.79,9.33]	[11.18,12.49,13.81,15.12]	[7.85,9.34,10.80,12.23]
60%	[6.04,7.70,9.29,10.84]	[13.05,14.58,16.12,17.65]	[8.84,10.45,12.02,13.57]
70%	[7.79,9.51,11.19,12.82]	[16.20,18.11,20.01,21.92]	[10.31,12.09,13.84,15.55]
80%	[8.14,9.81,11.43,13.02]	[22.18,24.79,27.40,30.00]	[10.95,12.80,14.62,16.42]
90%	[8.42,10.03,11.62,13.17]	[40.10,44.82,49.54,54.26]	[11.59,13.51,15.41,17.28]

Now we rank $FWACC_{0\%}$, $FWACC_{10\%},...,$ $FWACC_{90\%}$ shown as follow:

Step 1: In the process of standardizing generalized trapezoidal fuzzy WACC numbers, we have chosen 20 as the denominator since k is any real value. For example, at a 20% debt level, we translate the generalized trapezoidal fuzzy number $FWACC_{20\%} = [8.003, 8.990, 9.977, 10.964]$ into a standardized generalized trapezoidal fuzzy number $FWACC^*_{20\%}$ shown as follows:

$$FWACC^*_{20\%}$$

$$= \left[\frac{7.747}{20}, \frac{8.761}{20}, \frac{9.776}{20}, \frac{10.79}{20} \right]$$

$$= [0.387, 0.438, 0.489, 0.540]$$

Step 2: Based on Equations (3) and (4), we can get the centroid point $(\hat{x}_{\tilde{A}^*_j}, \hat{y}_{\tilde{A}^*_j})$ of the standardized generalized trapezoidal fuzzy number as follows: $FWACC_{0\%}$ is

[0.4895, 0.3889]; $FWACC_{10\%}$ is [0.4742, 0.3889]; $FWACC_{20\%}$ is [0.4634, 0.3889];... and $FWACC_{90\%}$ is [0.7221, 0.3889].

Step 3: Based on Equation (5), we can get the standard deviation ($s_{\tilde{A}_j^*}$) of the standardized generalized trapezoidal fuzzy number as follows: $FWACC_{0\%}$ is 0.063194; $FWACC_{10\%}$ is 0.063701; $FWACC_{20\%}$ is 0.065476; ... and $FWACC_{90\%}$ is 0.12248.

Step 4: Based on Equation (6), we can get a new point $(\hat{x}_{\tilde{A}_j^*}, \hat{y}_{\tilde{A}_j^*})$ = [0.4895, 0.475424] of the standardized generalized trapezoidal fuzzy number as follows: $FWACC_{0\%}$ is [0.4895, 0.475424]; $FWACC_{10\%}$ is [0.4742, 0.475227]; and $FWACC_{90\%}$ is [0.7221, 0.452369].

Step 5: Based on Equation (7), we can see that the ranking value score ($FWACC_{0\%}$) of the standardized gen- eralized trapezoidal fuzzy number $FWACC_{0\%}$ is 0.47648; the ranking value score ($FWACC_{10\%}$) of the standardized generalized trapezoidal fuzzy number $FWACC_{10\%}$ is 0.475509;... and the ranking value score ($FWACC_{90\%}$) of the standardized generalized trapezoidal fuzzy number $FWACC_{90\%}$ is 0.52394.

Moreover, in **Table 4**, the minimum ranking value score is the standardized generalized trapezoidal fuzzy number $FWACC_{50\%}$ of 0.46552, which minimizes the overall cost of capital. Hence, Boeing's optimal debt ratio is 50%. The ranking value score, which is 0.47648 when the firm is unlevered, decreases as the firm initially adds debt, reaches a minimum of 0.46552 at a 50% debt, and then starts to increase again. The optimal debt ratio for Boeing is shown graphically in **Figure 5**.

Table 4. A new ranking method for the generalized trapezoidal fuzzy numbers.

FWACC	step 1	step 2	step 3	step 4	step 5
$FWACC_{0\%}$	[0.416,0.465,0.514,0.563]	[0.4895,0.3889]	0.063194	[0.4895,0.475424]	0.47648
$FWACC_{10\%}$	[0.400,0.450,0.498,0.548]	[0.4742,0.3889]	0.063701	[0.4742,0.475227]	0.475509
$FWACC_{20\%}$	[0.387,0.438,0.489,0.540]	[0.4634,0.3889]	0.065476	[0.4634,0.474537]	0.47457
$FWACC_{30\%}$	[0.378,0.431,0.484,0.538]	[0.4578,0.3889]	0.068591	[0.4578,0.473326]	0.473326
$FWACC_{40\%}$	[0.392,0.455,0.517,0.580]	[0.4861,0.3889]	0.080829	[0.4861,0.468566]	0.46942
$FWACC_{50\%}$	[0.393,0.467,0.540,0.611]	[0.5025,0.3889]	0.094117	[0.5025,0.463399]	0.46552
$FWACC_{60\%}$	[0.442,0.522,0.601,0.678]	[0.5608,0.3889]	0.101633	[0.5608,0.460476]	0.471852
$FWACC_{70\%}$	[0.516,0.604,0.692,0.778]	[0.6472,0.3889]	0.112789	[0.6472,0.456137]	0.493887
$FWACC_{80\%}$	[0.547,0.640,0.731,0.821]	[0.6847,0.3889]	0.117626	[0.6847,0.454257]	0.50777
$FWACC_{90\%}$	[0.580,0.676,0.771,0.864]	[0.7221,0.3889]	0.12248	[0.7221,0.452369]	0.52394

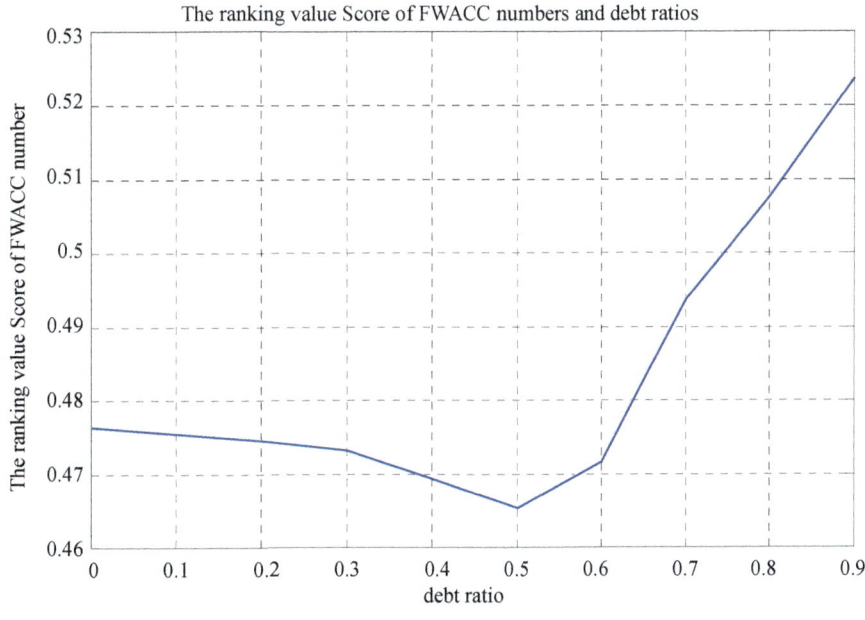

Figure 5. The ranking value score of trapezoidal fuzzy numbers and debt ratios

Using fuzzy logic to analyze WACC and optimal capital structure, we find that WACC follows a U-shaped curve. That is, the fuzzy WACC decreases initially with the increase of debt ratio. However, the fuzzy WACC begins to increase when the debt ratio exceeds 50%. Therefore, the lowest fuzzy WACC is achieved when the debt ratio is at the 50% level. For debt ratio of 50%, it means that the WACC will lie within the closed interval [0.5025, 0.463399] with a new ranking method. From another point of view, if a practitioner is comfortable with this new ranking method, then he/she can pick up any value from the closed interval [0.5025, 0.463399] as the WACC for his/her later use.

4. Conclusions

Due to the uncertainty in the capital markets and incomplete information, decision makers often possess only fuzzy information for the decision variables. This study combines fuzzy logic theory, the concept of WACC and optimal capital structure. Such integration allows decision makers to estimate the upper and lower bounds of the cost of capital given a debt ratio, hence making optimal decisions under uncertainty with fuzzy information. In general, the traditional WACC assumes implicitly that the level of cash flows to the firm is unaffected by the firm's financing mix, which might be unreasonable in the real world. This paper sheds light on making capital structure decisions. We suggest that the fuzzy WACC model can be used as an alternative way to estimate a firm's WACC. Furthermore, the fuzzy WACC model takes explicitly the issues of uncertainty, complexity, and imprecision. The fuzzy WACC approach allows the pre-tax cost of debt, the effective tax rate, the tax benefit, and the cost of equity to be fuzzy numbers; it also offers ranking means to find the optimal debt ratio. Finally, we would like to stress that advanced decision methods such as fuzzy capital structure and fuzzy WACC open the door of opportunity to explore the optimal debt ratio for a firm, and give further insight into the real uncertainty of the cost of capital. The proposed model may give practitioners a better understanding of the problem when making the financing mix choices.

5. References

[1]   W. F. Sharpe, "Capital Asset Prices," *Journal of Finance*, Vol. 13, No. 3, September 1964, pp. 425-442.

[2]   J. Lintner, "The Valuation of Risk Assets and the Selection of Risky Investments in Stock Portfolios and Capital Budgets," *Review of Economics and Statistics*, Vol. 47, 1965, pp. 13-37.

[3]   R. F. Bruner, K.M. Eades, R.S. Harris and R.C. Higgins, "Best Practices in Estimating the Cost of Capital: Survey

and Synthesis," *Financial Practice and Education*, 1998, pp. 13-28.

[4]   H. J. Bierman, "Capital Budgeting in 1992: A Survey," *Financial Management*, Vol. 22, 1993, p. 24.

[5]   L. J. Gitman and P. A. Vandenberg, "Cost of Capital Techniques Used by Major US Firms: 1997 vs. 1980," *Financial Practice and Education*, Vol. 10, No. 2, Fall/Winter, 2000, pp. 53-68.

[6]   J. R. Graham and C. R. Harvey, "The Theory and Practice of Corporate Finance: Evidence from the Field," *Journal of Financial Economics*, Vol. 60, 2001, pp. 187-244.

[7]   G. Arnold and P. Hatzopoulos, "The Theory-practice Gap in Capital Budgeting: Evidence from the United Kingdom," *Journal of Business Finance and Accounting*, Vol. 27, 2000, pp. 603-626.

[8]   E. McLaney, J. Pointon, M. Thoma and J. Tucker, "Practitioners' perspectives on the UK cost of capital," *European Journal of Finance*, Vol. 10, 2004, pp. 123-138.

[9]   D. Brounen, A. De Jong and K. Koedijk, "Corporate Finance in Europe: Confronting Theory with Practice," *Financial Management*, Vol. 33, No. 4, 2004, pp. 71-101.

[10] N. Chopra, J. Lakonishok and J. R. Ritter, "Measuring Abnormal Performance: Do Stocks Overreact," *Journal of Financial Economics*, Vol. 31, 1992, pp. 235-268.

[11] E. F. Fama and K.R. French, "The Cross-section of Expected Stock Returns," *The Journal of Finance*, Vol. 47, 1992, pp. 427- 465.

[12] J.L. Davis, "The Cross-section of Realized Stock Returns: The PRE-COMPUSTAT Evidence," J*ournal of Finance*, Vol. 49, No. 5, 1994, pp. 1579-1593.

[13] B. M. Barber and J.D. Lyon, "Firm Size, Book-to-market Ratio, and Security Returns: A holdout sample of financial firms," *Journal of Finance*, Vol. 52, 1997, PP. 875-883.

[14] R. Roll, "A Critique of the Asset Pricing Theory's Tests," *Journal of Financial Economics*, Vol. 4, No. 2, 1977, pp. 129-176.

[15] F. Black, "Beta and Return," *Journal of Portfolio Management*, Vol. 20, No. 1, 1993, pp. 8-18.

[16] S. P. Kothari, J. Shanken and R. G. Sloan, "Another Look at the Cross-section of Expected Returns," *Journal of Finance*, Vol. 50, No. 1, 1995, pp. 185-224.

[17] W. F. Sharpe, "Factor Models, CAPMs and the APT," *Journal of Portfolio Management*, Vol. 11, 1984, pp. 21-25.

[18] R. Lister, "Cost of Capital is Beyond Our Search," *Accountancy*, Vol. 138, No. 1360, 2006, pp. 42-43.

[19] D. Lund, "Taxation, Uncertainty, and the Cost of Equity," *International Tax and Public Finance*, 9, 2002, 483-503.

[20] C. Mayer, "Corporation Tax, Finance and the Cost of Capital," *Review of Economic Studies*, Vol. 53, No. 1, 1986, pp. 93-112.

[21] S. J. Chen and S.M. Chen, "Fuzzy Risk Analysis Based on the Ranking of Generalized Trapezoidal Fuzzy Num-

bers," *Applied Intelligence*, Vol. 26, No. 1, 2007, pp. 1-11.

[22] C. H. Cheng and D.L. Mon, "Fuzzy System Reliability Analysis by Confidence Interval," *Fuzzy Sets and Systems*, Vol. 56, May 1993, pp. 29-35.

[23] C. H. Cheng, "A New Approach for Ranking Fuzzy Numbers by Distance Method," *Fuzzy Sets and Systems*, Vol. 95, No. 1, 1998, pp. 307-317.

[24] T.C. Chu, "Ranking Fuzzy Numbers with an Area Between the Centroid Point and Original Point," *Computers and Mathematics with Applications*, Vol. 43, 2002, pp. 111-117.

[25] A. Damodaran, "Corporate Finance: Theory and Practice," John Wiley & Sons, 2001.

21

Case Study on Business Risk Management for Software Outsourcing Service Provider with ISM[*]

Jiangping Wan[1,2], Dan Wan[1], Hui Zhang[1]
[1]*School of Business Administration, South China University of Technology, Guangzhou, China*
[2]*Institute of Emerging Industrialization Development South China University of Technology, Guangzhou, China*

Abstract

This paper identifies the risks of CN Group which is working at software outsourcing projects between HongKong and Guangdong, discovers the causal relationships among the risk factors, and constructs corresponding risk structure model with Interpretive Structural Modeling. Five original risk factors are identified, including contracts risk, requirements definition and change, lack of communication, political and legal environment differences, and exchange rate fluctuations. Finally, a risk management model of CN Group is put forward and three advices are proposed for software outsourcing business operation: project planning, project requirements, and communication.

Keywords: Software Outsourcing, Project Management, Risk Factor, Interpretive Structural Modeling, Empirical Analysis

1. Introduction

Software outsourcing is a major characteristic of economic globalization, a new form of innovation networks and strategic alliances, and also a strategic instrument for nurturing and promoting enterprises' core competitiveness. Outsourcing service providers who undertake software outsourcing face both opportunities and challenges [1]. With an increasingly competitive outsourcing market, it has been the industry's top priority to explore the risk management for China's software outsourcing business. The widespread failures of software outsourcing projects have attracted scholars to focus on the risks of the software outsourcing project [1]. Kliem & Ralph had discovered six risk factors leading to the failure [2].

However, these studies only implement isolated risk management in limited processes, without comprehensive consideration from the enterprises' operation level. In this context, issues studied in this thesis include: 1) What risks do software outsourcing enterprises confront? 2) How do software outsourcing enterprises respond to these risks? 3) Have there been appropriate risk management models for software outsourcing enterprises to

effectively carry out risk management? 4) How do software outsourcing enterprises guarantee the correct implementation of these risk management models?

There are many risks in the course of risk management of the software outsourcing enterprise, the risk factors contact each other and store each other, forming a multi-level, multi-link network structure. Therefore, the risk management of software outsourcing actually covers the whole process of the software life cycle; the risks can not be seen independently. Interpretive Structural Modeling (ISM) is the most practical technology of the structure modeling, and is most widely used in analyzing software outsourcing risks in the system with many variables, complex relationships and unclear structure. In this paper, we constructed a risk structure model for CN Group which is working software outsourcing projects between HongKong and Guangdong, and then found out some original risks to propose several solutions.

2. Software Risk Management

Literature 3 shows the comparison of 6 risk management models (**Table 1**). The core of Boehm's risk management theory is to maintain and update a list of the top ten risks [4]. Software risk management principles of CRM (Continuous Risk Management), include a comprehensive

[*]This research was supported by Key Project of Guangdong Province Education Office (06JDXM63002), NSF of China (70471091), and QualiPSo (IST-FP6-IP-034763)

view, positive strategies, open communication environment, integrated management, continuous process, a common goal and coordinative working. CRM model proposed by SEI demands to pay close attention to risk identification and management in all stages of project life cycle [5]. Riskit method can provide systematic risk management processes and technologies of early stage, aimed at completely indicating and managing the causes of risk, the trigger events and their impacts, and assessing risk with reasonable steps. Riskit method provides the detail implementation template to each activity of the risk management [6]. SoftRisk model is proposed by Keshlaf and Hashim. The core of this model is to continuously identify and control risk, and manage risk through updating and maintaining the list of top ten risks which are based on Boehm theory [7]. IEEE risk management standard defines risk management processes during software development life cycle [8]. It systematically describes and manages the risks emerging in product or service life cycle, including the following activities: planning and implementing risk management, managing project risk list, analyzing risk, monitoring risk, handling risk, and evaluating risk management process. Software Risk Management process area is the third level of CMMI [9], which is to identify potential factors that could jeopardize key objectives so that countermeasures can be planned and implemented when necessary to ease the negative impact and eventually realize the organizational goals.

The practice of software risk management involves two primary steps each with three subsidiary steps by Bohem is illustrated in **Figure 1** [4].

The first primary step, risk assessment, involves risk identification, risk analysis, and risk prioritization: 1) Risk identification produces lists of the project-specific risk items likely to compromise a project's success. Typical risk identification techniques include checklists, examination of decision drivers, comparison with experience (assumption analysis), and decomposition. 2) Risk analysis assesses the loss probability and loss magnitude for each identified risk item, and it assesses compound risks in risk item interactions. Typical techniques include performance models, cost models, network analysis, statistical decision analysis, and quality-factor (like reliability, availability, and security) analysis. 3) Risk prioritization produces a ranked ordering of the risk items identified and analyzed. Typical techniques include risk-exposure analysis, risk-reduction leverage analysis (particularly involving cost-benefit analysis), and Delphi or group-consensus techniques.

The second primary step, risk control, involves risk-management planning, risk resolution, and risk monitoring: 1) Risk-management planning helps prepare you to address each risk item (for example, via information buying, risk avoidance, risk transfer, or risk reduction), including the coordination of the individual risk-item plans with each other and with the overall project plan. Typical techniques include checklists of risk-resolution techniques, cost benefit analysis, and standard risk management plan outlines, forms, and elements. 2) Risk resolution produces a situation in which the risk items are eliminated or otherwise resolved (for example, risk avoidance via relaxation of requirements). Typical techniques include prototypes, simulations, benchmarks, mission analyses, key-personnel agreements, design-to-cost approaches, and incremental development. 3) Risk monitoring involves tracking the project's progress toward resolving its risk items and taking corrective action where appropriate. Typical techniques include milestone tracking and a top-10 risk-item list that is highlighted at each weekly, monthly, or milestone project review and followed up appropriately with reassessment of the risk item or corrective action.

Table 1. Comparison of risk management models.

Model	Characteristic	Model complexity	Core activities of model
Barn-Boehm Theory	Identify risks and maintain a list of the top ten risks	low	Risk identification
CRM model of SEI	Continuous risk management, emphasizing on communication of risk	low	communication
Riskit method	Continuous risk management, manager expectation's influence on risks, modeling risk with a graphical tool, Riskit analysis diagram, and with software support	high	Standard definition of risk management
SoftRisk risk management model	Continuous risk management, maintain a list of the top ten risks, risks statistic	middle	statistic
IEEE risk management standard	Continuous risk management, continuous improvement, executives developing standards, being able to manage project and organizational risks	middle	Risk management description table
CMMI risk management process area	Continuous and prospective risk management, continuous process improving	middle	Risk database

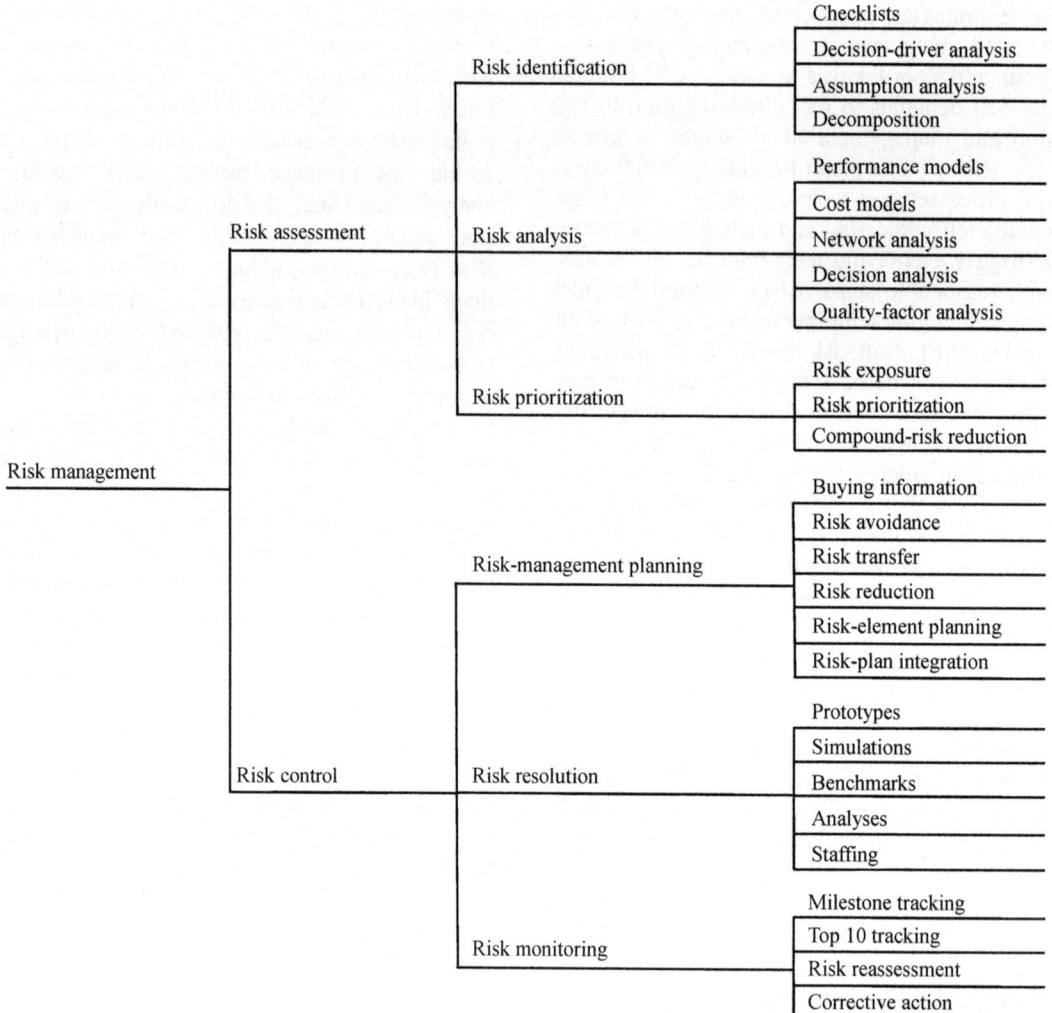

Figure 1. Software risk management steps.

3. Analysis on Risks of CN Group

CN summarized its risks having the following characteristics.

1) The objectivity and universality of risk. As the uncertainty of loss, a considerable part of the risk of CN Group can not completely controlled. These objective risks exist not only in software outsourcing project life cycle, but also in the operations of CN group. Although the CN group wishes to fully understand and control risk, but until now it can only change the conditions of risk existence and occurrence, reduces risk frequency and mitigates risk damage in limited space and time, but cannot eliminate it.

2) The contingency of a particular risk and inevitability of a number of risks. In the software outsourcing projects of CN Group, the occurrence of any specific risk is caused by many risk factors and other factors together, thus it is a random phenomenon. However, some risks can be controlled and forecasted through observation and statistical analysis of substantial risk accident data.

3) The variability of risk. This refers to the various risks changing in terms of quality and quantity in the entire project process. As the project goes on, some risks will be controlled, some will occur and get handled, and at the same time new risks may rise in every stage of the project. Especially in large projects, due to more risk factors, the variability of risk is much more pronounced.

4) The diversity and multi-level of risk. CN Group is a software outsourcing company, and responsible for several large software outsourcing projects. These software outsourcing projects have long life cycle, large-scale, broad scope and numerous risk factors of various types, resulting in that various risks will be confronted in its entire life cycle. Furthermore the intrinsic relationships between risk factors are complex, and cross-impacts of various risk factors between and external factors endow the multilevel risks.

4. Construct Software Outsourcing Risks Structure Model of CN Group with ISM

4.1. Identify the Risks of the Software Outsourcing Project

The major event sequence of ISM is in the following [10]: 1) Theme is selected. 2) Developer is identified. 3) Elements and contextual relation are identified. 4) Leader is identified. 5) ISM program is entered in computer. 6) Adequate computer time is allocated. 7) Facilities are ready. 8) Session plan is complete. 9) Computer contains elements and contextual relation. 10) Session can begin. 11) Element set is edited. 12) Reachable matrix is complete. 13) Total structure is available. 14) Amendments are complete. 15) Final structure is satisfactory.

According to major event sequence of ISM, We organized eight experts to form an ISM panel. Because of the consideration for confidentiality, eight experts all come from CN Group. ISM panel set problems and identified risk factors regularly (every three months). After several discussions, the members of ISM panel reached a consensus. Finally, 21 major risk factors of software outsourcing projects were found out. These risks can be illustrated in **Table 2**.

4.2. Construct Concept Model and Reachable Matrix

The concept model is constructed according to risk factors. After analysis, we propose a reasonable schedule of the relationships among risk factors of CN Group. It is illustrated in **Table 3**.

Table 2. Major risks software outsourcing of CN group.

Number	Risk factor	Description
S_1	Research and development risk	The operation problems caused by research and development
S_2	Human resources risk	The personnel structure is not rational, the key personnel and project managers are lack of experiences
S_3	The risk of requirement definition & change	The products was unclear, the requirement changed continually, resulting in increasing costs
S_4	Cultural differences	Cultural and values differences among different countries cause problems in work team
S_5	Enterprise decision-making blunders	By the wrong analysis of finance, technology, strategy, and the occasion
S_6	Contractor risk	By the inaccurate assessment of the contractor's core competencies and process capability
S_7	Contract risk	The contract defects and the wrong choice of contract type caused by the weak capability of contract
S_8	The lack of client support	In the information, communication, resources, technology, and finance is critical to the successfulness of the project
S_9	Software outsourcing project risk	By technology, personnel capacity, resources, or lack of responsibility
S_{10}	After service risk	Service quality such as software maintenance, technical support, and training services
S_{11}	Losing control of milestones	Lack of supervision plan and inattention of third-party commissioner
S_{12}	Inaccurate evaluation criteria	The evaluation criteria document defects about contract, commissioner rules, and software test plans
S_{13}	Exchange rate fluctuations	The project profit will also be affected
S_{14}	Financial risk	Financial risk caused by the lack of follow-up funds
S_{15}	Political and legal environment differences	Cause problems in trade, legal awareness, and other issues
S_{16}	Lack of communication	The coordination mechanisms of client, contractor, and supervision do not work
S_{17}	Client risk	On the software products, the capability of software outsourcing enterprises, and supervision
S_{18}	Market risk	Services change, the risk of sales, the operational environment risks, competitors risk, and so on
S_{19}	Merger / acquisition risk	As a company in Hong Kong, CN Group is possible to be merged by other enterprise
S_{20}	CMMI implementation risk	CMMI is too rigid to run smoothly in the entire company, so it can not help to improve the efficiency of operation
S_{21}	Marketing risk	Because of the unpredictable impact by uncertain factors, it is possible to loss or add income

Table 3. Relationship among major risks software outsourcing business of CN group.

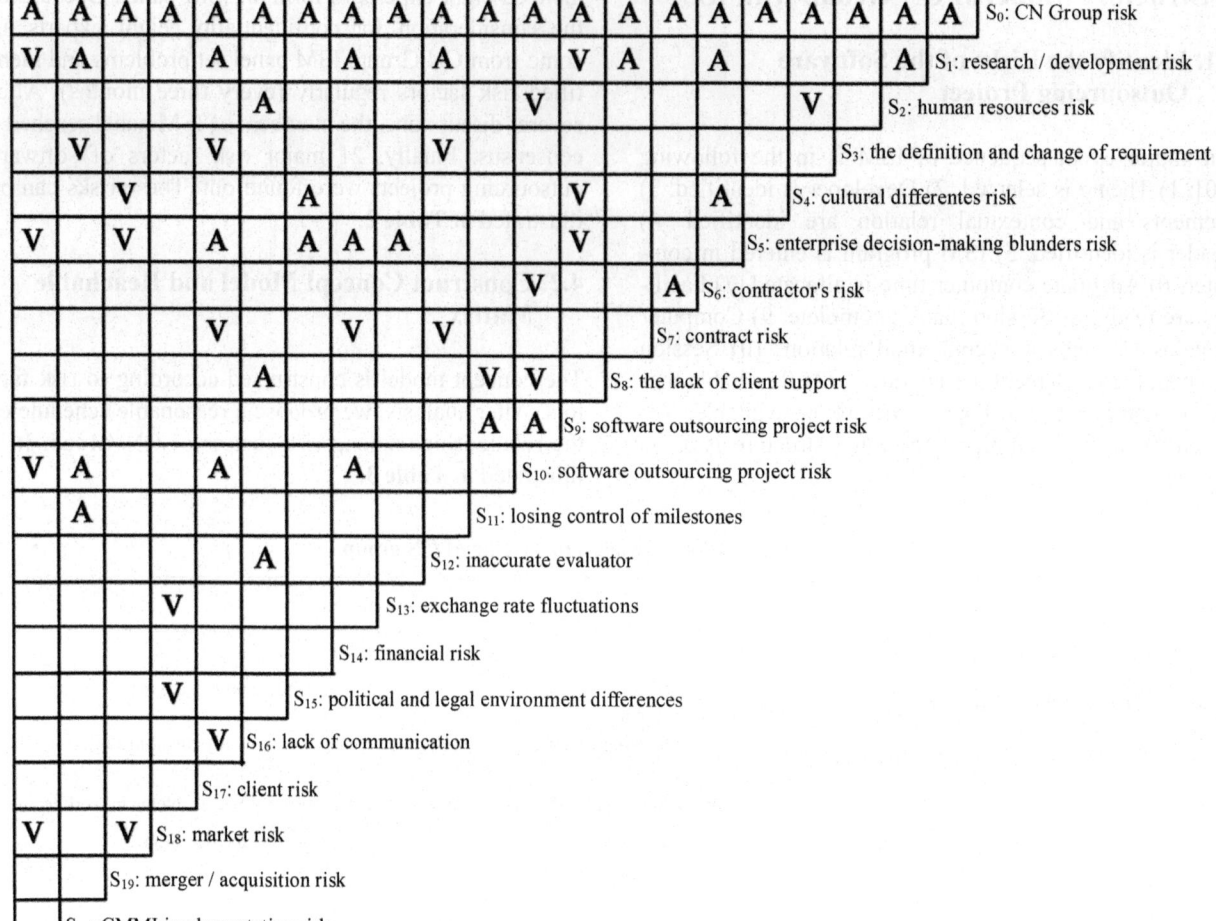

S₀: CN Group risk
S₁: research / development risk
S₂: human resources risk
S₃: the definition and change of requirement
S₄: cultural differentes risk
S₅: enterprise decision-making blunders risk
S₆: contractor's risk
S₇: contract risk
S₈: the lack of client support
S₉: software outsourcing project risk
S₁₀: software outsourcing project risk
S₁₁: losing control of milestones
S₁₂: inaccurate evaluator
S₁₃: exchange rate fluctuations
S₁₄: financial risk
S₁₅: political and legal environment differences
S₁₆: lack of communication
S₁₇: client risk
S₁₈: market risk
S₁₉: merger / acquisition risk
S₂₀: CMMI implementation risk
S₂₁: marketing risk

There into: ①V denotes the row factor has effected on the column factor (the row factor result in the column factor); ②A denotes the column factor has effected on the row factor; ③blank denotes the row factor and the column factor are unrelated.

4.3. Establish a Re-Order Reachable Matrix After the Class Division

Class division means dividing different risk factors into different levels for the purpose of providing a risk factors structural framework with good hierarchy and causal relationships for risk analysis and risk management.

1) Reachable matrix shows all the direct or indirect impact relationships between different factors. 2) Reachable set R (Si). The reachable set of Si is a set of system elements those can be reached by Si in Reachable matrix or directed graph, denotes as R (Si). 3) Antecedence set A (Si). The antecedence set of Si is a set of system elements those can reach to Si in Reachable matrix or directed graph, denotes as A (Si).

Table 4 is illustrated the first level of Reachable set and antecedence set of risks in CN Group.

Using Boolean algebra operational rules on the adja-cency matrix, we can get a Reachable set. Because R(S0) = R(S0) ∩ A(S0), the highest factors set of the first layer L1 = {S0}. By redlining the corresponding rows and columns, we can get the Reachable set and antecedence set of the second layer. In the same way, the highest factors set of the second layer L2 = {S9, S19, S21}; the highest factors set of the third layer L3 = {S1, S4, S5, S10, S11, S18}; the highest factors set of the fourth layer L4 = {S2, S6, S8, S12, S13, S14, S15, S17, S20}; the factors set of the lowest layer L5 = {S3, S7, S16}. The re-order Reachable matrix is as follows (**Figure 2**).

4.4. Construct the Structural Model

According to the re-order reachable matrix, we can construct the risk structural model of CN Group. They can be illustrated by **Figure 3**. (There are 50 pairs of relationships here).

Table 4. The reachable set and antecedence of the first layer.

	R(S_i)	A(S_i)	R(S_i)/A(S_i)
S_0	0	0,1,2,3,4,5,6,7,8,9,10,11,12,13,14,15,16,17,18,19,20,21	0
S_1	0,1,9,21	1,2,6,8,12,14,17,20	1
S_2	0,1,2,4,10	2,16	2
S_3	0,3,12,17,20	3	3
S_4	0,4,9,19	2,4,6,15	4
S_5	0,5,9,19,21	5,13,14,15	5
S_6	0,1,4,6,10	6,7	6
S_7	0,6,7,12,14,17	7	7
S_8	0,1,8,10,11	8,16	8
S_9	0,9	1,4,5,9,10,11	9
S_{10}	0,9,10,21	2,6,8,10,14,17,20	10
S_{11}	0,9,11	8,11,20	11
S_{12}	0,1,12	3,7,12,16	12
S_{13}	0,5,13,18	13	13
S_{14}	0,1,5,10,14	7,14	14
S_{15}	0,4,5,15,18	15	15
S_{16}	0,2,8,12,16,17	16	16
S_{17}	0,1,5,10,17	3,7,16,17	17
S_{18}	0,18,19,21	13,15,18	18
S_{19}	0,19	4,5,18,19	19
S_{20}	0,1,10,11,20	3,20	20
S_{21}	0,21	1,5,10,18,21	21

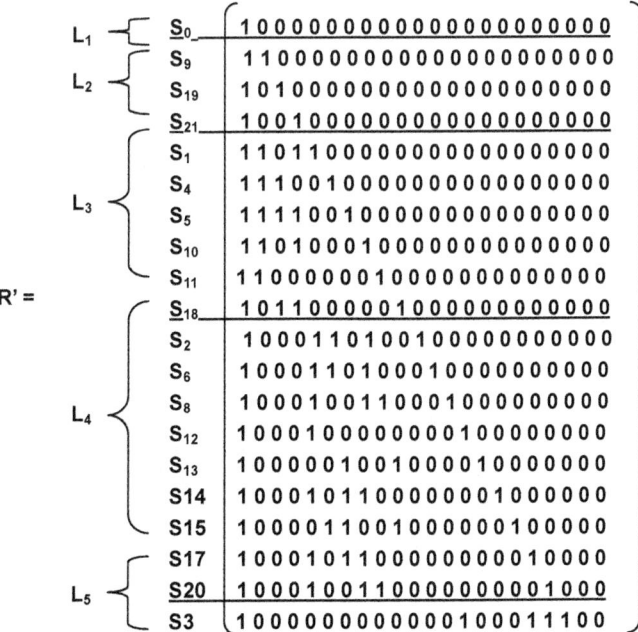

Figure 2. The re-order reachable matrix R'.

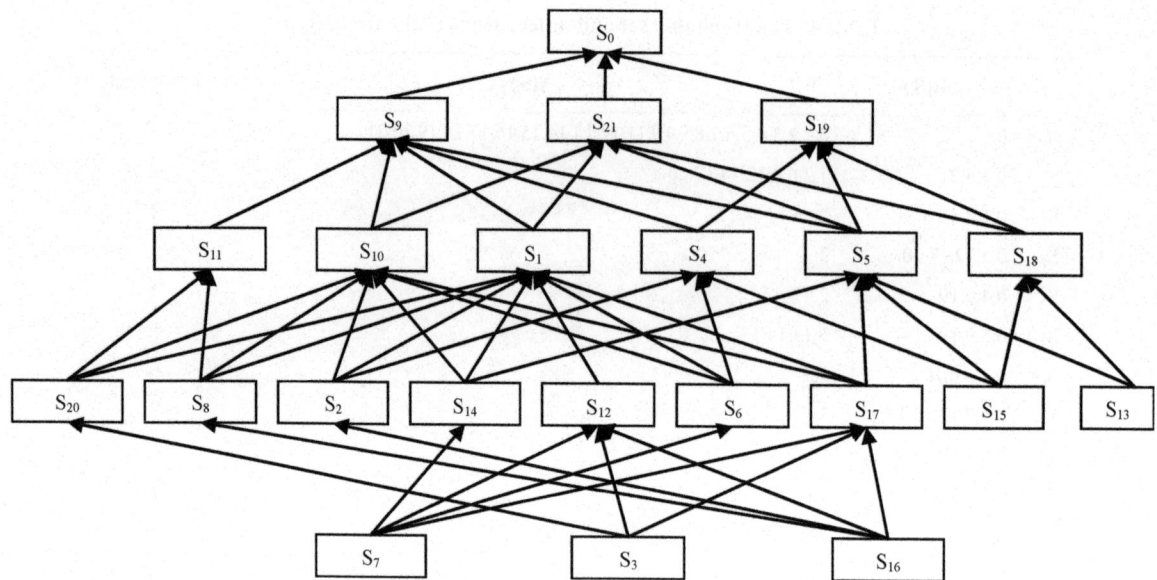

Figure 3. ISM based business risk structural model for CN Group.

It can be seen from **Figure 4** that this model is a directed five-level hierarchical structure model, and that the bottom-line arrows indicate low-level factors affecting high-level factors. By replacing risk factors code with the actual risk factors, the interpretative structure model of CN's software outsourcing business risk is established.

5. Analyze the Interpretive Structural Model

After the analysis, we discover the software outsourcing business risks of CN Group constitute of factors in five level structures (**Figure 4**).

1) The lowest level constitute of contract risk, lack of communication, and the risk of requirement definition and change. They are the key factors affecting the successfulness of software outsourcing projects; although political and legal environment differences and exchange rate fluctuations are in the fourth layer, they are the bottom of the risks of CN Group; especially, the factors contract risk, lack of communication, and the risk of requirement definition and change occur in the early stages of operation of software outsourcing projects, having significant impact on the successfulness of CN Group's project.

2) The factors of the second layer is the direct risk factors resulting CN Group to crisis, including software outsourcing project risk, merger / acquisition risk, and marketing risk. Three risks separately belong to the project management, marketing management and enterprise management, but they are significant and correlative closely.

3) The software outsourcing project risk mainly due to losing control of milestones, research and development

risk, after service risk, cultural differences, and enterprise decision-making blunders risk. The deeper reasons are CMMI implementation risk, the lack of client support, human resources risk, contract risk, financial risk, inaccurate evaluation criteria, contractor risk, and client risk. The original risks are contract risk, lack of communication, and the risk of requirement definition and change.

4) Marketing risk mainly due to enterprise decision-making blunders risk, market risk, research and development risk, and after service risk. The deeper reasons are financial risk, human resources risk, client risk, political and legal environment differences, and exchange rate fluctuations.

5) Merger / acquisition risk mainly due to cultural differences, enterprise decision-making blunders risk, and market risk.

6. Risk Management Model of CN Group

The existing risk management process in CN Group has included general processes for risk warning, analysis, plan, response and tracking in the outsourcing risk management model (**Figure 5**).

Risk early warning is the regular or irregular action of software outsourcing enterprises. CN Group needs to appoint a risk warning manager, being solely responsible for the work of risk warning. Risk warning manager reports directly to the CEO.

Risk identification is an attempt to determine risk factors that threat software outsourcing business with a systematic approach. CN Group should start with focusing on the issue that what scope, schedule, cost and quality problems could possibly emerge in the risks they face,

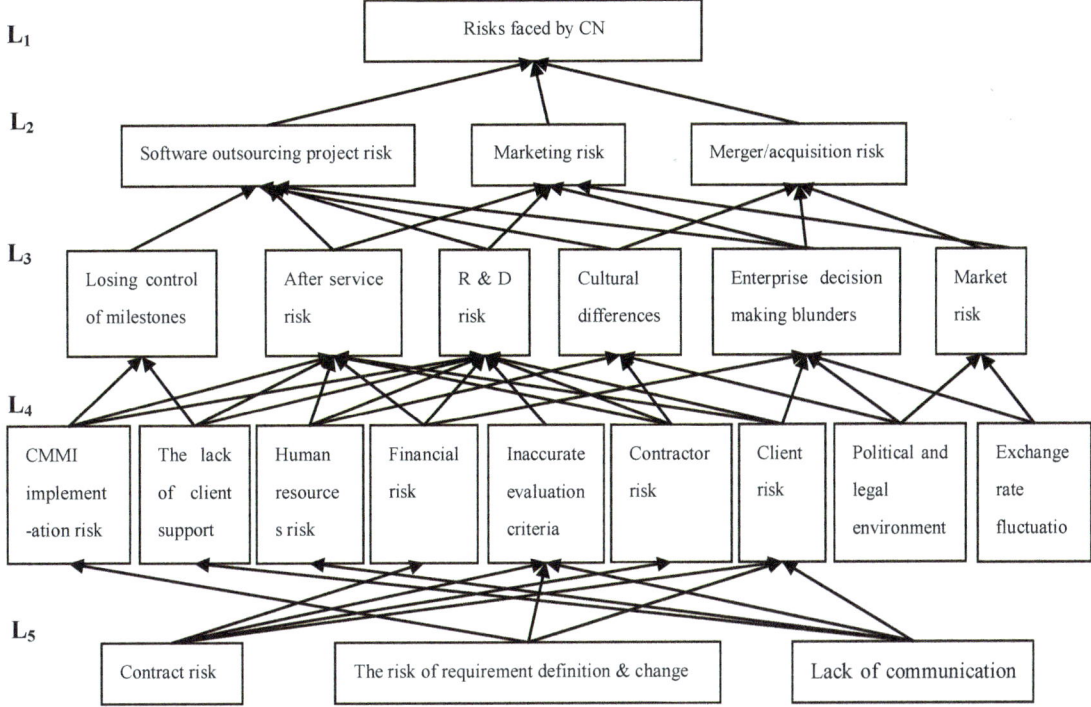

Figure 4. Interpretive Structure Model of CN's Software Outsourcing Business Risk.

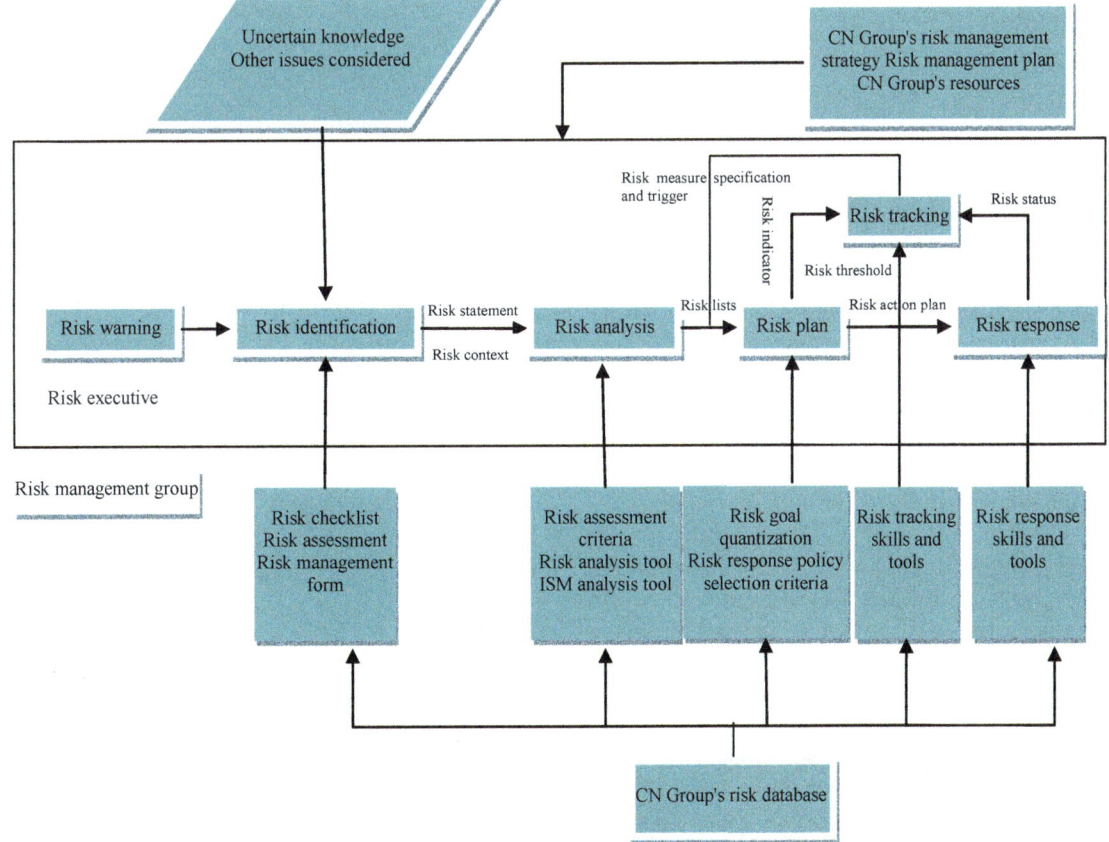

Figure 5. Risk Management of CN Group.

mainly to discuss and list the possible risks.

Risk analysis is divided into qualitative risk analysis and quantitative risk analysis. Qualitative risk analysis is a process to assess the impact of the identified risks and their likelihood. For example, we can clearly find out the causal relationship of risks involved in software outsourcing process through structural analysis on the risk of CN group with ISM model. Thus we can determine the root of the important risks from the complex risk signs.

Risk action plan should contain the following elements: responsibility, resources, time, activities, response measures, results and person in charge.

CN Group can choose the following types of risk-response strategies: 1) controlling risk. 2) accepting risk. 3) transferring risk. 4) avoiding risk. It should adopt different response strategies according to different conditions, different environment or different issues of software outsourcing process.

The role of risk tracking is to monitor the status of the risk and check the validity of risk counter measures and whether tracking mechanisms are in operation, continue to identify new risks and develop strategies to provide the basis for active risk control.

7. The Countermeasures for the Risk Management of Software Outsourcing Enterprises

We advise the enterprises working at software outsourcing projects between Guangdong and Hong Kong should pay attention to the following aspects for managing risks:

1) Project requirement. A clear project requirement is the fundamental of the right project planning and implementation, so the contractor should gain some insight into the client's requirement before the project implementation, and discuss uncertain requirement with client. For the changes in the process of implementation, all participants should reach a consensus in the end. In requirement analysis, the contractor should carefully analyze the client's requirement, and then collect the client's complete requirement through business modeling, conversation, questionnaires, and requirement meeting.

2) Project planning. Prior to the implementation of the project, the client usually puts forward the draft of the implementation plan of the project, project managers should confer with client on the integrity and feasibility of the project plan, project process, workload, resource allocation and project milestones.

3) Communication. The implementation of the software outsourcing project is a cooperation process of both. It is necessary to establish an effective communication channel to ensure the outsourcing business to be carried

out successfully. The contractor must confirm with client on which communication tools (telephone, fax, e-mail, online conversation, etc.) should be used under given circumstance, then determine format (for example, weekly format) and form of communication (for example, on spot, telephone, both project linkman).

8. Conclusions

This paper identifies the software outsourcing business risks of CN Group, and discovers the causal relationships among risk factors, and constructs corresponding risk structure model with ISM. Five original risk factors are found, including contracts risk, the risk of requirements definition and change, lack of communication, political and legal environment differences, and exchange rate fluctuations. Finally, risk management model is put forward for CN Group, and three advices are proposed: project requirement, project planning and communication to help software outsourcing providers between Guangdong and HongKong to find effective ways for software outsourcing project's success.

9. Acknowledgements

Thank for helpful discussion with Mr.Kevin Kuang, Dr.CK Wong, Mr. Chan Zening, Mr.An Yuguo, Mrs Huang Huajie and Mrs Hou Jianhua etc.

10. References

[1]   Y. Qin, W. J. Li and C .D. Pan, "The Development of Services Outsourcing in Multinational Companies and China's Countermeasures," *Science and Technology Progress and Policy*, Vol. 23, No. 4, April 2006, pp. 131-132.

[2]   R. Kliem, "Managing the Risks of Offshore IT Development Project," *Information Systems Management*, Vol. 21, No. 3, March 2004, pp. 21-27.

[3]   M. Z. Mao and X. W. Ge, "Analysis and Research on Risk and Management," *Science and Technology Management Research*, Vol. 24, No. 6, June 2005, pp. 148-151.

[4]   B.W Boehm, "Software Risk Management: Principles and Practices," *IEEE Software*, Vol. 8, No. 1, August 1991, pp. 32-41.

[5]   V. Scoy and L. Roger, "Software Development Risk: Opportunity, Not Problem," *Technical Report*, CMU/SEI-92-TR-30, September 1992.

[6]   J. Kontio, "Risk Management in Software Development: A Technology Overview and the Riskit Method," *The Proceedings of ICSE*, Los Angles CA, May 1999, pp. 679-680.

[7]   A. A. Keshlaf and K. Hashim, "A Model and Prototype

Tool to Manage Software Risks," *Proceedings of the First Asia–Pacific Conference on Quality Software*, October 2000, pp. 297- 305.

[8] IEEE Std, "IEEE Standard for Software Life Cycle Processes- Risk Management," Vol. 1504, 2001, pp. 1-24.

[9] CMMI Product Team, "Capability Maturity Model Integration V1. 1 for Software Engineering," CMU/ SEI, August 2002.

[10] J. N. Warfield, "The Mathematics of Structure," AJAR, Publishing Company, 2003.

Permissions

The contributors of this book come from diverse backgrounds, making this book a truly international effort. This book will bring forth new frontiers with its revolutionizing research information and detailed analysis of the nascent developments around the world.

We would like to thank all the contributing authors for lending their expertise to make the book truly unique. They have played a crucial role in the development of this book. Without their invaluable contributions this book wouldn't have been possible. They have made vital efforts to compile up to date information on the varied aspects of this subject to make this book a valuable addition to the collection of many professionals and students.

This book was conceptualized with the vision of imparting up-to-date information and advanced data in this field. To ensure the same, a matchless editorial board was set up. Every individual on the board went through rigorous rounds of assessment to prove their worth. After which they invested a large part of their time researching and compiling the most relevant data for our readers. Conferences and sessions were held from time to time between the editorial board and the contributing authors to present the data in the most comprehensible form. The editorial team has worked tirelessly to provide valuable and valid information to help people across the globe.

Every chapter published in this book has been scrutinized by our experts. Their significance has been extensively debated. The topics covered herein carry significant findings which will fuel the growth of the discipline. They may even be implemented as practical applications or may be referred to as a beginning point for another development. Chapters in this book were first published by Scientific Research Publishing Inc.; hereby published with permission under the Creative Commons Attribution License or equivalent.

The editorial board has been involved in producing this book since its inception. They have spent rigorous hours researching and exploring the diverse topics which have resulted in the successful publishing of this book. They have passed on their knowledge of decades through this book. To expedite this challenging task, the publisher supported the team at every step. A small team of assistant editors was also appointed to further simplify the editing procedure and attain best results for the readers.

Our editorial team has been hand-picked from every corner of the world. Their multi-ethnicity adds dynamic inputs to the discussions which result in innovative outcomes. These outcomes are then further discussed with the researchers and contributors who give their valuable feedback and opinion regarding the same. The feedback is then collaborated with the researches and they are edited in a comprehensive manner to aid the understanding of the subject.

Apart from the editorial board, the designing team has also invested a significant amount of their time in understanding the subject and creating the most relevant covers. They scrutinized every image to scout for the most suitable representation of the subject and create an appropriate cover for the book.

The publishing team has been involved in this book since its early stages. They were actively engaged in every process, be it collecting the data, connecting with the contributors or procuring relevant information. The team has been an ardent support to the editorial, designing and production team. Their endless efforts to recruit the best for this project, has resulted in the accomplishment of this book. They are a veteran in the field of academics and their pool of knowledge is as vast as their experience in printing. Their expertise and guidance has proved useful at every step. Their uncompromising quality standards have made this book an exceptional effort. Their encouragement from time to time has been an inspiration for everyone.

The publisher and the editorial board hope that this book will prove to be a valuable piece of knowledge for researchers, students, practitioners and scholars across the globe.

List of Contributors

Hany A. Shawky
Center for Institutional Investment Management, School of Business, University at Albany, Albany, USA

Achla Marathe
Virginia Bioinformatics Institute, Virginia Tech, Blacksburg, USA

Marcel van Marrewijk
Research to Improve, Trusting Companies International and Virtu et Fortuna, Vlaardingen, Netherland
Van Linden van den Heuvellsingel 7, Vlaardingen, The Netherlands

Tao Zhang, Guijun Zhuang and Yuanyuan Huang
School of Management, Xi'an Jiaotong University, Xi'an, China

Panagiotis E. Petrakis
Department of Economics, Division of Economic Development, Athens National and Kapodistrian University, Athens, Greece

Maik Wagner
Department of Business Statistics, Friedrich-Schiller-University Jena, Germany

Karin Sanders, Matthijs Moorkamp, Nicole Torka, Sandra Groeneveld and Claudia Groeneveld
Department of Organizational Psychology and Human Resource Development, University of Twente, Enschede, The Netherlands

Emanuela Giusi Gaeta
University of Rome "Tor Vergata", Rome, Italy

Carlos E. Escobar Toledo and Claudia Garcia Aranda
Faculty of Chemistry, National University of Mexico, Mexico City, Mexico

Bertrand Mareschal
Solvay School of Business Administration, Université Libre de Bruxelles, Brussels, Belgium

Rajiv K. Sinha
Griffith School of Engineering (Environment), Griffith University, Nathan Campus, Brisbane, Australia

Sunita Agarwal
University of Rajasthan, Jaipur, India

Krunal Chauhan, Vinod Chandran and Brijal Kiranbhai Soni
Vermiculture Project, Griffith University, Brisbane, Australia

Guglielmo D'Amico
Università "G. D'Annunzio" di Chieti, Dip. di Scienze del Farmaco, via dei Vestini, Chieti, Italy

Jacques Janssen
Jacan &, EURIA, Université de Bretagne Occidentale, 6 avenue le Gorgeu, Brest, France

Raimondo Manca
Università "La Sapienza", Dip. di Matematica per le Decisioni Economiche, Finanziarie ed Assicurative, via del Castro Laurenziano, Roma, Italy

Sammer Markos, Nhien-An Le-Khac and M-Tahar Kechadi
School of Computer Science & Informatics, University College Dublin, Belfield, Dublin, Ireland

William J. Trainor Jr.
East Tennessee State University, Johnson City, USA

Tiaojun Xiao, Xinxin Yan and Jiabao Zhao
School of Management Science and Engineering, Nanjing University, Nanjing, China

Shafali Jain, Tripta Thakur and Arun Shandilya
Department of Electrical Engineering, National Institute of Technology, MANIT-Bhopal, India

Mattias Ankarhem
Ministry of Finance, Stockholm, Sweden

Sven-Olov Daunfeldt
The Ratio Institute, Stockholm, Sweden
Dalarna University, Borlänge, Sweden

Shahiduzzaman Quoreshi
University of Bergen, Bergen, Norway

Niklas Rudholm
Dalarna University, Borlänge, Sweden
The Swedish Retail Institute, Stockholm, Sweden

Chih-Chiang Hwang
Department of Finance, National Dong Hwa University, Taiwan, China
Department of Health Business Administration, Tajen University, Taiwan, China

Shin-Yun Wang
Department of Finance, National Dong Hwa University, Taiwan, China

Jiangping Wan
School of Business Administration, South China University of Technology, Guangzhou, China
Institute of Emerging Industrialization Development, South China University of Technology, Guangzhou, China

Dan Wan and Hui Zhang
School of Business Administration, South China University of Technology, Guangzhou, China

CPSIA information can be obtained
at www.ICGtesting.com
Printed in the USA
LVOW05*1914240118
563840LV00003B/40/P